D1527324

Science and Spectacle

Studies in the History of Science, Technology and Medicine
edited by John Krige, CRHST, Paris, France.

Studies in the History of Science, Technology and Medicine aims to stimulate research in the field, concentrating on the twentieth century. It seeks to contribute to our understanding of science, technology and medicine as they are embedded in society, exploring the links between the subjects on the one hand and the cultural, economic, political and institutional contexts of their genesis and development on the other. Within this framework, and while not favouring any particular methodological approach, the series welcomes studies which examine relations between science, technology, medicine and society in new ways e.g. the social construction of technologies, large technical systems.

Other titles in the series

Volume 1   *Technological Change: Methods and Themes in the History of Technology*
edited by Robert Fox

Volume 2   *Technology Transfer out of Germany after 1945*
edited by Matthias Judt and Burghard Ciesla

Volume 3   *Entomology, Ecology and Agriculture: The Making of Scientific Careers in North America. 1885-1985*
Paolo Palladino

Volume 4   *The Historiography of Contemporary Science and Technology: Whose History? Whose Science?*
edited by Thomas Söderqvist

Volume 5   *Science and Spectacle: The Work of Jodrell Bank in Post-war British Culture*
Jon Agar

Volume 6   *Molecularizing Biology and Medicine: New Practices and Alliances*
Soraya de Chadarevian and Harmke Kamminga

Other Volumes in Preparation

Making Isotopes Matter: F.W. Aston and the Culture of Physics
Jeff Hughes

This book is part of a series. The publisher will accept continuation orders which may be cancelled at any time and which provide for automatic billing and shipping of each title in the series upon publication. Please write for details.

Science and Spectacle
The Work of Jodrell Bank in Post-war British Culture

Jon Agar
University of Manchester, UK

harwood academic publishers

Australia • Canada • China • France • Germany • India • Japan • Luxembourg
Malaysia • The Netherlands • Russia • Singapore • Switzerland • Thailand
United Kingdom

Amsteldijk 166
1st Floor
1079 LH Amsterdam
The Netherlands

British Library Cataloguing in Publication Data

Agar, Jon
    Science and spectacle : the work of Jodrell Bank in post-war British culture.
    – (Studies in the history of science, technology and medicine; v. 5)
    1. Jodrell Bank Experimental Station 2. Popular culture – Great Britain –
    History 3. Great Britain – History – 1945 – I. Title
    522.1'942716

ISBN 90-5702-258-3

Contents

List of Tables

List of Illustrations

PREFACE AND INTRODUCTION

Spectacle is perhaps more frequently encountered in histories of early modern court culture, theatre, or, following situationist provocateur Guy Debord, the analysis of image-saturated modern societies, than in the history of twentieth century science. In the 1950s, the British government, consulting engineers, industrial firms, academic scientists at Manchester University, and a private foundation all contributed, in differing ways, to the construction of an emblematic instrument: a large steerable radio telescope at Jodrell Bank. In this book I draw on various historiographies to interpret this icon as a spectacle of science.

When I began thinking about science and spectacle, two categories drawn from recent historical writings on science, that of 'Big Science' and 'display', initially promised to be useful. I argue in Chapter One that the macro organisation of science in post-1939 Britain was marked by novel sites, structures, audiences and subjects. Several share the characteristics of what has been labelled 'Big Science'. The term has also been used by several authors to describe radio astronomy. Large scale organised research has a long history, but 'Big Science' can be usefully reserved for a style of organisation exemplified by the Manhattan Project, the post-war nuclear science and high energy physics installations such as Brookhaven, Fermilab and CERN, and arguably the space projects such as Apollo and the Space Telescope, and latterly the Human Genome Project.

There have been two notable recent attempts to review and revise 'Big Science', the nexus broadly marked by influx of 'money, manpower, machines, media and military' as an analytical category.[1] Capshew and Rader have traced the various meanings of Big Science: as pathological opposite to healthy little science, as a quantifiable phenomenon, as associated with big instruments, as 'industrialised science', as a collection of ethical problems such as accountability, as science 'governmentalised', as a holistic 'form of life', and as a specific culture or institution. Having demonstrated how

---

[1] Capshew, J.H. and Rader, K.A., 1992. Big science: Price to present. *Osiris* 7, pp3-25.

'murky' (as Hevly has described it[2]) the concept can be, Capshew and Rader make a useful distinction between qualities of large 'scale' and 'scope' that mark Big Science. The qualities of scale are: the vertical integration of people and material resources, the centralisation of control, and the concentration of work processes within a circumscribed locale. The qualities of scope are: 'co-ordination amongst geographically dispersed investigators or facilities', a reliance on communication networks, and decentralised, horizontal integration.

It is qualities of scale that Hevly draws out, and expands upon, as the characteristics of Big Science, although 'Big Science is not simply science carried out with big or expensive instruments'. Like Capshew and Rader, Hevly highlights 'concentration of resources', adding that this process occurs into 'a decreasing number of research centers', at which 'special facilities' are dedicated towards 'specific goals' or missions. At such institutions, the workforce is typically 'specialised', both hierarchically as groups with group managers, but also into 'theoreticians, experimenters and instrument builders'. Although this latter distinction is highly tailored to the discussion of particle physics, Hevly broadens the discussion to note the institutionalised but often contested roles given to the groups of experts, in particular to engineers, in this division of labour. Hevly makes a valuable observation that "Big Science, drawing on earlier rhetoric concerning science and power, depends on the attachment of social and political significance to scientific projects, whether for their contribution to national health, military power, industrial potential, or prestige". This 'attachment' can be usefully seen as an active process, enroling public and political forces, often to secure government, foundational or industrial support. The number of different bodies supporting a Big Science project makes divergent interests likely: the tension between security demanded by the military and the openness of a project of public prestige is particularly acute.

Networks of contact and exchange between government, university and industry marked several significant research projects during the Second World War (see Chapter One). These networks framed the organisation of British post-war research, and are also characteristic of Big Science. Most Big Science literature has taken North American science as its object. I now consider whether this historiography can be used to discuss the new British sites for science.

British space science (with its Antipodean launch sites and collaboration) and the International Geophysical Year (a world-wide programme of research in 1957-1958) shared the 'horizontal integration' characteristics that Capshew and Rader termed large 'scope' science. However, although it is tempting to

---

[2] Hevly, B., 1992. Reflections on big science and big history. In Galison, P. and Hevly, B. (eds.) 1992, *Big Science: The Growth of Large Scale Research*. Stanford: Stanford University Press, pp355-363.

declare IGY the large scope post-war Big Science project that paralleled the large scale projects such as the joint European particle physics research organisation CERN, it can also be usefully placed in a lineage of extended, collaborative projects, interconnected with expressions of nationalism (such as the 'magnetic crusade'), and internationalism (such as the astronomical Carte du ciele). Big science can perhaps be extended back to Lawrence's 1930s laboratory, but not back into the 19th century without distortion and loss of analytical sharpness.[3]

The British nuclear physics establishment at Harwell displayed the large numbers of staff vertically integrated into hierarchical teams that Capshew and Rader identify with big 'scale' science. Harwell also combined the government, academic and military interests that Hevly finds a feature of Big Science. Likewise CERN certainly was marked by many of Hevly's features: the concentration of resources, the expensive machines, the government funding, and the heterogeneous organisation of the work-force. However, this is to an extent not surprising, as the historiography was developed primarily to discuss American high energy physics.

Whereas the American historiography of Big Science can be used with advantage to discuss the sites of high energy physics, it cannot be transferred with entire success. With the case of CERN it captures the large, co-ordinated teams of technicians, scientists and administrators working with large expensive equipment. However, CERN had no direct connection with military or industrial organisation: Krige and Pestre can only gesture towards the huge laboratory generating 'a pool of expertise which could be drawn on by various technologically advanced sectors of the economy, including those of interest to the so-called "military-industrial complex", a functional argument stressed in a wider context by Mukerji.[4] Furthermore, Krige and Pestre have undermined the solidity and seeming inevitability of Big Science by highlighting the contingencies within CERN's early history.[5] Where the military agenda of the British atomic programme (including Harwell) was explicit, the historiography does not cope well with the specificities of British government establishments.

Finally, Big Science cannot adequately discuss the use of large and

---

[3] A good case has been made against the easy periodisation equating big science with post-1939 organisation of research, so that, despite massive federal spending and the Manhattan Project, the (now) Lawrence Berkeley Laboratory can be presented as a pre-war example of big science. See: Seidel, R., 1992. The origin of the Lawrence Berkeley Laboratory. In Galison and Hevly (1992), pp21-45.

[4] Krige, J. and Pestre, D., in Hermann, A., Krige, J., Mersits, U. and Pestre, D., 1987. *History of CERN*, Vol. 1, p542. Mukerji, C., 1989. *A Fragile Power: Scientists and the State*. Princeton: Princeton University Press, pp3-38.

[5] Krige, J. and Pestre, D., Some thoughts on the early history of CERN. In Galison and Hevly (1992), pp78-99.

expensive instruments within small, university-style groups. This is exemplified by nuclear physics research within British universities, and also by astronomy before satellites and interplanetary probes. As Galison has described the position of the huge telescopes at Mount Palomar and Mount Wilson: "while the telescopes could be built only by co-ordinated teams of engineers, scientists, and industrialists, they were used primarily by small groups of observers . . . prewar astronomy had come to demand large-scale equipment while remaining traditional at the level of scientific practice".[6] This sketch could be transposed to describe radio astronomy in Britain.

Radio astronomy provides, and has provided, an excellent subject for a historian or sociologist of science working in Britain. Michael Mulkay, David Edge and Steve Woolgar from a sociologically informed perspective, and Ben Martin and John Irvine from the perspective of science policy, have profitably made use of radio astronomy as a case study. The location of three of the important radio astronomy groups of the 1950s in Britain fortunately meant that sources would be near at hand. Moreover, collections of sources, in particular the Jodrell Bank Archive held at the John Rylands Library in Manchester and government papers at the Public Record Office and Radiocommunications Agency, are extremely rich, and largely unexamined by previous scholars. There was therefore the opportunity of utilising fertile archival material, not only to pursue an inquiry of my own, but also to be informed by and engage with scholars of cognate disciplines.

While Big Science historiography proved useful in highlighting interesting aspects of the Jodrell Bank projects, there was danger in mobilising it programmatically. Detailed contextual study revealed that although many of the ingredients were present (money, manpower, machines, media, and military), they interacted in unexpected ways. The securing of valuable resources (the allocation of quiet frequencies, as well as money) relied upon networks connecting the radio astronomers with civil servants and politicians. The construction of equipment depended upon relations with industrial firms and consulting engineers. Perhaps most importantly, the relations between the observatory and an outside public had to be carefully built and managed. In each of these cases 'radio astronomy' had to carry different meanings to interest different groups. Edgerton has expertly dissected, and dismissed, the idea propagated by declinist historians that Britain's investment in research and development is closely connected with economic performance.[7] Having demolished the economic factors as the sole justification for science, we must understand basic research in political and cultural terms: contextually, what was it *for* and what did it *mean*?

The invention of meaning is tracked carefully in this book. In particular

---

[6] Galison, P., The many faces of big science. In Galison and Hevly (1992), p1-17.

[7] Edgerton, D., 1996. *Science, Technology and the British Industrial Decline, 1870-1970.* Cambridge: Cambridge University Press.

the fashioning and presentation of the large steerable Radio Telescope was crucial to its 'success', as well as of those individuals chosen to be associated with the instrument. The availability and growing significance of relatively new media, for example televisual technologies, meant that techniques of presentation had to be developed. Issues of interpretation also proved difficult. In understanding such matters the recent historiography of display is valuable. In an influential analysis of 'scientific production as performance', Schaffer has shown how 18th century natural philosophers produced a 'theatre' of electrical phenomena, in which those 'privileged' could bring out the active and hidden powers of nature.[8] The task of these dramatic and popular displays was, he writes, to "exploit control over these powers to draw out and make manifest the theological and moral implications for the audience". The management of scientific spectacle therefore supported the theological and moral authority of key actors. Two implications are also stressed by Schaffer, and others writing in the historiographical strand of display.

First, the constitution and maintenance of authority was a valued and protected technique. Exclusion of 'false' claimants was vital. Schaffer records that "the most important desideratum for the survival of natural philosophy was . . . the institution of some system of policing of its own practitioners". Likewise, Morus addresses the struggle for authority between two groups of natural philosophers with differing 'technologies of display'.[9] In my account of science and spectacle in post-war British science, technologies of display are also important in the bestowal of authority, a process dependent on managed exclusion. However, with the Jodrell Bank Radio Telescope the groups involved, and the issues at stake, turn out to be different in many ways to those of 18th and 19th century natural philosophy.

Second, scientific spectacle was difficult to control: the practitioner could not direct the spectator's interpretation. Schaffer shows how in the late 18th century spectacle and 'direct experience' of nature could lead to allegations of delusion and superstition. Golinski similarly traces the problematic display of phosphorus in the early Royal Society: as a spectacle "phosphorus could be a device for extending public appreciation of the new experimental philosophy, but it could also become a target for criticism".[10] The Royal Society's authority suffered if public appreciation extended to women, children and "persons of differing conditions". Moreover, chemical experiments were liable to failure during public demonstration, or of mutating

---

[8] Schaffer, S., 1983. Natural philosophy and public spectacle in the eighteenth century. *History of Science* 21, pp1-43.

[9] Morus, I.R., 1993. Currents from the underworld: Electricity and the technology of display in early Victorian England. *Isis* 84, pp50-69.

[10] Golinski, J., 1989. 'A noble spectacle: phosphorus and the public culture of science in the early Royal Society', *Isis* 80, pp11-39.

in meaning in the passage from spectacle to spectator. Where I think 'spectacle' can be usefully distinguished from display is the greater extent of organisation that creates, and attempts to guide, interpretation: for Jodrell Bank in the late 1950s spectacle is a central organising principle.

The historiography of scientific display therefore urges the historian to pay as much attention to reception of meaning as to its production. When studying spectators, elite scientific culture can be seen intersecting with a popular culture: indeed *interaction* has been identified a preferable locus for historical study, rather than studying separate spheres.[11] Recent cultural history has persuasively argued against understanding popular audiences as passive. For example Natalie Zemon Davis stresses the creativity of popular culture.[12] Popular scientific culture should not be seen as a simplified version of an elite's, but instead 'more complex than the mere imposition of a dominant culture or some autonomous analogue of it'.[13] These warnings guide my account of the interaction between the spectacle of the Radio Telescope and the spectators in Chapter Three. Visitors (welcome and unwelcome) to Jodrell Bank did creatively appropriate the claims and instruments of the radio astronomers. However, as I argue in the conclusion, the organisation of the establishment itself operated to position and discipline their actions.

Finally, as well as drawing on insights from the historiographies of Big Science and display to understand the interaction of spectacle and its audiences, this book also examines knowledge-making practices at work. Practice and skill have been prominent themes of recent historical and sociological writing on science[14], although they have been mobilised in many different, sometimes conflicting ways.[15] Here, the historiography of practice is a guide to help understand the manipulative, experimental work of radio astronomers. In particular, I relate the practical work of interpreting the output of radio telescopes to the organisation of the observatory, and, crucially, to the orientation of the establishment as a scientific spectacle.

---

[11] Chartier, R., 1984. Culture as appropriation: Popular cultural uses in early modern France. In Kaplan, S.L. (ed.), 1984, *Understanding Popular Culture: Europe from the Middle Ages to the Nineteenth Century.* Berlin: Mouton, pp229-254.

[12] Davis, N.Z., 1975. *Society and Culture in Early Modern France.* Stanford: Stanford University Press, p225.

[13] Cooter, R. and Pumfrey, S., 1994. Separate spheres and public places: Reflections on the history of science popularization and science in popular culture. *History of Science* 32, pp237-267. Shapin, S., 1990. Science and the public. In Olby *et al.* (eds.), *Companion to the History of Modern Science.* London: Routledge, p994.

[14] Golinski, J., 1990. The theory of practice and the practice of theory: Sociological approaches in the history of science. *Isis* 81, pp492-505.

[15] Baigrie, B.S., 1995. Scientific practice: The veiw from the tabletop. In Buchwald, J.Z. (ed.) 1995. *Scientific Practice: Theories and Stories of Doing Physics.* Chicago: Chicago University Press, pp87-122.

Knowledge-making practices, socially embedded (and difficult to recover), were located at a nexus both where knowledge was created, and where the relations between spectacle and visitor were reproduced. For radio astronomy this meant the resolution of either order or 'interference'. These mundane practical processes of valuation therefore link epistemology and sociotechnical organisation.

OUTLINE OF THE BOOK STRUCTURE

Chapter One introduces the context of post-war British science. Four aspects of this context are highlighted: the increase in government expenditure on research through the loosely structured Haldanian system of research councils, the growth of universities alongside an expansion of education, and the emergence of new sites, and changing audiences, for science. I discuss CERN as an example of these new centralised, and only partly academic, sites. As I show in Chapter Two, radio astronomical projects, in particular the plan for a large, steerable radio telescope at Jodrell Bank, marked a similar concentration of resources. I follow the promoters of the Radio Telescope, and link its history with the post-war context that I have discussed: the loose funding policy structure, and the transformations in sites and expenditure in education and science.

I argue that the influx of money associated with the expansion of the universities, along with expensive projects supported by the economies of post-war science, problematised the university as a site for science. In the mid-1950s it was debated within government whether universities should conduct the new scale science. How a university such as Manchester, which was in the van of the expansion of tertiary education, managed a project such as the Radio Telescope, was inevitably a focus of these debates. I therefore study the history of the Radio Telescope's support in order to trace the negotiated and contested boundary between academic and government science. I support this interpretation by demonstrating that similar debates existed around other sites, such as agricultural and medical research establishments that straddled this boundary.

As the cost of the telescope spiralled, more supporters had to be convinced to back the project. Already the telescope was receiving money from the Department of Scientific and Industrial Research (DSIR) and the University Grants Committee (UGC). Now the private Nuffield Foundation and other government and military bodies, such as the Air Ministry and Ministry of Supply, were mobilised. I show how the telescope was interpreted differently for these new audiences, and how these interpretations partially translated into material design changes. Criticisms of these design changes, led by the Public Accounts Committee for their own purposes, heightened the debate over large scale science in the university. Linking Chapters Two and Three

I discuss two attempts via public routes to secure private funding: a failed attempt after Sputnik to persuade Prime Minister Harold Macmillan to help Jodrell Bank, and an appeal to industry, commerce and private funds to clear the debt.

At the conclusion of the discussions over siting of expensive research, the radio telescope remained in university control. This resolution depended on the presentation of the instrument to the public as an object of prestige. This constructed quality was crucial in enrolling the interests of bodies such as the Royal Astronomical Society, and was an important resource for promoters of the telescope within Whitehall. In Chapter Three I examine this public presentation. I show that DSIR portrayed the instrument as a 'great public spectacle' of Britain and British science. I trace this spectacle in news releases, public lectures and film. There were continuities, and differences, between the spectacle of the Radio Telescope and other public presentations of science in post-war Britain such as the Festival of Britain examined in Chapter One. The construction of an instrument of public prestige illustrates once again the connection between malleability of interpretation and the heterogeneity of the supporting bodies.

The sustenance of the prestige of the instrument depended on the maintenance of a specific spatialised relation between its users and its public. This relation was that of astronomers and engineers as insiders, and the public held back as an audience. I discuss how a spatial solution to the problem of public astronomical authority depended upon the division and management of visitors, a solution that was imported from the famous Californian optical observatories at Mount Wilson and Mount Palomar. The prestige of the instrument relied on visitors, having been divided and categorised, receiving different and guided displays. These displays occurred at the boundary between Jodrell Bank and the outside world, marked for example by press conferences, films and visitor centres. I establish that spatial politics were therefore crucial in supporting the telescope as the icon and spectacle of science, which allowed large scale science to continue at universities.

Also in Chapter Three I link the spatial politics of instrumental prestige to the authority of the insider. I show how, because of the new scale of research, both engineer and scientist could claim credit for the project. This shift was picked up by the PAC who made engineer-astronomer relations a focus of its criticisms, illustrative, it claimed, of the unsuitability of bursars to manage the increased funds associated with increased education. In contrast to public displays of harmony, there was an internal controversy over *who* would 'control' the telescope. The contest between engineer and astronomer for credit was resolved, like the connected problem of insider-public relations, through boundary conflicts. The resolution included the disappearance of the engineer and the public identification of the Telescope (and hence British science) with the radio astronomer Lovell.

The radio astronomers imagined the effect if the public were allowed too close to their work: they would destroy the productive quiet of the observatory, their presence was a 'danger' that would 'disturb' and 'interfere'. Discussion of the public in these terms persuaded the government and university to ensure that the instrument's public spectators were held back and in place. I label this interpretation a discourse of interference. In Chapter Three I show how the discourse of interference evaluated visitors, thereby maintaining the public-insider boundary, upon which the processes of public authority and credit conferral rested. In Chapter Four I show that the discourse of interference also provided the means to interpret and evaluate the products of the Radio Telescope: inscriptions such as pen-recordings. Astronomical authority, the credit allocated within the community of astronomers, was grounded on clean, valued inscriptions untouched by interference. The discourse of interference was therefore a fundamental, if mundane, component of the radio astronomers' knowledge-making practices. Electrical interference was also described in spatialised terms: as penetrating from outside the observatory, often embodied in the public.

This nexus of interference, authority and public-insider boundaries is therefore examined in detail in Chapters Four and Five. I discuss the politics of frequency allocation, nationally and internationally. I follow the attempts by radio astronomers from Cambridge and Manchester to secure clear and quiet bands in the radio spectrum (the radio spectrum itself provides another example of the association of space and authority). These attempts resulted in two reciprocal changes: the accommodation of radio astronomy as a 'new user' within the radio spectrum, and in the deflection of other users creating zones of fifty mile radius around the two observatories. This reciprocity between frequency and physical space was also found in the repeated comments within Cabinet committees that radio astronomy be moved to quieter sites.

In Chapter Four I show how the astronomers countered institutions such as government departments, the armed forces, and commercial companies in their attempts to create a productive quiet within the Jodrell Bank observatory. This account is of the securing of valuable resources (frequency allocations) and therefore it has close parallels with the account of the securing of money in Chapter Two. In Chapter Five, I discuss how the astronomers opposed the presence of urban activities: local housing development, electricity supplies, restaurants, traffic, and electrified railways. In parallel to Chapter Three the public were seen as threatening, embodying interference and pressing at the boundaries of Jodrell Bank. The campaign for and against development each rested on local networks: of local business, district and county councillors, local press and pressure groups. The campaigns culminated in the 1960s in public inquiries, in which the discourse of interference was used again both to hold the public back and to interpret the products of the Telescope, this time within the Courtroom. I demonstrate again the link between public authority and spatialised organisational politics.

Spectacle is therefore understood in this book as having several components: as a public icon made to be edifying (and malleable enough to carry different meanings for different groups[16]); as an organisation that works by valuation of incoming bodies, and demands discursive and knowledge-making practices which reproduce this organisation; and finally as an extensive network that links radio astronomers and engineers to other groups: the maintenance of spectacle necessitated a heavy investment in local, national and international politics. Finally, although examined in detail elsewhere, my account shows that spectacle involves particular spatial organisation.[17] Spatiality appears in my account of radio astronomy at Jodrell Bank in three ways. First, in the challenge to the university as a site for science. This is closely connected with the innovations in organising research, in particular, as large scale science. Jodrell Bank assumed special significance in the debates over this challenge. It itself was therefore the site of the second spatiality in my account: the spatiality of the discourse of interference, linking the construction of prestige, the public-insider boundary, and organisational authority, manifested in talk of 'disturbance', 'penetration' and 'danger'. The third spatiality is again linked: the space of the radio spectrum, reciprocally connected to physical space. The use and change of each space was associated with power and authority relations.

---

[16] A 'boundary object' in the sense of Star, S.L. and Griesemer, J.R., 1989. Institutional ecology, 'translations' and boundary objects: Amateurs and professionals in Berkeley's Museum of Vertebrate Zoology, 1907-39. *Social Studies of Science* 19, pp397-420.

[17] Agar, J., Screening science: Spatiality and authority at Jodrell Bank. In Agar, J. and Smith, C.W.(eds), *Making Space for Science*. London: Macmillan, forthcoming.

ACKNOWLEDGEMENTS

I have received a great deal of help in writing this book. Thanks in general go to members of the Unit for the History of Science (as it was then named before its cultural turn) at the University of Kent at Canterbury, and the Centre for the History of Science, Technology and Medicine at the University of Manchester. I received valuable and insightful comments from Crosbie Smith, Ben Marsden, Elizabeth Pidoux, Graeme Gooday, Simon Schaffer, Yakup Bektas, Geof Bowker, Alex Dolby, Simon Chaplin, John Pickstone, Paolo Palladino, Joan Mottram, Sally Horrocks and Kathryn Packer. I am particularly indebted to Jeff Hughes for reading and criticising a penultimate draft. Much of my research time was spent in archives, and I am grateful to staff at the John Rylands University Library at Manchester, the Public Records Office and OfTel, and H.C. Daniels of the Radiocommunications Agency, for help with access to the primary sources.

CHAPTER 1

Science in Post-war Britain

In this chapter I provide a thumbnail historical account of the organisation of science and government in twentieth century Britain. I show how the loose funding structure of this organisation remained largely unchanged from the years immediately after the First World War. I contrast this static structure with the pivotal transformations of science in society that took place during the Second World War. I review three areas of war-time transformation: a shift to goal-orientated research, the installation of scientific advisors at high-level in Whitehall, and the recognition of these changes within public bodies. I argue that the Second World War forged 'an influential network of contacts between scientists, civil servants, the military and industry.

I follow how these convulsive changes constituted a very different dynamic context for science in society to that of the interwar years. I analyse three components of this new context: the increase in expenditure on research, the expansion of the education sector, and the emergence of new subject areas and forms of scientific organisation. I outline the histories of key novel British scientific organisations: the nuclear physics programmes at British universities, Harwell and in Europe, the Royal Aircraft Establishment at Farnborough, the General Post Office research laboratories, and the space science and International Geophysical Year projects. I show how it was in a post-war context defined by the growth of this new geography of institutions that radio astronomy emerged. I review the histories of radio astronomy, in particular that presented by Edge and Mulkay, and the accounts given by participants. Finally, in an examination of the techniques of radio astronomy at Jodrell bank, I emphasise the work and organisation needed to produce ordered records of astronomical phenomena. This order was made to contrast with the interference I discuss in Chapters Four and Five.

THE CONTEXT OF BRITISH SCIENCE

The institutions that presided over the division and allocation of government funds for science remained largely unaltered from the Edwardian period up to the mid-1960s. This static structure is in contrast with three axes of change found in accounts of twentieth century science: the ascendancy of the authority of the scientist within the advisory structures of government[1], the development of qualitatively different organisational forms involving new disciplines[2], and (particularly after 1939) increasing levels of expenditure.[3]

THE GOVERNMENT FUNDING OF SCIENCE

As the first world war ground to a halt, Lord Haldane subjected the British 'machinery of government' to a lengthy review.[4] One area towards which Haldane directed his rationalising gaze was the organisation of scientific and industrial research. Haldane argued that whilst government funding of research was necessary, it had to be organised in such a way that the research was free from direct ministerial control. This 'Haldane Principle' grounded and created the system of 'research councils': bodies possessing the executive authority to divide and allocate a sum of government money subject to parliamentary scrutiny, but independent of the departmental control of the minister (the Lord President of the Council) responsible for them to parliament. The councils formed were the Medical Research Council (MRC, out of the slightly older Medical Research Committee set up in 1913), the Agricultural Research Council (ARC, in 1931) and the Department of Scientific and Industrial Research (DSIR, in 1918).[5]

The ideology of the Haldane Principle research councils is deeply imbued with the rhetoric of the desirability of the 'freedom' and 'independence' of science. It can only be consistent with the account of science as, ideally, an autonomous, intellectual and largely non-political pursuit. As Varcoe has

---

[1] McGucken, W., 1984. *Scientists, Society and State: the Social Relations of Science Movement in Great Britain 1931-1947*, Columbus: Ohio State University Press.

[2] Hermann, A., Krige, J., Mersits, U and Pestre, D., 1987. *History of CERN*, 2 Vols, Amsterdam and Oxford: North-Holland Physics Publishing. Gowing, M., 1974. *Independence and Deterrance, Britain and Atomic Energy, 1945-52*, 2 Vols, London: Macmillan.

[3] Rose, H. and Rose, S., 1969. *Science and Society*, Harmondsworth: Penguin. Wilkie, T., 1991. *British Science and Politics since 1945*, Oxford: Blackwell. Varcoe, I., 1974. *Organizing for Science in Britain: a Case Study*, Oxford: Oxford University Press. Vig, N., 1968. *Science and Technology in British Politics*, Oxford: Pergamon Press. Gummett, P., 1980. *Scientists in Whitehall*, Manchester: Manchester University Press.

[4] Hennessy, P., 1989. *Whitehall*, London: Fontana, pp. 292-299.

[5] 'Department' because it received a direct vote from Parliament, and had a sizable civil service staff.

pointed out, Haldane's description of research councils in theory may not correspond to the actions of the councils in practice: 'the mere existence of a set of administrative arrangements geared especially to the organisation and promotion of research...is no guarantee that the research will express a defensible, consistent set of priorities'.[6] Moreover, various 'exigencies', argues Varcoe, such as 'contingent circumstances', 'accumulated commitments to outside elements' and adaptations to 'earlier situations of crisis and threat', further deflected the behaviour of research councils from Haldane Principle ideals. Two initial comments can be made. Firstly, that these arguments imply that a contextual understanding of the actions of the research councils should be sought. Secondly, that a critical attitude should be taken to the argument that the Haldane research council system was a 'hands-off' organisation of research, funding non-political and 'insulated' scientists, as anything except a crude first approximation.[7] A more productive methodology would view the Haldane Principle as part of the wider repertoire of rhetorical strategies, such as the desirability of academic 'freedom', that were available to promoters of projects during the period.

To complete this review of the structures of government funding of science I examine in more detail the two bodies that feature significantly in my account of radio astronomy: the Department of Scientific and Industrial Research and the University Grants Committee. The DSIR was set up in 1916 as an organisational response to perceived deficiencies in the supply of key commodities needed for the war effort. For almost fifty years, the DSIR constituted 'one of the main instruments by which the state supported civil science and by which the state encouraged British industry to exploit scientific knowledge and convert science into industrial and economic development'.[8] It differed from the MRC and ARC in that it possessed an Advisory Council restricted so that it could neither instigate research proposals, nor be responsible for all industrial research in government. Also unlike the MRC and the ARC, it was not defined in relation to a specific discipline, and had a wide and diffuse remit.

The responsibilities of the DSIR fell into three main areas. First, it managed an expanding number of government experimental stations, often under a 'research board': the National Physical Laboratory had passed to its control in 1918, and it was soon joined by other establishments such as the Building and Fire Research Stations. Varcoe has described the 'inflexible' organisation of these government establishments: any change in number or grading of staff needed Treasury approval, pay was generally low (although

---

[6] Varcoe (1974), p. 6. See also Alter, P., 1987. *The Reluctant Patron: Science and the State in Britain, 1850-1920*, London: Berg.

[7] Wilkie (1991), p. 34. cf my discussion of the effect of the plurality of funding sources later.

[8] Wilkie (1991), p. 27.

women were paid the same as men, a practice regarded as 'abnormal' when reviewed within Whitehall).[9] Where establishments did well they generally had the support of a profession, were based on an 'organised body of theoretical knowledge', and possessed an energetic director.[10] The geographical distribution of the government establishments was largely in a crescent to the west of London.[11] Second, the DSIR sought to promote industrial research. The major organisational instrument in enacting this policy was the Research Association: a co-operative scheme between industrial firms supported by government money in which research of common interest was carried out, with resulting patents placed in a pool available to all co-operating firms. Although their reception depended on the industrial sector involved, firms were largely unenthusiastic about the research associations. The third responsibility of the DSIR was for research in the universities. The Department funded studentships and postdoctoral awards, thereby creating a career structure for scientists for many for the first time in the interwar period. However, despite increasing 'steadily' during the interwar years, expenditure on university research 'remained limited in scope' until the post-war years.[12]

Responsibility for supporting research in the universities was shared with the DSIR by the University Grants Committee (UGC). The UGC, although part of the administrative structure of the Treasury, was provided with an annual vote of money that it distributed to fund university education. A gradual division of bureaucratic labour evolved, called the 'dual-support system', in which 'universities provide money from their UGC grants for the provision and running of university departments and for the salaries of academic and other staff, while the research councils make specific grants to individual scientists within those departments for selected projects'.[13] A smaller sum was also available to researchers (almost entirely at universities) through the grant allocated at the discretion of the Royal Society, an elite body composed and reflecting the interests of established scientists. Finally, it should be emphasised that there were closer links between industry and academia in the interwar years than has been, until recently, thought. Firms such as ICI demanded the output of qualified scientists and engineers, whereas Metropolitan-Vickers could claim in 1949 that ten university professors had passed through their research department.[14]

---

[9] Varcoe (1974), p. 40.
[10] Varcoe (1974), p. 41.
[11] Hall, P., Breheny, M., McQuaid, R. and Hart, D., 1987. *Western Sunrise: the Genesis and Growth of Britain's Major High Tech Corridor*, London: Allen and Unwin.
[12] Varcoe (1974), p. 62.
[13] Gummett (1991), p. 159.
[14] Edgerton, D.E.H. and Horrocks, S.M., 1994. 'British industrial research and development before 1945', *Economic History Review* 47, pp. 213-238.

Other government bodies, distinct from the research councils and the UGC, were involved with research. Many of the departments of state expanded research and development: in particular the armed services (the Air Ministry, Admiralty, War Office, and later the Ministry of Supply and Ministry of Aviation) and the General Post Office built up extensive research facilities.[15] The scale of research at these establishments was certainly considerable, although surprisingly little is known about them. For example, by 1939 whereas about £14m was being spent by the government on research and development, only £4m of it was categorised as civil.[16] There was a fundamental policy difference between the departments of state and the DSIR: the departments supported research only as far as it affected their administrative responsibilities, and they therefore had no direct involvement with policies for the production of scientific 'manpower', or the general promotion of research, in particular 'basic' research.

WORLD WAR II AND BRITISH SCIENCE

There is a standard historiography of British science that views the Second World War as a discontinuity in the relations of science in society. For Vig, 'World War II was...the great turning point in government-science relations in Britain'.[17] For Rose and Rose, science in society was reshaped by 'the sudden change in the intellectual environment that the outbreak of the Second World War produced'.[18] This transformation occurred on many levels. Rose and Rose find 'three themes of general importance [that] arise in these war years and mark the way for what was to come subsequently': 'the rapid development of war research', 'the growth of centralised bodies for scientific decision making', and the 'public recognition of the need to lay down plans for the post-war retention of many of these structures'. I will examine each of these three themes in turn.

War Research

Three qualitative remarks should be made about the nature of the 'war research'. First, the research was directed towards specific goal-orientated

---

[15] Williams, F.E., 1976. 'The story of Dollis Hill', *Post Office Electrical Engineering Journal* 69, pp. 140-145, for GPO. Edgerton, D.E.H., 1991. *England and the Aeroplane: an easy on a militant and technological nation, London: Macmillan.*

[16] Vig (1968), p. 12-13. cf an FBI estimate of 5.4m spend by industrial firms by 1938 on R&D, Vig (1968), p. 10.

[17] Vig(1968), p. 13

[18] Rose and Rose (1969), p. 58

projects, in particular nuclear physics, code-breaking, and radio and radar engineering. Indeed, at a 'meta-level', a mode of analysis was formed to quantify war measures: operational research. Second, these projects received more resources in the form of equipment, capital, personnel and priority than pre-war programmes. Third, there was a shift in the place and organisation of the projects. Whereas before the war the researcher had usually worked either in a university, an industrial laboratory or a govenment research establishment, the war mobilised and mixed these sites. A university physicist, for example, uncovered through Whitehall's Central Register might be posted to work on radio direction finding at the Telecommunications Research Establishment (TRE), on valves at GEC, or code-breaking at Bletchley Park. A network of contacts between government, university and military was weaved at sites such as TRE and structures my account of the growth of radio astronomy in the decade after 1945.[19]

Rose and Rose argue that a notable aspect of 'war research' was secrecy: 'the procedures whereby aspects of this research - such as the decision to develop atomic weapons - remained deliberately hidden from parliamentary scrutiny'. The site of research was guarded and private. However, from the scientists' perspective the shift was the opposite: they became 'in the know', part of extensive networks of contacts within the government, the armed services and industry.

The Promotion of Scientific Advisors in Government

McGucken has told a convincing story of the growing links between scientists and the state during the first half of the twentieth century. Pressure from a spectrum of bodies, such as the Association of Scientific Workers, the British Science Guild, the Royal Society and the British Association, groups that often represented different interests and pursued different projects led to increasing accessibility of government decision making to scientists. Before the war, such representation and advice was patchy and likely to be resisted. An important exception was the Committee for the Scientific Survey of Air Defence (under Henry Tizard, and involving amongst others Patrick Blackett), which supported the development of radio direction finding (RDF) from the mid-1930s.[20]

In 1940, a public but anonymous campaign by scientists argued through a fast-selling Penguin paperback, *Science in War,* that there existed in science

[19] Calder, A., 1969. The People's War: Britan 1939-45, London: Cape, pp. 457-477. Rowe, A.P., 1948. *One Story of Radar,* Cambridge: Cambridge University Press. Bowen, E.G., 1987. *Radar Days,* Bristol: Adam Hilger. Lovell, 1991. *Echoes of War: the Story of H2S Radar,* Bristol: Adam Hilger.

[20] Clark, R.W., 1965. *Tizard,* Methuen: London, pp. 112-145. Clark, R.W., 1962. *The Rise of the Boffins,* Phoenix House: London, pp. 44-49.

"vast potential forces insufficiently co-ordinated".[21] In private, the claim was being made by scientists that formal scientific advice to government at the highest level was necessary. Churchill, who preferred the individual advice of F.A. Lindemann, reluctantly relented, and a Scientific Advisory Committee was appointed.[22] An Engineering Advisory Committee was appointed the following year, although this body was later effectively replaced by the appointment of three scientific advisors to the Ministry of Production.[23] At a more secret level, a Defence Services Panel was set up to consider defence research, and, discreeter still, the Maud Committee planned the British 'tube alloys' program in atomic weaponry.[24] This promotion of scientific advisors during the Second World War was part of 'the torrent of irregulars diverted from mainstream careers' that brought dynamic fresh blood into the war-mobilised Whitehall.[25]

The Retention of War-time Organisation

McGucken states that as the war drew to a close there existed a recognition within government circles of the contribution of the boffins, and a state of 'general gratitude towards science'. The war was seen as a vindication of the planners' arguments of the 1930s, and there was pressure on Clement Attlee's incoming interventionist Labour government to institionalise wartime arrangements. Moreover, the scientists attempted to solidify the war-time advisory structures into ones of permanant peacetime influence. Herbert Morrison, appointed Lord President of the Council in Attlee's government, formed a Committee on Future Scientific Policy in 1945, consisting of Sir Alan Barlow as chair, Edward Appleton, Patrick Blackett, Alfred Egerton, Geoffrey Crowther, George Nelson and later C.P. Snow and Solly Zuckerman.[26] This Committee accepted and recommended a proposal of Tizard's for two permanant peacetime advisory bodies: the Advisory Council on Scientific Policy (ACSP), and the Defence Research Policy Committee (DRPC). These bodies were formally set up in 1947. Along with the existence

[21] Anon, 1940. *Science in War,* Harmondsworth: Penguin Books. Quoted in McGucken (1984), p. 188. *Science in War* had its roots in the 1930s debates over the planning of science.
[22] McGucken (1984), p. 196 and passim. The SAC consisted initially of W. Bragg, A.C.G. Egerton, A.V.Hill, Edward Appleton, Edwin Butler and Edwar Mellanby.
[23] The EAC initially consisted of Lord Falmouth, Henry Tizard, James Beard, A.P.M. Fleming, W.T. Halcrow, B.W. Holman, C.C. Paterson, H.R. Ricardo, H.R. Ricardo, and Robertson.
[24] Gowing, M., 1964. *Britain and Atomic Energy, 1939-1945,* London: Macmillian.
[25] Hennessy (1989), p. 89.
[26] McGucken (1984), p. 321.

of Scientific Advisors to many of the government departments, and the other formal and informal contacts between government and science, these bodies symbolised the intertwined networks of advice and influence that were in existence by the mid 1940s. As Vig states 'scientists (as well as economists and other specialists) were integrated into government administration and planning in a way they had not previously'.[27] These networks allowed people, equipment and knowledge to be exchanged in a post-war economy of science, government and industry.

Rose and Rose note that there was 'public recognition' of the desirability of the 'retention of many of these structures in the shape of permanent government policy-making bodies for the conduct of research and development'.[28] Vig also mentions a 'mystique' of science amongst the public: a 'mystique about the potential benefits of scientific applications in peacetime'.[29] There existed a strong movement, centred on rhetoric of 'planning' and growing from the impingement of war-time organisation on many people's lives, that gathered momentum as the war turned in the Allies' favour. It was from this shift that Beveridge's proposals for the welfare state, and the support for Attlee's Labour Party, arose. However, the role of science within this broad movement towards 'planning' in many sectors of government, in particular its reception by public groups, has not been adequately examined.[30] The science that had been represented by newspaper and filmreel as crucial to 'winning the war' through radar and the atomic bomb (or nearly averting defeat through V2 rockets) could also be used to justify the rational planning of society. Two trends therefore marked the post-war world: the growth in the private networks of exchange and influence scientists and government, and the public enthusiasm for the application of science in the planned post-war reconstruction.

RESEARCH IN POST-WAR BRITAIN

Three developments in the organisation and practice of post-war science are highly significant: the increase in expenditure on both civil and military research, anxieties about the output of scientific 'manpower' and the related expansion of the universities, and the emergence of new subject areas within novel organisations.

---

[27] Vig (1968), p. 13.

[28] Rose and Rose (1969), p. 59.

[29] Vig (1968), p. 14.

[30] Barnet has argued the paradoxical claim that this 'New Jerusalem' culture of planning contined within it a blinked anti-technical education bias. Barnett, C., 1986. *The Audit of War: the Illusion and Reality of Britain as a Great Nation*, London: Papermac.

Increased Expenditure on Research

Although expenditure increased, the structure that channelled the funds remained largely unchanged. Gummett has argued that 'those who favoured autonomy for the research councils held their own for four decades', with the 'most serious challenge perhaps arising within the Barlow Committee' in 1946.[31] Members of the Barlow Committee discussed the organisation of science from three positions. A 'radical position' was promoted in particular by the science advisors Blackett and Zuckerman (along with Tizard, and chairman of the Scientific Advisory Committe and Royal Society president, Sir Henry Dale). This group advocated 'strong central co-ordination of all government-supported scientific activity'.[32] A 'moderate position', called for by ex-Chancellor of the Exchequer Sir John Anderson, stressed the benefits of the status quo, with the Lord President responsible for science, relatively autonomous research councils, and specialised facilities developed by other government departments. This existing struct.re would be supplemented by an expanded peacetime Scientific Advisory Council, but this body would include neither government scientists nor the secretaries of the research councils or the Royal Society. A third position countered the moderates' proposed reduction in the roles of research council and Royal Society representatives, but also wished, in the words of Royal Society physical secretary Sir Alfred Egerton, to "avoid ...too definite planning". The outcome of the debate satisfied this third position, with the structure only changed by the formation of the ACSP and DRPC, although not with the large supporting staff recommended by the radicals on the Barlow Committee. As Gummett notes, the dominant (and cited) reason for the decision not to place all government research and development under a Ministry of Science was the overriding 'Whitehall tradition of the responsibility of each minister for the work of his own ministry'.[33]

Therefore, in the immediate post-war years the key figures and institutions of British science confirmed, after considerable internal debate, a loose organization of bodies supporting and funding science.[34] Such bodies were held together by formal but restricted subject boards, and informally by the overlapping networks of civil servants and scientists that sat on them. Further important institutional changes in the organisation of science over the subsequent few years, such as the National Research and Development Corporation (NRDC), and Nature Conservancy, also occurred in governmental

---

[31] Gummett (1980), p. 189.

[32] Gummett (1980), p. 218. McGucken (1984), p. 320-328.

[33] Gummett (1980), p. 220.

[34] This diverse, heterogenous structure was mirrored at a lower level by the structure within the DSIR. See Varcoe (1974), pp. 58-60.

milieux of 'low co-ordination' at the centre.[35] The only central co-ordination was that executed by the Treasury with which each research council, and departmental minister, independently negotiated. Parliamentary scrutiny of these arrangements for the organisation of science was either perfunctory (as in the powerful Select Committee on Estimates), or retrospective (such as the equally powerful Public Accounts Committee or PAC).[36] This loosely structured environment of 'autonomous' research councils and separate government departments is crucial for understanding the development of Jodrell Bank.

If the framework of government funding of science remained largely unchanged, then this must be contrasted with the transformation in the scale of the expenditure that passed through it. Vig has estimated the total expenditure on 'research' by the British government to have risen from £10m in 1939, to £220m in 1955-56, and to £425m in 1964-65.[37] Gummett has compiled figures for government expenditure on 'civil research and development' that can be compared. The sum distributed by research councils rose from £2.9m in 1945-46, to £11.2m in 1955-56, and to £40.3m in 1963-64.[38] In particular, expenditure by the DSIR climbed from £2.3m in 1945-46, to £7.5m in 1955-56, and to £25.4m in 1963-64. To this should be added money allocated for research at the universities by the UGC, which was: £1.5m in 1945-46, £11.0m in 1955-56 and £31.2m in 1963-64.[39]

A number of initial comments can be made on these figures. First, expenditure rose considerably over the immediate two post-war decades. Furthermore, total expenditure on research grew by a slightly higher rate, as the contribution from industry rose from a quarter in 1955-56 to a third in 1961-62.[40] The bulk of government money was not spent within government

---

[35] For the NRDC see: Hendry, J., 1989. *Innovating for Failure: Government Policy and the Early British Computer Industry*, Cambridge MA and London: MIT Press. Also Varcoe (1974), p. 48.

[36] Walkland, S.A., 1965. 'Science and Parliament: the role of Select Committees of the House of Commons', *Parliamentary Affairs* 18, pp. 266-278.

[37] Vig (1968), p. 2. To put this in a different perspective, the federal expenditure on research in the United States over the same period was: $74m in 1940, $1,600m in 1952 (equalling the wartime high), $8,000m in 1960, and $15,000 in 1964. For an excellent account of how such sums transformed the campuses at MIT and Stanford, see: Leslie, S., 1993. *The Cold War and American Science: the Military-Industrial-Academic Complex at MIT and Stanford*, New York: Columbia University Press.

[38] Gummett (1980), p. 39. From Council for Scientific Policy, Report on Science Policy, appendix II, Cmnd 3007, (1966); and Advisory Council on Scientific Policy, Ninth Report, Cmnd 11, (1956).

[39] Includes a small (but inseparable) figure of money channeled through 'learned societies', predominantly the Royal Society.

[40] Gummett (1980), p. 37.

research establishments. Indeed, as Gummett concludes: 'R&D in the UK from 1945 to 1964 was mainly financed by government but performed by industry'. Second, defence research and development formed the dominant portion of expenditure, although civil R&D was still substantial. This is connected to the extraordinary concentration of science capital (in the form of money, equipment and personnel) in a few sectors. For example, Vig records that under the Conservative administrations of Churchill, Eden and Macmillan research expenditure was 'very heavily concentrated in atomic energy and nuclear physics'.[41] To this must be added aviation, for as Gummett records in 1963-64: £31.2m was spent by the Ministry of Aviation on civil R&D[42], £45.0m through the Atomic Energy Authority, and £7.8m on the National Institute for Research in Nuclear Science (NIRNS).

There are several reasons why government expenditure on research increased so sharply. Capital that had been invested in expensive and potentially long term projects instigated during the Second World War was continued. Projects such as atomic and aviation research were justified by the Cold War tensions that rapidly came to determine policy. The commitment to the development of an independent atomic research programme after the McMahon Act had effectively severed collaboration with the Americans provides a clear example of this point. Such projects were supported within Whitehall by the increased role of scientific and expert advisors, and outside by what Vig has called the 'bipartisan harmony' over the expected contribution of science. Finally, the increased funding interlinked with the expansion of education in the post-war years, a subject to which I now turn.

The Expansion of Education

Plans for the expansion of education were formulated during the war: the Education Act passed in 1944 envisaged greater numbers entering secondary education, with knock-on effects on university numbers. The combined effect of demobilisation and expansion meant that student numbers rose from 55,000 in 1938 to 84,451 in 1952.[43] Stress was placed within this expansion on scientific and engineering subjects. The Barlow Committee, in a 1946 report on 'scientific manpower', estimated that although the demand for qualified scientists and engineers would rise to 90,000, the actual output by 1955 would only be 64,000. The report, accepted by the government, demanded a doubling of trained scientists by the mid-1950s.[44] Scientific research at the

---

[41] Vig (1968), p. 20.
[42] Although note that, since the Ministry of Aviation took over most of the Ministry of Supply's responsibilities, this figure does not just record expenditure on aviation.
[43] Varcoe (1974), p. 63.
[44] Sir Alan Barlow (ch), Scientific Manpower: Report of a Committee Appointed by the Lord President of the Council, Cmd 6824, 1946.

universities was funded according to the 'dual-support' system which I have outlined above in my discussion of the UGC.

An expansion of the UGC's and the research councils' allocations for science accompanied the expansion of the universities. For example the DSIR expenditure on postgraduate allowances and senior research awards was less than £14,000 in 1939, but grew to £600,000 in 1956-57, and £1,750,000 in 1963-64.[45] Concern for levels of scientific 'manpower' was a continuing feature of the 1950s. By 1957, although university enrolment had stood at 89,000 in 1956-57 (including 32,000 in science and engineering), the government announced a further expansion over the 1957-62 quinquennium: an overall enrolment of 106,000 by the mid-1960s of which two-thirds of the new students would be in science and technology.[46]

Novel Post-War Sites for Science

A proportion of the qualified scientists and engineers produced in the post-war expansion of education continued research at the new sites for science that were soon established. In this section I introduce the new geography of establishments where they worked. I consider the case of CERN at length as it has several points of contact with the Radio Telescope project at Jodrell Bank.

The scientists and engineers who had collaborated in wartime government and industrial research sites returned to civilian life with prestige, contacts and escalated expectations. This description closely fits the nuclear physicists. Five university physics departments responded positively to an invitation to outline research programmes, issued by the Nuclear Physics Committee of the Ministry of Supply in 1946.[47] This initiative led to large capital grants (of the order of £100,000 each) from the DSIR to build facilities in the prestigious field of nuclear physics. Birmingham under Mark Oliphant constructed a 1.3 GeV proton accelerator; Cambridge began a linear accelerator of energy around 300-400 MeV; the 400 MeV proton-synchrotron at Liverpool was the largest instrument of its kind in Europe until the CERN 600 MeV was completed in 1957; whilst electron synchrotrons were built at both Glasgow and Oxford. These instruments were operated within traditional university physics departments, consisting of small groups of researchers, technicians, and administative staff. No British facility could compare with

[45] Varcoe (1974), p. 62.

[46] Vig (1968), p. 21. The overall figure was raised to 124,000 the following year, along with a supplementary building grants for the construction of new universities (of which Sussex was the first).

[47] Krige, J. 1989. 'The installation of high-energy accelerators in Britain after the war: big equipment but not "Big Science"', in De Maria, M., Grilli, M. and Sebastiani (eds.), *The Restructuring of Physical Sciences in Europe and the United States, 1945-1960*, Singapore: World Scientific, pp. 488-501.

the collaborative university laboratory at Brookhaven or Berkeley with its extensive military-industrial links. The size and cost of the British university accelerators provoked tensions within the university context, a theme I will return to throughout this book.

British nuclear physics was also carried out at the Atomic Energy Research Establishment at Harwell[48], where the emphasis was on applied nuclear physics: the conduct of research on piles, and the production of isotopes. Attlee's Labour government set up Harwell with the recent memories of extensive American wartime collaboration, but in the context of increased American protectionism on nuclear matters exemplified by the McMahon Act which imposed 'draconian policies' restricting communication and co-operation.[49] Initially, the establishment was oriented towards the military: Harwell's director from 1945 to 1959, Sir John Cockcroft, was responsible only to Minister of Supply and his Permanent Secretary. Harwell's policy-making apparatus stood largely separate from the newly instigated structures that advised on the remainder of civil and defence science: Tizard, as chair of both the ACSP and DRPC was largely excluded.[50] Several large instruments were constructed, including cyclotrons, an electron synchrotron, and a linear accelerator. From the early 1950s, with the establishment of the United Kingdom Atomic Energy Authority (UKAEA) in 1954, Harwell increasingly 'became responsible for research and development on civil nuclear power, growing to 6,000 staff by 1956'.[51] The large numbers of staff at Harwell were organised into hierarchical team structures. As an institution, it was the centre of the post-war economies of science, as students, isotopes and techniques circulated, albeit in a highly regulated manner, between university, government and industry.[52]

The commitment that British physicists had made to their university and government projects made them wary of European collaboration, even though the pooled resources may have led to more powerful research machines. Several schemes for European co-operation on a nuclear physics project were floated in late 1949 and early 1950. Over the next year, a small group

---

[48] Harwell was the largest site. Other nuclear research and development was undertaken: in particular, weapons research at Aldermaston and the production of fissile material at Risley.

[49] Gowing (1974), vol 1: Policy Making, pp. 104-112.

[50] Gowing (1974), p. 36. Although this situation was briefly rectified by the appointment of Cockcroft as chair of the DRPC from 1952-1954. Gummett (1980), p. 32.

[51] Gummett (1980), p. 129.

[52] With important consequences for the geography of British science: Harwell spawned several new sites between Oxford and West London, including the fusion research at Culham, radio isotopes at Amersham, and the SRC Atlas Computing Laboratory. See Hall et al (1987), p. 120.

of nuclear and cosmic ray physicists met with science administrators, and a proposal for a European accelerator laboratory was agreed. At this stage British physicists were reticent, offering 'co-operation without commitment'.[53] There were reasons for British reticence: Britain was 'already ahead of her European associates in the field of accelerator design, development and construction', and had, moreover, just completed (but not yet exploited) several large and expensive machines. Furthermore, it was the post-war policy of bodies such as the Royal Society to continue the 'traditional forms of scientific collaboration - exchange of personnel... attendence at conferences, circulation of preprints', over "new centralized international laboratories in subjects where active research is being carried out on a large scale".[54] Finally, the European project was contrary to Labour policy of supporting closer ties between the United States and Europe (exemplified by NATO and the Marshall Plan), and the continuing links with the Commonwealth.

Mild enthusiasm for a European project amongst elite British physicists was tied to conditions: James Chadwick, professor at Liverpool University wanted the proposed institute under Neils Bohr at Copenhagen, and supported Sir George Thomson's suggestion of offering the Liverpool cyclotron as Britain's contribution to a Copenhagen centre. At a conference in Paris in December 1951, the promoters of a European particle physics project were highly polarised: a group led by the French, Italians and Belgians who considered a big new accelerator 'essential', and a group opposing any new machine and favouring an institute under Bohr. Thomson, whilst offering the Liverpool cyclotron, also presented a financial argument: "Now the claims of other expensive branches of physics, like radio-astronomy, and indeed other branches of science, had to be heard".[55] The Cabinet Steering Committee on International Relations refused to sanction the signing of the draft proposals drawn up after Paris, worrying that Britain would be committed to an expensive project, and one that was contrary to Foreign Office policy on involvement with international organisations. However, the offer of the Liverpool cyclotron remained in an attempt not to look unco-operative.

A new wave of lobbying by Cockcroft, Thomson and Chadwick in the first half of 1952 'paid off': Lord Cherwell (a figure of renewed importance with the election of Churchill the year before) was favourable. Also, the Secretary of the DSIR, Sir Ben Lockspeiser, agreed to the cost of CERN falling on the DSIR vote so long as "the various departments could agree

[53] Krige, J., in Hermann et al (1987), p. 435.
[54] Royal Society International Relations Committee, International Research Laboratories. Draft Brief for UK Delegation to ECOSOC, 1948. Quoted by Krige in Hermann et al (1987), p. 437.
[55] Quotation from Krige, in Hermann et al (1987), p. 451.

that the UK join the [provisional CERN] Council".[56] From this point on the DSIR 'became increasingly involved in the project'. On 23 June 1952, despite the recommendations of the now pro-CERN Cabinet Steering Committee, the Treasury rejected what it viewed as an open-ended financial commitment to an expensive scientific project.

A distinct shift in the British attitude towards CERN occured in mid-1952: a group of younger physicists at Harwell, convinced that a European large accelerator was now likely and intent on British science remaining 'competitive', advocated Britain joining the full CERN.[57] Of the 'elder statesmen' Cockcroft, Herbert Skinner, and Blackett sympathised with the young Harwell group. A significant factor in persuading them was the perceived success of the bevatron at the communal Brookhaven in the United States, especially when compared to the "dispersion of effort" amongst the five British universities.[58] Chadwick and Thomson remained committed to an organisation under Bohr, and against a new big accelerator. Chadwick considered Britain "close to bankruptcy" and therefore not able to afford membership. Aware of this new commitment amongst British physicists, and swayed by Cherwell's approval, Lockspeiser agreed to persuade ministers that the involvement of HMG in CERN was desirable. Krige speculates that a certain amount of self-interest entered into Lockspeiser's decision: 'these moves occured at a time when the DSIR found itself again slipping into second place behind the scientific services of the defence departments which, in response to the cold war, had received a new injection of funds', and CERN presented a way 'to ensure that the DSIR had a stake in the most glamorous and prestigious area of civil science'.[59]

Although the Chancellor, R.A. Butler, again initially rejected the case for British membership of CERN in August 1952, he was finally persuaded (concurring with a memorandum written by Lockspeiser) in December after opt-out clauses were incorporated in the CERN convention. Krige gives several reasons for Butler's decision: the final consensus amongst physicists, the opt-out clauses, the approval of Cherwell, an 'overall improvement in the British economy' between mid-1952 and mid-1955, and surprisingly an 'acceptence in government circles that scientific research in general, and accelerator physics in particular, were expensive and expansive'. Moreover,

---

[56] Reported in Letter, Rackham to Verry, 7 April 1952. From Krige, in Hermann et al (1987), p. 463.

[57] Krige notes that this Harwell group had 'worked on the development of radar during the war where they acquired skills readily transferable to the accelerator domain', and now constituted 'the most experienced nucleus of accelerator builders'.

[58] The words belong to the University College space scientist Harry Massey. From Krige, in Hermann et al (1987), pp. 485-486.

[59] Krige, in Hermann et al (1987), p. 489.

the nuclear physicists benefited by association from 'the new priority given to rearmament and weapons development' from 1951 to 1959.[60] Lockspeiser was able to sign the CERN convention for Britain in July 1953.

Research at CERN was structured into teams and administrative hierarchies, and organised around expensive, large scale machines requiring permanent teams of experimentalists and instrument builders. A similar pattern was found on a national scale was found at the British National Institute for Research in Nuclear Science (NIRNS). NIRNS was set up in 1957 to provide 'centralised reserach facilities for teams from universities and other institutions on a scale which individually they could not mount', and 'complement' work at CERN.[61] As a 'national research centre' it is deeply significant, as it represents a break from siting facilities (other than international ventures such as CERN) at universities.

The history of British space science has several connections with that of CERN and radio astronomy. Massey and Robins, participants in the rocket and satellite research programmes, have described its development in terms of the confluence of meteorological research and Second World War technology.[62] In this account one strand was the radiophysical research of the ionosphere under Edward Appleton, and the meteorological research programme overseen by the Gassiot Committee of the Royal Society. The second strand was the trajectory of rocket technology, passing at the war's end from the V2 engineers at Peenemunde to a welcoming Russia and the United States, and thence in part to Britain.[63] This confluence was a happy circumstance: it was a 'fortunate fact that by 1953, while there were a number of scientists whose research would be greatly expanded if space research techniques became available, technological progress through defence requirements had proceeded to a stage where it could be utilised successfully'.[64] This historiography of fortune should not obscure the networks of contacts that cemented post-war science. In 1953, the Ministry of Supply made rockets (now thoroughly tested at RAE) available to university scientists. Scientists at Queen's University, Belfast, University College of Wales, Birmingham University, and Imperial College all expressed enthusiasm. A meeting at RAE of the Gassiot Committee in February 1954 recommended that the Royal Society Secretary, David Brunt, make a direct

---

[60] Krige, in Hermann et al (1987), p. 501.

[61] Gummett (1980), p. 172.

[62] Massey, H. and Robins, M., 1986. *History of British Space Science*, Cambridge: Cambridge University Press.

[63] In the first few years after 1945 American scientists launched 60 improved V-2s (renamed the WAC Corporal, Viking, and Aerobee); the USSR launched 20 V-2s in 1947; and 3 British V-2s took off from Cuxhaven in Operation Backfire.

[64] Massey and Robins (1986), p. 1.

appeal to the Treasury for £100,000 for civil rocket research: half to go to university grants, and half to the Ministry of Supply for costs. Treasury agreement to the proposal came in mid-1955, with the funds channelled through the Air Ministry. A Gassiot sub-committee, chaired by Massey and approved by Ministry of Supply chief scientist Sir Owen Wansbrough-Jones, outlined a research programme. These experiments were launched on Skylark rockets from Woomera, and required extensive 'co-operation' between the Royal Society, RAE and the Australian Weapons Research Establishment.

University scientists and technicians constructed the experimental apparatus for the Skylark programme, but the final assembly, launch and data collection took place at military sites. Viewed by a university scientist, the experiments still remained apparently small scale. However, involved with and supporting each launch were a large number of bodies: university physics departments, the Royal Society, scientists, engineers and bureaucrats at government and military establishments in Britain and Australia, as well as the networks of communication and transport necessary for collaboration.

The collaboration was extended in the great international scientific venture of the 1950s: the International Geophysical Year (IGY).[65] The suggestion by American science administrator Lloyd Berkner that the 25th anniversary of the 2nd Polar Year of 1932-33 be marked by another such programme of joint research found strong support amongst the relevant international unions: the International Astronomical Union (IAU) and the International Union of Geodesy and Geophysics. This persuaded the International Council of Scientific Unions (ICSU) to organise IGY for 1957-58. During the Year 'about sixty countries participated, taking observations over eighteen months at hundreds of stations under plans drawn up by a special committee and with the results collated by a small international secretariat'.[66] IGY was seized upon by the Royal Society as an opportunity to demonstrate its continued national importance. The British involvement centred around a Royal Society expedition, organised by its National Committee for IGY, to Halley Bay in Antarctica. Researchers at Manchester University constructed and operated duplicates of their Jodrell Bank radar apparatus at Halley Bay to study meteor trails in the ionosphere. The National Committee, although 'very sceptical' about their likely appearance in IGY, discussed preparations for tracking the American earth satellites announced by Eisenhower. I will discuss in this book the reception and use of the satellites, in particular the surprise Soviet Sputniks, within Britain.

---

[65] Fraser, R., 1957. *Once Around the Sun: International Geophysical Year 1957-1958*, London: The Scientific Book Club. Wilson, J.T., 1961. *IGY: the Year of the New Moons*, London: Michael Joseph, 1961. Sullivan, W., 1961. *Assault on the Unknown: the International Geophysical Year*, London: Hodder and Stroughton.

[66] Rose and Rose (1969), p. 183.

A Novel Popular Audience for Science?

We have seen that science was held in particular high regard both within government, and arguably by a wider public in the immediate post-war years. We have also seen how a lack of scientific and engineering 'manpower' was seen as a severe problem, and efforts were made to expand rapidly the output of qualified graduates. In this section I want to examine the interactions between the managed display of science and the dynamics of a popular audience for science in the 1950s. I begin with a key early 1950s interface between elite science and the public (as well as nation state and subject): the Festival of Britain.

In 1951, the Festival of Britain opened, an expression of the post-war culture of planning that Roy Strong has described as having 'made visible a brave New World' for those 'wearied of war and its aftermath, austerity'.[67] Partly because the Festival bequeathed the South Bank complex it has been regarded as significant in the history of post-war British arts, but far less so in the history of science. Some contemporary observers wistfully compared the Festival to the industrially dominated Great Exhibition of 1851: 'the Festival of Britain is not so manifestly a scientific occasion'. Interestingly, this commentator, Herbert Dingle, the isolated Professor of History and Philosophy of Science at the University of London, goes on to claim: 'yet in an even greater degree it is permeated by the spirit of science, for this is pre-eminently a scientific age'.[68] Forgan has recently explicitly called for a reclamation of the Festival: she rightly argues that 'the role of science was far more significant than has hitherto been acknowledged'.[69]

Images of science and technology were deeply embedded as a key component in the rhetoric and iconography of progress before the beginning of the century. Science and technology had already been on display at expos and world fairs: for example at the Chicago World Fair of 1893 'visitors to the fair were amazed by seemingly endless displays of electricity: whirring dynamos and motors, dancing fountains, futuristic kitchens, and an elevated railway'.[70] However, a detailed examination of the Festival of Britain reveals nuances in the use of science that stem from its particular post-war British context. The organisation of the Festival began under the Attlee government

---

[67] Roy Strong in Banham, M. and Hillier, B. (eds), 1976. *A Tonic to the Nation: the Festival of Britain 1951*, London: Thames & Hudson, p. 8.

[68] Dingle, H. (ed.), 1951. *A Century of Science, 1851-1951*, London: Hutchinson's Scientific and Technical Publications, p. vii.

[69] Forgan, S., 'Festivals of science and the two cultures: science, architecture and display in the Festival of Britain 1951', forthcoming.

[70] Platt, H., 'City lights: the electrification of the Chicago region, 1880-1930', in Tarr, J.A. and Dupuy, G., 1988. *Technology and the Rise of the Networked City in Europe and America*, Philadelphia: Temple University Press, pp. 246-281.

in 1947, and ended under the lukewarm administration of Churchill's returning Conservatives. Elite scientists and government advisors were well represented in organising committees, and a Council for Science and Technology under Sir Alan Barlow was set up, amongst others, alongside the pre-existing Arts Council.[71] Ian Cox, an ex-geologist who had also worked for the BBC and the London Press Service, was appointed to the key position of Director of Science and member of the eleven-strong Executive Committee.

The Festival Council approved twelve official exhibitions, of which two are of most interest here: the South Bank Exhibition and the Exhibition of Science at South Kensington. The latter was essentially a permanent extension of the Science Museum, and was subsidiary to the South Bank, as the official history records:

> Science, as a field in which Britain has made outstanding contributions, already provided much of the material at the South Bank where its application to contemporary life was to be emphasised. The exhibition at South Kensington would develop this story further.[72]

The story, on the twin Festival themes[73] of the Land and People of Britain, was narrated at the 'centrepiece' of the South Bank: the Dome of Discovery. Exhibitions based on narrative themes were, as Forgan points out, a recent innovation. A sense of the story can be gleaned from the *Guide*, written by Cox.[74] An ideal visitor would enter the Dome and be confronted first with displays of great British exploration, continuing the trail to see and hear of such subjects as agriculture, the earth, the sea and the sky. At each stage science was to the fore: 'providing the most suitable weapons' for pest control, telling the spectator the composition of the sea, and detailing the structure of the ionosphere. The visitor passed through Outer Space[75], the Living World and the Physical World, ending the first 'Upstream' theme of 'Land' with nuclear research and its numerous applications. Outside the Dome, the 'Downstream circuit' of 'People', although focusing on British

---

[71] Members were: Barlow (chair), Sir Wallace Akers, Sir Stanley Angwin, Sir Edward Appleton, Ian Cox, Sir Alfred Egerton, Sir John Fryer, Sir William Halcrow, E.H. Havelock, Sir Harold Himsworth, Sir Ben Lockspeiser, Sir Edward Mellanby, Professor Andrew Robertson, Sir Edward Salisbury, Sir William Slater, and Sir Frank Smith.

[72] Anon, *The Story of the Festival of Britain 1951*, London: HMSO, 1952, p. 9.

[73] Themes 'devised by Ian Cox'.

[74] Cox, I., 1951. *The South Bank Exhibition. A Guide to the Story in Tells*, London: HMSO.

[75] Penrose Angwin was Theme Convener, Display Designers were Austin Frazer and Eric Towell.

institutions and character, also displayed medical science. The scientific image was reiterated in the Skylon (an emaciated suspended rocket shape).

King George VI, broadcasting from the steps of St Paul's Cathedral, declared the Festival open with a message proclaiming it as a 'visible sign of national achievement and confidence' (and a reminder of 'how vital a part is played in industry by scientific imagination and research'.[76] 8,455,863 people passed through the turnstiles of the South Bank Exhibition, 213,744 made the extra trip to South Kensington.[77] Over eight million also enjoyed the Festival Pleasure Gardens, a funfair in Battersea Park reluctantly approved by the Festival Committee and distanced from the South Bank.

It is difficult to recover how the Festival's narrative was received and reshaped by its audience (who were, of course, far less diligent in writing up their experience than the organisers). However, if the message was heard at all as it was intended to be, the passage of people through turnstiles circulated a particular linkage of science and national identity in 1950s Britain. The Festival of Britain promoted a spectacular pageant of science, discovery and exploration as elements of a national rebirth.

The nuclear research pinnacle of the Dome of Discovery's Upstream Circuit reflected both the public interest in the atom, but also Britain's commitment to the atomic project. The closely linked military and civil programme aimed at producing both weapons that would signify national status, and a new energy industry.[78] Managing display was an important aspect of this endeavour, both to interpret the work for national and international audiences, but also to act as a recruiting mechanism. Harwell, for example, held open days. In August 1956 the new Queen's triumphant opening ceremony of Calder Hall (the first atomic power station to feed electricity into a national grid) suggested national preeminence in reactor design and a possible export product. As Sir Edwin Plowden, Chairman of the UKAEA expressed the sentiment in the foreword of a promotional book:

> Atomic energy is news. It has been for all of its short history... In any true perspective the opening of Calder Hall must balk large, particularly for this country.[79]

However the presentation of nuclear science as national spectacle would raise unique problems, not least issues of defence security. Barely a year after the opening of Calder Hall, the fire at the neighbouring Windscale

---

[76] Anon (1952), pp. 17-18.

[77] Anon (1952), pp. 31-32. The numbers include repeat visits.

[78] Cathcart, B., 1994. *Test of Greatness: Britain's Struggle for the Atomic Bomb*, London: John Murray.

[79] Jay, K., 1956. *Calder Hall: the Story of Britain's First Atomic Power Station*, London: Methuen, p. v.

plutonium factory began the slow processes of reappraisal of the nuclear programme, within Whitehall, the media, and the public at large.[80] Closely following the Windscale accident, an attempt at managing a public display of apparent nuclear success, Harwell's Zero Energy Thermonuclear Assembly (ZETA), ended ignominiously. ZETA began as an experiemntal apparatus to investigate the production of energy from nuclear fusion. Harried by persistent questioning, Cockcroft declared that it was "90 per cent certain that the neutrons [produced by ZETA] were of thermonuclear origin".[81] A primed press recast the announcement in familiar atomic rhetoric of an imminent age of energy plenty, the Scientific Correspondent of the *Manchester Guardian* proclaiming:

> Life would be transformed out of recognition. Prosperity of a kind the world has not yet seen might be just round the corner.[82]

However by May 1958 Harwell scientists revised their opinion that the neutrons were the result of fusion, and soon the press were said to have promulgated "undue optimism" over the ZETA results. Risk and inflated expectations made nuclear physics an unstable icon. The example of ZETA illustrated how although scientists increasingly recognised that they had to play to a public gallery (as well as a political one) to win support for their work, they also realised that careful management of public display was required. Moreover, the public audience for science was undergoing change.

Displays of nuclear science were intended for various audiences, part of which bought popularizations (of science in general) in both book and periodical form in increasing numbers. Regular titles such as *Endeavour* and *Discovery* continued into the post-war years, and they were joined in 1946 by *Science News* published by Penguin. Edited first by John Enogat when it was a shilling an issue, and later by J.L. Crammer, A.W. Haslett, and finally Archie and Nan Clow, *Science News* described itself as a 'guide into the jungle' of scientific writing, with an emphasis on 'new developments...the foremost fringe of scientific developments'.[83] The paperback format carried around ten articles (with a central section of illustrations), a research report by Haslett and correspondence. *Science News* could be bought both at

---

[80] See: Arnold, L. 1992. *Windscale 1957: Anatomy of a Nuclear Accident*, Dublin: Gill and Macmillan.

[81] Hartcup, G. and Allibone, T.E., 1984. *Cockcroft and the Atom*, Bristol: Adam Hilger, p. 206. Hendry, J. and Lawson, J.D, 1993. *Fusion Research in the UK, 1945-1960*, London: HMSO.

[82] Maddox, J., 1958. *A Plain Man's Guide to Zeta*, Manchester Guardian Pamphlet. See also: Jukes, J.D., 1959. *Man-Made Sun. The Story of Zeta*, London: Abelard-Schuman.

[83] *Science News* (1946) 1, pp. 7-8.

booksellers and by subscription, a system shared by its hardback monograph equivalent, W.A. Foyle's Scientific Book Club. By 1949, when subscribers numbered over 7000, a member of the Scientific Book Club could purchase editions of books at from one fifth to one third the price in the bookshop.[84]

It is difficult to generalise about the size and structure of the readership of 1950s science popularizations. Some information can be deduced from the success of the launch of *New Scientist* in 1956 (responsible, in part, for the decline of *Science News* which ended three years later after 54 issues).[85] From the start *New Scientist* was well-connected. Sir Cyril Hinshelwood, President of the Royal Society, wrote on bacteria for the first issue, and he was followed by other eminent names.[86] The classifieds offered jobs in university, government and industrial laboratories; major firms such as ICI and Shell placed regular full-page advertisements. The employment-seeking graduates created by the expansion of education following Barlow formed an important and sizable readership.

Appearing a few months after the opening of Calder Hall, *New Scientist* was a bullish supporter of the nuclear programme. Tom Margerison, Scientific Editor (and staff writer with Nigel Calder), argued in November 1956 that the 'only solution' to reliance on Middle East oil was 'to develop atomic energy more rapidly than the Government had planned', a stance reiterated repeatedly by the columnist 'Geminus'. Indeed the journal vigorously lobbied for the place of science in general:

> If Britain is to remain a first-class economic Power our Government, our Parliament and our people must become far more keenly aware of the ascendancy of science...

The magazine covered in depth spectacular and prestige projects, such as the International Geophysical Year, satellites and, later when 'radio astronomy [had] replaced nuclear physics as our chief intellectual sounding board', large radio telescopes.[87] *New Scientist* used coverage of the spectacular to

---

[84] Authors reprinted by the Scientific Book Club included nearly all the familiar contemporary names of science popularization and popular science: Julian Huxley, J.B.S. Haldane, James Jeans, Ritchie Calder, J.G. Crowther, J. Bronowski, Captain J.Y. Cousteau, and so on.

[85] The early *New Scientist*s cost one shilling an issue, by which time *Science News* had risen to 2/6.

[86] The opening Editorial modestly claimed: 'We who launch it believe we are doing so at a time when the need for the magazine is obvious and urgent. We have been encouraged in our project by the approval – in many cases the enthusiasm – of leaders of science and industry whom we consulted in the preparatory stages'. *New Scientist* (22 November 1956) 1(1), p. 5.

[87] Editorial, *New Scientist* (22 August 1957) 40(2), p. 5.

claim and address a young constituency in a period when organizations that represented such groups, for example the Association of Scientific Workers, struggled to recruit.[88]

In this section it has only been possible to discuss science and the public in 1950s Britain through negative means: drawing conclusions from the organisation of displays, the likely readership of books, and the setting up and success of new periodicals. This evidence is enough to show at least the *existence* of an audience for a possible spectacle of science. Only later, when the 'odd' correspondence to Jodrell Bank is discussed in Chapter Three, will a less passive public be recovered.

HISTORIES OF RADIO ASTRONOMY

In this section I discuss the emergence of radio astronomy in the years immediately following the Second World War. I analyse in detail the historiographies of the two major accounts of British radio astronomy: Lovell's *The Story of Jodrell Bank* (1968), and Edge and Mulkay's *Astronomy Transformed* (1976). I indicate their strengths, but also show lacunae which I examine further in the subsequent chapters.

Narratives and Sources

Narratives of the history of radio astronomy are found in the following forums: explicitly in books and articles written by participants, implicitly in other interventions by participants (such as films and academic papers), in newspaper stories, in scholarly works within the disciplines of sociology of science and science policy, and in the output of historians of science. Two broad but important points should be noted. First, these narratives have drawn from, and been retold by one another: sequences and themes recur until they form a spell of solidity, of 'fact'. Second, each narrative was written from a position, a specific cultural location, and written for a reason: they are interventions directed towards an audience. Therefore attention should be paid to changing orders, to absences and presences, in the narrative sequences.[89]

Textual authority was constituted from the management and arrangement of 'sources'. The source of lived experience underwrote the participants'

---

[88] Horner, D., 1986. 'Scientists, trade unions and labour movement policies for science and technology, 1947-1964', thesis, Aston University, p. 87.

[89] Woolgar, S., 1979. 'The emergence and growth of research areas in science with special reference to research on pulsars', unpublished PhD, Cambridge University. Woolgar provides a systematic analysis of the discrepancies between discovery accounts, arguing that the discrepancies provide a useful historical resource.

accounts, such as the collected recollections in Sullivan's edited volume[90], or the director of the Cambridge radio astronomy group, Martin Ryle's contribution to *Search and Research*.[91] The accounts of the history of Manchester University's radio astronomy station at Jodrell Bank, written by Bernard Lovell, were more complex, and will be considered in depth later. Lovell extended his claim of participatory authority by incorporating his own documents and private diaries to support his histories. Moreover, he used his histories, as well as the device of mobilising private documents, continually in his personal and institutional strategies. History in the hands of Lovell formed a repertoire to be mobilised, and constituted a public self-fashioning. The most impressive attempt to synthesise the intellectual and social development of radio astronomy in Britain was Edge and Mulkay's rich and detailed *Astronomy Transformed*.[92] Edge and Mulkay (one an ex-Cambridge radio astronomer and the other a sociologist of science), used four types of source data: the published and public 'research papers, proceedings of learned societies, symposia and conference proceedings', interviews with a 'significant proportion of those contributing to...radio astronomy' between 1945 and 1960, the participants' histories, and the 'more objective data' such as 'patterns of citation'.[93] These publications, based on these sources, have been digested in part of North's recent 'big picture' history of astronomy.[94]

The Early History of Radio Astronomy

Britain, Australia, USA, France, and Holland started the 1950s as the major observing nations in radio astronomy and remained so, Canada and the USSR joined them during the decade, whereas Germany, Japan, and Sweden were also 'active...if more modestly'.[95] In this section I review the early histories of work in Britain, Australia, Holland and the United States.

---

[90] Sullivan III, W.T. (ed), 1984. *The Early Years of Radio Astronomy: Reflections Fifty Years After Jansky's Discovery*, Cambridge: Cambridge University Press.

[91] Ryle, M., 1971. 'Radio Astronomy: the Cambridge Contribution'. In Wilson, J.P (ed), 1971. *Search and Research*, London: Mullard, pp. 11-54. Also in this category is Hey, J.S., 1973. *The Evolution of Radio Astronomy*, London: Elek.

[92] Edge, D.O. and Mulkay, M.J., 1976. *Astronomy Transformed: the Emergence of Radio Astronomy in Britain*, London: John Wiley and Sons.

[93] Edge and Mulkay (1976), pp. 2-3.

[94] North, J.D., 1994. *The Fontana History of Astronomy and Cosmology*, London: Fontana Press, pp. 542-566.

[95] Edge and Mulkay (1976), p. 49. For Sweden see: Hard, M., 1993. 'Technological drift in science: Swedish radio astronomy in the making, 1942-1976'. In Lindqvist, S., 1993. *Center on the Periphery: Historical Aspects of 20th-Century Swedish Physics*, Canton: Science History Publications, pp. 378-397. For France, Canada,

The three major groups in Britain were all born from war-time work. The war-time task of the group under Hey at the Army Operational Research Group (AORG) was to study the reports on the efficiency of all army radar equipments, to identify sources of interference, and ...investigate anything that might impede the effective operation of Britain's radar. The investigation of 'interference' led Hey to identify strong radio emissions from the sun, and the phenomena of transient ionospheric 'echoes' that could be confused with V-2s. The AORG was based at Malvern, final home of the TRE and its successor the Royal Radar Establishment. Although it continued as a small group through the 1950s, the importance of the AORG lies in its part in the network of contacts formed at TRE. The knowledge and practice of the radar phenomena identified by Hey was transplanted back into university departments with the dispersal of government establishments, in particular TRE, at the war's end.

Martin Ryle, returning to Cambridge, was helped by J.A. Ratcliffe, the head of the Cavendish Radio Physics Group, to recruit ex-TRE researchers to begin a programme on radio emissions from the sun, utilising ex-TRE and ex-RAE equipment. The Cambridge radio astronomy group grew slowly, marked early on by a concentration on the design and development of 'new research techniques'. At the end of the 1940s, attention at Cambridge shifted from solar research to a research programme dominated by the production of 'surveys' of radio 'sources' with novel and progressively larger 'arrays' of aerials. The technical strategy of the Cambridge group in the 1950s was a commitment to these special purpose interferometer arrays, along with the complex techniques, in particular 'aperture synthesis' required to reduce the data.

At Manchester, too, physicists returned to the university department. Langworthy Professor in Physics, Patrick Blackett returned to resume active directorship of the physics laboratories having had a good war: serving on the Maud Committee on nuclear weapons and the Ministry of Supply RDF Applications Committee, as well as conducting influential research and development at RAE, AA Command, Coastal Command and the Admiralty, where he was Director of Naval Operational Research.[96] Blackett, a radical member of the Barlow Committee, was determined that Manchester should spearhead the expansionary policies for education that the Committee called

USSR and Japan see: Salomonovich, A.E., 'The first steps in Soviet radio astronomy', Ginzburg, V.L., 'Remarks on my early work on radio astronomy', Denisse, J.F., 'The early years of radio astronomy in France', Covington, A.E., 'The beginnings of solar radio astronomy in Canada' and Tanaka, H., 'Development of solar radio astronomy in Japan up until 1960', in Sullivan (1984).

[96] Lovell, A.C.B., 1976. *P.M.S. Blackett: a Biographical Memoir*, Bristol: John Wright & Sons, a book version of the Royal Society Obituary.

for. He had a strong local and national ally in Sir Ernest Simon, later Lord Simon of Wythenshawe, who was also later a powerful ally of the promoters of the Radio Telescope.[97]

Blackett and Lovell, who returned to Manchester when demobilised from TRE, recruited radar researchers and equipment to begin a programme on Blackett's subject of cosmic ray showers, which they identified as the source of Hey's transient radar echoes and a subject on which they had published jointly during the war.[98] The group established itself in a university-owned field, a botanical research site named Jodrell Bank, twenty miles south of Manchester. Blackett's policy of departmental expansion was to encourage rapid growth in a diversity of projects under team leaders, in contrast to channelling all the department's resources into cosmic rays. So as the Jodrell Bank Research Station grew, and when in 1946 the echoes that the radar sets displayed were identified with meteors, the cosmic ray research branched into an expanding meteor astronomy programme. Later in the 1940s, a 218 foot bowl of wire was constructed firstly as part of the radar research, but was quickly and flexibly used in other areas. Edge and Mulkay locate in the 218 foot telescope the beginnings of a 'technical strategy' of large dish, 'multipurpose' instruments, of which the 240 foot Radio Telescope was the centrepiece. They were used either singly, or in combination with smaller, movable aerials as interferometers.

The Australian group based at the Radiophysics Laboratory of Commonwealth Scientific and Industrial Research Organisation (CSIRO) near Sydney, was, like Hey's AORG, a government establishment that continued war-time radar work into post-war radio astronomy.[99] Its Chief was Edward G. Bowen, who had worked at TRE and the MIT Radiation Laboratory during the war. The research programme of the radio astronomy group, headed by J.L. Pawsey, was broadly similar to Cambridge's, with concentration on the development of arrays to use on solar and survey work.

The Dutch scientists involved with radio astronomy were a rarity, say Edge and Mulkay, in that they were 'established optical astronomers' who

---

[97] Simon, E.D., 1944. *The Development of British Universities*, London: Longmans.

[98] Blackett, P.M.S. and Lovell, A.C.B., 1941. 'Radio echoes and cosmic ray showers', *Proceedings of the Royal Society of London A* 177, p. 183. See also Lovell, A.C.B., 1993. 'The Blackett-Eckersley-Lovell correspondence of World War Two and the origins of Jodrell Bank', *Notes and Records of the Royal Society of London* 47, pp. 119-131. Blackett had held influential government advisory posts, as well as carrying out innovatory operational research, during the war. He is a central figure in the post-war networks of science.

[99] Robertson, P., 1992. *Beyond Southern Skies: Radio Astronomy and the Parkes Telescope*, Cambridge: Cambridge University Press. Also, see the useful reminiscences by E.G. Bowen, W.N. Christiansen, F.J. Kerr, B.Y. Mills and R.N. Bracewell in Sullivan (1984).

'took the initiative, perceived the possibility of using radio techniques to pursue their scientific goals, and took steps to form and direct a suitably qualified team'.[100] This process started at Leiden under Jan Oort during German occupation of the Netherlands. Oort's group continued classical astronomical subjects but used different electromagnetic wavelengths: studies of the galaxy, in particular the hydrogen clouds that they predicted would radiate at 21 cm (1420 Mc/s).

Cosmic radio waves were first identified in America before the war, by the two lone figures of radio astronomy mythology: Karl Jansky and Grote Reber, retrospectively elevated to everpresent 'founding fathers' in the linear histories of radio astronomy, although their work was largely unknown in Britain or Australia (Hey was an exception).[101] Radio astronomy in the United States after the war started slowly, as has been noted by several authors.[102] Since 1945, as in Britain and Australia, sizable war-time radar and electronics programmes had been built up in the United States, this absence is surprising. Edge and Mulkay found three reasons: the "revolution" in optical astronomy, marked by the construction of telescopes such as Mount Wilson, 'absorbed many astronomers in the thirties and forties' making radio astronomy was not immediately appealing; secondly, this optical programme was expanding with even larger telescopes (the 200" Mount Palomar was completed in 1949); and finally the prestigious big science of nuclear physics drew into it many of the radar and electronics researchers.[103] Small radio astronomy groups did exist at MIT, the National Bureau of Standards, the Carnegie Institution, and from the mid-1950s, radio astronomy expanded rapidly at Harvard, Stanford, the Naval Research Laboratory (NRL), and, in particular, the combined university National Radio Astronomy Observatory (NRAO) at Green Bank, West Virginia.[104] However, as I argue in my conclusion, it is probably more productive to seek explanations for why non-American radio astronomy grew so fast, than asking why American radio astronomy was slow to develop.

Edge and Mulkay identify the emergence of an 'international research community' in radio astronomy as complete by the mid-1950s. Specialities within radio astronomy had appeared: radar work on meteors, and its extension to the moon, the planets and aurorae, ionospheric investigations via the 'scintillation' of discrete sources, radio emission from the planets, notably Jupiter, solar radio emission, mapping of galactic radio emission,

---

[100] Edge and Mulkay (1976), p. 35.

[101] Edge and Mulkay (1976), p. 11, p. 20.

[102] Sullivan, W.T. (1984), p. 191.

[103] Edge and Mulkay (1976), p. 264.

[104] Needell, A.A., 1987. 'Lloyd Berkner, Merle Tuve, and the federal role in radio astronomy', *Osiris* 2nd series 3, pp. 261-288.

and the study of discrete sources both individually and in surveys. The radio universe was startlingly different from the optical one: the few 'optical identifications' of strong radio sources seemed to consist of either rare or close objects: colliding galaxies in the case of Cygnus A, supernova remnants (the Crab Nebula in Taurus), and the relatively nearby Andromeda and Triangulum galaxies. The bulk of the radio sources remained unidentified, initially described as 'radio stars' indicating an origin within the galaxy, and later (following the few identifications) held to be extragalactic objects.

Two Historiographies of Radio Astronomy

Astronomy Transformed was an attempt to provide a 'case study showing how the social and intellectual aspects of radio astronomy have been linked together in one historical process', and thence to 'discuss the findings...in relation to previous writings on the development of areas of scientific inquiry'.[105] The book was explicitly limited: firstly by the restriction to the comparative study of three 'centres' of radio astronomical research in the 1950s: the off-shoot of the Cavendish Radio Group at Cambridge, Manchester University's research station at Jodrell Bank, and the Australian radiophysics group at Sydney; and secondly by a concentration within these groups on work on radio 'sources'. *Astronomy Transformed* centres on the controversy over radio source surveys that erupted between Cambridge and Sydney in the mid-1950s.

Edge and Mulkay relate the social organisation of research to the scientific and technical 'strategies' taken by the research groups. The dominant social process was that of 'competition' both within and between groups. Competitive pressures 'were at work inside the groups' and were 'effectively resolved by specialisation of interests and skills and that such specialisation, accompanied as it was by the use of common equipment and a concern with closely related areas of inquiry, gave rise to a fairly high level of collaborative research'.[106] Between groups, the competitive pressures resulted in 'differentiation' or dispute. 'Technical commitments' played an important role in these processes. Contrasting Jodrell Bank and Cambridge, they state:

> Over the years each group became increasingly committed to its own type of equipment and to distinctive observational methods. As the cost of increasingly sophisticated instruments rose, and as the time involved in planning succeeding stages of technical advance lengthened, so it became less and less possible for either group to bring about any sudden change in technique or radically to change its focus of scientific enquiry.[107]

---

[105] Edge and Mulkay (1976), p. 223.

[106] Edge and Mulkay (1976), p. 237.

[107] Edge and Mulkay (1976), pp. 354-355.

The technical strategies, say Edge and Mulkay, were the response to scientific questions posed by the unfamiliar radio universe, and their development essential in the closure of these questions.[108] Within Britain competition between groups resulted in differentiation, expressed and solidified in choices over techniques and instruments. They draw out several contrasts between the Cambridge and Jodrell Bank groups. The technical commitment to 'multipurpose' large dishes at Jodrell Bank was related to strong internal differentiation into 'teams'. They identify (via co-publication) four teams of radar workers: three with team leaders (Lovell, Tom Kaiser, and J.S. Greenhow) and one pair.[109] Radio and radar were split early on at Jodrell Bank, with 'tight-knit groups' of radio workers forming around R.D. Davies (on 21cm hydrogen emission), Palmer and Large (both on discrete sources). Research students became 'attached to teams' that maintained 'a constant research focus'. The senior figures, Lovell and Hanbury Brown, held together this social structure, in their administrative and evaluative roles. The processes of internal social differentiation and scientific and technical strategy were 'inter-related'. Edge and Mulkay refuse to give primacy to either, and instead argue for co-development: formation into teams meant that multi-purpose instruments were desirable, which reciprocally strengthened the team system. They therefore suggest that the design of the Mark I telescope (a 'multi-purpose, steerable, large paraboloid') was an expression of this combination of group dynamics and scientific strategy.[110] This differentiated structure is contrasted to the more 'integrated' social organisation of research at Cambridge.

Edge and Mulkay argue that 'the technical and intellectual development of the Cambridge group...can be interpreted in terms of a single-minded "state of the art" exploitation of the principle of aerial design known as

---

[108] Thus, with the source survey dispute between Sydney and Cambridge, although the 'shift towards more precise techniques produced, at first, sharp controversy – not only over the interpretation of the radio data...[but also] at a more fundamental level, over the validity and reliability of the radio measures themselves', 'technical consensus' was 'eventually' achieved. Edge and Mulkay (1976), pp. 110-111.

[109] Working with Lovell were Clegg, Ellyett, Aspinall, J.G. Davies, Closs, Banwell and Hughes. Browne, Bullough and S. Evans worked under Kaiser; and Watkins, Neufeld, Hall and Davis under Greenhow. The pair consisted of Almond and Hawkins. Edge and Mulkay (1976), p. 304.

[110] 'Relatively early...the idea of a major instrument, of potential use to the whole group, emerged: because the radar and radio interests had to be satisfied, a multipurpose, steerable, large paraboloid was an obvious design choice. The group therefore became committed, relatively early and irreversibly, to an investment in multipurpose "dishes" as the major components of their instrumentation'. Edge and Mulkay (1976), p. 331.

"aperture synthesis"'. This exploitation was co-ordinated by Ryle, and involved centrally 'every other veteran in the group'.[111] The technical commitment to aperture synthesis was inter-related to the dominant scientific strategy of producing surveys of radio sources that could be interpreted cosmologically (primarily in claims against the steady state cosmology of theorists Hoyle, Bondi and Gold), and to an integrated, compact and 'closed' social group. Edge and Mulkay sustain this account of distinctions between Cambridge and Jodrell Bank with their descriptions of recruitment and leadership at the research sites. The 'closed' Cambridge group had a lower turn-over of staff and students, recruiting largely internally from products of the Natural Sciences Tripos system, whereas Jodrell bank is described as being more 'open' to the wider scientific community: it was an identifiable research school through which future radio astronomers passed, symposiums and meetings of scientific societies were often held on-site.[112] The 'leadership' of Ryle was involved, 'the group remained actively committed to topics central to Ryle': he was a 'cited leader', defined by 'active engagement in research relevant to the groups's goals...on a detailed, day-to-day basis', in addition to his administrative responsibilities. Lovell, on the other hand, Edge and Mulkay characterise as 'distanced' from the team research, exhibiting 'supportive leadership'. In their account the scientific and technical strategy of using multipurpose instruments, and the attendant differentiated social structure, meant that Lovell had to devote his time to administrative work: the lobbying for resources to build and hold together the instruments, primarily the Mark I paraboloid. They therefore dismiss any explanation of the differences between Jodrell Bank and Cambridge that begins from the individualised differences of Lovell and Ryle, instead pointing to the 'scientific (ie cultural), technical and social constraints that have allowed two different styles of leadership to operate at the two centres'.[113]

Lovell has provided a leader's view of the construction of the major, multipurpose telescope of Manchester University in his *The Story of Jodrell Bank*, published in the late 1960s.[114] *The Story* is a valuable historical document, describing the early 'pioneer' years of meteor work using ex-army radar equipment, the construction of the 218 foot transit telescope, and centring on the development, from the first 'visions' to the completion and

[111] Edge and Mulkay (1976), p. 339.

[112] For example a Royal Astronomical Society (RAS) summer meeting in 1949, an RAS symposium in 1953, and a meeting of the International Astronomical Union (IAU) in 1955.

[113] Edge and Mulkay (1976), p. 346.

[114] Lovell, A.C.B., 1968. *The Story of Jodrell Bank*, London: Oxford University Press. See also: Lovell, A.C.B., 1984, 'The origins and early history of Jodrell Bank', in Sullivan (1984), pp. 193-211.

triumphant use, of a large steerable Radio Telescope.[115] The story of how a capital grant was obtained from the DSIR, the gradual but troublesome erection of the telescope by the construction companies, the design changes, the escalating cost and the subsequent trouble that these price rises caused are told in great detail. Dates and figures are supplied in abundance. Lovell provides extensive excerpts from his own working diaries to create credibility. *The Story* is affectingly heroic: a story of a great and patriotic scientific endeavour overcoming obstacles such as inclement weather, refractory and striking builders, and opposition from within government. I will discuss many aspects of *The Story of Jodrell Bank* during this book, but here I will comment briefly on some absences, which the candour of Lovell's style should not obscure.

Firstly, *The Story* (which sold very well) was not a new story to many of its readers: as I will show later the telescope was promoted from the beginning as a prestige project. Its financial 'troubles' were also public. A partial explanation of the book's surprising openness was that Lovell was dispelling a perception of profligacy by seemingly revealing all the facts about a triumphant, but nearly halted, project. Lovell, in 1968, was in the midst of promoting even larger (up to 1000 foot) telescopes: the Mark V and Mark VA. The public appear in *The Story* as a threat, a move that I will discuss at length later. 'We' (says Lovell) were 'resentful of publicity': the astronomers were 'waging a war with the Press whose unwelcome attention we had attracted'.[116] However, in the edifying narrative of *The Story*, the press too were won over, they 'became our friends' once the worth of the telescope had been revealed in the conclusion with its tracking of nation-threatening satellites. What I aim to show in this book is that the 'public' were crucial in holding the Jodrell Bank project together. The relations of the telescope with its public are examined in depth, and are shown to be more than just an at times threatening or receptive audience. The telescope had a problematic relationship with a public actively appropriating and consuming science, such as Hoyle's huge selling *The Nature of the Universe* (1951), and the publicised projects of IGY and Jodrell Bank. A second absence is one of seeming simplification: the heterogenous teams of astronomers working with various aerials and instruments largely disappear in favour of the Radio Telescope. Likewise, the crucial interventions of telescope's Consulting Engineer, H. Charles Husband, fade from view. I

---

[115] Nomenclature is significant: the name 'Mark I', shared with the famous Mark I computer constructed at Manchester University in the late 1940s, seems to be only widespread around the early 1960s, when a Mark II was planned, and the main instrument upgraded into the 'Mark IA'. During the 1950s the instrument was referred to as the 'Radio Telescope' (most often), the 'steerable radio telescope' or as the 'paraboloid'.

[116] Lovell (1968), p. 160.

examine the fluid processes that are fully matured and solidified by *The Story* in 1968 that led to these absences, and show that these too, like the role of the public, were vital in supporting the project. Both issues are matters of public self-fashioning: simultaneously of Lovell and Telescope.[117]

Turning from participants' accounts to those of historians and social scientists, many authors have used the term 'Big Science' to describe radio astronomy at Jodrell Bank and Cambridge. Edge and Mulkay locate the period when 'radio astronomy had escalated irreversibly into "Big Science" with the construction of large instruments (the Radio Telescope at Jodrell Bank, the 'first full "aperture synthesis" instrument' at Cambridge, amongst others in the world), and with the entrenchment of the radio astronomical interests in an established 'research oligopoly'.[118] Gilbert uses the term in his brief discussion of meteor research at Jodrell Bank[119], as do Martin and Irvine in their science policy comparison of the track records of radio astronomy centres.[120] How useful is such a description? I argued in my Introduction that the historiography of Big Science was too broad to be used without immense care, and best coped with the American institutions that it was composed to discuss. Jodrell Bank, as with Harwell and CERN, must be understood in the particular and subtle contexts of European, national and local cultures. Some aspects of 'big science' do however allow important aspects to be visible and be interrogated. In the case of Jodrell Bank, matters of 'media' and 'military' (along with associated 'publicity' and 'secrecy') are indeed highly relevant. However, it is best to recall Smith's somewhat dismissive comment in his account of the certainly Big Science Space Telescope, that a big instrument does not make Big Science.[121] The departmental contexts within which the large steerable Radio Telescope, and the Cambridge arrays, operated remained typically academic.

ORGANIZING WORK AND DISCOVERY AT JODRELL BANK

In terms of staff and equipment Jodrell Bank grew rapidly. In October 1948

---

[117] The telescope was renamed finally in the late 1980s as 'The Lovell Telescope' marking the final disappearance of Husband.
[118] Edge and Mulkay (1976), p. 53, and p. 251.
[119] Gilbert, G.N., 1976. 'The development of science and scientific knowledge: the case of radar meteor research'. In Lemaine, G., MacLeod, R., Mulkay, M., and Weingart, P. (eds.), 1976. *Perspectives on the Emergence of Scientific Disciplines*, The Hague: Mouton & Co, pp. 187-204.
[120] Martin, B. and Irvine, J., 1983. 'Assessing basic research: some partial indicators of scientific progress in radio astronomy', *Research Policy* 12, pp. 61-90.
[121] Smith, R.W., 1992. 'The biggest kind of big science: astronomy and the Space Telescope', in Galison and Hevly (1992), pp. 184-211.

the scientific staff stood at twelve, along with six technical staff and a half-time secretary.[122] Four years later the twenty scientists, seven technicians, two secretaries, groundsman, cleaner and cook were headed by the newly promoted Professor Lovell.[123] The UGC and DSIR were the main paymasters, while the Royal Society, chemical combine ICI and the Simon Fund were also occasional benefactors. Scientific, technical and administrative staff further increased as the steerable Radio Telescope became operational in 1957.

We know from Edge and Mulkay that the scientists at Jodrell Bank were organised as teams, which in turn reflected the growth and decline of lines of research. The remainder of this section will briefly describe these research programmes as they developed up to the 1960s, after which an important argument regarding the *organisation* of work and discovery can be made. The description follows the orientation of the lines of research: radar studies (of meteors, the moon, planets and the ionosphere), work on radio noise sources, the mapping of neutral hydrogen emission, and instrument design.

Jodrell Bank Research Programmes

The publications from Jodrell Bank show that after an initial engagement with cosmic rays[124] and solar radiation[125], the use of the ex-military radar equipment centred on an expanding research programme on echoes from meteor trails. The radio-physicists who came to Jodrell Bank possessed the manipulative skills necessary to make the equipment (a 'transmitter [that] worked on a frequency of 72.4 Mc/s and radiated 150 pulses per second each of 8 microseconds duration...peak power in the pulse was 150 kW...the transmitter and receiver were identical Yagi's and were directed vertically'[126]) work. However, although Hey had identified the transient echoes seen on radar screens with meteors during the war, identical skills of identification and interpretation had to be freshly learnt by the radio-physicists. Crucial to this learning was the interpretative calibration achieved through collaboration with an amateur astronomer, J.P.M. Prentice of the British Astronomical Association: Prentice, a skilled observer of meteors, possessed the knowledge

[122] JBA JBM/5/1. 'Report on Jodrell Bank. December 1945 - July 1948'.

[123] JBA JBM/5/1. 'Jodrell Bank Report. No. 5: 1951-1952'. Two years later the staff stood at 28 scientists, ten technicians (three senior, five ordinary and two junior), three secretaries, a groundsman, two cleaners and two cooks.

[124] Lovell, 1946. 'Cosmic rays and their origin', *Endeavour* 5, p. 74-79. This interest began during the War: Blackett and Lovell (1941).

[125] Lovell A.C.B. and Banwell, C.J., 1946. 'Abnormal solar radiation on 72 Mc/s', *Nature* 158, p. 517-518.

[126] Prentice, J.P.M., Lovell A.C.B. and Banwell, C.J. 1947. 'Radio echo observations of meteors', *Monthly Notices of the Royal Astronomical Society* 107, pp. 155-163.

of the optical night sky which the Jodrell Bank staff lacked. The meteor research programme productively diversified as the interpretative skills improved: the time, direction, duration and counting of the echoes were attributed significance. The radio-physicists could relevantly intervene in the debates of optical astronomers (over the nature of meteor orbits[127], new daytime meteor showers[128]), and meteorologists (electron content in the ionosphere and aurorae). As British radio-physicists began to intervene in astronomical debates they also began to fashion themselves as *radio astronomers*, for example by joining the Royal Astronomical Society (RAS) and publishing in its journals. The process of acquiring this new identity was relatively (and surprisingly) smooth.[129]

Jodrell Bank astronomers applied radar techniques in the investigation of other objects, work often supported by other sponsors. The drift of meteor trails in upper atmosphere winds, and the scintillation of radiation from bright discrete radio sources, was used to investigate ionospheric conditions. From the early 1950s, J.S. Greenhow and E.L. Neufeld, amongst others, reported on ionospheric conditions such as winds and turbulence supported by grants secured from the United States Air Force (USAF).[130] Inclusion as part of the Royal Society's International Geophysical Year expedition to Halley Bay in Antarctica extended the geographical coverage of the Jodrell Bank astronomers' ionospheric research. USAF's Air Research and Development Command funded such investigations because of its relevance to ballistic missile design.

Defence concerns could also be mobilised to support other radar developments at Jodrell Bank. In 1953, William Murray, supported by a DSIR student fellowship, and J.K. Hargreaves began a study of lunar radar

---

[127] Ellyett, C.D. and Davies, J.G., 1948. 'Velocity of meteors by diffraction of radio waves from trails during formation', *Nature* 161, pp. 596-597. Davies J.G. and Ellyett, C.D., (1949). 'The diffraction of radio waves from meteor trails and the measurement of meteor velocities', *Philosophical Magazine* 40, pp. 614-626. Almond, M., 1950. 'On interstellar meteors', *The Observatory* 70, p. 112-116.

[128] Clegg, J.A., Hughes, V.A., and Lovell, A.C.B., 1947. 'The daytime meteor streams of 1947 May-August', *Monthly Notices of the Royal Astronomical Society* 107, pp. 369-378. Lovell, A.C.B., 1948b. 'The daytime meteor streams, 1948, June-July', *BAA Circular* 300. Aspinall, A., Clegg, J.A., Lovell, A.C.B., and Ellyett, C.D., 1949. 'The daytime meteor streams of 1948. I Measurement of the activity and radiant positions', *Monthly Notices of the Royal Astronomical Society* 109, pp. 352-358. Ibid, ditto 'II Measurements of the velocities', *Monthly Notices of the Royal Astronomical Society* 109, pp. 359-364.

[129] Edge and Mulkay (1976), pp. 55-59.

[130] As well as regular reports for USAF, the upper atmosphere results were also published, in particular Edward Appleton's *Journal of Atmospheric and Terrestrial Physics*.

echoes in connection with the meteor radar team led by Tom Kaiser.[131] Using a fixed array transmitter and a small steerable radio telescope (incidentally the Festival of Britain dish) they showed that a long period fading of the radar signal was due to a phenomenon called Faraday rotation. Another postgraduate student, John V. Evans, took over the lunar work the following year, rebuilding the equipment. When Evans' postgraduate stipend ran out, USAF became the new financial supporters (funding secured by Lovell's good links with Harvard astronomer Fred Whipple). Here the USAF interest was the use of the moon as part of a secure passive communication circuit. The moon relay work also provided props for demonstrating the capabilities of the steerable 250 foot Radio Telescope: recordings of speech echoed from the moon formed an impressive component of Lovell's 1958 Reith Lectures (see Chapter Three). Finally, the lunar (and later planetary) radar techniques were mobilised as a means of saving the Radio Telescope project: by tracking Soviet and American satellites and probes after 1957. As I discuss in the following chapters, while payments from NASA eased the financial situation at Jodrell Bank in the late 1950s and early 1960s, the tracking of satellites also involved careful positioning of the Radio Telescope as a national symbol, a public presentation that relied on a deliberate ambiguity in its defence significance.

Radar astronomy, in particular meteor astronomy for which Jodrell Bank was recognised as a world centre by 1954[132], became less important for Jodrell Bank by the late 1950s. Research on radio noise sources became correspondingly more prominent in this period. However entry into this line of research was difficult: groups in other parts of the world, in particular Cambridge and Sydney had quickly established a reputation for source work reliant on the construction and combination of arrays of aerials. Jodrell Bank radio source strategy followed broadly followed two lines: exploiting the advantages of large filled dishes (such as sensitivity), or by investigating the smallest scale of sources by combining signals from ever wider-spaced antennas (long baseline interferometry). An example of the former strategy was ex-TRE radio physicist Robert Hanbury Brown and Cyril Hazard's detection of the Andromeda galaxy, followed by the programmatic mapping of other radio sources, using the 218 foot fixed paraboloid.[133] The second strategy was pursued from 1948 onwards. First, Lovell, with C. Gordon Little, collaborated with Ryle's Cambridge group in an investigation of radio

---

[131] Agar, 'Moon relay experiments at Jodrell Bank', in Butrica, A., *Beyond the Ionosphere*, NASA History, forthcoming.

[132] At which point Jodrell Bank's director had written the first monograph on the subject. Lovell, A.C.B., 1954. *Meteor Astronomy*, Oxford: Clarendon Press.

[133] Hanbury Brown, R. and Hazard, C., 1950. 'Radio-frequency radiation from the Great Nebula in Andromeda (M31)', *Nature* 166, p. 901. Hanbury Brown, R. and Hazard, C., 1953. 'A survey of 23 localized radio sources in the Northern Hemisphere', *Monthly Notices of the Royal Astronomical Society* 113, pp. 123-133.

source fluctuations using receivers spaced at increasing intervals.[134] Later, the team around Hanbury Brown and Henry Palmer attempted to measure the angular diameter of discrete radio sources by an interferometer made out of the 218 foot paraboloid and a small mobile dish. By increasing the baseline (13km in 1955, 20km in 1956 and 115.4km in 1961), thereby improving resolution, the team could show that the radio sources were both of very angular size (of the order of seconds of arc), and likely to lie outside this galaxy.[135] The steerable Radio Telescope was brought into both strands of source research from 1957.[136] The narrow view ('beam') of the large filled dishes that marked Jodrell Bank's 'technological strategy' meant they were unsuited to counting radio sources or mapping large areas of the sky. This restriction meant that Manchester radio astronomers only rarely engaged directly in the Cambridge-Sydney source count controversy.[137]

    The investigation of 'radio stars' also diversified. When Hazard returned from two years' national service in 1955 he used first the 218 foot fixed dish, and later the Radio Telescope, to observe the occultation of radio sources by the moon. Hazard used his observations to determine positions of radio stars accurate enough for optical telescopes to attempt to identify a corresponding object.[138] Another diversification of the discrete radio source program was the project to detect radio waves from the eruption of flare stars. This project, heavily dependent on access to time on the steerable Radio Telescope, was Lovell's first major observational commitment after the instrument had been completed.[139] Finally, like many other radio astronomy groups, a Jodrell Bank team took up studies of the radiation emitted by neutral hydrogen at a wavelength of 21cm (1420 Mc/s). Jan Oort's Leiden group had predicted, identified and mapped the distribution of

---

[134] However, according to Lovell, Ryle disagreed with Jodrell Bank's conclusions so Cambridge published separately. Lovell (1984), p. 203.

[135] For example: Morris, D., Palmer, H.P. and Thompson, A,R., 1957. 'Five radio sources of small angular diameter', *Observatory* 77, pp. 103-110. The team published regularly from the mid-1950s onwards.

[136] For example, Large, M.I., Mathewson, D.S. and Haslam, C.G.T., 1959. 'A high resolution survey of the Andromeda galaxy at 408 Mc/s', *Nature* 183, pp. 1250-1251, which was followed by a radio survey of the galactic plane. The Radio Telescope was (and is as part of MERLIN) often used as an element of an interferometer.

[137] Edge and Mulkay (1976), p. 166. They report one 'centrally involved' Jodrell Bank astronomer as stating that instead of pursuing source counts: 'Our policy was to try and find out what radio sources are by studying some of the more powerful ones in detail' (p. 144).

[138] Hazard, C., 1961. 'Lunar occultation of a radio source', *Nature* 191, 58. See Edge and Mulkay (1976), p. 199.

[139] Lovell, A.C.B., 1973. *Out of Zenith. Jodrell Bank, 1957-1970*, London: Oxford University Press, pp. 167-185.

this radiation: culminating in the collaboration with Sydney radio astronomers to produce a map of the galaxy which, they claimed, showed a spiral structure.[140] Such was the dominance of Dutch and Australian 21cm research that the Jodrell Bank group, starting with R.D. Davies (who arrived from Sydney in 1953) and D.R.W. Williams, had to work hard to find variations on the theme: for example using neutral hydrogen absorption lines as an indicator of radio source distance.

Research Work

In the above brief summary it has been convenient to adopt the characteristic narrative style of describing discovery: uncomplicated observation and statement of astronomical significance. However, this (usefully compact) narrative style is misleading in several ways: underplaying the difficulties of design, the highly significant *work* involved in reduction of observations, and finally the difficulty in sustaining claims in the community of radio astronomers.

A research team would typically either build or adapt equipment, or later when the big telescope was completed they would be allocated time on the instrument according to a committee's judgements. Instrumental innovation was encouraged. The capital sunk into the large fixed and steerable dishes meant that these aerials had to be the basis of the programmes. However there was flexibility in how they were used (for example combined with smaller mobile aerials), and in the design and arrangement of receivers. A good example of this freedom was the 'phase correlation interferometer' used by Palmer's team on the radio source angular diameter research discussed above. Instrument design and construction was always a central component of the Jodrell Bank research programmes, but it could also be, for a few staff, a specialty. Instrumental innovation could be a line of research in its own right: Hanbury Brown's remarkable development of the 'intensity interferometer', theoretically (and controversially[141]) with Richard Q. Twiss (then of the Services Electronics Research Laboratory) and in practice with Roger Jennison and M.K. Das Gupta is a good example. Hanbury Brown eventually left Jodrell Bank for Australia to continue this technique at optical wavelengths. Jennison also concentrated on technical and theoretical

---

[140] Oort, J.H., Kerr, F.J. and Westerhout, G., 1958. 'The Galactic System as a spiral nebula', *Monthly Notices of the Royal Astronomical Society* 118, pp. 379-389.

[141] The intensity interferometer ignores the amplitude phase of the photons arriving at the two separate aerials (which *would* be measured in a conventional interferometer), measuring (and later combining) only their intensities. Hanbury Brown recalls: 'physicists wrote to use from all over the world to tell us we didn't understand quantum theory'. Hanbury Brown, R. (1984), p. 230. See also Edge and Mulkay (1976), p. 146.

development[142], eventually writing a popular introduction on the subject.[143] Finally, Jodrell Bank employed full-time technicians, who, as we have seen, were outnumbered by scientific staff at a ratio of about two to one. Technicians' work is notoriously hard to recover historically[144], and I discuss them further with respect to staffing the Radio Telescope in Chapter Three.

As with the Cavendish laboratory, the institutional source of Ryle's group's technical skill[145], a vital support of a growing mid-twentieth century physics-based establishment was the networks of contacts between scientists and equipment suppliers.[146] Initially the availability of war-surplus to the ex-radar scientists meant these suppliers were military, and indeed it remained an occasional source in later years. However, contacts in the electrical industry were needed for further development. For example, the construction of sensitive, well-designed receivers necessitated constant intelligence of new amplifier technologies. The discussions surrounding the design of receivers for the steerable Radio Telescope in late 1954 provide a good illustration of the network of contacts. Hanbury Brown was excited by a valve he had seen in Leiden, Phillips' EC 56, and contacted the Ministry of Supply, writing:

> As you will realise this valve is as good, if not better than the best American valves and is very considerably better than any British valve I know.[147]

Hanbury Brown had visited General Electric Company (GEC) at Wembley and found they did not know the valve. Lovell, who also witnessed the vacuum tube at Leiden, contacted the electronics firm Mullards. Mullards initially prevaricated, stating that the Phillips had supplied 'specially selected valves' to the Dutch astronomers, and the low noise level was therefore not easily repeatable. Pressure from Cambridge and Manchester[148] persuaded

---

[142] Although Edge and Mulkay record that this was because Jennison had been "nudged" out of source work by the development of strong team structures around Palmer and R.D. Davies. Edge and Mulkay (1976), p. 327.

[143] Jennison, R.C., 1966. *Introduction to Radio Astronomy*, London: Newnes.

[144] Shapin, S., 1989. 'The invisible technician', *American Scientist* 77, pp. 554-563.

[145] Edge and Mulkay (1976), p. 127.

[146] On the centrality of industry to the Cavendish Laboratory see: Hughes, J., 1996. 'Plasticine and Valves: industry, instrumentation and the emergence of nuclear physics', in Gaudillere, J.P., Lowy, I. and Pestre, D., 1996. *The Invisible Industrialist: Manufactures and the Construction of Scientific Knowledge*, London: Macmillan.

[147] JBA CS1/5/2. Letter, Hanbury Brown to Findlay, 21 September 1954.

[148] Complaining to government bodies such as the CVD committee, as well as directly to industry. Francis Graham-Smith question to Hanbury Brown, 'Did you talk to GEC again and grumble about the backwardness if our valve industry' is a nice example of the latter. JBA CS1/5/2. Letter, Graham Smith to Hanbury Brown, 1 November 1954.

crucial that pen-recordings, and later representations, were tagged and kept: to keep track of *who* was working on *what*, but also so that previous results could be referred back to: the operation of the observatory generated *ordered records*, a form of organizational memory.

For the radio astronomer the end point of this work could be an isophote map, a measurement of the intensity of a radio source, or perhaps the determination of a position and its likely errors. Such knowledge claims began with a process of valuation at the level of 'raw data' (which I discuss at length later) and are 'refined' by repetitive labour, and are always relative to the organization and management of people and equipment. The knowledge claims, based on refined valued traces, are then published. For the Jodrell Bank astronomers, the journals *Nature, Proceedings of the Royal Society A*, the *Journal of Atmospheric and Terrestrial Physics*, the *Philosophical Magazine* and the RAS's *Monthly Notices* and *Observatory*, were common forums.[166] The status of these knowledge claims were negotiated, and sometimes ratified, in ways that will be now, through sociological and ethnographical studies, not surprising to this book's audience.[167] However, it will hopefully be evident by my Conclusion that the shaping of these narrow *knowledge* claims is not the most interesting aspect of a study of Jodrell Bank, nor possibly, the most important.

SUMMARY

In this chapter I have provided a historical account of the organisation of science and government in twentieth century Britain. I have demonstrated that the Second World War marked a discontinuity in this history. Whilst the loose structure of funding bodies remained largely unchanged since Haldane, British science changed qualitatively along three axes. First, government expenditure on both civil and defence research increased spectacularly: from £10 million in 1939 to £220 million in 1955-56. Second, the post-war expansion in both secondary and tertiary education meant a growth in university science. Manchester University was one of the loudest advocates for this expansion. Third, post-war research was marked by novel sites for science. Much of this new research grew from war-time projects: Harwell and CERN nuclear physics from the atomic weapon programme, and radio astronomy from the radar work at the Telecommunications Research

---

[166] In special cases, for example with the tracking of Sputnik and other satellites, and with Greenhow's team's ionospheric work, the forum of epistemological negotiation was military and of a slightly different character to that in public journals.

[167] And, indeed, with respect to the causes, and closure, of the radio source survey controversy we already have an excellent account in Edge and Mulkay (1976).

Establishment. This threefold growth depended on networks linking government, military and academic bodies, within which people, equipment, money and prestige could be exchanged. The network structures the context of British radio astronomy in the account that follows.

I described the early history of post-war nuclear physics and Britain's involvement in CERN at length. This history intersects with the development of British radio astronomy for five reasons. First, at a time in which crucial decisions were made about constructing radio telescopes, CERN represented a shift in policy away from 'dispersed' nuclear physics to centralised facilities. Second, connected to this was an acceptance, not least within the Treasury, of the new expense of 'pure' scientific research. Third, as Chadwick's estimation that Britain was "close to bankruptcy" in mid-1952 shows, this acceptance was difficult and remarkable. Fourth, alongside the shifts towards greater centralisation and expense of research facilities, the politics of supporting research changed. The rearmament between 1951 and 1959[168] benefited both nuclear physics and, as I discuss later, radio astronomy. Such benefit was indirect, for Krige's argument that the Department of Scientific and Industrial Research would be sympathetic to a glamorous and prestigious project because they were in competition with the defence departments who were expanding in-house research, can be made both for CERN and radio astronomy. It is therefore important to examine 'prestige' more closely. The fifth reason why the history of nuclear physics had consequences for the development of radio astronomy was the change in siting science. I have shown that CERN, Harwell and NIRNS marked a centralisation of facilities. They also marked a shift away from research within the university.

This tension between government and academia in the siting and organisation of research forms a theme in Chapter Two, where I suggest that it is a force shaping institutions combining a strong component of each, such as Jodrell Bank, and ARC and MRC Units. A study of this tension provides a case study for the analysis of the spatiality of the radio astronomy observatory as an organisation. In Chapter Three I consider how the economies of prestige and 'significance' mentioned by Hevly intersected with spatial politics of display and internal organisation. The telescope was embedded in a sociotechnical organisation that operated to generate ordered records, upon which (after much repetitive effort) claims about astronomical objects were made. In Chapters Four and Five the work needed to distance ordered records from noise is examined.

Finally, in the following chapter, I relate the design and construction of instruments at Jodrell Bank to the context of post-war British science. My account of the key technical choice of the large steerable dish is a more

---

[168] Vig (1968), p. 19.

symmetrical and less retrospective account of this choice than that given by Lovell. My account also diverges from that offered by Edge and Mulkay. Rather than relating technical choice only to the limited dynamics of the social groups of radio astronomers, I argue that the telescope's design and construction was shaped by its enrolment by a broad spectrum of bodies, including military, public and governmental.

CHAPTER 2

Funding a Spectacle of Science

In Chapter One I highlighted three aspects of post-war British science: an increase in expenditure on research through a 'loose' funding system, an anxiety over the production of 'manpower', and new disciplinary and institutional sites for science. In this chapter these concerns inform my query into a problem: why were so many resources committed to Jodrell Bank, the largest non-nuclear university-based scientific project in Britain?

The subject of money is missing from *Astronomy Transformed*. This is surprising for what is styled as an account of the emergence of a new and expensive discipline. This would be acceptable if the raising and spending of money could be separated from the other activities and meanings that surrounded Jodrell Bank. Money is certainly present in *The Story of Jodrell Bank*, where it appears in the, by turns, tragic and heroic narrative as it is granted and spent. In this chapter I study funding more broadly: as tied to the exchange of 'cultural capital', as part of wider trends and changes in the university site, and as part of the public fashioning of Jodrell Bank.

I discuss how some research at Jodrell Bank became tied to the use of multipurpose large dishes, and the decision to begin a project on a large, steerable radio telescope. I then look at how this project was promoted, from both sides: the promoters and the bodies that influenced the allocation of financial resources. These bodies included the Department of Scientific and Industrial Research (DSIR), the University Grants Committee (UGC), the Treasury, the Public Accounts Committee (PAC), the Nuffield Foundation and the Ministry of Supply. I claim that the different presentations and receptions of the instrument illustrate a 'malleability' of technological artefacts. I relate this malleability to the looseness and 'freedom' of the funding system. I locate the tensions of the funding of Jodrell Bank in a wider historical context: the organisational configuration of large-scale science. I claim that the trends associated with this phenomenon, in particular expense and government involvement, led to a problematisation of the university as a suitable site for science.

It is very important to note that the economies that I discuss in this chapter were restricted, and largely non-public. The economies of credit and credibility in this chapter were, crucially, not enough in themselves to sustain (or even begin) the activities at Jodrell Bank. They intersected with other economies, such as public and spatialised economies of spectacle, representations and authority, a story I take up in Chapter Three.

A 218 FOOT PARABOLOID

In the previous chapter I discussed how staff and equipment grew rapidly after 1945. As they expanded, so did the cost of running Jodrell Bank. Although in its first year expenditure was so 'negligible' that it could be 'debited to the Physics Department grant without special accounting', after March 1946 the accounts were separated and in July 'Professor Blackett allocated a specific sum from the Physics Department grant for the running of Jodrell Bank'.[1] Up to this time, the research had been done with easily built small aerials or by tinkering with existing radar equipment. The next project at Jodrell Bank therefore contrasted: 'My calculations on the cosmic ray problem indicated that success would demand much greater sensitivity than we possesed and the only way to get it...was to build a bigger aerial'.[2] The '218 foot paraboloid', a large bowl of wire fixed on the ground focussing radio waves on an aerial mounted on top of a tall metal pole, was funded by the DSIR to continue the search for cosmic ray echoes just as research was turning to studies of meteors. The securing of separate DSIR grants also began the gradual distancing of Jodrell Bank from the Physics Department.

Paraboloid big dishes allowed a flexible approach to research programme choice. Edge and Mulkay have viewed the 218 Foot Paraboloid as the beginnings of a 'commitment' at Jodrell Bank to large multipurpose dishes. When Robert Hanbury Brown joined Jodrell Bank in 1949 he found that by 'happy accident, they had built a powerful instrument with which...to study the radio emissions from space'.[3] This is, of course, retrospective, but it does indicate that contingencies entered into the construction of the instrument. Others can be easily found. Its location was mainly determined by where the trailer of receivers had stuck in the mud, its size determined by the position of hedges. The central tower was initially what could be made from Air Ministry surplus. Funding was also more unplanned than an interpretation as part of a 'commitment' would suggest. Lovell applied to the DSIR for £1000

---

[1] JBA JBM/5/2. 'Report on Jodrell Bank. December 1945 - July 1948'.

[2] Lovell (1968), p. 16.

[3] Hanbury Brown, R., 1984. 'Paraboloids, galaxies, and stars: memories of Jodrell Bank', in Sullivan, W.T. (1984), pp. 213-236.

'to complete...the aerial', and to his 'surprise' got it. It fulfilled the DSIR desideratum of 'timeliness and promise'. The 'planned development' view makes little sense in context. The construction of the transit paraboloid was possible through mobilisation of those largely contingent resources that were to hand. Edge and Mulkay are, however, correct in their appeal to the context of the projects of other close groups in order to understand the adoption of large dishes at Jodrell Bank. The aerial's form was justified by reference to what other groups were doing[4], by 'division of labour'. Paraboloids represented a mark of differentiation: Cambridge and Sydney were developing interferometers, so, as Hanbury Brown has commented, Jodrell Bank went for large dishes.

When the Royal Astronomical Society held a symposium at Manchester in July 1949, they could view, on a guided tour, the radar transmitters and photographic equipment used for meteor astronomy: 'the reception of the echoes...reflected from meteor trails, was observed on large cathode ray screens'.[5] However, the assembled Fellows could also take 'a lively interest in the recording of cosmic noise being received'. Here 'Mr V.A. Hughes exhibited recorder charts showing the region...the hissing sound of "Cygnus calling" was made clearly audible to the visitors'. The flexibility of dish aerials allowed a proliferation in research topics. Jodrell Bank astronomers used a small 30 foot steerable dish, and the fixed 218 foot dish, to study radiation from outside the solar system.

A LARGE STEERABLE DISH

Once the Manchester group had displayed the possibilities of the transit paraboloid, then it could be used in an argument for a fully steerable dish: the wire bowl fixed to the ground follows only a thin strip of the sky, so think how the benefits are multiplied if it can look anywhere! This is the argument Lovell used to his peers. Director of Manchester University Physical Laboratory and Nobel Laureate of that year, Professor Patrick M.S. Blackett, gave his backing on the condition that Lovell produced a plan and budget. Through Blackett the University was persuaded to finance a preliminary investigation. For Lovell this episode illustrated the organisational know-how of the Laboratory leader: if the University was involved at an early

---

[4] For example: Hanbury Brown (1984), p. 214. See Edge and Mulkay (1976), particularly Chapter Four, for the conscious 'division of labour' between early radio astronomy groups.

[5] RAS Symposium, 1949. 'The RAS at Manchester, July 1949. The daytime meteor streams of 1948 geophysical discussion at Manchester, 1949, July ionisation in the earth's upper atmosphere', *The Observatory* 69, p. 123.

stage, then a later approach to the DSIR for a large sum would become easier.[6] But appraisals of know-how were inextricably linked with marks of status in the post-war economy of science, and Blackett as the Director, government confidant and Nobel Prize-winner can be seen as the lynch-pin of the Jodrell Bank telescope project.

Finding an Engineer

Lovell approached a 'few of the largest engineering firms' in 1948 without success. 'The reasons were either that they were too busy on work of 'national importance' or that such a project [was] an impossible engineering undertaking'.[7] In *The Story of Jodrell Bank* Lovell described the early discussions with an unnamed company, which were unsatisfactory: he cited cost, disagreements over design (particularly the mount) and (implied) incompetence.[8] In the note attached to the grant application to the Scientific Grants Committee (SGC) of the DSIR, Blackett wrote that the £1000 from the University was used to get a design 'in light alloy by Head Wrightson Aldean...recommended by...Grubb Parsons'.[9] This was presumably Lovell's unnamed firm. Blackett went on: 'it now appears that a light alloy design will be more expensive than steel. We have an estimate from Messrs. Husband & Co for a straightforward steel structure'. Lovell stated later in *The Story of Jodrell Bank* that the engineering firm that provided 'the steel tube for the transit telescope' recommended Husband. However, in Blackett's words: 'I have formed a very favourable opinion of Mr. Husband, who has had very considerable experience on Government work, particularly for the Ministry of Supply...he was recommended for this project by the Ministry of Works'.

How is the variance in these two accounts to be explained? It is instructive to consider the intended audience. Lovell's account is semi-popular in that it is not solely aimed at his professional peers. It does however assume a degree of interest higher than that for a popular account. As I argued in Chapter One, it is also written with emphasis and detail that would seem odd if this was so. However, the book is not aimed at amateur astronomers or popular enthusiasts, but at the audience which was aware that there was a possible 'scandal' about the telescope's financing, and who could influence future decisions. As will be illustrated throughout this book, the relations between Husband and Lovell, explicitly criticised by the PAC, presented a

---

[6] Lovell (1968), p. 25.

[7] Lovell (1968), p. 26: 'the figure which had been talked about...was...£60,000 to £70,000...but we were quickly informed that [it] would cost at least half a million'. cf the final figure was in excess of £700,000.

[8] Lovell (1968), p. 26.

[9] PRO DSIR 2 497. Appendix by Blackett to Application for Grant, 7 June 1950.

sensitive topic for Lovell, who passes over the subject of the choice of engineer without comment (apart from professional praise). Blackett's audience is the SGC, so it is advantageous to stress the previous government work of Husband and, by implication, his reliability.

The Scientific Grants Committee of the DSIR

The SGC meeting on the 22 July 1950 discussed two proposals from Blackett and Lovell.[10] One was a request for £5000 'supplementary to the existing grant' for the 'investigation of galactic radio emissions'. The application was amended by a character reference for Lovell by Blackett[11] and a seven page memo entitled 'Radio Astronomy at Jodrell Bank' dated April 1950, and a complete bibliography for Jodrell Bank from 1947-50 (38 items). The memo was written for the Radio Astronomy Committee of the RAS, of which more below. The second application was for a capital grant of £154,800 and a recurrent grant of £15,800, for the 'Construction of a large radio telescope for investigating galactic and solar radio emission, meteoric phenomena, aurorae, lunar and planetary echoes'. This was a wide-ranging astronomical programme. The application was also appended with a memo, 'A Proposal for a 250ft Aperture Steerable Paraboloid for Use in Radio Astronomy', written by Lovell and dated January 1950. In the memo Lovell remarked that steerable aerials were being planned in other countries,[12] and he outlined a research programme. Two rhetorical strategies that will become familiar to us in following chapters as used by the promoters of the radio telescope were already apparent in these memoranda: the use of historical sequence to place the telescope in a position of naturalness, and the listing of numerous possible fertile research topics that could justify the project, and distinguish it from the 'single-purpose' interferometer arrays of Cambridge. Importantly, '[the telescope] possessed no features which make it in any way alternative to...interferometric techniques': Lovell deflected possible accusations that this expensive instrument would duplicate Cambridge results. Further substantial backing came from a Royal Astronomical Society (RAS) resolution attached to the grant application. In it:

> The Council of the RAS strongly endorses the proposals put forward...The Council considers that by the erection of this apparatus the prestige of Science in Britain

[10] PRO DSIR 2 497. Application for Grant, 7 June 1950.
[11] 'Lovell has done wonders in a short time and it is very difficult for him to estimate ahead with great accuracy - hence this application for additional money. He is, on the whole, one of the most business-like men I know and takes enormous trouble to get his estimates right'.
[12] PRO DSIR 2 497. It 'is known that steerable aerials are planned...or under construction in Holland (75ft), Canada (150ft) and America (200ft)'.

would be considerably enhanced...In giving its support the Council places on record its opinion that the investigations to be undertaken are of high scientific importance...The Council is impressed by the consideration that the construction of the proposed paraboloid would permit the continuation in the U.K. of new methods of astronomical research, which have been so greatly developed by the skill of scientists in the U.K., and which are independent of climatic conditions.

Peer Support: The Royal Astronomical Society

This endorsement was less smooth than Lovell's account of it in *The Story of Jodrell Bank* suggests. Blackett, winding up the 1948 RAS symposium at Jodrell Bank, 'after referring to Manchester's contributions to astronomy in the past...pointed out how appropriate a place it was, with its weather, for the study of radio or "blind" astronomy!'.[13] The lobbying continued through the creation and actions of a special RAS 'committee on radio astronomy'. Its convener, W.M.H. Greaves of the Royal Observatory, Edinburgh, saw the committee's 'job [as] to explore the ways in which radio technique can give information on astronomical problems and to bring what pressure to bear when financial help is wanted'.[14] The former function was never used, and it was the latter that motivated the radio astronomers. Blackett told Lovell that before any meeting, 'you, Ryle and Hey [should] get together previously and work out yourselves, if possible, a programme'.[15] Lovell wrote to Hey and Ryle suggesting a meeting, commenting as an aside that:

Actually, I have recently written a short note on the uses of a 200ft movable paraboloid...Of course, large sums of money are involved in such a project, and Blackett's view is that this is exactly the sort of project that should be put before the new committee in order that they could press for necessary finances.[16]

The Cavendish radio astronomers reacted sharply to the document, as can be ascertained from Lovell's reply to Ryle that he was 'very sorry if you felt that the draft document...tended to be rather overweighted by the suggestion for the big paraboloid'.[17] Indeed, the place of the paraboloid was not at this stage fixed. Lovell stated that head of the Cavendish radio group, J.A. Ratcliffe, had

clearly got entirely the wrong impression of the whole affair. Just because the initial suggestion for the 200ft paraboloid came from here we were particularly

[13] RAS Symposium, op cit.
[14] JBA CS7/19/1. Letter, Greaves to Blackett, 15 December 1949.
[15] JBA CS7/19/1. Letter, Blackett to Lovell, 19 December 1949.
[16] JBA CS7/19/1. Letter, Lovell to Ryle, 23 December 1949. Letter, Lovell to Hey, 23 December 1949.
[17] JBA CS7/19/1, Letter, Lovell to Ryle, 31 January 1950.

anxious not to appear to be pressing it in any way, since our view is that it is an instrument that the country should possess, quite independently of where it is situated. It may be that with the work to be done on it over the next 5 or 10 years, it would be best situated at Jodrell Bank, but at the moment that is...beside the point.

With these disagreements it was decided to avoid the issue for the time being, and no documents were circulated before the preliminary meeting in February 1950.[18] Persons invited were: Blackett, Lovell, Appleton, Chapman, Massey, Newton, Prentice, Hey, Ryle and Ratcliffe. The second (and last) meeting was held later in the month in the apartments of Appleton (who chaired the meeting) at the University of Edinburgh. The meeting, though tense,[19] managed the divergent interests of Cambridge and Manchester radio astronomers by giving similar ringing endorsements as quoted above to *both* groups.

In this way Britain's astronomical establishment could now be shown to have backed the proposal for explicit reasons of prestige, scientific merit, world-leading skills and cloudy skies. That Lovell and Blackett secured such a resolution reveals both their connections and the intense lobbying that occurred before the SGC met.[20] Influential civil servants were also lobbied. The minutes of the SGC meeting note that Item 37 was attended by Sir Ben Lockspeiser, Under-Secretary of the DSIR.[21] Before Lockspeiser attended the meeting (in itself not surprising given the size of the grant), Lovell had already secured his support.[22] The Committee recommended 'an immediate grant' of £3300 over a period of one year for 'design drawing and on site investigation'. More importantly the principle of a large, steerable, British radio telescope had been accepted and backed within part of Whitehall.

The SGC Again

During the next year Husband and Co prepared the 'Consultant Engineer Report', dated February 1951. This indicated that the telescope would be more expensive than initially thought. The grant application considered by the SGC on 2 May 1951 was for £279,140.[23] This meant that continual lobbying was needed to ensure the telescope's funding: 'it seems certain that Sir Henry Tizard, Blackett, and the Vice-Chancellor never wavered in their

---

[18] JBA CS7/19/1. Letter, Lovell to Blackett, 31 January 1950.

[19] Lovell (1968), p. 32.

[20] Lovell (1968), p. 32, gives the credit to Blackett.

[21] PRO DSIR 2 497. SGC meeting, Thursday 22 June 1950, at 10.30am.

[22] Sir Ben Lockspeiser, introduction to paper by Lovell, A.C.B., 1955. 'Radio astronomy', Journal Royal Society of Arts 103, pp. 666-682.

[23] PRO DSIR 2 501. Application for Grant, 2 May 1951.

determination to find some means of financing the project'.[24] Tizard was one of the group of British scientists to gain a substantial degree of power within the government during the war. The influential Committee for the Scientific Survey of Air Defence, known as the 'Tizard Committee', significantly included Blackett. Tizard had known Lovell 'during the war as an ingenious developer of airborne radar devices'.[25] In 1951, Tizard was Chairman of both the Defence Research Policy Committee and the Advisory Council on Scientific Policy, and was therefore a powerful ally, although his influence declined sharply with the return of Lord Cherwell and Churchill's post-war government.[26]

The grant application to the SGC was again appended: present were Lovell's memo of January 1950, Husband's Consulting Engineers Report[27], the RAS resolution and a message of support from the Vice-Chancellor. Also attached are a few comments from the Chair of the University Grants Committee (UGC), Arthur Trueman, in which hints of dissent can be found. While 'many members of my Committee would be keenly interested in the proposal and would on general scientific grounds support it very warmly', Trueman cautiously continued:

> 1) We are not sure what will be the sum available for recurrent purposes in the universities in the next quinquennium
> 2) ...I think your Committee ought to be warned that if this grant is approved it is by no means certain that from the licences then available to us, we should be able to make arrangements for the construction to be started, and carried on at the rate which would be desired[28]

In correspondence with the Vice Chancellor of Manchester University (Sir John Stopford), Trueman remarked that he was 'a little doubtful how far you could carry this additional commitment until you know what your position is likely to be in the quinquennium'. Trueman went on to say that whilst the UGC 'provided capital and the necessary licences for large new schemes for nuclear physics', it would be 'very reluctant...to accept, without careful consideration any claim to establish new priorities of this kind'.[29] Stopford, after consulting Blackett and Lovell, was able to allay these fears, pointing out that (quoting Blackett): 'with the exception of the extra £2000 recurrent

[24] Lovell (1968), p. 35.
[25] Clark, R.W., 1972. *A Biography of the Nuffield Foundation*, London: Longman.
[26] However, see Clark (1965), p. 401, who argues that Tizard had 'already began to ease himself out of his official responsibilities' by 1949. Clark, unfortunately, does not refer to Tizard's involvement with Jodrell Bank.
[27] The copy held at the Public Record Office has not kept the drawings.
[28] PRO DSIR 2 501. Application for Grant, 2 May 1951.
[29] PRO UGC 7 152. Letter, Trueman to Stopford, 4 May 1951.

expenditure...for which I asked in my letter of 22 May, neither Lovell nor I ever intended that any large extra recurrent grants should fall on University funds'.[30]

The meeting of the SGC recommended a grant of £279,140 over a period of four years, and the Chairman was requested to prepare a report to the Advisory Council. Why had the DSIR backed such a huge project? Firstly, the Department saw in the project a novel and bold programme of scientific research, satisfying their twin desiderata of 'timeliness and promise' which all successful projects had to possess. Secondly, a partial explanation is the central location of the key actors in the post-war economy of credit between British science and government: particularly in this case the networks that grew from TRE and radar development. However, the DSIR played a more pro-active role than this. The civil servants were amenable to the rhetoric used by Lovell of funding radio astronomy as demonstrating 'national leadership' in at least discipline. As I will show in the next chapter the DSIR explicitly promoted the telescope as a 'spectacle' of post-war British science. Such a creditable and prestigious object held two purposes for the Department. Externally, the telescope became a symbol of national prestige in the identity of the nation. Within Whitehall the telescope represented the new importance of civil science, at a time when the DSIR was losing ground to the executive departments in the responsibility for government-funded research.[31]

THE SIGNIFICANCES OF AN EXPENSIVE INSTRUMENT

The University as a Site for Science

Jodrell Bank created problems in that it was a large, civil, non-nuclear, university-based capital project, with no obvious predecessor. Its construction had to be 'played by ear' (not unlike the development of a new TRE radar device). The main funding bodies tried to articulate what kind of form the finished observatory should take. Ben Lockspeiser wrote to Trueman:

> The capital sum is considerable, and puts the equipment into the same class...as some of the new cyclotrons...there may be much to be said in favour of having it at a central institution where it is available for all who wish to use it rather than at a particular university. In fact Brookhaven was founded for this purpose.[32]

Lockspeiser's appeal to Brookhaven, the American nuclear physics institution

---

[30] PRO UGC 7 152. Letter, Stopford to Trueman, May 1951.
[31] Krige, in Herman et al (1987). Gummett (1980).
[32] PRO UGC 7 152. Letter, Lockspeiser to Trueman, 4 June 1951.

that was run for a consortium of Universities, illustrated an alternative institutional model for British radio astronomy. This appealed to the contemporary argument that Britain had made an error of policy by constructing accelerators at five universities. For example, Krige reports that the space scientist Massey, after criticising the policy of dispersing money amongst the five and thereby 'dissipating effort', argued that the Brookhaven model presented an alternative for British nuclear science in mid-1952.[33] Lockspeiser suggested an informal meeting to discuss the institutional form to be adopted. It took place on July 13 1951[34], and decided in favour of Manchester University as the institution, and Jodrell Bank as the site. Unfortunately, there is no record of the informal committee's reasoning. Although the decision smoothed the path of the grant through the Advisory Council of the DSIR, it did not resolve the tension of expensive scientific projects in universities, a point to which I shall return.

Instrumental Malleability

The budget soon ran into trouble. The following financial history of the telescope, was given by the DSIR:

> (iii) On the 18 July 1951, the Advisory Council recommended a grant, not exceeding £300,000 spread over 4 years. The Lord President approved this on 10 August 1951.
> (iv) On 17 August 1951, DSIR wrote to the Treasury referring to £287,000 but asking for £300,000 to allow for 'comparatively small increases...'.
> (v) The Treasury replied on 7 September 1951 saying 'we are prepared to agree to the grant of not more than £300,000 which you ask for'; but also saying 'you will therefore have to be prepared to fit the work of the radio telescope year by year into a total, which, apart from plain defence work, may not be greater than your present vote'.
> (vi) Lord Woolton [Lord President of the Council] had advised on 4 December (and replied on the 8 December) that this warning warranted some delay.[35]

The promotion of the Radio Telescope could have stalled at this point were it not for the mobilisation of another link in the network of contacts that characterised post-war science. In the Autumn of 1951, Sir Henry Tizard,

---

[33] Krige, J., 'Chapter 13: Britain and the European laboratory project, mid-1952 - December 1953', in Hermann et al (1987), pp. 485-486.

[34] Present were: Sir Ben Lockspeiser, Sir A. Trueman, Sir Harold Spencer Jones, Professor R.O. Redman, Professor F.J.B. Stratton, Dr G.M.B. Dobson, Professor Sir David Brunt, Dr I. Heilbron, Dr E.C. Bullard, Professor P.I. Dee and Professor Sir George Thomson.

[35] PRO DSIR 2 512. Memorandum, 'Manchester University Radio Telescope: Revised Estimates'.

recently retired from chairing both major government science policy bodies, the ACSP and DRPC, recommended to the trustees of the Nuffield Foundation that they should support the Radio Telescope, underwriting it to up to £300,000. He did this by a letter kept 'secret from Blackett, Lovell and Sir Ben Lockspeiser... If the trustees turned the idea down, he would say no more'.[36] The trustees[37] responded favourably, but decided to wait until they knew how much money the DSIR would commit. That nationalistic arguments were used to sway the trustees is apparent from their reaction quoted by Clark that radio astronomy was 'a field in which Great Britain leads the world, and should continue to lead'.[38] Lord Nuffield himself was more sceptical.[39] Lord Nuffield, William Morris before his ennoblement, had founded the Nuffield Foundation in 1943. The Foundation's financial resources had soared along with Morris Motors stock in the post-war automobile boom. As a believer in private enterprise he opposed the use of Foundation money to support what he saw as a speculative government project. According to the Nuffield Foundation's 'biographer' the arguments that persuaded Nuffield were first that radar (now a device of high status and proven military value) was once 'esoteric', and secondly that 'the radio telescope might one day be directed if need be on the steppes of Russia'. This was the first use of cold war rhetoric and the defence interpretation of the telescope. This interpretative malleability of the telescope became apparent as the bodies that supported the instrument became more heterogeneous.

The DSIR's financial history of the telescope briefly noted the Nuffield Foundation's decision:

(vii) On 30 January 1952, the Secretary suggested to the Lord President that, as the Nuffield Foundation would share our costs, we might go ahead.
(viii) In March 1952, Manchester submitted a revised estimate for £335,449.[40]

This, Lovell states, was due to a 'general rise in prices... without a nut being

---

[36] Clark (1972), p. 103.

[37] The trustees included Sir John Stopford, VC of Manchester University. Clark reports that Stopford managed the complication of the 'dual roles' in a 'splendidly correct' way.

[38] Letter, trustees of the Nuffield Foundation to Tizard, in Clark (1972), p. 103.

[39] I have a very small amount of evidence to suggest there was some antipathy between Nuffield and Lovell. In a letter discussing a film project about the construction of Jodrell Bank (see next chapter), a Treasury official, approved the Foreign Office inspired engineering emphasis of the film, 'because of Nuffield Foundation's attitude to Professor Lovell'. PRO INF 12 664. Letter, Senior to Ross, 16 July 1954.

[40] PRO DSIR 2 512. Memorandum, 'Manchester University Radio Telescope: Revised Estimates'.

changed'.[41] The DSIR report goes on:

> (ix) On 20 March, the Nuffield Foundation told the Lord President they had set aside £200,000 for the telescope.
>
> (x) The formal letter of announcement, dated 10 April 1952, was sent to the University promising the £336,000 (£168,000 DSIR, £168,000 Nuffield).

This money was tied to conditions, in particular 'Rainford [the Bursar] would place contracts on receipt of agreed specifications between Husband and [Lovell]', and any contract of £5000 or more needed 'the prior consent of DSIR'.[42] This also meant the consent of the Treasury.

Within a year more money was needed. This increase was mainly due to design change and rising costs. In 1951, astronomers at Harvard, Leiden and Australia detected neutral hydrogen emission on the 21cm wavelength. This allowed radio astronomers to compete with optical astronomers in galactic observations. Lovell was concerned that Jodrell Bank should have a share of it. For the telescope to work at 21cm, the mesh needed to be closer. This meant more wire, and therefore more weight and greater cost. The mount needed to be stronger to support the heavier dish. The weight of the structure increased from about 900 tons to 1177 tons, the total cost to £445,046.[43]

An application for extra grant was made and discussed at the SGC meeting of 6 May 1953. Lovell states that 'it went awry right from the start'. However, subject to two conditions the Committee recommended an increase of the grant to £239,616 (with Nuffield contributing an extra £32,000). The conditions were that Lovell obtain 'written assurance from a competent aero-dynamicist that...proper allowances had been made for wind' and 'that Manchester University should be invited to consider the possibility of increasing its contribution' though the 'additional grant should not be made conditional upon such added contributions'. The Committee was making a show of being fierce. I.G. Evans, the Assistant Secretary at the DSIR, reported to Lovell 'in spite of the attack made...they were basically of the opinion that the project should proceed'.[44] The University increased its token contribution to running costs to £3300, and the aero-dynamicist, Professor W.A. Mair, was an old acquaintance of Lovell's.

The decision to provide extra money was approved at the Advisory Council on 20 May 1953.[45] The reasons for the continued backing were essentially

---

[41] Lovell (1968), p. 43.

[42] Lovell (1968), p. 48.

[43] PRO DSIR 2 512, op cit, but also see £459,896 in Lovell (1968), p. 51.

[44] Lovell (1968), p. 52.

[45] The SGC reported to the ACSP, the chair of which was the Lord President of the Council, who took responsibility for science at Cabinet level.

those of the initial decision: the principle of a large radio telescope had been accepted. However, the announcement of the additional funding was accompanied by a caveat 'warning...of the embarrassment that an application for any further increase would create in the Department'.[46]

More money was indeed asked for. The two main reasons for this both had extensive further ramifications. Metropolitan Vickers who were contracted to provide the servo drive motors for the telescope asked for £55,000, nearly twice their original estimate of £28,600.[47] Lockspeiser was sympathetic to the claims of the company[48], and the attitude of his DSIR hardened against further grant requests. Although the motors were finally supplied by Metropolitan Vickers, this was only secured after pressure from Treasury to place the contract with a British firm (Siemens was its main rival). The second reason was a series of design changes, which drew intense criticism from the Public Accounts Committee, embarrassed the government departments and nearly resulted in legal action between the consulting engineer and the university. This subject is still a sensitive issue. The Treasury papers dealing with it are closed for 50 years.

Lovell states that '[d]uring 1953 and early 1954 it seemed to me that for various reasons, radio telescopes were likely to become of great importance in the world of the future'.[49] By this he means that not only the telescope could be modified to respond to radar, and therefore would become a sensitive part of a ballistic missile tracking system, but as a instrument capable of generating research relevant to long range bomber navigation. In February 1954, the Air Navigation Committee (ANC) of the Aeronautical Research Council 'considered a paper by Professor Lovell on the use of the radio emissions from the sun and the radio stars for astro navigation'.[50] Spencer Jones, Astronomer Royal and the ANC's chairman, advised the ANC that the '250 foot steerable paraboloid, now in course of installation...would be suitable for the proposed investigation, provided a minor change in design were made'.[51] A.G. Pugsley of Bristol University's Department of Civil Engineering wrote that the modifications necessary would be a tighter mesh

---

[46] PRO DSIR 2 295. Advisory Council on Scientific Policy, 20 May 1953.

[47] PRO DSIR 2 501. Papers in PRO DSIR 2 270 indicate that Metropolitan Vickers also under-estimated their bids for the Liverpool cyclotron.

[48] Lovell (1968), p. 76, records that Lockspeiser and the Chairman of Metropolitan Vickers discussed this at their club.

[49] Lovell (1968), p. 84.

[50] PRO AVIA 54 1944. Note, 'Air Navigation Committee: report and recommendation', February 1954. Lovell was a membe of the ARC. See also Lovell, A.C.B., 1992. *Astronomer by Chance*, Oxford: Oxford University Press, pp. 234-238.

[51] PRO AVIA 54 1944. Letter, Spencer Jones to E. Jones (Principal Director of Scientific Research (Air), Ministry of Supply), 5 March 1954.

for the higher frequencies (higher even than the 21cm Hydrogen line). This would weigh more and so a strengthening of the support would also be needed. With this demonstration of interest it seemed that Jodrell Bank would receive money through the Ministry of Supply if such modifications were made. A meeting between Lovell and Husband took place on 1 March 1954, as Lovell privately explained later to Manchester University:

> ...I had been asked by a highly placed official in the Ministry of Supply to get some idea from the engineer of the cost of modifying the telescope to work on 10cm.[52]

Husband's (and Pugsley's) estimate was that the redesign would cost an extra £46,500. However, the Ministry of Supply support fell through in late April 1954, partly due to the traditional Treasury antipathy to multiple government departments funding single projects, but also to internal disquiet. Robert Cockburn, then Scientific Adviser to the Air Ministry (and ex-TRE), considered there was 'no direct defence interest in the use of the Jodrell Bank telescope' either as 'a means of intercepting interesting signals at very long range by means of scattered propagation' or in 'the use of stellar noise as means of navigation'.[53] The data for navigation was already being produced in the United States at the Naval Research Laboratory, and, aware of the problems presented to other government departments by the Radio Telescope, the Ministries internally concurred that they 'should not get entangled with the finances and difficulties of that white elephant'.[54] There was then a misunderstanding at Manchester, in that Lovell was apparently surprised and alarmed to find in mid-August 1954 that the redesign of the bowl had been carried through.[55]

The design changes (see Figures 2.1 and 2.2) revealed the telescope's malleability in a very real sense. They reflected efforts to mobilise support from new constituencies, the incorporation of changing commitments, and the outcome of radio frequency negotiations (for which see Chapter Four). However, once inscribed into the designs and built into the technology of the telescope, they became difficult to change: the telescope was *malleable* but

---

[52] JBA CS7/34/1. Memorandum by Lovell, 'Comments on the engineer's "Note on the Jodrell Bank Telescope", undated (1955).

[53] PRO AVIA 54 1944. Memorandum, 'Jodrell Bank Telescope', by Cockburn, 22 March 1954. Interestingly, at this stage even Blackett thought (as summarised by Cockburn) that 'Lovell should concentrate on justifying the £430,000 which he has already received'.

[54] AVIA 54 1944. Note, PDQRD(A) to PDLRD, 3 May 1954.

[55] Lovell explained to the University: 'I had no indications whatsoever that in spite of this letter [of 26 April 1954, telling Husband that the Ministry of Supply had backed out] the engineers had stopped work on the original structure. My first knowledge that the bowel ['e' crossed out] had been redesigned was contained in a letter I received from the engineer on August 13th, 1954'. JBA CS7/34/1. Memorandum by Lovell, ibid.

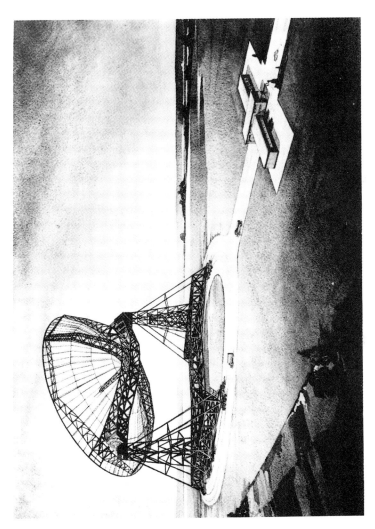

Figure 2.1 Husband's drawing of the Radio Telescope, before the design changes.
Source: Lovell, A.C.B., 1954a. 'The new radio telescope at Jodrell Bank', *Discovery* 15, p185.

(Drawing copyright: Mott MacDonald & Sheffield)

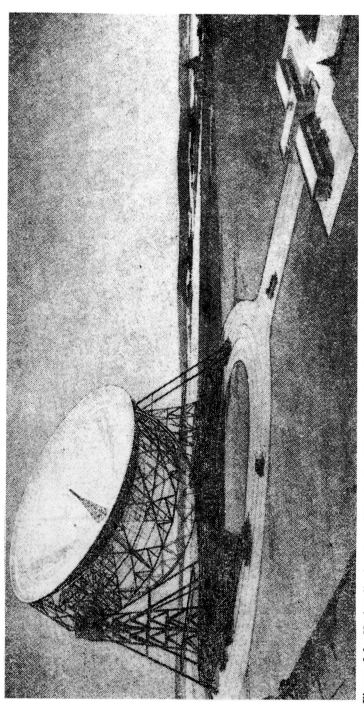

Figure 2.2 Husband's drawing of the Radio Telescope, after the design changes.

Source: Lovell, A.C.B., 1956b. 'Radio astronomy and the Jodrell Bank Telescope. *Proceedings of the Institution of Electrical Engineers* 103, pp711-721.

(Drawing copyright: Mott MacDonald & Sheffield)

not *fluid*. Although the status and significance of the telescope were usefully malleable, allowing different versions to be mobilised for different audiences, the steel structure proved expensively firmer. But the telescope was now adapted to receive even higher frequencies, and its defence interpretation would be still available to Lovell (particularly in protecting the telescope's complex but *fully steerable* mount in negotiations with the DSIR).[56] The malleability was a result of the different interests in the telescope, which was accentuated by the loose research council structure of funding science.

The Radio Telescope and the Financial Competence of Universities

During 1954, the gaze of the Public Accounts Committee (the powerful parliamentary select committee that reviewed, retrospectively, budget overspends) turned on the Radio Telescope. The PAC called Lockspeiser before it on March 25 of that year, declaring that it was 'most anxious to satisfy any apprehension as to the adequacy of the system of financial control [of the universities]'.[57] The Committee pursued its own particular agenda: its target was the accountability of university finance and it was calling for the full inspection of their books by the Comptroller and Auditor General[58], and hence under the surveillance of the Treasury. The publicised telescope, read as an example of a university's lack of financial control, could become enlisted as a powerful weapon in the PAC's armoury. The UGC and DSIR met informally prior to the PAC hearing:

> We discussed the general question of the placing of large and expensive to run machines... You agreed, I think, that we should have in the future to consider how far it was right to leave the erection and maintenance of such machines to universities or how far they might be more directly DSIR commitments.[59]

An aspect of the organisation of post-war science, the location of large projects in universities, became an issue of controversy within Whitehall and Parliament, with the pressure stemming from the Treasury and the PAC. The

---

[56] For interpretative flexibility of technology see: Pinch, T.J. and Bijker, W.E., 1987. 'The social construction of facts and artifacts: or how the sociology of science and the sociology of technology might benefit each other', in Bijker, W.E., Hughes, T.P. and Pinch, T.J. (eds.) 1987. *The Social Construction of Technological Systems: New Directions in the Sociology and History of Technology*, Cambridge MA: MIT Press.

[57] *The Times*, 8 September 1954.

[58] Briggs, A., 1969. 'Development in higher education in the United Kingdom', in Niblett, W.R. (ed), *Higher Education: Demand and Response*, London: Tavistock, p. 95-116. Parl. Papers HCP (1953/4) 67-I, paragraphs 888-975 for a particularly pointed debate between the PAC and Sir E. Hale (UGC) on 23 February 1954.

[59] PRO UGC 7 152. Letter, Blount (DSIR) to Murray (UGC), 25 February 1954.

university, as a *site* for research science, beyond teaching laboratories, was in flux. It was because Jodrell Bank had been forced into the public realm (see next chapter) that it became the focus for such discussions.

After some detailed questioning by the PAC over the reasons for the increase in expenditure agreed in 1953, Lockspeiser stated that there would be no further increases unless 'scientific demands...entirely new came up which would compel us - literally compel us - to make the review'.[60] This closing of the orthodox internal routes of funding the telescope, made the public representation of the telescope ever more important. The financing of the telescope came up again before the PAC in 1957 and 1958 and will be discussed later, along with the wider issues of the university site for science.

In August 1954, Lovell became aware that Husband's design change discussed in April had been implemented. But there was no question of extra money being available to strengthen the bowl. Lovell records in *The Story of Jodrell Bank* that a meeting between Hanbury Brown, J.G. Davies and himself agreed that they could 'save the budget by abandoning all aspects which were not absolutely necessary, such as any idea of driving it in the azimuth'.[61] However, Lovell was again able to exploit the interpretative malleability of the telescope, and mobilise defence concerns. As a member of the Air Warfare Committee of the Ministry of Supply, he was aware of the state of the early warning system. The coastal radar stations did not possess a dish as large (and hence as sensitive) as the projected Radio Telescope. This would be the case until the Ballistic Missile Early Warning System (BMEWS), which surrounded the United States and Canada, was extended to include Britain (Fylingdales was begun in 1960, 'initially cost £45 million, and started operation in 1963'[62]). He contacted Cockburn, now Controller of Guided Weapons and Electronics at the Ministry of Supply, who arranged a meeting between Sir Harry Garner, Chairman of the Guided Weapons Advisory Board, and Lockspeiser. Garner, reports Lovell, had a particular 'interest in having the telescope completed quickly and in a steerable condition'. Although no aid could be directly given by these other Ministries, it seems to have swayed the DSIR's mind. During 1951 and 1952, the DSIR had been told that, because of the rearmament pressures of the Korean War, the civil research programme must be reshaped according to defence interests, and probably these pressures continued.[63] On 2 October 1954, Charles Cawley (Assistant Director (HQ), DSIR) wrote that there was 'further discussion of the position in the Department' and he requested information on 'additional

---

[60] Parl. Papers HCP (1953/54) 67-I, paragraph 2512.

[61] Lovell (1968), p. 91.

[62] Campbell, D., 1986. *The Unsinkable Aircraft Carrier*, London: Paladin, pp. 84-86.

[63] PRO DEFE 11 15. Memorandum, 'Ministry of Defence. Transfer of civil scientific effort to defence', 17 March 1952.

sums'. On December 15 1954, the Advisory Council (with Lockspeiser secretary) discussed the telescope. Quoting his diary, Lovell states that it 'had taken the very definite view that every effort should be made to finish off the telescope in its original steerable form'.[64] Appeal to defence interests also secured Ministry of Supply and United States Air Force support for lunar echo and meteor ionisation work at Jodrell Bank.[65]

This episode is significant in relation to Edge and Mulkay's account of the Cambridge and Manchester radio astronomy groups differentiating and commiting themselves to different 'technical strategies'. The adoption of the 'technical strategy' of steerable multipurpose radio telescopes at Jodrell Bank cannot be smoothly derived from competitive specialty dynamics: it stemmed from the heterogeneity of the funding structure, an environment made up of bodies with divergent interests in the project.

Soon more money again was needed. Husband suggested a solid sheet bowl in December, and a scale model was tested at the National Physical Laboratory. These tests revealed the problem of 'bowl flutter', a destructive resonance effect. To counteract this, a 'braking' mechanism was necessary. This item, along with further cost increases from Metropolitan-Vickers, meant that the budget for the telescope was over-running even with the extra £50,000 approved by the DSIR Advisory Council.

Friction now appeared between the DSIR and the UGC. In a letter from Cawley (DSIR) to Hale (UGC), he noted that 'it is going to be extremely difficult' to find the money voted by the Advisory Council.[66] This was read by the UGC as an attempt to shift responsibility for the finance of the telescope away from the DSIR at the end of the quinquennium (August 1957). There was immediate discussion within the UGC over the telescope. A meeting within the UGC attended by Sir Edward Hale (Secretary, UGC), Howard Mallaby (Deputy Secretary, UGC) and Sir Keith Murray (Chair, UGC) noted:

> Cawley's letter implies...that the DSIR expects us to take over the radio telescope at the end of this quinquennium, just as they expected us to take over nuclear physics research. These confident expectations on the part of the DSIR must, I feel, be checked.[67]

---

[64] Lovell (1968), p. 106. Again note the how Lovell repeatedly draws from his diary as an authoritative source. A 'study contract for...passive early warning radar' was later placed with Marconis for work at Jodrell Bank. PRO AVIA 65 1638. Minutes, 'Record of meeting...to discuss guided weapons progress', 7 August 1957.

[65] JBA ACC/56/5. Letter, Lovell to Wansbrough-Jones, 12 January 1956. See: Agar, J., 1996. 'Moon relay experiments at Jodrell Bank', in Butrica, A. (ed.), *Beyond the Ionosphere*, NASA History.

[66] PRO UGC 7 152. Letter, Cawley to Hale, 24 January 1955.

[67] PRO UGC 7 152. Minute sheet, written by Murray, 31 January 1955.

The meeting went on to note that, whilst the DSIR proposals should be examined on its merits, there were two main reasons against assuming responsibility for what 'is likely to be a very troublesome child'. Firstly, it had 'not yet reached weaning age and I would want a firm assurance that it will be completed by 1957'. Secondly, it had 'many of the characteristics which made the finances of nuclear physics so unpalatable to both DSIR and ourselves'. Murray doubted that the '£500,000 [would]...by any measure meet the total capital expenditure'. Interestingly, he went on: 'Nor does there seem to be a great confidence that the machine [would] be a success'. Indeed, in a significant phrase, was 'this Jodrell Bank enterprise really a desirable, valuable and necessary adjunct to Manchester University?'. Furthermore 'the life story' of 'this ailing and costly infant...may well become interesting to the PAC'. In a letter to Cawley, Hale stated: the 'implication that the UGC should accept financial responsibility is one we cannot readily accept'[68], and to Stopford he went on: 'we should very much like an opportunity to have your opinion on [the Radio Telescope's] value to the University' and suggested a 'private discussion'.[69] Stopford replied 'it would be best if you could both visit Jodrell Bank'.[70] Before this visit, the DSIR tightened the screws:

> I stated wrongly that our grant comes to an end at the end of the quinquennium. In fact...the grant ends on 31 March 1956. Before the new quinquennium, therefore, the University will be faced with the problem of financing the project for a period of 16 months.[71]

Hale replied that this was a 'much greater shock...[that] we have no provision for'.[72] The experience of financing the telescope made the departments question the wisdom of the funding system. In a letter to Murray, Blount (Deputy Secretary, DSIR) discussed this. He distinguished small sums used flexibly to back research of 'timeliness and promise'.[73] This was necessary because 'new ideas occur haphazardly, and not conveniently... when plans are made for a new quinquennium'. These were 'quite different' from 'big undertakings':

> Even if the UGC and the university decided that the development of the radio telescope was not going to be worth while...it would really not be possible to abandon the venture: too big a vested interest has been created and there has been so much publicity that [it] would be politically most embarrassing.

[68] PRO UGC 7 152. Letter, Hale to Cawley, 4 February 1955.
[69] PRO UGC 7 152. Letter, Hale to Stopford, 4 February 1955.
[70] PRO UGC 7 152. Letter, Stopford to Hale, 10 February 1955.
[71] PRO UGC 7 152. Letter, Cawley to Hale, 14 February 1955.
[72] PRO UGC 7 152. Letter, Hale to Cawley, 16 February 1955.
[73] PRO UGC 7 152. Letter, Blount to Murray, 15 February 1955.

Two vitally important processes are clearly apparent here. Firstly, the resources that were being committed to the new longer-term ('vested interest') expensive-instrument post-war science were straining the research council system of funding science at universities. Secondly, while it was concluded that the telescope project was unstoppable because it was highly public, conversely it was also because it was highly public that Jodrell Bank was the site where these anxieties found expression.

Blount wondered whether, since Murray was an assessor on the Advisory Council and the SGC, he might 'pick up any proposals which might subsequently grow into an embarrassment to you or the universities'. Murray replied that big undertakings could be a source of embarrassment, pointedly adding: 'especially when your grants terminate during a quinquennium'.[74] He doubted that 'a lay mind' could spot 'apparently innocuous projects' and suggested the introduction of 'an amber light into the system'.

Meetings were arranged between Cawley, Blount, Murray and Hale at the Athenaeum on March 14; and between Stopford, Lovell, Hale and Murray on March 16 at Manchester.[75] The Athenaeum meeting considered the radio telescope as part of its wider context of support for 'large machines'.

The most impressive argument that could be used to justify support for the Jodrell Bank project was the physical presence of the half-finished telescope. A report of the visit to Jodrell Bank noted that: the Bursar would provide more exact estimates of expenditure, Lovell would provide a summary of the 'work and significance of the station'[76], the 'secretary and I would consider whether the UGC should undertake to fill the gap or part of it' and '[W]e should ask the DSIR to accept liability for subsequent non-recurrent expenditure and expenditure on 'apparatus for research arising out of use of the telescope". Furthermore, in 'subsequent private discussion, the V-C assured us that the University as a whole was behind the Jodrell Bank experiment'. A following minute sheet of Murray's goes on: 'I admit that, as a layman, I was immensely impressed...[by the] zest and enthusiasm...and support of the university'[77], and even though '[I] realise that this may make too easy a way out for DSIR and may not therefore prevent them doing the same sort of thing again...We could make an emergency addition to the Manchester block grant without [creating] awkward precedents'.

Bodies that could be brought to the telescope under the astronomers' guidance were more easily convinced of its value. A letter to Blount from

---

[74] PRO UGC 7 152. Letter, Murray to Blount, 16 February 1955.

[75] PRO UGC 7 152. Letter, Stopford to Hale, 9 March 1955. Letter, Blount to Murray, 10 March 1955.

[76] PRO UGC 7 152. Report of Hale and Murray, written by Murray, 18 March 1955.

[77] PRO UGC 7 152. Minute sheet by Murray, 19 March 1955, by which Hale has pencilled in 'So was I - E.H.'.

Murray said: 'I shall be prepared to ask my Committee to contribute to this £17,700 from the now almost infinitesimal reserves left to us', as long as the DSIR met the remaining capital cost, paid for insurance and would not 'offer temporary support for research...likely to become sufficiently onerous for its cessation...requiring intervention'.[78]

The DSIR replied with 'delight' that the UGC were using their reserves.[79] However, it felt that Manchester was being 'a little ingenuous' in expressing surprise at the early cessation of funds, 'certainly Lovell discussed it with Lockspeiser last autumn'[80], and it queried whether the UGC should not have been aware of this, since all 'papers are received in your office'. For a while, the negotiations over which goverment department should be responsible for the telescope rested.

A meeting of the UGC on 5 May 1955 considered the proposals. The Committee agreed to provide the £17,700 recurrent grant. With respect to capital expenditure, it noted the following communique from the DSIR:

> We are at present waiting for the University to make an application for a supplementary grant...Assuming that this is within the limits set by our Advisory Council...we intend to provide money.[81]

It also noted that inquiries were being made about insurance, and assurances sought from the DSIR over the cessation of future grants.

However, the full extent of the telescopes's financial situation was only revealed in October. Not only had the weight of steel needed risen to nearly 1700 tons, but also 'United Steel Structural Co. [were] claiming £135 per ton instead of £114 per ton in the contract'.[82] The capital cost of the telescope now stood at £630,000, with only £390,000, plus the extra £50,000, promised.

On 27 October 1955, the Chief Finance Officer of the DSIR (S.H. Smith) visited Jodrell Bank with the Manchester University Bursar (Rainford). The possibility of a deal emerged in which Manchester would receive the £50,000, and the DSIR would match pound for pound anything Manchester could raise on the remaining debt.

---

[78] PRO UGC 7 152. Letter, murray to Blount, 29 March 1955.

[79] At the same moment, the DSIR had persuaded the Nuffield Foundation to fund two magnetic surveys, totalling £50,000 (which otherwise the DSIR would have had to fund). The DSIR argued that if it had to pay any more for Radio Telescope "it could only be done by breaking promises to universities and other bodies already made (which was unthinkable) or by cutting down (including perhaps some sackings) in the units and stations controlled by the DSIR itself". Clark (1972), pp. 105-106.

[80] PRO UGC 7 152. Letter, Blount to Murray, 15 April 1955.

[81] PRO UGC 2 36. Minutes, 5 May 1955.

[82] Lovell (1968), p. 121.

Brief negotiations ensued with the Royal Society about a 'possible IGY contribution to the radio telescope: channelling Royal Society IGY money to the telescope, despite previous 'estimates...based on the [assumption] that no special arrangements would be required for the telescope on behalf of IGY'.[83] The justification was that the telescope would then be completed and able to take part in the international effort. Sir David Brunt replied that the Royal Society was unable to contribute, partly because the available funds were tied to 'specified purposes', but also because there was 'a strong feeling that it is not appropriate for the Royal Society to step in to clear up a mess left by the DSIR'.[84] Brunt could only advise resubmitting a request to the DSIR, stressing the IGY angle, whilst strengthening existing contacts.[85] As Brunt recounted:

> yesterday afternoon at a meeting of DSIR I sat next to Blackett, who has now become a member of the Advisory Council of DSIR...I explained to him the precise situation with regard to your telescope...he is going to raise this question at the meeting of the Advisory Council

However, the DSIR decided in December that no more money could be committed until a Committee of Inquiry, with an independent chairman, looked into the telescope. The dates of the inquiry were fixed for 18-20 January 1956. It consisted of Mansfield Cooper (chair and Manchester University law professor), Matheson (Manchester University engineering professor), Smith-Rose and Saxton (Radio Research Station), Verry, Greenall and Smith (DSIR, alo representing the Nuffield Foundation), Scruton (National Physical Laboratory) and Thomas (Building Research Station).[86] The UGC was not represented. There was then a considerable delay before the Committee of Inquiry made its report.

The Committee of Inquiry's conclusions began to be known to the astronomers in August. However, its conclusions circulated around Whitehall as early as April 1956. In a briefing made by Blount of the DSIR for his minister the Lord President, he notes that the DSIR's Advisory Council

---

[83] JBA CS7/3/3. Letter, Lovell to Sir David Brunt (Royal Society Secretary and Vice-President), 9 November 1955.

[84] JBA CS7/3/3. Letter, Brunt to Lovell, 11 November 1955.

[85] Lovell wrote the letter, copying it to Blackett, emphasising the IGY angle as Brunt had suggested. He stated: 'apart from the inherent value of the scientific programme it seems to me from a prestige point of view the telescope is Britain's one chance of producing a new instrument comparable in importance with the American and Russian satellites'. The satellites being a projected highlight of the International Geophysical Year. JBA CS7/3/3. Letter, Lovell to Cawley, 14 November 1955. Letter, Lovell to Blackett, 14 November 1955.

[86] Lovell (1968), p. 133.

endorsed the telescope project since 'the reasons which led Sir Ben Lockspeiser to recommend the previous grant still stand':

> Radio astronomy is a field in which the way has largely been pioneered by Britain and it would be disastrous to the *prestige* of this country if we failed to complete the instrument as originally planned [my italics][87]

For the DSIR, it was crucial to finish the telescope because the Department was deeply implicated with the construction of the telescope as an object of national prestige. The Department read the Committee of Enquiry's [sic] 'Conclusions and Recommendations' as recording, firstly 'a very unsatisfactory position...between the University and its Consultants...', and secondly 'a position in which funds are nor [sic] available to complete the telescope, unless further Government grants are forthcoming or the University can raise new funds, or both'. Thirdly, and revealingly, the DSIR interpreted the Committee of Enquiry as recording that:

> the formal responsibility for completing or abandoning the project rests with the University, which has no legal claims on the DSIR or the Nuffield Trust for additional financial support: but having regard to the publicity which the project has inevitably received and its importance as a scientific advance and to national prestige, ways and means virtually must be found for seeing it through.

Since the DSIR had explicitly promoted the project as an object of public national prestige, then it could be accused creating the problem. Blount therefore stressed the desirability of the 'DSIR, *which is to say, the Government*, playing a full part in seeing it through [my italics]'. Blount hoped that the 'cogency of these reasons' would convince the Lord President 'to authorise me to seek the necessary Treasury sanction to proceed', whilst being aware that 'I have to meet the Treasury's normal critical examination... but also persuade the Treasury to agree to face the already critical Public Accounts Committee'. Blount was also aware that this commitment would mean large cuts in other projects: 'we shall have to save on other work the extra amount we now contemplate spending on this'.[88]

A Site Committee had to be set up to oversee the telescope's construction. The Committee of Inquiry accepted a capital cost of £650,000, of which £260,000 needed to be found. The Treasury did indeed allow the DSIR to

---

[87] PRO DSIR 17 182. Letter, B.K. Blount to the Lord President, 11 April 1956. In particular, he goes on, Britain must not fail 'to complete it in time to play the important part planned for it during the International Geophysical Year'.

[88] This was the only way to convince the Treasury: 'we must and do expect to have to find the additional grants proposed out of the total resources [already voted to DSIR] – so that an additional call on the Exchequer will not in fact be involved'.

grant £130,000. There were however '4 pages of conditions', not least of which was one insisting that the university gave a written guarantee that the sum was not greater than that recoverable by legal action (against Husband for changing the design). These were unacceptable to Manchester University.

In October 1956, Mansfield Cooper, erstwhile chairman of the Committee of Inquiry, became Vice-Chancellor of Manchester University. He immediately wrote to the UGC and, noting that they had not been kept informed (somewhat surprisingly), suggested a meeting.[89] This was arranged for 10 October. A note of the meeting was made by Murray:

> [The University] has taken Counsel's opinion twice and each has confirmed that there has been a breach of contract by the consultant [Husband] and that they have got a strong case against him.

There was a small doubt that the university had not waived its right to bring case by not prosecuting Husband earlier.[90] However, Murray continued:

> I, personally, was very perturbed by the possible consequences vis-a-vis the PAC and the Treasury if it was established that the university was to blame for this over-expenditure. Anything that could be done therefore to make it as clear as possible that the blame lay elsewhere seemed to me highly desirable, not only from the point of view of Manchester, but of *the Universities as a whole* (my italics).

Here again the UGC interpreted the telescope in terms of its own anxieties: the destabilising PAC criticisms of the telescope had significance with regard to the status of all universities. This was echoed by an internal note added to Murray's by Hale:

> This Jodrell Bank trouble has been a nightmare to me qua its possible effect on public confidence in the capacity of universities to control the expenditure of public money... this ought to be the determining element of policy here.

With this policy agreed, Murray told Mansfield Cooper to seek further comment from the Vice-Chancellor of Bristol, Philip Morris.[91] Filling in Morris, Murray informed him that he had not told Mansfield Cooper that 'certain people in the Treasury itself, where the issue has been discussed by DSIR, are already citing the Manchester problem as evidence supporting the PAC view'.[92] Morris's main conclusion was that the matter 'should be cleared

---

[89] PRO UGC 7 152. Letter, Mansfield Cooper to Murray, 1 October 1956.

[90] PRO UGC 7 152. Letter, Mansfield Cooper to Murray, 6 December 1956, contains the two opinions of Counsel.

[91] Morris was chair of the Vice-Chancellors and Principals committee.

[92] PRO UGC 7 152. Letter, Murray to Morris, 11 October 1956.

up as far as possible by rigorous examination and by the clear establishment of actual or constructive faults on the part of any concerned'.

Treasury opinion on the matter can be gauged from a further series of correspondence. In March 1957, Frank Turnbull, Under-Secretary of the Treasury, wrote to Hale, noting: 'You may have heard about this from the university side, but I do not think you have been consulted from our side about the main problem'.[93] This was:

> Manchester University seem to have failed to keep adequate supervision over the consulting engineer and have concealed from DSIR until too late the legal possibility or recovering money from him. As a result an unnecessary burden has been placed on the Exchequer.

With this letter was accompanied 'the main papers' held by the Treasury.[94] Why were the Treasury revealing these? Hale was worried by Turnbull's phrase: 'the possibilities of bringing pressure to bear through the DSIR grant are limited, so the ultimate question is whether, if Manchester University are eventually judged to be at fault, anything can be done through the UGC'. Hale retreated: '[the UGC would be] very reluctant to become involved...at this late stage'.[95] Furthermore: the 'PAC's attitude to our Committee does not encourage me to hope that they would be impressed by any exculpation of the university by our Committee'. Hale's personal opinion was that Husband had 'forced the hand of the university into proceeding with the new design', and, but for overriding factors, the UGC would like to have seen Husband sued. These factors, Hale drily pointed out, came from considering the importance of 'getting value for the money sunk in the telescope' with its 'high rate of obsolescence' and commitments to International Geophysical Year.

In March 1957, the Comptroller and Auditor General, Sir Frank Tribe, published a report on the escalating cost of the telescope. Its contents were widely reported (unfavourably) by the newspapers. It was at this point that the telescope's financial troubles were made public. Also in March, Sir Harry Melville, ex-Superintendent at TRE and successor to Lockspeiser as Secretary at the DSIR[96], and S.H. Smith (Finance Officer for DSIR) were called before the PAC. Melville's answers implied that it was Husband who was at fault:

---

[93] PRO UGC 7 152. Letter, Turnbull to Hale, 8 March 1957.

[94] Unfortunately, only a list of contents is present. However of note is the fact that the Comptroller and Auditor General was involved and made a report in January 1957.

[95] PRO UGC 7 152. Letter, Hale to Turnbull, 13 March 1957.

[96] Melville had been a professor of chemistry at the University of Birmingham, and moved to Whitehall as Secretary to DSIR in 1955. He was a TRE Superintendent between 1943-1945.

[Q] If this was a University project, who had changed the design without obtaining approval of the University, the engineer or Prof Lovell?
[A] Oh, no, quite clearly the engineering consultant changed the design without concurrence of the University.[97]

However Melville did not seem well briefed. He got the size of the telescope wrong, and believed that Lovell lived by the telescope 'in apartments'[98] and that he was 'unaware of any [design] changes until the steelwork arrived'. The PAC then turned to the fees payable to Husband, whom they saw as standing to profit from the increase in expenditure. The possibility of an extra grant was discussed. The PAC then linked the case of the telescope to their concerns over university finance:

> (Chair)...would you agree that the expenditure has not been properly controlled and administered by the University?
> (Melville) I think we would be bound to say that in this instance Manchester University's financial administration is not without criticism.
> (Chair) Of course, this does not give us very much satisfaction when we think of the Treasury Minute of January...which said that non-recurrent grants to universities are properly controlled and properly administered.[99]

The PAC report was published on 13 August 1957, and there was much criticism in the press. As will be seen in the next chapter, press conferences were explicitly managed at Jodrell Bank by the DSIR to protect the telescope, and divert attention away from PAC criticisms. The UGC privately warned Manchester University that not only would that university suffer financially, but worse: Geoffrey Heyworth (Chairman of Unilever, and member of the UGC) told Sir Raymond Streat (outgoing Chairman on the Cotton Board and incoming Chairman of the University Council): 'we [are] heading straight for the disaster of bureaucratic direction of all the Universities'.[100]

The situation at the end of the summer in 1957 was that the DSIR would provide £130,000 of the remaining debt subject to conditions. This left £130,000 to be found by Manchester. Melville had given assurances to the PAC that no more money would be made available from government departments.

---

[97] Parl. Papers HCP (1956/7) 75-I, paragraph 1839.
[98] Parl. Papers HCP (1956/7) 75-I, paragraph 1849.
[99] Parl. Papers HCP (1956/7) 75-I, paragraphs 1945-1946.
[100] Streat, R. (Dupree, M., ed.), 1987. *Lancashire and Whitehall: the Diary of Sir Raymond Streat. Volume Two: 1939-57*, Manchester: Manchester University Press, p. 928. See also Footnote 127.

Sputnik

On 4 October 1957 the Russians announced that they had launched the first earth staellite, Sputnik, as part of the International Geophysical Year. The Jodrell Bank telescope, which had recently received critical media attention, was immediately linked with the satellite, a process which I examine closely in Chapter Three. This association (of the telescope with satellites, and hence with important anxieties of national security) allowed contrasts to be drawn between the telescope's great utility and its debt. With the internal orthodox route of seeking funds closed by the Treasury, these contrasts were used in an attempt to publicly shame the government into clearing the telescope's debt. An attempt was then made by the allies of the radio astronomers to combine this public campaign with a private lobbying of government at the highest level. The public campaign will be discussed next chapter, but the internal lobbying fits well with this chapter's concerns.

Initially, a fresh attempt to mobilise the defence interpretation of the telescope seemed unlikely: the scientific advisor to the Ministry of Supply, Sir Owen Wansbrough-Jones, had made a rare public statement five days following the satellite launch that Sputnik had '"little to do with defence"'. He read it otherwise as being just a '"great scientific experiment"'.[101]

In his biography of Lovell, Dudley Saward wrote that Sir Robert Renwick ('a well known financier and industrialist', but also ex-wartime co-ordinator of airborne radar research and production) and himself had written a letter praising the readiness of the telescope to track the satellite, and that it appeared in *The Times* on the 16 October 1957.[102] In Saward's account, Renwick 'was looking at the necessity of having the telescope as an effective defence weapon, as well as an instrument for the exploration of outer space', and after consulting with Lovell forwarded this information to Macmillan in the form of a memo.[103] Macmillan, on the return from a meeting with Eisenhower in Washington, was then able to reply when 'subjected on 29 October in the House of Commons to questions about the Russian satellite', with reference to Jodrell Bank.[104]

---

[101] *The Times*, 'US Ready to Discuss Control of Outer Space, "Little to do with Defence": Ministry Scientist's View', 9 October 1957. The article went on to the reception of signals from the satellite by the BBC and at the Mullard at Cambridge, as well as a pointer to the article on radar tracking at Jodrell Bank.

[102] Saward, D., 1984. *Bernard Lovell: a Biography*, London: Robert Hale, p. 190; his description of Renwick, p. 312. Renwick was on the Board of AEI and had connections with numerous other companies. He was Controller of Communications, Air Ministry and Controller of Communications Equipment, Ministry of Aircraft Production, 1942-1945.

[103] Saward (1984), pp. 191-192.

[104] Saward (1984), pp. 193-194.

However, examination of the government sources on the episode reveals a less straightforward account. The lobbying of Macmillan was similar in character to the use of contacts and networks with the Royal Astronomical Society and, as will be seen later, with radio frequencies. The Macmillan memorandum was carefully worded: after giving the technical statistics, it noted that

> the telescope has been built for two purposes: firstly to receive the radio emissions which are generated in the remote parts of the universe, secondly as a giant radar system...it has been realised for some time that this instrument would be the most powerful radar equipment in the Western world and would be particularly suited to the tracking of satellites.[105]

Whereas it had been intended to use the telescope on the American satellites 'to obtain fundamental data which would be necessary as a first stage in the detection and tracking of enemy long range missiles', the surprise Soviet Sputnik had now allowed 'the potentialities of the instrument' to be 'demonstrated'.[106] Having belatedly cashed in the public capital generated by the media, Renwick in his covering letter made the link: provided 'Manchester University is relieved from its financial embarrassment and supplied with sufficient funding...you have, I suggest, something of immense value for defence purposes to offer the Americans'.[107] With Macmillan, about to leave to Washington to attempt to negotiate an 'escape from the inhibitions of the McMahon Act and make possible Anglo-American exchange of information on nuclear weapons development' and a 'joint approach to the development of guided missiles',[108] this was rhetoric designed for immediate appeal. After gaining the information from the DSIR that the telescope was 'the only instrument in the UK which could detect the presence of a rocket motor in an object so small as the Sputnik' and that 'the Americans have no comparable instrument',[109] Macmillan gave the short reply that he 'was glad to have this paper on the eve of [his] departure for Washington'.[110]

In November, Lovell wrote to Renwick again. Jodrell Bank, he claimed, had 'had to assume the national responsibility for keeping track' of the

---

[105] PRO PREM 11 2484. 'Note on Jodrell Bank Telescope'.
[106] The note was accompanied by an 'attached photograph [showing]...a part of the radar trace as the instrument tracked the rocket from the Arctic Circle into Russia'.
[107] PRO PREM 11 2484. Letter, Renwick to Macmillan, 22 October 1957.
[108] *The Times*, 18 October 1957.
[109] PRO PREM 11 2484. Letter, Privy Council Office to de Zulueta (Private Secretary to Prime Minister), 22 October 1957. Melville of the DSIR did know there was 'one in Australia' but he was 'not sure whether it is in full working order'.
[110] PRO PREM 11 2484. Letter, Macmillan to Renwick, 22 October 1957.

Sputnik satellites'.[111] But whereas he was 'delighted to be in a position to assist the Minstry of Supply and many other interested bodies at home and in America', it meant that the Jodrell Bank 'resources [were] strained' and 'distracted by the financial worry over the cost of the telescope'. Lovell suggested that the 'Russians will soon send a rocket to the moon', when 'no doubt all eyes will once more turn to Jodrell Bank', which lacked the more powerful radar equipment to track a rocket that far. After 'private speculation at Jodrell Bank as to the extent of the equipment which would be required', he outlined the apparatus needed:

> The technology and the valves are available (although the transmitter valves may only be available in the US at present) we feel the cost would be considerably [sic] - probably £100,000...This would indeed be a magnificent apparatus capable of radar research on other planets as well as its immediate application to the tracking of the moon rocket.

This letter was again forwarded to Number 10 by Renwick, with the comment that 'this installation is, of course, of vital importance to the world and...is becoming of great National Interest'.[112] Furthermore, 'in these days when the prestige of the country is so vital, I do really feel that a gesture on the part of the Treasury...would have the unstinted support of the whole country'. However, these attempts to use the public identification of the telescope with the satellite to mobilise Prime Ministerial support of the telescope failed. Macmillan's Private Secretary, de Zulueta, confessed to the Treasury that although Lovell had emphasised 'the importance of the Jodrell Bank telescope in tracking Sputnik', he did 'not know what value the telescope really [had] in this connection', and that the 'Prime Minister has no special interest in this except that someone mentioned it to him when he was in Manchester'.[113] De Zulueta said although he 'suppose[d] that we shall have to reply', he also went on that 'Prof Lovell was at one time employed in one of Sir Robert Renwick's companies and this might explains [sic] Sir Robert's interest'.[114] The Treasury were also unmoved: although they were the 'villains of the peace [sic] in Lovell's mind, the payments for the telescope have always been on DSIR votes and their defence before parliament has been on behalf

---

[111] PRO PREM 11 2484. Letter, Lovell to Renwick, 12 November 1957.

[112] PRO PREM 11 2484. Letter, Renwick to de Zulueta, 14 November 1957. The letter was also sent to Charles Hill.

[113] PRO PREM 11 2484. Letter, de Zulueta to Collier, 15 November 1957.

[114] In fact the only previous formal connection between the two was that they had worked together during the Second World War, Lovell at TRE and Renwick as Controller of Communications Equipment, Ministry of Aircraft Production.

of DSIR minutes'.[115] Their strategies were resisted. Melville, the Secretary to the DSIR, who had been short-circuited in the appeal and (importantly) did not have interests that coincided with the astronomers at that moment, wrote angrily to the Manchester University Vice-Chancellor:

> I was very disturbed recently to learn that Prof Lovell had made yet another unofficial move to obtain support for his cause[116]

Moreover, Melville continued, it was carried out in an 'unorthodox way', and he hoped that the VC would 'dissuade Prof Lovell from further private lobbying of this kind', since it would 'only make life even more difficult for all of us'. But Lovell had made 'unofficial' moves before, manipulating similar public symbols of prestige and national interest, so why did this one fail? The behaviour of key actors, in particular the DSIR, could not be controlled by the astronomers, and in this context their interests were not aligned. The public authority of Lovell and Renwick which, as we will see, had been painstakingly constructed from the assembly of texts and film and the appropriation of the Soviet satellite was easily deconstructed within the Cabinet Office. Prestige was for consumption outside of government.

The Radio Telescope Appeal

The appearance of Sputnik was not decisive in the government funding of Jodrell Bank. However, in both Saward's and Lovell's narratives, the tracking of the satellites did provide the turning point in the telescope's financial history: 'at last we were drawing away from our days of misery and disgrace...at Jodrell we had seized our chances'.[117] The remaining debt on the telescope had to be cleared by private appeal: but, I argue, the association of the telescope with satellites was also not generally decisive in persuading industry to donate to the Telescope Appeal.

I claim that the techniques used to promote and support the telescope to industry were qualitatively similar to those used to persuade government: indeed both can be located in the wider post-war networks of contacts and economy of science. The relevance of the telescope to a broad array of interests had to be manufactured, and this attempt at manufacturing relevance started in late 1955, as soon as the financial predicament of the telescope was known, and *before* Sputnik. Lovell had first contacted Renwick at this time asking, 'in view of [Renwick's] interest and long association with this

---

[115] PRO PREM 11 2484. Letter, Collier to Simpson (Office of Lord President of the Council), 18 November 1957.

[116] PRO PREM 11 2484. Letter, Melville to Mansfield Cooper, 29 January 1957.

[117] Lovell (1968), p. 217.

[the radio] industry', whether he could 'offer any advice...in particular if [Renwick] could suggest any firms who might be in a position to respond'.[118] Renwick agreed to help and 'have a word with all my friends in the bigger firms connected with the Radio Industry'.[119]

Lovell wrote to Mott, Director of the Cavendish Laboratories, for advice, asking if he 'could tell me in confidence how you achieved such striking success in the finance of Ryle's programme' (the radio firm Mullard had recently contributed £100,000).[120] Mott replied that a network of connections supported Cambridge radio astronomy:

> Ratcliffe should really have the credit for our success in getting money for Ryle's work. A friend at the Ministry of Supply advised us to approach Mullards and to ask them how best to get the radio industry to join in giving us support. Mullards said they would prefer to do it themselves, if their name was associated with the project.[121]

The campaign then began to demonstrate the coinciding interests of industry and telescope. Mott had suggested that the campaign should start with local industry. P.A. Smith, a Director of ICI who had a major regional base at Wilmslow and who funded ICI Fellowships at Jodrell Bank, expressed sympathy: 'it may be argued that radio astronomy is not very close to [ICI's] normal activities. Nevertheless we all understand that the development of the physical sciences is important for all of us'.[122] Smith offered a 'purely personal suggestion' that Lovell should 'enlist the help of several industrial concerns', specifically local electrical and engineering companies: 'I wonder whether Sir Vincent Ferranti might be able to offer substantial constructive suggestions...various of our directors in London are on sufficiently good terms with important people in the electrical industry to broach the subject'.[123] Lovell wrote to Sir Vincent de Ferranti at Hollinwood in Lancashire 'to see if we can enlist your sympathy and assistance' (Ferranti Ltd specialised in electronics, particularly for defence systems):

---

[118] JBA CS7/3/3. Letter, Lovell to Renwick, 31 October 1955.

[119] JBA CS7/3/3. Letter, Renwick to Lovell, 3 November 1955.

[120] JBA CS7/3/3. Letter, Lovell to Mott, 10 November 1955.

[121] JBA CS7/3/3. Letter, Mott to Lovell, 11 November 1955. J.A. Ratcliffe was the senior researcher in the Cavendish radio group.

[122] JBA CS7/3/3. Letter Smith to Lovell, 18 November 1955. As Lovell replied: 'I realise that our work may not be directly connected with ICI; on the other hand we have ICI Fellows here who have done magnificent work on the properties of the upper atmosphere and high speed missiles using the radio telescope'. JBA CS7/3/3. Letter, Lovell to Smith, 18 November 1955.

[123] JBA CS7/3/3. Letter, Smith to Lovell, 18 November 1955.

I expect that the structure of the radio telescope at Jodrell Bank will be familiar to you. As you probably know the instrument is really a gigantic radar scanner...[124]

Lovell invited de Ferranti to Jodrell Bank 'to show you...the telescope and also the wide field which our research covers', but the industrialist declined, offering instead a private meeting at the Ferranti factory. De Ferranti doubted that the range of Jodrell Bank research was wide enough to interest his company. In reply Lovell picked up on an issue mentioned by de Ferranti at the meeting, a project with which Ferranti were involved of the Canadian Defence Board called JANNET, essentially a communication system based on radar scattering by meteors: 'if one is searching for a plausible connection between the interests of Messrs Ferranti and the radio telescope, one would find the relationship here'.[125] Lovell attempted to strengthen this link by persuading Arthur Porter (of the Department of Electrical Engineering at Imperial College, London, and who had strong links with Ferranti) to write to Sir Vincent 'giving any reason why he should support the telescope'.[126]

Others were also enlisted. The science journalist, Ritchie Calder, was asked to appoach Leverhulme.[127] L.H. Bedford of English Electric was reminded of 'the general interests of your company in much of our research programme'.[128] Lovell informed GEC that 'the radio and electronics industry and, in fact, all the industries concerned with defence in the electronics field have so much to gain from our work here, and from the presence of the telescope in Great Britain'.[129] Lovell tried to connect the telescope to specific

---

[124] JBA CS7/3/3. Letter, Lovell to de Ferranti, 22 November 1955.

[125] JBA CS7/3/3. Letter, Lovell to de Ferranti, 29 November 1955.

[126] JBA CS7/3/3. Letter, Lovell to Porter, 29 November 1955. Porter had worked with Professor Douglas Hartree on the differential analyser at Manchester University in the 1930s. Lovell, as a young member of the physical laboratories had assisted Hartree's team 'during one summer term and vacation'. PRO DSIR 17 265. Note by Hartree, 1939.

[127] JBA CS7/3/3. Letter, Lovell to Calder, 24 November 1955. However, the Leverhulme Trust 'were legally powerless to give money for buildings or structures...it was obligatory on them under their Trust Deed, to be absolutely satisfied that the money they gave was for academic work which would not otherwise be done'. Fortunately, effective power in the Trust was not with Lord Leverhulme ("a nice young man, nothing to do with business of course, but doing admirably as Lord Lieutenant of Cheshire") but with Geoffrey Heyworth, Chairman of Unilever. The Leverhulme Trust had to support Jodrell Bank 'in an indirect way', through fellowships. Streat (1987), p. 927.

[128] JBA CS7/3/3. Letter, Lovell to Bedford, 24 November 1955.

[129] JBA CS7/3/3. Letter, Lovell to Espley (GEC Laboratories), 25 November 1955.

interests of the companies where possible. With Rolls Royce, he stated the 'fundamental work which we are doing on the evaporation of meteors moving into the atmosphere at very high Mach numbers is bound to be of interest to any firm concerned with high speed flight'.[130] When the defence electronics company GEC asked Lovell to 'expand' on the 'interests of industry in your project'[131], Lovell could list three reasons: prestige, the production of defence-relevant techniques and manpower both in the future, when: 'the highly specialised techniques which have been developed here for the study of extraterrestrial radio signals will provide the fundamental scientific capital on which the country always draws in emergencies', and in the present, with for example, the radar study of meteors and the ionosphere, which was:

> fundamental to any industry concerned with the future of guided weapons, missiles and rockets...In [the case of meteors] we are dealing with *nature's missiles* moving into the atmosphere...and I think we are the only team in the country with the relevant facilities to study [these problems] [My italics].

Other electrical and engineering companies (such as EMI) were approached in late 1955 and early 1956. As with Ferranti, Lovell used contacts to strengthen the requests. This applied to both nationally - significant firms[132], and local ones.[133] A request for funds from foundations in the United States was also considered.[134] A small group of well-connected sympathisers, including Renwick and Lord Simon of Wythenshawe, co-operated in lobbying industry to support the telescope.[135]

The official appeal, the Radio Telescope Fund, was launched by the

---

[130] JBA CS7/3/3. Letter, Lovell to Griffith (Research Department of Rolls Royce), 29 November 1955.

[131] JBA CS7/3/3. Letter, Espley to Lovell, 1 December 1955.

[132] For example when Lovell wrote to Sir John Cockcroft (Director of Harwell) that: '...it would be important to obtain the direct interest of Sir Ewart Smith, the Deputy Chairman (of ICI)...I am trying to find someone who knows Sir Ewart well enough to get him along to Jodrell Bank, since he was at Fort Halstead durng the war I am wondering if you could help...'
JBA CS7/3/3. Letter, Lovell to Cockcroft, 5 December 1955.

[133] Lovell wrote to G. Derek Lockett (who lived in the same village as Lovell, and reappears in Chapter Five) saying that he was 'appealing either to national firms who have an interest in the presence of this telescope in Great Britain...or local firms... who might wish to have their name associated with it as a local enterprise'. Lovell hoped that Lockett's 'acquaintance with the balance sheets of many companies [might] enable you to advise me on the likelihood of success'.
JBA CS7/3/3. Letter, Lovell to Lockett, 8 December 1955.

[134] JBA CS7/3/3. Letter, Lovell to Whipple, 12 September 1956.

[135] JBA CS7/3/3. Letter, Lord Simon to Sir Hugh Beaver, 29 March 1956.

University in November 1958. The informal and formal appeal was separated by the Inquiry.[136] It is significant that many of the companies which did donate to the Fund had been enlisted before the tracking of satellites began. The appeal, both informal and formal, provides an excellent insight into the connections of post-war science. During the lobbying, pictures and public lecture reprints were included with the begging letters. Public lectures were also the occasions of personal persuasion (for example Sir George Nelson of English Electric was in the audience for, and was spoken to after, Lovell's Kelvin Lecture of 1956).[137] The crucial role of public presentations and showmanship is examined in Chapter Three. The manufacture of the telescope's relevance to industry displays yet again the interpretative malleability of the instrument.

The Fund's largest donations were of £10,000 from Henry Simon Ltd and Simon Carves Ltd, which both had links with Lord Simon of Wythenshawe. In December 1959, the total donations stood at only £65,781. A meeting of the Board of Visitors in mid-1959, when the total stood at a similar figure, thought that 'further progress did not look promising'.[138] The government vacillated over the debt, wanting to be seen neither to reward bad practice by the consulting engineers, nor as unsympathetic to science at a time when the opposition were explicitly critical of science policy.[139] The debt was finally cleared by a donation of £50,000 by Lord Nuffield in 1960 (on condition that the radio astronomy laboratories be named after him).[140] By this time the telescope's utility as a tracker of satellites had been demonstrated.

Doubts Remain

The government departments were still in 1958 trying to find a structure

---

[136] It also prevented the Vice-Chancellor approving either what a 'member of the DSIR staff most closely concerned with Treasury negotiations has suggested that [Lovell] attempt to obtain the necessary money from the United States' or that Lovell 'should arrange for a direct approach to be made either by the Minister of Supply or Minister of Defence to the Treasury'. JBA CS7/3/3. Letter, Lovell to Vice-Chancellor, 4 September 1956.

[137] JBA CS7/3/3. Letter, Lovell to Sir George Nelson, 4 May 1956.

[138] JBA CS9/1/4. Minutes of Board of Visitors to the Radio Telescope, 2 June 1959.

[139] Vig (1968). As the Minister of Works warned the Lord President: the government should definitely say either no or yes, otherwise 'the impression will clearly be given that we have only moved at the behest of Socialist pressure and our opponents will get all the benefits from the extra payment and we shall only earn further disrespect for the delay'. PRO CAB 1775. Letter, Harmar Nicholls to Lord Hailsham, 11 February 1959.

[140] Clark (1972), p. 106.

whereby the telescope could be funded and the cost divided between university and government. Again the parallel is drawn to the large nuclear physics machines as the nearest precedent. These were dealt with using the 'Hale Formula'. This was drawn up between the Atomic Energy Authority and the universities. In the Hale Formula the universities (and hence the UGC) met the cost of academic salaries and other predictable expenditure, whereas the AEA met that which was closely related to the maintenance and running of the big machines. The AEA was also asked to meet large scale capital expenditure either on existing machines financed by the DSIR or on new large items of equipment. In the event the AEA withdrew but the DSIR took up their responsibilities as set out above. In February, Rainford wrote to the DSIR suggesting this arrangement to deal with a request for an extra grant of £15,200 for special equipment.[141] Although the PAC report ruled out any new expenditure, the DSIR were sympathetic to this line of approach:

> Indeed we have tried to persuade Lovell to use orthodox methods of obtaining supplementary funds rather than peddle his modern version of the 'for want of a nail the battle was lost' - because no-one will give me a few thousand pounds I can't get Venus!'[142]

The Treasury were however reluctant 'to put the radio telescope in a special category', and noted that it could 'involve the university bidding one side against the other'.[143] A meeting was held at the Treasury on the 16 April between the Treasury, the DSIR and the UGC. The discussion centred on whether Manchester had been allocated enough money adequately to cover the additional expenditure and if not how it should be provided. The Treasury evidently thought that the 'whole background' unsatisfactory, as the following statement from a Treasury civil servant, Knowles, shows: 'apart from the merits of this specific request (and I don't doubt that Lovell will get the money from someone) it throws up again the very unsatisfactory division of responsibility for financing scientific research'.[144]

Knowles then said he and Slater (also of the Treasury) were jointly preparing a memo on 'financial responsibility for scientific research in universities', and with respect to this the 'further telescope request' should be borne in mind. In the meantime the UGC had expressed reluctance to adopt the Hale Formula: 'we do not consider the analogy [with the nuclear machines] a good one'.[145] Another meeting was held, this time just between

---

[141] PRO UGC 7 152. Letter, Rainford to DSIR, 28 February 1958.

[142] PRO T 218 132. Letter, Elkington to Grant (Treasury), 31 March 1958.

[143] PRO T 218 132. Internal memo, Dingley to Slater, 15 April 1958. The speculation that 'the Government [might] wash its hands of the whole affair' is crossed out.

[144] PRO T 218 132. Letter, Knowles to Grant, 30 April 1958.

[145] PRO UGC 7 152. Letter, Felton to Dingley, 30 April 1958.

the Treasury and the DSIR on the 5 May. The Treasury were concerned not to allocate any new funds unless they could be clearly identified as new research, as this might 'attract further adverse comment from the PAC'[146] and any mistake would 'seriously undermine the financial independence of this university'. A letter following the meeting spoke of not even considering special new projects 'for a year or so'.[147] An application for a new special project was in fact made in the following September. After careful consideration the Treasury felt it 'could be defended if necessary before the PAC'.[148] Even then this was because 'a refusal of this equipment grant might cause a greater political embarrassment to Ministers than any comments of the PAC (which will probably be rather glad anyhow to fade out of this affair if possible)'.[149] The opinion of the Treasury is made clear in the following statement, made just before it agreed to the DSIR allocating its grant:

> Financial control by DSIR over Manchester University was weak, and control by the University over Professor Lovell perhaps even weaker. As a result the planning and progress of the project tended to get ahead of both the estimates and the financial attention...The real charge is that Lovell and the engineers didn't really put the full facts on the table...until too late to stop work.[150]

THE CONTESTED BOUNDARY BETWEEN GOVERNMENT AND UNIVERSITIES

In this chapter I have attempted to make sense of the support for a large steerable radio telescope at Jodrell Bank in terms of the context of a heterogenous funding structure. I have ascribed interests to the bodies relevant to the story (Manchester University, DSIR, UGC, Treasury, Ministry of Supply and the PAC), and used those interests to account for their actions.

---

[146] PRO T 218 132. Minutes of meeting, 5 May 1958.

[147] PRO T 218 132. Letter, Grant to Elkington, 21 May 1958.

[148] PRO T 218 132. Internal memo, Knowles to Wright and MacPherson, 14 October 1958. The DSIR invited an application to be made to cover 'running and maintenance costs' on the basis of the Hale Formula.
JBA CS7/3/3. Letter, Lovell to Rainford, 24 October 1958.

[149] A factor in this withdrawal was a legal move by Husband to force a retraction of Melville's PAC statement that the engineer and the astronomer had not communicated at vital stages of the project. This legal move did not go beyond pressure on the Lord President (Lod Hailsham) who refused to comment. However, the PAC did have to issue a statement saying that 'it is clear that the evidence given to the Committee of last session was gravely inaccurate'
CAB 124 1774. Letter, Quirk to Simpson, 22 September 1958.

[150] PRO T 218 132. Internal memo, Griffiths to Knowles, 15 October 1958.

The DSIR backed the telescope for reasons of scientific 'timeliness and promise', because of the networks of connections between the would-be astronomers and government strengthened during the war, and for 'prestige' both national and internal. The words 'national prestige', donating cultural capital, litter the memoranda where the backing of the telescope was discussed. When the money needed escalated, other interpretations were mobilised. I related this interpretative malleability to the heterogenous environment that embedded the telescope, out of which its supporters and detractors had to construct the instrument's meaning. The astronomers, the radio industry, and the Ministry of Supply could interpret the telescope as a 'giant radar scanner'.the PAC, the University, and the UGC all clearly read the telescope with respect to their positions in debates over the accountability of university finance.

The discussions over what was the appropriate institutional form to house the radio telescope began even before the price rose. I have shown that this debate continued throughout the 1950s: how far should such a project be a university (through the UGC) or government (DSIR) affair? I will now show how this tension over where research should be sited can be located in a wider context.

In March 1952, the Vice-Chancellor of the University of Glasgow, Sir Hector Hetherington, anxiously wrote to Hale of the UGC. The Treasury had accepted the PAC view that the accounts of the Agricultural Research Council stations within universities should be available for inspection. The ARC stations had been chosen because an overwhelming proportion of their income came direct from a research council, and very little came from the university's block UGC grant (over which the University had full control). The anxiety lay in that the Treasury, on this seemingly minor point, had accepted a general argument from the PAC: that the 'accounts of all bodies which receive the greater part of their income from public funds, should be open to inspection by the Comptroller and Auditor General'.[151] As Hetherington said:

> there is, so far as I see, nothing to stop the operation of the same principle in relation to our general Treasury grant. Nowadays that constitutes "the greater part" of the income of all Universities.

Hale replied that the PAC's motives could be understood, with the post-war expansion of education 'here is a Vote which has increased tenfold...there have been some pretty bad extravagances in other fields of expenditure since the war, and it would be surprising if they did not fear that there might be a skeleton in this cupboard which they are not being allowed to inspect'.[152]

---

[151] PRO UGC 7 548. Letter, Hetherington to Hale, 14 March 1952.
[152] PRO UGC 7 548. Letter, Hale to Hetherington, 21 March 1952.

During the 1950s the same argument by the PAC and allied parts of the Treasury was made in turn about the ARC Long Ashton Research Station (Bristol University) and National Institute for Research in Dairying (Reading), the Institute for Research in Plant Physiology (Imperial), the School of Agriculture (Cambridge), the Poultry Genetics Station, the Welsh Plant Breeding Station, and the Medical Research Council (MRC) units such as the Institute of Cancer Research (University of London). The UGC and the Vice-Chancellors saw these as 'supplementary or peripheral components of the Universities'[153], for the attack on which there were two options: 'either the necessity of the University to make a definite stand...[on] the slope or to allow the slide to continue'.[154]

In an effective holding action the UGC along with the sympathetic parts of the Treasury agreed to form a Committee on Parliamentary Control of Finance. Hale happily reported to Herbert Brittain in the Treasury of their choice to chair the Committee that 'you could not choose a more suitable person than Sir George Gater'.[155] The Gater Committee was to report on 'universities methods of contracting and or recording and controlling expenditure [by non-recurrent grants]'.[156] Gater and his colleagues consulted the V-Cs, the relevant government departments and Unilever (representing industry). The UGC concluded with satisfaction in 1956, when it published the Gater Committee's Report as a white paper, that 'in general the Report has been welcomed throughout the universities'. Its thoughts were disseminated through the media.[157] This should hardly be surprising given that the body had been appointed by the UGC and overseen by allies in the Treasury.

The PAC and the Comptroller and Auditor General saw the wider issue as one of accountability to Parliament of public money, and any dissent was a 'silly controversy'.[158] The Vice-Chancellors saw the 'threatened intrusion of the Comptroller and Auditor General', as being an 'obvious danger' that the inspection of these institute's accounts would lead to the inspection of 'University finance in general'.[159] The UGC and the parts of the Treasury

---

[153] PRO UGC 7 548. Minute of meeting of Murray, Morris (V-C of Bristol), and Hale, 18 March 1954.
[154] PRO UGC 7 548. Letter, Morris to Murray, 9 July 1954.
[155] PRO UGC 7 549. Letter, Hale to Brittain, 18 March 1954.
[156] PRO UGC 7 549. Letter Hale to Dame Evelyn Sharp (Ministry of Housing and Local Government), 29 March 1954.
[157] PRO UGC 7 550. Press cuttings.
[158] PRO UGC 7 548. Letter, Tribe (Comptroller and Auditor General, the Exchequer and Audit Department) to F.E. Figgures (Treasury), 24 February 1955.
[159] PRO UGC 7 548. Letter, J.F. Wolfenden to Hale, 2 July 1952. This language is very close to that used to describe inteference, as I will discuss in Chapters Three, Four and Five.

closest to the UGC concurred. From the viewpoint of the research sites the issue was seen as being about Haldane-style 'freedom' of research, as Lord Iveagh, a Director of one of them, reported:

the financial control of research institutes could lead to an undesirable limitation of freedom and...an abrogation of the principle...that they should be removed from state control.[160]

The increased post-war expenditure on education had heightened tensions on the issues of university autonomy and financial control. This tension manifested itself in the contests at the boundary between the authorities of academia and government: at the 'peripheral' research units that combined total government financial support with a university site. It is therefore of no surprise then to find the telescope also viewed as a trojan horse into the finances of the 'universities as a whole', more dangerous still in that it had been highly publicised.

Just as university funding had risen, so in particular had funding on science, as I discussed in my introduction. The funding of science and technology in universities was therefore of double sensitivity. I will now extend the account of university research to show that the new organisation and funding of science strained the university as a site for science.

The scale of the new science seemed to call for a restructured DSIR. As the Director of the Cavendish wrote to Lovell in 1955:

I suppose you and we are in the same difficulty, you with regard to our project and we with regard to nuclear physics, because the DSIR has tied itself up with a quinquennial grant. The DSIR's Nuclear Physics Committee has strongly recommended that we embark on a new project, likely to cost £250,000 upwards, but the DSIR see no chance of providing us with any money [for 2 years]...I want to get this quinquennial business discussed; it seems to me essential for us to press that the body which handles these big projects in universities is not tied to a quinquennial estimate[161]

However an alternative to a DSIR restructured to allow flexible imbursement to universities, was a DSIR taking a more active role: running and maintaining facilities at a central non-university site.

In 1958, the Advisory Council for Scientific Policy (a body of scientists that advised on policy issues, see Chapter One) considered the issue of the respective responsibilities of the research councils, the Royal Society and

---

[160] PRO UGC 7 548. Lord Iveagh (Chairman of the Governing Board, NIRD) to Vanpemeer, 29 February 1952.

[161] JBA CS7/3/3. Letter, Mott to Lovell, 14 November 1955.

the UGC for the promotion of scientific research in universities.[162] The ACSP 'endorsed the principle of the advisibility of having a multiplicity of sources of research funds'.[163] The UGC drafted a memorandum which was circulated and approved by the Royal Society,[164] and the Research Councils: DSIR, MRC, ARC and the Nature Conservancy.

The motor behind this discussion had two components. Firstly, the increase in money passing through the Research Councils was set to continue.[165] Alexander Todd, chair of the ACSP, felt 'that some of the present difficulties undoubtedly stemmed from the rapid expansion of the universities, particularly in science and technology departments'.[166] Secondly, the character of research that the research councils funded was changing:

it has...to be recognised that the equipment needed by science departments, particularly for research is constantly increasing in size and complexity, and includes a number of items far more expensive than departments could in practice be expected to finance from their annual allocation of funds.[167]

Examples explicitly cited in the UGC memorandum included 'electronic computers', and 'electron microscopes'; the Radio Telescope clearly fell into this category.[168] The UGC noted that 'the DSIR is prepared to entertain applications for grants to finance the purchase of expensive equipment, not

---

[162] Indeed Lindor Brown of the Royal Society considered these meetings to be 'one of the best things that has ever come out of the ACSP', which provides an interesting conjunction to Gummett's reassessment of the effectiveness of the ACSP (see Chapter One). PRO UGC 7 771. Letter, Lindor Brown to Murray, 5 November 1958.

[163] PRO UGC 7 771. Letter, Murray to Fraser (Treasury), 27 February 1958.

[164] PRO UGC 7 771. Letter, Lindor Brown (UCL, and Biological Secretary of the Royal Society) to Hale, 13 March 1958.

[165] For example, reserach grants from the DSIR were set to increase from £470,000 in 1958-59 to £1,760,000 in 1963-64, and postgraduate training grants from £660,000 to £1,560,000 in the same period. PRO UGC 7 771. Draft letter, Melville to Aitken, 19 May 1959.

[166] PRO UGC 7 771. Minutes of the ACSP, 12 May 1958.

[167] PRO UGC 7 771. Memorandum by UGC, 'Financial responsibility for scientific research in universities', 1958.

[168] The Radio Telescope controversy also confirmed Gater's conclusions that the increased expenditure on research demanded tighter and more explicit methods of handling contracts between university and contractors. The Treasury proposed (after consultation with DSIR and Manchester University that 'as a condition of corresponding non-recurrent grants made by government departments to Universities in the future, that the Gater recommendations be observed...'. PRO CAB 124 1774. Memorandum, 'Draft reply (further revised' to PAC on Radio Telescope', 9 December 1957.

only for particular research projects, but also for developing the fields of knowledge in which they are interested'.[169] This 'developing' contrasted with the UGC's ideal of university independence. The danger as viewed by the UGC (and sympathetic part of Treasury) was that 'the DSIR [would] come to have too large a finger in the universities' pie, to our disadvantage and to the possible disadvantage of the independence of the universities'.[170]

In a memorandum which carried the approval of the interested bodies, the UGC outlined a policy which carefully delineated which body should fund what. The UGC and DSIR roles were kept separate: 'the UGC pays for the running expenses of established lines of work, while the DSIR pays for the unforeseen researches and for researches on new lines or in new fields which would otherwise not be established'.[171] It was considered 'not desirable that a single governmental colossus should bestride the whole university world [which]...is what would inevitably occur if the present functions of the UGC and of the research councils' were combined. The longer-term large scale research would be accommodated by a new form of grant, the details of which were hammered out by an ad hoc DSIR committee chaired by Blackett.[172]

The tensions that the agreed memorandum managed can be gauged by three reactions: from the Treasury, the Royal Society and the universities.

The Treasury were uneasy for two reasons. Firstly, as Cawley of the DSIR reported to Murray at the UGC: 'they fear that the division of function is vague and ill-defined and will therefore lead to overlapping and wasteful expenditure'.[173] All three parties, bearing in mind the contemporary wrangles over the Radio Telescope, knew that this particularly applied to the new expensive, long term research under discussion. The second fear of the Treasury, at least of those parts nearer the PAC and Audit office was the financial control of the universities. Transactions in the independent bursars' offices meant that 'the increase in DSIR expenditure will result in more Greek Bibles and more research in medieval literature'.

The Royal Society accepted the settlement, which conserved their role in the disbursement of grants for science, with enthusiasm. This is not surprising given some events that occurred in the mid-1950s. With the increase both in the numbers of grants and the size of individual grants, the Royal Society was concerned that, in this governmentalisation of British science, it should

---

[169] PRO UGC 7 771. UGC memorandum, op cit.

[170] PRO UGC 7 771. Internal note, Syers to Chairman of UGC, 26 September 1958.

[171] PRO UGC 7 771. DSIR memorandum, 'The division of function between the UGC and DSIR in supporting research in science and technology at universities', August 1958, summarising the UGC memorandum.

[172] PRO DSIR 17 615. 'Report to Council by the Ad Hoc Committee on Longer-Term Support by the DSIR for Research in Universities', 1958.

[173] PRO UGC 7 771. Letter, Cawley to Murray, 13 August 1958.

retain its influence. At the beginning of the 1950s the Royal Society acted as an extra research council, dividing and allocating a grant from the Treasury. However, the Treasury did not believe that the Royal Society was equipped to handle the increased scale of post-war science, as one of its civil servants stated:

> If and when there is to be any increase in the grants, it would almost bound to be an increase in the sums spent through DSIR, which is accountable to Parliament and has the administrative machinery to handle them, rather than through the Royal Society...[174]

Sir David Brunt, Royal Society Secretary was reported at the time to be 'rather unhappy', and refused to endorse Blackett's proposals for grants for special research. The new scale of research had strained the traditional bodies, such as the Royal Society, which organised British science.

The universities were also still worried about the shifting organisation of science. R.S. Aitken, chair of the Committee of Vice-Chancellors and Principals and V-C of the University of Birmingham, wrote that although the V-Cs were 'sensible and appreciative of the increase in UGC grants' and even 'fully appreciative of the prospect that Research Council money is likely to come to the Universities in considerably increased amounts', there remained anxieties. In particular:

> Looking ahead in this context...they do not wish to see much control of research policy passing to the Research Councils.[175]

If this happened, Aitken argued, then as in 'Eire, South Africa, Australia and New Zealand', there would be 'the growth of the doctrine that the job of the Universities is teaching while the research lies with government organisations', a trend that the V-Cs would 'deplore'.[176]

The facilities for nuclear research had been combined together to be one organisation, the National Institute for Research in Nuclear Science (NIRNS) only two years previously in 1957. The expense of the machines (in particular a 7 GeV proton synchrotron) had been the explicit reason for the institutional form.[177] It is therefore understandable that the Vice-Chancellors kept an

---

[174] PRO T 218 191. Letter, Playfair (Treasury) to Blount (DSIR), 12 November 1955, quoted in letter Hogg (DSIR) to Grant (Treasury), 12 July 1956.

[175] PRO UGC 7 771. Letter, Aitken to Murray, 1 July 1959.

[176] The UGC, as ever, were sympathetic to the universities' interests: as Murray reassured Aitken: 'I know that my Committee is aware of the dangers that might arise if an excessive responsibility passed to the Research Councils'. There would be no 'wholesale transfer of responsibilities'.
PRO UGC 7 771. Letter, Murray to Aitken, 2 July 1959.

[177] Massey and Robins (1986), p. 109.

anxious and watchful eye on the trends in the organisation and site of science. It is worth noting in passing that the new price and scale of research did not just affect relations at the level of university and government, but also strained the boundaries within universities. As the Board of the Faculty of Science at Manchester University noted as early as 1949:

> Certain pieces of special apparatus are now coming into use in the scientific laboratories of this country...many of these are very expensive and will serve the needs of several Departments. Indeed, nearly all the Departments of the Faculty might be interested in one or more of these instruments...[178]

Which Department would control, maintain and supervise the instruments had to be carefully managed between disciplinary interests.

SUMMARY

In this chapter I have traced some of the means used to secure money for the Radio Telescope at Jodrell Bank. I have shown that the actions and interests of several bodies, governmental, industrial and academic, have to be taken into account. It became apparent that the telescope could carry many messages: there existed an interpretative malleability, whereby each body could interpret the telescope according to their position. Interpretative malleability was as much a resource as a hindrance to the promoters of the telescope.

The malleability of the instrument's meaning can be directly related to the structure of the millieu in which the promoters worked. This milieu consisted of a loose collection of bodies: governmental Research Councils such as the DSIR, the executive departments of government such as the Ministry of Supply, and the University Grants Committee, as well as the universities, disciplines and private foundations. The meaning of the instrument was shaped according to the structure of this milieu.

I have discussed how this milieu was itself changing. The Radio Telescope was significant in two intertwined debates in the 1950s: how should long-term expensive scientific projects be organised, and what projects should be under government, and what should be under university, control.

In the next chapter I will analyse how these tensions were played out and partially resolved in the *public* sphere. I will look at the techniques of promotion. I will also show how the promotion related to the construction of the authority of the astronomer, and examine a debate over who could claim public 'credit' associated with the great instruments of post-war British research. There was a spatial solution to this contest over authority.

---

[178] JBA UNI/10/1. Minutes of Board of the Faculty of Science, 8 November 1949.

CHAPTER 3

'A Great Public Spectacle': Prestige, Position and Power at Jodrell Bank

This...is the story of the planning and construction of the Giant Radio Telescope at Jodrell Bank, Cheshire. What is a Radio Telescope? It is no less than man's newest instrument for probing the mysteries of the universe by the reception and analysis of radio waves coming from outer space...Observations made with radio telescopes have opened up an entirely new field of astronomical research, in which British scientists have taken the lead. With this great new instrument at their disposal they will be still better equipped to maintain that lead, and to be pioneers in a new voyage of discovery for mankind as a whole.[1]

In the previous chapter I showed how financial support for a large steerable Radio Telescope was mobilised in government departments and private foundations. I argued that for this support to be sustained against strong criticism, various bodies had to regard its construction and capabilities as significant to their interests. However, just as important as this process of private lobbying was to the completion of the telescope was the construction of the *public* significance of the instrument.

Not least because of the heterogeneity of bodies involved in the project each stage in this process was contested. During the formation of representations, such as press releases or documentary films, radio astronomer and engineer conflicted over attribution of credit. Government departments promoted the instrument as an object of 'national prestige' and public spectacle for their own reasons. The media, here press, film and radio, shaped both the content and interpretation of the instrument in transmitting its representation. Finally, the public appropriated the instrument for different purposes, to the frustration of other actors. In these conflicts the control of space was a crucial resource, and was intimately linked to *authorisation* of

---

[1] JBA CS7/23/7. Anvil Films Ltd, 'The Giant Radio Telescope', script for *The Inquisitive Giant*, film treatment for the Central Office of Information, Beaconsfield, December 1954.

actors both within the organisation and as public figures.

PUBLICITY AND THE MANAGEMENT OF VISITORS

Whilst building the network of resources necessary to secure the radio telescope's backing, Lovell wrote to Ryle (who shared a similar interest in preserving a suitable image of their discipline) that he had 'recently become very worried about the dangers of publicity on Radio Astronomy arising from the construction of our new Radio Telescope'.[2] The immediate worry was an advertisement for United Steel which had featured the telescope and had been published 'without any consultation'. Lovell expected the DSIR to provide protection, but was 'alarmed to find that the Press Officer at the DSIR was unable to exercise any official control over such events'. In fact the DSIR Chief Information Officer, Lt. Col. Walter G. Hingston, had advised that 'a fairly steady output' of unauthorised uses of the radio telescope was to be expected. The DSIR's flagship project, one which symbolised both the prestige of the country externally and the prestige of the department internally, could not be shy of publicity.

Lovell wrote a very similar letter on 'the dangers of publicity' to the consulting engineer, Husband. The radio astronomer made a distinction between those who were brought to the site and those who were not: 'in cases where official press representatives are sent to the Station...we do our best to make sure that their account is accurate'.[3] However, even then there was 'no ultimate control over what they publish', which led to 'embarrassment'. Like the DSIR, the engineer's attitude differed from Lovell's:

> Undoubtedly a lot of nonsense has appeared from time to time concerning the purpose of the Telescope, but on balance I think the widespread nature of the articles and advertisements have helped us greatly...[4]

The important aspect for the engineer was that in 'whatever is published by anyone, it would seem important in connection for an unusual design of this nature, for us to protect our normal copyright'. Where the astronomers, engineers and DSIR civil servants agreed was that the presentation of the telescope should be managed. The astronomers concurred that representational control was required, to limit publicity that was

---

[2] JBA CS7/15/2. Letter, Lovell to Ryle, 5 June 1953.

[3] JBA CS7/35/2. Letter, Lovell to Husband, 5 June 1953.

[4] JBA CS7/35/2. Letter, Husband to Lovell, 10 June 1953. Husband thought that a well-publicised telescope made 'manufacturers keenly interested in supplying parts and offering delivery dates'.

'embarrassing ...especially when extravagant and unscientific claims [were] made'. In the case of visitors, it was the bodily proximity of the 'extravagant' needed careful management.

Hingston, as Chief Information Officer, sought information about other sites of popular astronomical pilgrimage. The Californian optical observatories had a 'serious problem' of '150,000 visitors per year both at Palomar Mountain and Mount Wilson'.[5] The visitors consisted of 'two classes' which required different management. First, 'the general public', who were provided with 'a visitor's gallery in the dome of the 100-inch on Mount Wilson and in the dome of the 200-inch on Palomar Mountain'. Such a gallery was a

> glassed-in structure at the side of each dome and...provided with a stairway and entrance completely separate from that used by the scientific staff. Since it [was]...glassed-in all of the scientific operations [were]...completely protected from heat and dust and other disturbances created by the visitors.

The public were carried right up to within sight of scientific activity, but were barred from the private site by the glass wall. There was also a 'small museum' which 'displayed photographs taken with the telescopes on the mountain and a certain amount of descriptive material'. To 'answer the questions that so many of our visitors have', 'four page give-away leaflets' were supplied, as well as a 'fairly elaborate book'.[6] This is a clue as to the character of who was constituting 'the public': they were more than seekers of diverting entertainment, they also had 'questions'. The second group was made up of 'profesional scientists, trustees of one of the supporting institutions or other celebrities'.[7] These people were 'given a special conducted tour', and were taken 'in the scientific area and allowed to see something of what goes on *behind the scenes*' (my emphasis). The presentation of the tour required skill. It was 'not conducted by one of the scientific staff but by one of the permanent employees on the mountain selected because of long contact with the project'. What was happening at these Californian institutions was the emergence of organisational and spatial arrangements to separate out a 'public' (and 'a good many borderline cases') away from 'scientific groups', and alter their treatment accordingly.

The experience of Mount Wilson and Mount Palomar provided a template on which Hingston proposed a solution to the management of the telescope

---

[5] JBA CS7/15/1. Letter, I.S. Bowen (Carnegie Institution of Washington, California Institute of Technology) to Hingston, 20 August 1953.

[6] This book, *Frontiers in Space*, cost fifty cents. It was sold 'by the wife of one of our employees' who received the remuneration of fifteen cents per sale.

[7] Also 'an occasional college class in astronomy although we have refused to give this special service to other school groups'.

as 'a great public spectacle'.[8] As a representative of the DSIR interest he argued that 'it would be neither correct nor politic for Manchester University to refuse to give facilities to see the work'. Hingston saw several reasons why the telescope would prove an attraction: it would be 'visible for many miles in all directions' and 'nearness' would 'increase the sense of power and awe', it would be 'the largest moving object on land' ('powerful moving objects, for example express railway engines and ships attract what may almost be called worshippers'). These reasons (as expressed to the radio astronomer) did not coincide with the DSIR's intended 'purpose of the telescope': prestigious astronomical research. However, there would also be 'considerable, although possibly ill-informed, interest in the researches being done', due to contemporary enthusiasm over 'inter-planetary travel', the sales of Fred Hoyle's *The Nature of the Universe*, and 'on a lower level, space-ships, flying saucers, and science fiction'. Other groups 'not likely to be satisfied with gazing at the structure from a distance' were 'scientific societies, school and college societies', and 'journalists, news reel cameramen, sound and television broadcasters'.

Hingston expanded the Californian bifurcation of visitors into six categories each requiring specific attention. 'Workers in the same or allied fields or research' could be received by those employed at Jodrell Bank. Without 'organisation' no other category of visitor could be left 'without interfering'. 'Distinguished personages'[9] were 'very time wasting' but could not be refused, and likewise 'Overseas Visitors' on official visits. The 'Press, Broadcasting and Film Personnel' required 'special handling': it would be 'essential for someone to be employed to deal with Press Relations'. Hingston's category of 'People Interested in Science' consisted of 'local scientific societies', 'branches of the famous scientific and technical institutions', and 'numerous scientific societies in Universities, schools and colleges'. Finally, there was 'the general public', "gawpers" asking to see the telescope' from the 'big centres of population around Manchester and Liverpool and in the Potteries', and anywhere within 'an easy car's journey'. Such numbers would 'provide a very real threat to the work at the Experimental Station'.

Hingston presented three choices of 'methods' to deal with visitors whilst suggesting one viable option. Firstly, 'erect a fence round the site and refuse to see all visitors'. However, the distinguished and important would still have to be entertained. 'Refusal to co-operate' with the press, Hingston

---

[8] JBA CS7/15/1. Memorandum by Hingston, 'The Problem of Visitors to the Jodrell Bank Experimental Station', September 1953.

[9] The 'Senate of the University, Boards of Faculties and benefactors of the University; Cabinet Ministers, Senior Civil Servants, distinguished scientists, friends of the Nuffield Foundation and Members of Parliament. And their friends'.

noted, 'might harm the project by making further funds difficult to raise if required and also make government help to other fundamental research projects at Universities more open to attack'.

Whilst appealing to the astronomers' ambitions for further expansion at Jodrell Bank (as well as a solidarity amongst 'fundamental' scientists), Hingston was carefully insisting on the government department's role in the presentation of the flagship telescope project. The Chief Information Officer's final reason why not all visitors should be excluded was a curious one: 'feeling of superiority might be engendered in the staff of the Experimental Station with consequent contempt for men and women of the world outside'. As explanation, Hingston said 'this would be wrong for those running a project financed by the University, a charitable organisation and public funds'. The heterogeneous support for the telescope occasioned suitable public presentation and careful organisational self-fashioning. The other two 'methods' of management were 'to admit all categories of visitors except No.6 (the General Public)', or finally, 'to admit all Visitors', a policy that he immediately dismissed as impossible.

Any solution must 'cause minimum disturbance to the research', 'cost nothing or must be self-supporting', and be such that the 'visitors should go away satisfied'. Hingston proposed:

> The entire site would be surrounded with a fence difficult to climb thus protecting the research staff from *interference*. Outside the fence, but close to the telescope an information or observation room would be built and staffed by information officers.[10]

The information officers would 'give talks to parties at stated times' and would 'give more personal attention to important people'.[11] The costs would be recouped from sales of leaflets, brochures, photographs, reprints, books on astronomy, 'car park rights', and the 'sale of rights to run a tea room by the car park', although 'care should be taken to retain copyright on general articles about the work'. As at Mount Wilson and Mount Palomar the visitors would be managed. Imported from California was the setting up of organisational structures, along with concurrent spatial modifications, to guide the display of science, and to simultaneously mark off its privileged sites. Hingston's efforts can be seen as part of a spatial solution to the problem of astronomical authority.

---

[10] JBA CS7/15/1. Memorandum by Hingston, op cit, my emphasis.
[11] There was an implied distinction based on gender over who dealt with the 'Distinguished Personages': the 'Information Officer in charge' (a 'He') would be 'able to talk fluently (but accurately and soberly) about the work...[and be] reliable, tactful abd resourceful', whereas the Assistant Information Officer might also act as a 'salesman or saleswoman'.

PHOTOGRAPHS AND THE 'GRIP OF PUBLICITY'

It is a commonplace to note that photographs do not portray the 'real object' but instead the meaning can vary immensely when read by different persons. The astronomers were acutely aware of this, but the instability that could be problematic was also a resource: they made use of the malleability of imagery whilst simultaneously being anxious over others usurping their control. I will discuss the making of films later, but here I give evidence to show that the astronomers sought the restriction of photographs of the telescope.

Whilst the telescope was a mass of steel and scaffolding under construction, 'Messrs. Airviews Limited', a company based at Manchester Ringway Airport, began taking aerial photographs of the telescope and selling them to the media. Lovell wrote to Hingston asking for action to stop Airviews.[12] Again, the DSIR, as primary funder of the telescope project and target of Public Accounts Committee criticism, were as concerned as the astronomers that the telescope should be seen as a success. They might therefore have been sympathetic to Lovell's reasoning that Airviews photographing meant 'that your [ie DSIR's] grip on the publicity [was] being loosened'. With the Airviews photograph becoming an issue within a month of the defence role of the radio telescope swinging support for the project in Whitehall, Hingston may have read a security implication in Lovell's ambiguous statement that it was 'also undesirable for other reasons that such photographs should be published'.

The solution proposed by Lovell, however, that no photographs of the telescope should be circulated to the press, could not be accepted by the DSIR who backed the telescope as a prestigious British scientific project. Lovell wrote again within three weeks of the first letter that the 'publicity arrangements on the radio telescope' were 'getting out of hand' since not only were Airviews continuing to fly over the telescope, but the government publicity office, the Central Office of Information, had 'more or less instructed' the astronomers 'to allow their official photographer...[to] take photographs'.[13] Lovell, although not wanting to risk 'bad relations by sending away this photographer', sought an assurance that the photographs would 'on no account be released in this country', and any future photographing be conducted under watchful supervision on the DSIR and Jodrell Bank press days, wherein lay 'the only hope of canalizing this sort of activity'. For their flagship project, the DSIR required that some pictures be released, but concurred with Lovell's suggestion for the 'canalizing' (that is to say direction) of the press, Hingston wrote:

---

[12] JBA CS7/15/1. Letter, Lovell to Hingston, 8 November 1954.
[13] JBA CS7/15/1. Letter, Lovell to Hingston, 25 November 1954.

I will arrange a rota system, by which each of the agencies can send up a man in turn at, say, monthly intervals, to take photographs only. He would be escorted by either of my Press Officers, and the ...Resident Engineer.[14]

The 'canalizing' of visual representations of the telescope extended to the 'captioning of the photographs'. This would not 'provide a problem' since Hingston would 'give a general caption about the building of the Radio Telescope for placing on every photograph and the particular captions for the individual photographs would be very short and agreed on the spot with the Resident Engineer'.

There remains the question of why Lovell was worried. Hingston saw the problem as working out how the photographic agency's 'wants could be provided without disturbing [the astronomers'] work'. The separation and demarcation of the public domain from a domain of scientific work was, I argue in this and following chapters, important in the construction of the Jodrell Bank observatory. However, the answer was not quite so passive as just the provision of a 'quiet' space for research: the 'grip of publicity' suggests an awareness of the possibilities of image manipulation actively wielded in the pursuit of personal and institutional projects.

ON LOCATION: 'THE INQUISITIVE GIANT'

The arguments that the actors had over photographs also marked the construction of more complex representations of the telescope. In the 1950s, audiovisual projects presented a relatively new discursive axis for scientific actors. In this section I show how a film, called *The Inquisitive Giant,* provided a site for articulating and partially resolving two key issues of this chapter: the telescope as a public instrument of national prestige, and the management of the divergent interests of engineers, government departments and radio astronomers. In particular, the tensions over the film can be seen as part of an ongoing conflict: who should be visibly accredited by association with the prestigious public instrument.

The idea for some sort of film of the telescope was floated as early as September 1952. Lovell wrote to Hingston that: 'the foundations of the telescope are now being put in and I am sure that when it is complete we shall have many regrets if there is no documentary film of its construction'.[15] Lovell had in mind a short film, starting immediately to capture the 'noise...of the pile drivers'.

From the standpoint of the DSIR, Hingston saw the advantages of a film project. He wrote back that 'it should be possible to make films of scientific

---

[14] JBA CS7/15/1. Letter, Hingston to Lovell, 1 December 1954.
[15] JBA CS7/14/2. Letter, Lovell to Hingston, 23 September 1952.

interest and of wide general interest', both of which would be of great value
to this country's prestige'.[16] In contrast to Lovell, the civil servant could
envisage a bigger and more expensive film project.

Discussion about the virtues of a film continued in the DSIR in 1953. In
an internal memorandum, Hingston gave three reasons why a film should be
made.[17] First, it had 'already proved of greater public interest than any other
project [he] had handled'. Second, it therefore had great potential as a
much-needed symbol of national prestige: 'it would bring credit to Britain',
he argued, 'it should be more effective propaganda than the films on our
social system, housing and justice'. The intended audience was not merely
domestic: a suitable presentation of the telescope 'would raise prestige of
our scientific ability and of our genius for constructional engineering', and
be 'a useful factor in gaining orders and contracts overseas'. The Great
Public Spectacle, which demonstrated British leadership in at least one
discipline, could generate lucrative spin-offs. Third, Hingston argued to his
peers that, with the DSIR itself implicated in the symbolic status of the
expensive telescope it must take care in its display. Thus if the film were not
made

> there is likely to be adverse criticism of the sponsors of the work, which must
> inevitably come to be focussed on the DSIR because it is a Government
> Department.

Hingston thought that with 'plenty of money' the project had the
hyperbolic elements to be 'the greatest scientific and engineering film ever
made'. His problem was who could be trusted to carry it out. There were
three alternatives: the DSIR's own film unit, the film unit of a commercial
company, and the Central Office of Information (COI).

Asking the COI to make the film would present a difficult policy shift for
the DSIR. As its senior mandarin, Sir Ben Lockspeiser, had confided to his
minister, the Lord President of the Council, 'the use of films' was very rarely
'worth the high cost' involved.[18] For this reason the DSIR had not used them,
and it did not have a budget allocation with the COI. Hingston also did not
think the 'COI distribution methods... good', and he favoured asking the
'Shell Petroleum Company to make the film on behalf of the University'.

In Hingston's opinion, the Shell Film Unit had a 'very high reputation for
making scientific films of integrity', they possessed the advisory talents of
Sir Arthur Elton ('probably the greatest authority in the world on documentary

---

[16] JBA CS7/14/2. Letter, Hingston to Lovell, 30 September 1952.

[17] JBA CS7/15/1. Memorandum by Hingston, 'Film of the Radio Telescope',
December 1953.

[18] PRO DSIR 17 182. Letter, Lockspeiser to the Lord President of the Council, 20
September 1950.

films'[19]), it had 'ample money', and 'an excellent world wide distribution system'. Hingston assured his colleagues in the DSIR that there was no 'danger of the film being used to advertise the products of the Company'. The Shell Film Unit was also certainly skilled in the presentation of science as an expression of national prestige. Its Public Relations Officer, Ian Cox, was Director (Science and Technology) of the 1951 Festival of Britain. As discussed in Chapter One, the Festival's centrepiece, the Dome of Discovery was designed around a 'narrative' so that a viewer carried away a memory of 'creditable British exploration, invention and industrial capacity'.[20] Even in 1951 radio astronomy could be used to express sentiments of national achievement:

> [a] radio telescope...was operated from the Dome of Discovery, with its 'dish' aerial mounted on the top of the Shot Tower. This was beamed on the moon and visitors could see on a cathode ray tube signals being transmitted there and their reflection back about two and half seconds later.[21]

The presentation of the radio telescope, consisting of a dish aerial on a gun mounting, played on the familiar 'swords and ploughshares' trope. Cox recalls that 'radio signals from much deeper in outer space were also on show'. It was experience such as this that Hingston hoped to call upon to help construct the new telescopic narrative.

The Shell Film Unit was first reportedly 'thrilled at the idea'[22], but then, barely a month later, Hingston reported to a colleague in the Foreign Office that he had 'heard (unofficially) that they are refusing our request with regret because radio astronomy cannot be connected in any possible way with Shell products'.[23] Tarred by no brush, as it were.

The DSIR did not initially consider the break with Shell irreversible. The Shell Film Unit had made films on subjects as diverse as malaria in Sardinia

---

[19] JBA CS7/15/1. Memorandum by Hingston, ibid. Sir Arthur Hallan Rice Elton gained his skills in the presentation of national symbols in the Empire Marketing Board Film Unit in the 1930s. He spent the Second World War as Supervisor of Films at the Ministry of Information. He was a founder member of both the Film Centre Ltd in 1938, and the Scientific Film Association from 1943.

[20] Misha Black in Banham and Hillier (1976), p. 84. The Dome was built by Freeman and Fox, the construction company (a rival of Husband & Co) who later in the 1950s built the large steerable Parkes radio telescope at Sydney. See:

[21] Ian Cox in Banham and Hilliar (1976), p. 69.

[22] JBA CS7/15/1. Memorandum, Hingston, 'Film of the Radio Telescope', December 1953.

[23] PRO INF 12 664. Letter, Hingston to R.H.K. Marrett (Information Policy Department, Foreign Office), I January 1954. Interestingly, oil products were also problematic for the organisers of the Festival of Britain. See Forgan (forthcoming), p. 9.

and road safety for children. A high level approach by the Secretary of the DSIR to Shell's Managing Director, Sir Francis Hopwood, repeating the proposition was expected to be a formality.[24] However, with Shell intransigent, the DSIR had no other commercial option, as Hingston expressed it:

> The scientific integrity of the film would be of the first...importance. The Shell Film Unit could be relied upon to maintain this integrity but I cannot rely on other sponsors...in practice we [would] be dealing with high-powered PROs whose one and only object in life is to "sell" their organisation

Faced with this problem of control, the DSIR were forced to use the COI.[26] The Lord President promised 'full support if it is necessary in pushing this project through'.[27] The job of film production was given by the COI to Anvil Films of Beaconsfield, who in 1954 began recording footage of the spectacle under construction.

There remained the question of who would pay for the film. The DSIR found a willing sponsor in the Foreign Office. The two departments coincided in the wish to fashion the instrument as a public object of national prestige.[28] The Foreign Office viewed the purpose of the film as '(a) to display overseas British primacy in scientific research, and British ability to develop the results of research in industrial and technical projects', and '(b) to show a major achievement of British structural engineering'.[29] Both departments were therefore happy with Anvil Films projection of the film:

> the film should leave the audience feeling...that Britain has shown courage, great imagination, and well justified faith in her own scientists and engineers in devoting at this time so much material, labour, and skill to the furtherance...of pure scientific research[30]

---

[24] JBA CS7/15/1. Draft letter to Sir Francis Hopwood, undated.

[25] PRO INF 12 664. Letter, Hingston to Marrett, 1 January 1954.

[26] The COI were not impressed: 'Instead of coming to us in the first place they hawk this idea themselves to Shell Film Unit, make an adverse memorandam about out budgeting procedures ...then go direct to the Foreign Office, and finish up by saying that time is short'. PRO INF 12 664. Internal minute, Langston to Hadfield, 15 January 1954.

[27] PRO INF 12 664. Internal minute, Ross to Langston, 30 January 1954.

[28] Holly Senior of the Foreign Office saw the project as an 'omnidirectional' and 'most valuable prestige film'.
PRO INF 12 664. Letter, Senior to Langston (COI), 13 January 1954.

[29] PRO INF 12 664. Specification sheet, 18 May 1954.

[30] PRO INF 12 664. Report, 'The Radio Telescope at Jodrell Bank: investigation and report for the Central Office of Information', by Anvil Films Ltd, July 1954.

In a phrase that indicates that not all post-war projects could be the Great Public Spectacle of British science, Anvil Films noted that the purity of the telescope meant that it was 'certainly not designed to facilitate the killing of large numbers of our fellow beings'.

£10,000 was allocated by the Foreign Office to make the film a significant proportion of the total budget for 1954/55 of £26,100.[31] The intended audience was 'all available audiences overseas, through commercial cinema, television and non-theatrical outlets', as well as 'commercial or television and non-theatrical distribution in UK'. Using the film, the Foreign Office aimed to sell British science and engineering abroad. Since technology is easier to sell than knowledge, this inevitably meant the Foreign Office expressed a preference for an emphasis on engineering and construction work[32], a point of contrast to which I will return.

The film, like other aspects of the Great Public Spectacle, could not function without the pre-existing repertoire of popular astronomical interests. As Hingston wrote to the Foreign Office about a receptive audience:

> as a representative of a scientific organisation I hardly dare to say that this radio telescope is right in the modern young persons' line of thought of space-ships, travel to the moon and thoughts on whether there are human beings on other planets.[33]

The COI and Foreign Office concurred: 'Mr Price [COI] stressed the importance of the human touch, linking the project to the man in the street and a London background. The film should say here is something in which Britain leads the world'.

As I discussed in Chapter Two, the University, the astronomers, consulting engineers, the DSIR and the UGC all became anxious that the telescope would cost far more than the original estimates in 1954. I also showed that in that year the PAC, searching for evidence of university financial laxity, explicitly criticised the relations between Lovell and Husband. The PAC saw a lack of communication between the two as the reason for the costly design changes of the telescope. At the same moment as Sir Ben Lockspeiser, under-secretary of the DSIR, was summoned to give evidence to the PAC at which he stated that there would be no further increases unless 'scientific demands...entirely new came up which would compel - literally compel us - to make the review'[34], the DSIR reinterpreted the significance of the Jodrell

---

[31] PRO INF 12 664. Internal note to O'Connell, 5 May 1954.

[32] 'This emphasis on the engineering side was satisfactory to the Foreign Office'. PRO INF 12 664. Letter, Senior to Ross, 16 July 1954.

[33] PRO INF 12 664. Letter, Hingston to Marrett, 1 January 1954.

[34] Parl. Papers HCP (1953/54) 67-I. paragraph 2512.

Bank telescope. The Anvil film treatment portrayed the telescope as 'a tribute to the mind and spirit of Man himself'.[35] In particular, 'man in two *complementary* types...the scientist, the seeker, the dreamer of dreams, the thirster after knowledge...and his *essential* partner, the practical engineer' (my italics). The script was in part a carefully worded defence against the specific PAC criticism: inadequate dialogue between 'two types of men in whom Britain has always been fortunate' - university scientists and the contracted engineers. As Lovell wrote to the COI:

> It is important...to give the impression of the constant interplay between the engineers and the scientists during the years in which the telescope has been designed and built.[36]

Soon after this, however, Husband felt the film was not representing him equitably, as Lovell reported to Hingston: the engineer complained after receiving a 'revised film script...no notice [had] been taken of the criticisms' and he threatened to 'take legal action'.[37] Husband's complaint was that 'the film departs from the facts'.

Husband was irate that he was not being represented to his satisfaction at the press conferences. Whilst the engineer had helped send a group of photographers up in a crane, Lovell had briefed the main press without him:

> Even if for some reason it was impossible to send across the field for me, you had only to make a clear statement that my firm is entirely responsible for the design of the Radio Telescope...In fact I find you made no such reference...[38]

The engineer, who was 'always being urged by the Board of Trade and the Foreign Office to arrange for as much publicity as possible', found that he was not allowed a voice (despite the film declaring astronomer and engineer to be 'complementary'). Husband thought that he was not being given 'credit where credit is due'. It was in this immediate context that Husband took 'legal advice as to how far a documentary film of this nature can be allowed to depart from the facts', and attempted to challenge the narrative of the film which placed Lovell centrally. A controversy arose as to who was responsible

---

[35] JBA CS7/23/7. Anvil Films Ltd, op cit.

[36] JBA CS7/39/4. Letter, Lovell to Mayne (Films Division, COI), 15 February 1955. The script was duly changed, as the instructions to Anvil Films went: 'insert occasional scenes throughout sequence showing discussions between Professor Lovell and Mr Husband'.
PRO INF 12 665. Memorandum, 'Giant Radio Telescope: proposed amendations to film treatment', undated (February 1955).

[37] JBA CS7/15/1. Letter, Lovell to Hingston, 31 March 1955.

[38] JBA CS7/33/1. Letter, Husband to Lovell, 28 March 1955.

for the design of the telescope (and by extension the 'credit' that may accrue). Lovell replied to Husband's assertion of 'entire' responsibility by reserving the original primary 'scientific design' as the astronomers' own: 'many of the principles of this design were, of course, settled before we met you'.[39] In a strategy that Lovell repeated in *The Story of Jodrell Bank*[40], he responded to this challenge to the historical narrative by offering the personal authority to be found in a textual source, as he wrote to Hingston: 'I have fortunately got a detailed diary of all events, including the early years before Husband came into the picture' [sic].[41] The controversy centred around whether Lovell had been in possession of 'realistic or even useful designs for a 250 ft. telescope' before the first meeting between astronomer and engineer.[42] In the film this point of tension is managed by a scene portraying the first design meeting in which Lovell produces what are evidently very sketchy designs from his inside pocket.[43] A similar argument, over responsibility for design, occured in 1955 over the redesign of the bowl ('to meet', in Husband's words, 'some special "radar" requirements') and was managed by negotiating the scripted history of the telescope.[44]

I will now turn to how the narrative of *The Inquisitive Giant* was made to tell a suitable story: one which presented a spectacular image of the instrument, positioned particular individuals in relation to it, and responded to its the unfolding financial fortunes. The script was written after consultation with Lovell, Husband, the Foreign Office and the DSIR, and after several drafts and intense negotiation over key scenes. After a deliberately mysterious opening sequence in which a 'shadowy figure of man - a radio astronomer' was seen moving amongst darkened metal girders and speaking 'a technical jargon that will seem rather incomprehensible, but have the ring of authenticity', the main narrative unfolds.[45]

---

[39] JBA CS7/33/1. Letter, Lovell to Husband, 7 April 1955. The letter was checked by Robert Hanbury Brown before sending.

[40] As discussed in Chapter Two.

[41] JBA CS7/15/1. Letter, Lovell to Hingston, 31 March 1955. Also: JBA CS7/33/1. Letter, Lovell to Husband, 12 April 1955: 'I have refreshed my memory of the exact historical sequence of the events in 1948-1950 by referring to the original documents. I feel quite certain that the film sequence...can be adjusted to the satisfaction of us both'.

[42] JBA CS7/33/1. Letter, Husband to Lovell, 14 April 1955. As Husband put it, if Lovell did have the plans, 'you have done us both a great dis-service in the matter of time and expense by not disclosing these to me...'. Husband sceptically reflected: 'there are plenty of pictures and descriptions of rockets to reach the moon...but very few, if any, of these are backed up by sound engineering calculations and design'.

[43] Film, *The Inquisitive Giant*.

[44] PRO INF 12 665. Letter, Husband to Mayne, 25 March 1955.

[45] JBA CS7/39/4. Script for *The Inquisitive Giant*, 1955.

The film repeated the two rhetorical strategies found within the memoranda produced for the RAS and DSIR, described in Chapter Two, of historical sequencing and of listing of myriad possible projects. Beginning with Stonehenge it tells of 'man's perennial fascination by the heavens above him'[46], passing through Ptolemy, Copernicus, the telescopes of Galileo, Newton, William Herschel, Lord Rosse, and at Mount Wilson and Mount Palomar, leading inexorably to the Jodrell Bank radio telescope. The flow of the narrative gave the construction of the British telescope apparent historical necessity. Up until Rosse 'with these great telescopes, Great Britain led the world in astronomical observations'. The apparent aberration in the sequence when the American telescopes are named was given a climatic explanation: 'But Britain suffers the disadvantage of a climate that renders impossible observation of the sky for long period [sic] of time. The largest telescopes yet built by man...have been built in the United States...'.[47] The COI recorded that the film treatment was how the 'Foreign Office and ourselves...would like this film to be built up'.[48]

In the film the telescope was centralised within scientific programmes, and thus constructed as necessary, by the listing of possible projects (an identical strategy as that used in the textual medium of the memoranda): the study of interference from solar flares was 'of immediate practical importance', research could be carried out on meteors, the moon's surface, 'wind currents' yielding 'valuable information to the meteorologist', as well as radio sources.

Authenticity was assembled from astronomical imagery: stills of the historical forebears, dramatic footage of scaffolding and girders in the erection of the telescope, pen recordings and optical astronomical photographs.[49] The seamless sequence that led to the radio telescope recruited both historical and contemporary astronomers, but the latter had the ability to resist. Lovell wrote letters to Grote Reber (an ancestral figure in stories of radio astronomy), Pawsey at Sydney, Ryle at Cambridge, and Hey at Malvern requesting their televisual presence.[50] Pawsey made available footage

---

[46] JBA CS7/23/7. Anvil Films Ltd, op cit.

[47] JBA CS7/39/4. Script, *The Inquisitive Giant*, 1955.

[48] JBA CS7/39/4. Letter, Mayne (COI) to Lovell, 24 January 1955.

[49] Editorial effort was required to make the link between the metal structure with its attendant radio equipment and pen recordings and 'astronomy'. For example, the sequence on solar flares begins with optical photographs and then cuts to 'the recording chart showing the "radio" equivalent'.
JBA CS7/39/4. Script, op cit.

[50] JBA CS7/39/4. Letter, Lovell to Reber, 25 April 1955. Letter, Lovell to Pawsey, 25 April 1955. Letter, Lovell to Ryle, 25 April 1955.

of the Australian telescopes[51], and Hey (after initially declining) appeared briefly in the film.[52] Only a portrait photograph was available of Reber and a desk made 'to give the impression that Reber or someone has just left' was mocked up in his place.[53] The other ancestral figure of radio astronomy, Karl Jansky, was included in a similar way, by creating

> an aerial system similar to that used by Jansky...and provide someone of roughly the same build who could imitate Jansky in the half gloom conditions in which we will shoot it.[54]

Martin Ryle resisted the interpretation that the script made: 'if it were to be a film on British Radio Astronomy...it would be a different matter', he replied to Lovell, 'but clearly it is intended to be concerned with your new telescope'.[55] Lovell recognised that the film required the authoritative endorsement of his peers, as he wrote to Warren at Anvil Films. It was 'very distressing': 'my own position would become impossible if neither he nor Hey would agree to appear'.[56] Either, Lovell suggested, 'let the film be bad' or 'come to some arrangement with Ryle' so that in the film it was 'made clear...that the big radio telescope [was] only one of the streams of the development of radio astronomy in this country'. When such an arrangement was offered, Ryle still resisted the historical narrative : he thought it not 'fair to the Cavendish, nor to those who have supported us, if the Cavendish work were only to appear as references to early and quite obsolete types of equipment'.[57] However, he did agree to the compromise that preserved the impression of 'timeliness and promise' necessary for further grants in both programmes:

> there should be some brief account of the various *types of investigation* which future Radio Astronomy seemed to promise; the fact that some of these could best be done with interferometers might even be mentioned...

A change in the historical narrative 'leaving it clear that other programmes have led on to the construction of other instruments' was thus agreed to. In

---

[51] JBA CS7/39/4. Letter, Pawsey to Lovell, 9 May 1955.
[52] JBA CS7/39/4. Letter, Hey to Lovell, 2 May 1955.
[53] JBA CS7/39/4. Letter, Warren (Anvil Films Ltd) to Lovell, 18 October 1956.
[54] JBA CS7/39/4. Letter, Warren to Hanbury Brown, 14 July 1955.
[55] JBA CS7/39/4. Letter, Ryle to Lovell, 4 May 1955.
[56] JBA CS7/39/4. Letter, Lovell to Warren, 6 May 1955. This argument was explicitly made by Blackett in his criticisms of the script, see: Letter, Lovell to Ryle, 6 May 1955.
[57] JBA CS7/39/4. Letter, Ryle to Lovell, 26 July 1955.

order to carry authority the film had to manage the division of scientific labour between Cambridge and Manchester.

The film re-constructed not only the telescope's historical predecessors but also the process by which it received assent. Out of all the bodies involved in securing funds for the telescope, *The Inquisitive Giant* focuses on one that played a marginal but symbolic role: the Royal Astronomical Society (RAS), the group of astronomical peers. For the purpose of the film, the RAS sub-committee meeting that approved the telescope was moved from Edinburgh to Burlington House.[58] The sub-committee was promoted to being a full meeting of the RAS, and Sir Edward Appleton to playing the role of RAS President. Lovell wrote to Appleton outlining the sequence in which 'there should be a few seconds shot of [Lovell] explaining the project, with a suitable short speech from yourself, and the audience reaction'.[59] Appleton expressed approval.[60] The sequence was filmed, showing Appleton declaring to his audience of fellow astronomers that

> this proposed Radio Telescope would permit us to continue in the United Kingdom new methods of astronomical research which have already been so greatly developed by the skill of British scientists and which are independent of climatic conditions.[61]

The audience was directed and shown to respond by 'listening and then applauding'.[62] The authoritative status of the telescope was thus displayed by such televisual methods of virtual witnessing.[63]

The Inquisitive Giant needed a soundtrack that befitted the tale of national prestige. Vaughan Williams expressed interest but was ultimately unable to take up the offer.[64] A suitable replacement was found in Peter Racine Fricker, who held ideal credentials in the eyes (and ears) of the COI: 'our suggestion is Peter Racine Fricker, who wrote the score for the Crown Film WHITE CONTINENT [for International Geophysical Year], having previously won the Festival of Britain competition. He is a composer of great intelligence and austerity who would...be absolutely right for this subject'.[65]

---

[58] JBA CS7/39/4. Letter, Lovell to Warren, 7 April 1955.

[59] JBA CS7/39/4. Letter, Lovell to Appleton, 12 January 1956.

[60] JBA CS7/39/4. Letter, Appleton to Lovell, 21 January 1956.

[61] JBA CS7/39/4. Script of *The Inquisitive Giant*, 1955.

[62] Such spontaneity belies the fact that the audience was filmed on a different day: Hunter, who appears to Appeton's left on the podium has a double in the audience.

[63] Shapin and Schaffer (1985), p. 60, for virtual witnessing.

[64] JBA CS7/15/1. Letter, Hingston to Lovell, 26 January 1955.

[65] PRO INF 12 666. Letter, May to Cockburn, 21 May 1957.

The finished film was judged a suitable visual and musical representation of the Radio Telescope, and was marketed by the COI. *The Inquisitive Giant* was 'ordered by the BBC, British Movietonews, and BCINA for use by them and for the USA by NBC, CBS and Telenews'.[66] It was displayed to public visitors on site at Jodrell Bank as part of the carefully arranged interface outlined by Hingston which I have already discussed.[67] Through *The Inquisitive Giant* the conflicting and confluent interests of the heterogeneous bodies of the telescopic project were managed, the telescope was fashioned as a project of national prestige, and its potentially troublesome legitimacy was secured through a reconstruction of peer assent. The interest and care taken by all parties in *The Inquisitive Giant* contrasts with other film projects. The telescope made an appearance in other films that promoted national prestige, for example a COI production made for the British pavilion at the Brussels Exhibition.[68] The Realist Film Unit used the telescope for a film on the ionosphere, but was treated with relative indifference.[69] Many requests to use the telescope as a mere dramatic backdrop were turned down.[70]

Whilst the film illustrates the point that the construction of public representations simultaneously involved the authorisation and accreditation of actors, one key actor had entirely disappeared from the finished film: the assenting public. When the film's narrative had first been planned, it was to end in the following manner. Having passed through the construction 'at last we see the finished telescope, towering, immense, dwarfing all the surrounding buildings - yet with the seeming delicacy of an open girder structure'.[71] Then there was to be 'the opening ceremony': the telescope enclosed by 'the crowd, the celebration, like the launching of a big ship'. But in the completed film the crowd scene had, significantly, vanished.

---

[66] PRO INF 12 666. Internal note, F. Watts to Frances Cockburn, 3 December 1957.

[67] Allan Chapman, personal communication.

[68] JBA CS7/41/4. Letter, Lovell to Parkinson, 13 January 1958.

[69] JBA CS7/39/4. Letter, Strasser (Realist) to Palmer, 29 May 1956.

[70] JBA CS7/31/4. Internal letter, Lascelles to Lovell, 2 March 1960. Lascelles reported on one such project: 'They wish to use Jodrell Bank or an Atomic Station as a background to a scientific film. But on reading the script the science they envisage is largely fictional and very crude – flashing lights and flickering dials. The main reason for the film, as I see it, is nothing but a background for clothing or otherwise the heroine (sic!) [sic] in as many different poses as possible – they have in mind Jayne Mansfield or Marilyn Monroe in this role... the part is supposed to be a being of extreme intelligence and I must in all fairness, that her physical beauty is only supposed to be a projection of the mind of mortal man'. He adds 'the film's basic theme of redemption by sacrifice is not peculiar to Jodrell Bank'.

[71] PRO INF 12 664. Report, 'The Radio Telescope at Jodrell Bank: investigation and report for the COI', Anvil Films Ltd, July 1954.

MANAGING THE PRESS

The completion of a large instrument or building, or launch of a ship is usually marked by the ritual of an 'opening'. The Jodrell Bank radio telescope was intended to be no exception. Lockspeiser, the Secretary of the DSIR, judged that the Duke of Edinburgh would be a suitable symbolic personage to perform the ceremony. Lovell was unsure of the 'ethics of these matters', and asked the Manchester University Vice-Chancellor to 'liaise with the DSIR and the Nuffield Foundation with regard to arrangements'.[72] The delays in the construction of the telescope meant the postponement of its opening. At a Site Committee meeting in the Autumn of 1956, Lovell suggested that 'from a national point of view' the 'ceremony could be performed on the date of the opening of IGY'.[73] The Royal Society, who co-ordinated the British contribution to the International Geophysical Year, expressed approval; and later reported that 'His Royal Highness was favourably disposed'.[74] There was still the concern from the University that the event might be an 'anticlimax': that the telescope would not be in a 'fit condition to be formally opened'.[75] However, this could also be a reason for setting an opening date: it would give Husband 'the necessary leverage to speed up deliveries'.[76] The chair of the Site Committee, Sir Charles Renold, outlined in a memorandum the 'minimum requirements' that would define the suitable 'condition': the 'structural fabric' must be completed, the 'scaffolding cleared away', the 'main structure' must 'be capable of being rotated by power' and set up so the 'reception of radio signals can be demonstrated'.[77] If this could be achieved then a 'dramatic and impressive' public display of the efficacy of the telescope could be performed:

> ...on pressing the button...the telescope [would] sweep over one or more of the remote radio sources in the depths of the universe. The resulting signal could be displayed on a number of pen recording instruments, and these could be used to initiate a local series of events such as the unfurling of flags...[78]

Husband suggested using 'the big bowl as the public address system for the

[72] JBA CS7/39/5. Letter, Lovell to Stopford (VC), 8 December 1954.
[73] JBA CS7/39/5. Letter, Lovell to Mansfield Cooper (VC), 29 September 1956.
[74] JBA CS7/39/5. Letter, Martin to Lovell, 5 November 1956.
[75] JBA CS7/39/5. Letter, Mansfield Cooper to Lovell, 26 November 1956.
[76] JBA CS7/39/5. Letter, Lovell to Mansfield Cooper, 30 November 1956.
[77] JBA CS7/31/2. memorandum by renold, 'Radio Telescope: Opening Date', circulated to members of the Site Committee, 6 December 1956.
[78] JBA CS7/31/2. Letter, Lovell to Husband, 13 December 1956.

occasion'.[79] Lovell replied that 'this might give a very confusing impression to the uninitiated as to the use of the telescope'.[80] A balance must be struck between an opening 'dramatic' enough to hold the attention of the media, and a ceremony that made the purpose of the telescope clear: hence the preference for a 'radar demonstration' linking the telescope to an astronomical object, possibly the strong radio sources in Cassiopeia or Cygnus, or even better the (visible) moon, the 'target likely to create an impression'.

The opening of the telescope was an attempt to display a singular meaning of the telescope. However, the interpretative flexibility of the instrument made this canalisation extremely difficult. The intended audience of this show was the media: radio, the press, news reel and television. This act of communication was contested both in the construction of the radio telescope message, and in its reception. For example, in early 1957, the *Sunday Pictorial* attempted to run a feature suggesting that Jodrell Bank was a poor choice for the telescope's site because of electrical interference. This was more than merely 'time wasting and annoying', as Blackett wrote to Lovell:

> I have been busy myself at the DSIR and with Lord Simon trying to get the financial side clear. Publicity of the *Sunday Pictorial* sort could do a hell of a lot of harm.[81]

Blackett considered 'the right party line' to be that 'of course the site was not perfect, that there were heaps of valuable results to get...even if some desirable experiments were not possible, [and] that talk about alternative sites etc was purely mischievous'. To make these points, Blackett's connections were invaluable:

> I immediately rang [the reporters'] boss, Cecil King, the chairman of the Sunday Pictorial, whom I know personally, and asked him to get the article cancelled altogether as it would achieve nothing useful and a great deal of serious difficulty. He agreed to do this.

The reporters had 'tried to gain entry to Jodrell Bank...but were refused permission', they had tried to access Lovell at his home where they were 'informed...that [Lovell] had an agreement with the Bursar and the Engineer' that there would be no 'publicity until the opening of the telescope', and they had later rung Lovell 'making enquiries about [electrical] interference

---

[79] JBA CS7/31/2. Letter, Husband to Lovell, 31 December 1956.

[80] JBA CS7/31/3. Letter, Lovell to Husband, 4 January 1957.

[81] JBA CS7/41/3. Letter, Blackett to Lovell, 24 January 1957.

on the site'.[82] Here was interference personified in the form of press reporters: they 'think nothing of penetrating to one's own house and disturbing one with telephone calls in the middle of the night'.

If the DSIR, the astronomers and the University Bursar thought that the financial insecurity of the telescope required the careful management of the telescope's image, the Engineer considered that this image should bear his name. Husband complained of the 'apparently uncontrolled publicity...taking place at the present time', who gave 'no acknowledgements whatever to any of the contractors, or ourselves, which seemed to me to be very unfair'.[83] The telescope must advertise engineering prowess as well as scientific prestige. This plea was repeated by other contractors.[84] There were several reasons why such pleas for control could not be met: private possession of the Jodrell Bank land was not enough ('the photograph in *The Times*...was obtained by the use of a telescopic lens'[85]), because of past debts (Lovell declared himself 'personally responsible for the appearance of the telescope in Sir Edward Appleton's Reith Lectures...Since Appleton was so actively responsible for furthering the cause of the telescope...it would have been exceedingly difficult to have refused'), and most importantly because too many parties had an interest in the telescope for the controlled image to be singular.

Thus Hingston of the DSIR, expecting the 'PAC report to appear in July or August', wished to 'divert the attention of the newspapers from the financial aspects of the telescope to its scientific interest and importance'. This could be done at a press conference, but the divergent interests of Husband were problematic: Hingston would not, 'under any consideration, think of holding this with Husband present...[he] would divert the conference into exactly those channels which we wish to avoid'. All parties agreed on the virtues of publicity 'arrangements...in a properly organised fashion', but conflicted as to what this fashion should be. The University, more concerned with the repercussions of the PAC's charges of financial incompetence, viewed Husband's worries as 'injured vanity'.[86] But for the consulting

---

[82] JBA CS7/41/3. Letter, Lovell to Blackett, 26 January 1957.

[83] JBA CS7/41/3. Letter, Husband to Renold, 1 May 1957.

[84] It is difficult to estimate the demands of the contractors as they are filtered through Husband to the Site Committee. Husband mentions Brush Electrical Engineering Ltd, who later made unauthorised use of pictures of the telescope.

[85] JBA CS7/41/3. Letter, Lovell to Mansfield Cooper, 7 May 1957. See also: *The Times*, Wednesday 17 April 1957, 'Jodrell Bank Nearing Completion'. *The Times* at this time had few pictures inside, but a regular pictorial backpage of miscellaneous but striking photographs: the telescope shared the page with a waterborne police station, a 'mechanical man' in Milan, a fire in Covent Garden, and the Prime Ministers of Australia and Japan.

[86] JBA CS7/41/3. Letter, Mansfield Cooper to Lovell, 8 May 1957.

engineer the discharge of credit from the symbolic, if precarious, telescope project was of material consequence to future ambitions, as Hingston was aware:

> The contractor for building anything rarely gets publicity except in his local press and in the technical journals. For example, do you know who is the contractor for the Dounreay Breeder Reactor?[87]

In the late 1950s to be identified with the telescope was to be at almost nuclear heights of progressive symbolism. However, as Hingston acutely observed in summing up the invisibility of the engineer, 'As was said at the last press do at Jodrell Bank, "Lovell is the telescope, and the telescope is Lovell"'.

In May 1957, after discussions between the University Vice-Chancellor and the DSIR, it was decided that 'the best way of handling the mounting national interest' was to place the responsibility for the telescope's publicity in the hands of 'the publicity section of the DSIR'.[88] The insiders' view of governmental machinery would be invaluable in limiting the financial troubles of the telescope, as the Vice-Chancellor put it:

> The question of publicity may become vitally important in discussions with the Treasury and with Parliament and I think... it will be necessary for us all to walk very closely hand in hand with the Department...and in all matters of publicity to be guided by them because they are aware of certain cross currents and nuances of opinion which we can't be expected to know.

The parallel inquiries by the PAC meant that the DSIR intensified their interest in the operation of the Radio Telescope as a spectacle of science, and insured that Manchester University took extreme care over its presentation. To put this policy into action a notice was circulated 'to be signed by all members of the Jodrell Bank research and teaching staff'.[89] Because of 'mounting national interest', all 'members of staff should avoid giving information or entering into discussions about the Jodrell Bank telescope with any members of the press, BBC or television services': such matters should be referred to Hingston.

The PAC reports were critical that the DSIR 'did not see fit to inquire more closely into the university's arrangements with the consulting engineers and into the system of control over the design and construction work'.[90]

---

[87] JBA CS7/41/3. Letter, Hingston to Lovell, 15 May 1957.
[88] JBA CS7/41/3. Letter, Mansfield Cooper to Lovell, 21 May 1957.
[89] JBA CS7/41/3. Notice, 27 May 1957.
[90] *The Times*, Wednesday 14 August 1957, p. 5.

Hingston's press conferences (divided into three: '26th June as the Press Day,...25th June as TV and Film Day and 27th June as the day for the Technical Press'), like *The Inquisitive Giant*, were platforms to defend against this charge. For example, the BBC were 'very anxious to include the Radio Telescope in their [International Geophysical Year] broadcast...and for reasons of national prestige it is clearly of importance that it should be included'. However Hingston 'made it a condition that [the BBC]...also mention Husband and something about the engineering feat of building the telescope'.[91] The opening had to be delayed until the instrument was movable, but a stage on which to present the telescope was needed before then, and the press conferences played this role:

> these conferences are being held...for a quite specific purpose, namely in the hope of off-setting the effect of any hostile criticisms which may come as a result of the PAC examination[92]

The conferences, as well as defending past funding, also sought to protect future ambitions. As with radio frequency allocation, the radio astronomers were well aware that their positions would be weakened if the views of Cambridge and Manchester were seen to conflict.[93] Indeed, relations with Cambridge were one of the two 'certain questions' that were expected to be asked.[94] Ryle, who had 'a mutual interest in this since the same question will be asked at his opening ceremony in July' visited Jodrell Bank in May, and the answers were prepared and coordinated. Two points were stressed, allowing the astronomers to appear unified yet both to be able to claim resources later: their groups had 'a long tradition of individual friendship and cooperation' even 'actual collaboration', but the 'new Cambridge telescope...is a specialised instrument as *distinct* from the Jodrell Bank telescope'.[95] This repeated the argument found in *The Inquisitive Giant.* that Cambrdige and Manchester radio astronomy projects were separate but equally valid.

The press releases of 1952 had cast the telescope in terms of national prestige: 'the pioneering work of research scientists at Manchester and Cambridge Universities has given Great Britain a prominent, even pre-

---

[91] JBA CS7/41/3. Letter, Hingston to Lovell, 22 May 1957.

[92] JBA CS7/41/3. Letter, Mansfield Cooper to Lovell, 19 June 1957.

[93] Discussed in Chapter Five.

[94] JBA CS7/41/3. Letter, Lovell to Hingston, 31 May 1957. The other was the effect of the 'electrification of the railway line'.

[95] JBA CS7/41/3. 'Notes on conversations with Ryle about probable questions at the press conference', 31 May 1957.

eminent position' in radio astronomy.[96] But this prestige had been tempered, explaining the Nuffield Foundation's involvement as due to government economy: 'although the DSIR was anxious to help, it seemed likely that in view of existing commitments, the need for economy in Government expenditure might make it necessary to postpone the project'. However, by 1957 the detailed press release makes recurrent, heightened reference to 'prestige'. The press release concluded by portraying the telescope almost like Henry V: promising a Britain reborn from war and set to regain Great Power status:

> British astronomy achieved distinction in the eighteenth and nineteenth centuries, when the Earl of Rosse and Sir William Herschel pioneered the construction of large telescopes. Unfortunately the country's leadership was doomed to capitulation to those living in a more favourable climate...Now the devices of war have been transformed into a revolutionary method for the exploration of space, independent of cloud or fog. In the study of the universe and nearby space, with its important ramifications in more practical matters, Britain can once more compete without handicap.[97]

These stirring words, prophesising 'the greatest radio telescope in the world' that 'will soon be operating within these shores', repeated much of the narrative found in televisual form in *The Inquisitive Giant*. Again references are made to the different but valid programme of Cambridge[98], to practical spinoff[99], and to national security. A full three months before Sputnik, allusions were made to the ability of this patriotic instrument to defend 'these shores': 'It is obvious that the interests in this aspect of radio astronomy extend far beyond the study of meteors...into...meteorology, ballistics and high-speed flight at great altitudes'.[100] The engineering press release that accompanied the scientific one noted that design changes to this instrument of 'great credit to British workmanship' now allowed 'it to be used to track moving objects in space'.[101]

---

[96] JBA CS7/41/1. DSIR press release, 'Exploration of the universe. A giant radio telescope', 25 April 1952. Accompanied by DSIR press release, 'The discovery of radio stars. The new science of radio stars', 25 April 1952.

[97] JBA CS7/15/3. DSIR press release, 'Radio astronomy. The uses of the radio telescope', 26 June 1957.

[98] JBA CS7/15/3. Ibid. Large dishes are described as 'an alternative approach' to that of Cambridge or Sydney.

[99] JBA CS7/15/3. Ibid. The telescope promised means of distinguishing and investigating the 'serious upheavals' caused by interference from solar radiation.

[100] JBA CS7/15/3. Ibid.

[101] JBA CS7/15/3. DSIR press release, 'Building the radio telescope. The engineering problems involved', 26 June 1957. Accompanied by DSIR press release, 'The Jodrell Bank radio telescope. Various facts', 26 June 1957.

The firms contracted to supply and build parts for the telescope shared in the display. Hoffmann Manufacturing proudly claimed that their 'ball and roller bearings' took 'all the weight on the Radio Telescope at Jodrell Bank'. The troublesome United Steel said the telescope had 'gripped the imagination of everyone connected with its design and construction'. These sentiments were echoed by the many other, often locally-based, contractors.[102]

However carefully managed the message given out at these displays, the reaction of their audience could not be assured. For example 'Swinger' of *The Master Builder*, declared that he or she was:

greatly privileged to attend the press visit to see the giant radio telescope at Jodrell Bank and to listen...spellbound to the story - of why it has to be as large, why it had to be designed as precisely as it was, how a fantastic number of obstacles were overcome and how and why England now has this tremendous lead over all other countries.[103]

But Swinger's eye spotted 'misleading' engineering information, and thought the 'publicity of this amazing venture...sadly bungled', although not because of the content of the press conferences, but because of the 'sudden release of...pent-up material': 'the campaign...appears to be designed to stigmatise the whole project as an ultra-expensive white elephant'. It is illustrative of the difficulties of directing a specific meaning for the telescope if at least one member of the press could reinterpret the message entirely opposite to that intended. However, Swinger did appreciate the potential prestige of the project: 'there ought to be an enclosure, like there is at London Airport where...I can take my USA [sic] and other friends and show off what we can do in this country'. Indeed, 'there ought to be excursions from Blackpool and Morecambe Bay, there ought to be ice cream stalls...it should be fully exploited'. Although the vice-chancellor could dismiss such views as 'ridiculous', they added urgency to his promise to tackle the 'problems of visitors'.[104]

---

[102] JBA JBM/2/4. Press releases. The firms' press releases were collected into one envelope to be given to reporters. Included were: United Steel Structural Co Ltd of Scunthorpe, Kirkstall Forge Engineering Ltd of Leeds, Brush Electrical Engineering of Loughborough, F.H. Wheeler of Sheffield, Orthostyle Ltd of Scunthorpe, The Cementation Co of London, Mills Scaffold Co Ltd of London, B. Thornton Ltd of Huddersfield, Alfred Wiseman & Co Ltd of Birmingham, Herbert Morris Ltd of Loughborough, W. & G. Sissons of Sheffield, Thos. W. Ward Ltd of Sheffield, Davy and United Engineering Co Ltd of Sheffield, Thomas Cotton Ltd of Mansfield, Lockheed of Liverpool, W.J. Whittal & Son Ltd of Birmingham, Renold Chains Ltd of Wythenshawe, Cooper Roller Bearings Co of King's Lynn, Z. & W. Wade of Whaley Bridge, Dunlop Rubber Co Ltd, and Hoffmann of Chelmsford.

[103] *The Master Builder*, July 1957.

[104] JBA CS7/39/5. Letter, Mansfield Cooper to Lovell, 2 August 1957.

THE 'PROBLEM' OF VISITORS RENEWED

Such managed show of meaning was forced because of the heterogeneous bodies interested in the telescope. As was shown in Chapter Two, a network of actors, that is to say more than one interested body, was necessary to secure resources, in particular funding. Such binding together of fragmented interests was always problematic and could unravel if they proved too divergent. One strategy that the DSIR, university and astronomers used to try and secure further resources was by a popular appeal. However, it is very important to distinguish between 'the public' as *constituted* by these bodies, and the bodily presence and actions of the public themselves. In their management of the telescope's meaning (via press release, press conference, or film) there seems to be an intended public audience. However, the content of these displays can be decoded as being specifically targeted at a much smaller group of actors that might choose to support the telescope project. Also, 'the public' that appeared in the memoranda on visitors was a representation, not an actual presence. Popular interest in astronomy and cosmology was a cultural configuration at odds with that attributed to the constructed 'public'.

At the same moment as great effort was being made in the presentation of the telescope, the question of 'arrangements for handling visitors' again became acute. The effect of the publicity was 'a great surge of weekend visitors and trespassers to Jodrell Bank'.[105] Indeed 'men who were posted at the entrances had to turn hordes away'. Lovell had complained earlier in the year about both 'trespassers' and 'visitors'. Trespassers 'either drive in boldly or otherwise climb the fences surrounding the telescope', and he demanded 'the same kind of protection and privacy as is enjoyed by a laboratory in the University'.[106] 'Visitors' were categorised in a manner similar to Hingston's four years before: 'individuals or parties who come at the request of a responsible University Officer for financial or other reasons', 'visiting scientists and other persons of importance who want to see over Jodrell Bank for general interest' and the 'mass of individuals'.[107] Of the latter group: 'if it is decided to attempt to deal with these then any solution must keep them away from the laboratories and immediate grounds'. This worried the astronomers more than it did the University, as the Vice-Chancellor put it: 'I would not care to raise what to [the University Officers] will seem a minor issue whilst the broader question of financing the telescope is causing them so much concern'.[108]

---

[105] JBA CS7/39/5. Letter, Lovell to Mansfield Cooper, 3 July 1957.

[106] JBA CS7/39/5. Letter, Lovell to Mansfield Cooper, 23 January 1957.

[107] Lovell noted that '3 years ago we were already handling 3,000 visitors per year, and there are now 20,000 accumulated requests in our files'.

[108] JBA CS7/39/5. Letter, Mansfield Cooper to Lovell, 30 January 1957.

Lovell wrote to the Vice-Chancellor that he would 'oppose...to the utmost [any] conscious effort to attract thousands of visitors from all over the country' as being 'incompatible with the scientific work of the establishment'.[109] In a memorandum, based on Hingston's, Lovell stated that if nothing was done, the 'staff will leave because they cannot do research and the station will cease to be effective in research although it possesses the finest equipment in the world'.[110] The category of 'schools, scientific societies' would mount to over 3000 persons per year, and admitting them would be 'a valuable educational function'. However, they would need 'detailed guidance and information, and a closer look at the telescope and some of the associated apparatus...they have to come "inside the fence"'. A solution involving specialised staff and buildings was proposed. This was in contrast to how the 'general public' were to be managed. The telescope 'might attract nearly 100,000 visitors per annum', but 'Jodrell Bank is not Blackpool and there is no precedent in the country for the mass handling of visitors in connection with scientific projects'. Lovell advocated no resources should be given to 'dealing with visits from the general public', indeed they 'must be restrained by fencing and gates'.

This seeming reluctance to allow the presence at Jodrell Bank of the 'thousands' whilst simultaneously apparently addressing them via the media, can be resolved if the bulk of these visitors were not the intended audience of the telescopic message (those involved in the funding and accreditation processes were). The imagined effect of the 'thousands' is also revealing:

> The argument that they would not be allowed to straddle the fences of the station is irrelevant...the interference which this would bring into the neighbourhood would completely undermine the efforts which we have made over the past years to restrain the town planners and infiltration of grid lines etc.[111]

The 'thousands' were described in precisely the same manner as electrical interference: both were 'intrusive', 'threatening', and discursively located at the boundaries of Jodrell Bank. The identification of visitors with interference was part of the discursive construction by the astronomers of a 'public'. Furthermore, I argue in Chapter Four that an ambiguity, and a consequent anxiety, was present in this discourse. The pen-recordings produced by the telescope were ambiguous: a 'spike' could represent either an astronomical object or local interference, and differentiating between the two was the root

---

[109] JBA CS7/41/3. Letter, Lovell to Mansfield Cooper, 6 June 1957.

[110] JBA CS7/39/5. Lovell, 'Memorandum on the problem of visitors at Jodrell Bank and a proposal for a solution', 18 June 1957.

[111] JBA CS7/39/5. Lovell, 'Memorandum', op cit. I discuss the measure taken to 'restrain' town planners and grid lines in Chapter Five.

of astronomical authority. The discourse of the 'public' was constructed to separate astronomers from 'visitors', and differentiating between these two was the source of organisational authority. However, this configured 'public' had to carry the heterogeneous interests of the bodies that supported the telescope. The dilemma lay in the need to 'protect' the 'privacy' and integrity of Jodrell Bank (therefore portraying visitors as an interfering 'disturbance'), whilst the financial problems of the telescope meant an appeal through the same 'public' was necessary. The anxiety for the astronomers was that the other bodies that supported the telescope could exploit this ambiguity in divergent ways: the DSIR and the COI required the telescope to be on display to visitors. As Lovell complained: 'I have had a good deal of correspondence recently with the Central Office of Information who continually make requests to be given permission to bring visitors to Jodrell Bank'.[112] At this point the ambiguity of the status of the visitors was therefore problematic to the astronomers, and precisely as in the case of radio interference, they viewed it in terms of disruption and disturbance.

The discourse of interference, in terms of which visitors (and as I will discuss in Chapter Four, disturbances to representations) were discussed, was therefore moulded to the heterogeneous institutional politics which surrounded the telescope project, and which secured its resources. What was stressed by the astronomers was the need to keep the 'general public' at a 'distance'. The management of the public was achieved spatially: through organisational structures and practices which could sort and regulate entry at the boundary, and to exclude audiences if necessary.

DEMONSTRATING THE TELESCOPE, COMMUNICATING WITH SATELLITES

In the mid-1950s plans were made for the International Geophysical Year: it would symbolically unite the research programmes of scientists from all nations, working on trans-national objects such as 'the earth' and 'the Antarctic' during a year of peak solar activity. It was ironic that such a show of united, disinterested science was the stage for a great act of national technological propaganda: the launching of the first artificial earth satellite, Sputnik. In the last chapter I discussed the attempts by the promoters of the Radio Telescope to use the public association of the instrument with satellites to lobby within Whitehall for the clearing of the remaining debt. Here, I describe how this association was made.

---

[112] JBA CS7/39/5. Letter, Lovell to Mansfield Cooper, 21 February 1958.

Sputnik Historiography

On the surface there appears to be a case for regarding the launch of Sputnik as a discontinuity in post war history: it seemed to symbolise Soviet technological parity with the United States. Furthermore, the rocket launcher meant that the States was under direct military threat for the first time in the 20th century, and it contradicted received wisdom about the technological prowess of the Western powers. Walter McDougall has analysed the American reaction to the launch.[113] There was indeed a 'post Sputnik panic', of which there were two explanations at the time: mismanagement by the Republicans who had not dealt with the interservice rivalry, budget ceilings and antipathy from the 'big bomber boys' that paralysed the American satellite projects; and a more 'general American malaise' the roots of which were familiar folk-devils (a 'flabby education', the 'denigration of scientists', 'complacency' and even 'consumerism'). But McDougall argues against a discontinuity in the wider history of post-war politics: 'the national state remained supreme, cooperation [between armed services] was a muted form of competition, and military rivalry incorporated the strategic canopy of space'. Sputnik accelerated trends that were already present: it 'stimulated the rapid development of space technology' but this development was 'not in turn transformed by it'; the response to the Russian satellite was the grafting of 'scientific advice onto the existing political corpus, as if scientists could inform policies, without politics informing science'. McDougall therefore sees the key reaction to the Soviet satellites to be 'the triumph of a technocratic mentality in the United States that extended not only to military spending, science and space, but also to foreign aid, education, medical care, urban renewal, [etc]'.

McDougall argues that the appearance of such 'technological optimism' in America was soon followed in Europe and elsewhere. However, I would contend that although McDougall's arguments convince with respect to the effect of the satellite on the promotion and prestige of a particular American technocratic managerial group (possibly even a 'managerial revolution') linking govenment, industry and academia, they do not necessarily extend elsewhere. The reception of the satellite and how its symbolic power was discharged among social groups was very contingent on national and local contexts. I examine how British groups made use of Sputnik, and I argue they interpreted it very much according to their own concerns.

Sputnik in Britain

On the 5th of October 1957, *The Times* reported that 'Moscow radio

---

[113] McDougall, W. A., 1982. 'Technology and statecraft in the Space Age: toward the history of a saltation', *American History Review* 87, pp. 1010-1040.

announced last night that Russia yesterday launched an earth satellite'.[114] Russian scientists had sprung the news on a surprised IGY meeting held at the Soviet Embassy. The Embassy must have been pleased with its display as *The Times* repeated the awed statements of the American organisers of IGY: Joseph Kaplan said it was 'really fantastic' and a 'remarkable achievement', Lloyd Berkner offered his congratulations. *The Times* on the following Monday carried seven articles on the satellite. The lead headline was on 'US disquiet at power of satellite launch: proof of rapid Soviet advance in rockets'.[115] Sputnik had made an 'enormous impression on American minds', along with a 'note of fear' because of 'American scientists' estimate that it must have taken something like an inter-continental ballistic rocket to launch a satellite of nearly double the expected weight', whereas 'hitherto the official tendency has been to belittle Russian advances towards the "ultimate weapon". The article focused on American surprise and shortcomings, Russian expressions of the purely scientific significance of the launch, and 'alarm at some of the underlying implications' for national security. The lead editorial reiterated the themes. Two shorter articles followed on the 'Prestige value to Moscow' by 'Our Science Correspondent', and 'Moscow on "Paving the Way to Interplanetary Travel"' by 'Our Special Correspondent'. These seem to tally with McDougall's account of the reception of Sputnik. However, there were also articles 'Observations at Cambridge: Work with Radio Telescope' and 'Disappointment at Jodrell Bank' separated only by 'Missile Propulsion Problem Solved: Military Significance'. At Cambridge 'six transits of the Russian satellite were traced by radar telescope [sic]...apparently the only observations of this kind in Britain', altogether 'a piece of masterly improvisation', whereas at Jodrell Bank, Lovell was reported as saying "it is absolutely stupendous, about the biggest thing that has happened in scientific history". But he was:

> "scientifically absolutely helpless and frustrated" because the new radio telescope at Jodrell Bank, Cheshire, of which he is in charge, will not be ready to track the satellite and make use of its presence in space for several weeks.

This was an interpretation contested by consulting engineers, who were still in possession of the telescope whilst it was under construction. The day after the launch Kington (of Husband & Co) had offered to 'come forthwith to Jodrell Bank in order to carry out any movements [Lovell] might require on the 250ft telescope to track the Russian satellite', Husband was 'very disappointed' at Lovell's refusal.[116] He argued:

---

[114] *The Times*, 5 October 1957.

[115] *The Times*, 7 October 1957.

[116] JBA CS7/31/3. Letter, Husband to Lovell, 8 October 1957.

> Whilst not finally tuned up to the best we hope to achieve it is capable of holding
> directional accuracies greater than those originally specified. The Telescope is in
> fact operational, although not formally handed over by my firm to the University.

Kington had reported that Lovell's fear was that 'anyone might think the big
instrument itself was not serviceable', and Husband had had:

> considerable difficulty in restraining Kington from contacting the Air Ministry in
> order to fit up himself on the big telescope a short wave receiver so that at least
> an attempt could be made to track the satellite by virtue of the "messages" which
> are being radiated from it.

The Consulting Engineer said that the 'only reason' he had not allowed this
was 'that we might have been accused subsequently of exceeding our terms
of reference'. This was, of course, the specific criticism made by the PAC
about the relations between the engineers and the astronomers (a link that
had already been explicitly noticed in the coverage of Sputnik in *The Daily
Express*). Husband detailed how radar instrumentation and an 'automatic
position recorder in azimuth and elevation' could be installed at minimal
cost. Indeed the firm manufacturing the telescope control system, Dunford &
Elliott, offered to contribute immediately material and human resources to
share in the tracking. Husband questioned Lovell's stated intention 'to fit the
telescope for plotting the tracks of artificial satellites after it has been handed
over to the University'. The opportunities to make use of Sputnik seemed
clear to the Engineers, as Husband expressed it to Lovell: 'I do beg of you
for the sake of both our reputations that some immediate joint action be
taken...'.

Why was Lovell reluctant to take this 'immediate joint action' and use the
telescope for tracking the Soviet satellite? The expression to Kington suggests
that Lovell might have been worried that the first public display of the
telescope in action must be when the instrument could be relied upon to
perform. However, the hesitation has more to do with possession of the
telescope. Lovell explained his actions to the Vice-Chancellor: it was 'an
unusual and most undesirable state of affairs that a consulting engineer should
attempt to dictate the research policy of a University department about whose
functions he knows extremely little'.[117] This was clearly an argument that
would appeal to an officer appointed to protect University interests. Lovell's
explanations give wider insights. Firstly, there was negotiation and contest as
to what was 'possible': thus Lovell denied Husband's assertion that the
telescope was 'in fact operational':

---

[117] JBA CS7/31/3. Letter, Lovell to Mansfield Cooper, 10 October 1957.

> After the weekend it became clear that Husband was prepared to take emergency
> measures to overcome many of the outstanding difficulties with the telescope if
> we would cooperate in using our lunar echo equipment...

For Lovell, therefore, the work on the satellite had demonstrated that Husband
had been footdragging over the completion of the telescope: he had 'within
a little over twenty-four hours, accomplished feats on which he [had] hitherto
refused to give a time-scale to the Site Committee'. But Husband interpreted
the week's events differently: as the University again not giving the engineers
due credit for their achievements. Secondly, in Lovell's explanation there
was the assertion of his authority and responsibility for policy, which included
the separation of the 'scientific' from other activities. Thus he said that 'the
radio telescope [was] a most unsuitable instrument for work with the Russian
satellite', whereas there were also 'some scientific plans of a long-term and
fundamental nature for using the Jodrell Bank telescope on the American
satellite which it can deal with adequately'. What made the distinction? The
work with the American satellite was 'in the IGY programme, and [had]
been accepted by the Royal Society as part of the British programme', and
furthermore 'the primary function of this instrument is to explore the remote
parts of the universe,...plans for using it on satellite work have a relatively
low priority'. The scientific character of the telescope needed to be strongly
asserted: it use was not to be 'dictated' by engineers, nor was it to be
military:

> I reminded the Ministry of Supply only three days before the launching of the
> Russian satellite that there is no instrument in this country capable of tracking
> it by radar, and that they had previously rejected a suggestion that they should
> provide funds for the modification of one of our smaller telescopes at Jodrell
> Bank for this purpose.

This again illustrates the malleability in the telescope's purpose, but the key
point is that through discussions of what was 'suitable' and 'possible' the
telescope's scientific nature was being distinguished. When Lovell stated
that 'all the forces at Jodrell Bank which could be usefully deployed on the
real scientific programmes connected with the satellite', he was rhetorically
asserting the scientific status of the site, as he was spatially asserting it in
the memoranda on visitors.

However, the telescope was used to track the satellite. This late action
was partly to counter contests of Lovell's internal organisational authority,
and continued only so long as the interpretation of the public display of the
working telescope could be guided. Lovell stated that he was willing to make
such a deal since 'it seemed that we should shorten the difficult final stages
of the telescope completion by many months' and 'because of the increasing
public concern about the lack of use of the telescope coupled with a certain

private pressure on me from London'.[118]

The extra money needed to finance the tracking of Sputnik was also disputed between astronomer and engineer. A contract had been previously agreed between Jodrell Bank and the Ministry of Supply to attach some equipment made by Marconi for 'the extraction of ionospheric data'.[119] This contract was secret: no findings from it were to be published in the scientific press. The Ministry of Supply suggested charging the Sputnik work to this account. Lovell was unhappy with this arrangement for 'a number of reasons, not least of which is that the contract in question has a restricted clause in it'. Initial Jodrell Bank work on satellites was indeed funded by the Ministry of Supply, as part of a programme (to use the Radio Telescope) on 'probable interference of meteors and aurora with the radar location of long range missiles', which was planned as early as November 1956.[120] Husband made two claims: that his company (and contractors who were involved in tracking, such as Dunford and Elliott) should be compensated, and that the hectic events now meant that 'any hope of completing the tests on the telescope and handing it over to [the university]... must now be abandoned'.[121] The 'possession' of the telescope represented a gambit in a continuing conflict over 'control' of the telescope. Rainford, the university bursar, Lovell and Husband, contested the issue of compensation until the Jodrell Bank satellite work settled into a regular programme, funded through the Royal Society.[122]

The Times reported on 'Plans Speeded for Radar Track of Satellite: All-night Work at Jodrell Bank'.[123] The hesitation and dispute between engineer and astronomer were not on display:

> After it was learnt this afternoon that radio signals from the Russian earth satellite were not being heard...Professor A.C.B. Lovell called a hurried conference...Mr H.C. Husband, the designer of the radio-telescope, who was present at the conference, said it was hoped to start using the instrument to track the satellite by radar within the next 24 hours...

---

[118] From the evidence presented in Chapter Two, the pressuriser from London can be identified as Renwick.

[119] JBA CS7/36/2. Letter, Lovell to Rainford, 12 November 1957.

[120] PRO WO 195 14270. Ministry of Supply. Advisory Council on Scientific Research and Technical Development. Radar and Signals Advisory Board. Lovell, 'The radar detection of the Russian earth satellites and carrier rocket and its bearing on the missile detection problem', 10 March 1958. This was a restricted report.

[121] JBA CS7/36/2. Letter, Husband to Rainford, 8 November 1957.

[122] JBA CS7/36/2. Letter, Lovell to Massey, 5 November 1957, gave a capital expenditure of £6,500, and running expenses of £1,500 per annum, and a maximum average weekly commitment of 'twenty four hours per week'. Letter, Lovell to Martin, 21 October 1959, indicates that these figures were accepted.

[123] *The Times*, 9 October 1957.

With the help of Sir John Dean of the Telegraph Construction & Maintenance Co Ltd, who volunteered emergency high frequency cable to connect the telescope to the laboratories[124], radar echoes from the satellite rocket were recorded.[125] The compromise reached whereby the telescope was allowed to track the satellite as the Engineers wanted but for only a few days so as not to disrupt the scientific programmes was expressed in the press statement issued ten days after the launch of Sputnik. The 'ability of the Jodrell Bank Radio Telescope to detect by radar the Russian Rocket has now been demonstrated', and the dispute over the possession of the telescope was made a virtue: 'this display of its power and adaptability has now been made possible by the cooperation of the engineers who still have some work to carry out on the telescope'.[126] The negotiated settlement was made explicit by Lovell in the statement:

> We are anxious that this work should not be hindered since the telescope is required for use on its full research programme as soon as possible...I have agreed that the telescope should continue on the satellite programme for only another three nights...

The reason given was the astronomical 'staff, who are already exhausted', and had 'many teaching duties in the University', even though 'the engineers have offered to staff the telescope throughout the night'.

At Jodrell Bank the satellite was used to show the public harmony of engineers and astronomers, and the successful demonstration of working telescopes. Other groups interpreted it in different ways: Kurt Mendelssohn, a German physicist working at the Clarendon since the 1930s, wrote that 'the military significance of the space satellite launched by the Russians tends to overshadow the far greater menace of their general technological superiority'.[127] The root of this superiority was education: 'the Russians are spending a far greater proportion of their national income on the training, equipment, and living standards of a large number of scientists', whereas in Britain, 'the UGC now precludes any sizable expansion of academic scientific education'. At the Conservative Party conference, a day later, the Conservative chairman Lord Hailsham (later the extremely laissez-faire Minister for Science) demurred: the satellite was indeed 'a triumph of technical education', but since, he claimed, the satellite was 'largely the product of Kapitsa [the ex-Cavendish physicist working in the Soviet Union

---

[124] JBA CS7/31/3. Letter, Husband to Lovell, 9 October 1957. For the point that the cable allowed the physical connection of the two see: Saward (1984), p. 189.

[125] JBA CS7/31/3. Letter, Husband to Lovell, 12 October 1957.

[126] JBA CS7/41/3. Press release, 'Statement for press by Prof. A.C.B. Lovell', 14 October 1957.

[127] *The Times*. Letter, 9 October 1957.

since the 1930s, it was]...also a triumph for British technical education'.[128] Although he was 'melancholy' that 'we gave the Americans the atomic bomb and the Russians the satellite', both demonstrated that there was no need for concern about British education.[129] A series of letters to *The Times*, under the rubric 'Lessons of the Satellite', read the satellite's significance in terms of public versus grammar school education. Hewlett Johnson, the Dean of Canterbury, compared the 'great financial resources' that allowed the building of 'extensive and expensive' laboratories at the King's School to the 'cramped' equivalent at Simon Langton (also in Canterbury), and drew the conclusion that the 'broad, progressive and solid' education in Russia would not allow a similar 'highly educated minority and semi-educated mass'.[130] The sentiments of the left-wing Dean were immediately challenged by a string of letters, objecting to the characterisation of both grammar and public schools, but particularly the latter.[131] Finally, the British Interplanetary Society, a part-enthusiast, part-professional group promoting British space science, wrote that it was 'simply a matter of money' not education that the Soviets had their satellite: 'the only reason for this country not having this type of equipment is that it has been thought better to concentrate first on such projects as the radio telescope'.[132]

The Soviet satellite was therefore appropriated differently by British groups, and contrasts with the reception of Sputnik within the United States. For Jodrell Bank, Sputnik was used to demonstrate the efficacy of their radio telescope. Why was this necessary? For the same reasons as guided the production of *The Inquisitive Giant*, and the press conferences: to manage internal divisions and contests of responsibility, and to counter criticism of the construction of the telescope by the constitution of public authority. The opportunity that the satellite presented had to be managed with care, as the Vice-Chancellor wrote to Lovell when 'the Press...[was] full of the evidence given before the Public Accounts Committee' and 'our negotiations with the DSIR and the Treasury have reached a highly critical stage': 'I enjoin you

[128] *The Times*, 'Conservatives in Conference: Satellite's Challenge to British Education', 10 October 1957.

[129] Nuclear schemes provided ample proof: 'Our atoms for peace project, of which Calder Hall was a shining example, is likely to be of greater and more enduring benefit to mankind than the atomic bomb or the satellite. In this we lead the world...'.

[130] *The Times*. Letter by Hewlett Johnson, 9 October 1957.

[131] *The Times*. Letter, Robert Boothby, 10 October 1957; letter, Frank Barber, 11October 1957; letter, George Snow (Headmaster, Ardingly College), 11 October 1957; letter, R. Birley (Chairman, Headmaster's Conference, Eton College), 12 October 1957; letter, R.W. Chapman, 14 October 1957; letter, Henrietta Bower, 15 October 1957; letter in reply, Hewlett Johnson, 17 October 1957.

[132] *The Times*. Letter, H.J. Wickenden, 14 October 1957.

to be extremely cautious in any statement that you now make to the Press'.[133]
In particular:

> Say as little as you can, short of losing their good will, and nothing at all I think
> on the relations between the University and the engineers.

A public connection between the satellite and the radio telescope had been
constructed, a link that had been foregrounded by earlier press conferences.
I discussed in Chapter Two how this newly forged connection was mobilised
with little immediate success within Whitehall and the Prime Minister's
Office.

THE POSITION OF THE ENGINEER

I have shown that throughout the period when the Radio Telescope was
under construction, and in particular as it neared completion in the years
after 1954, there existed disagreements between the Engineer and the
University. Many of these tensions were over issues of public accreditation.
For example, Husband objected to being pushed aside during the press
conferences. The rationale given by the DSIR was that his presence would
highlight the strong PAC criticisms which the conferences were designed to
deflect. In *The Inquisitive Giant* an engineering emphasis was encouraged by
the Foreign Office, so Husband was allowed a visible presence, and even
declared to be 'essential' and 'complementary' to the radio astronomers.
However, even under these sympathetic circumstances there was conflict
between engineer and astronomer over 'responsibility of design', which
translated into disputed 'credit where credit is due'. The harmony between
engineer and astronomer that the tracking of Sputnik was publicised to show,
hid in the private space behind the press line at Jodrell Bank a fierce argument
over 'possession' and 'control' of the instrument. In this section I present
more evidence to demonstrate a new tension in the role of the engineer, and
I link the demands for, and responses to, public accreditation to changing
modes of organisational authority within 'scientific' establishments.

The huge, heavy structure of the radio telescope required a delicate and
highly accurate mechanism to direct and guide it. This control mechanism
utilised feedback: the system directed the telescope, and this position was
fed back, along with attendant errors, to be recomputed. Like other
subsystems of the telescope, this electrical servomechanism grew from war-
time developments: 'it was Professor Blackett, who, as an expert on naval
gunnery control, put [Husband] in touch with the Admiralty Research

---

[133] JBA CS7/41/3. Letter, Mansfield Cooper to Lovell, 23 October 1957.

Establishment at Teddington'.[134] The control system of the telescope was 'based on apparatus which had already been developed for the automatic training of guns'. J.G. Davies was appointed to the Jodrell Bank scientific staff to adapt this basic system to direct the Radio Telescope, working closely with Herman Lindars of Dunford and Elliott Ltd who were awarded the control contract and who 'produced the practical design of the electrical and mechanical control mechanism, based on earlier gunnery control and Dr Davies' calculations'. A prototype 'computor' [sic] with an accuracy of 4 minutes of arc was tested at Jodrell Bank in 1955.[135]

Complaining of the 'possessive and copyright...attitude which Husband takes over the radio telescope', Lovell wrote to the University Bursar in April 1956 advising that:

> This is entirely an original computing system developed at Jodrell Bank by J.G. Davies...I think it is important that the University should protect itself over this device since there is widespread interest in the computor for control of other radio telescopes, and other similar systems.[136]

However, this dispute of public accreditation stemmed from a deeper conflict over responsibility and authority within the organisation of Jodrell Bank. At a Site Committee meeting in October, Husband stated that the error in the positioning of the telescope may be +/- 2", double that given in the original specification.[137] Lovell 'expressed concern', and wrote to the Bursar:

> the manner in which Husband is now evading these scientific issues with me is causing me anxiety. I have a scientific responsibility for the design of the telescope which I can no longer maintain unless the present position is immediately rectified.[138]

Husband, confident in the engineering abilities of Brush (who were building the driving system that produced the feedback signal) reassured Lovell that the one minute of arc accuracy was still attainable.[139] Lovell was not satisfied and demanded a direct meeting, circumventing Husband, to discuss accuracy.[140]

---

[134] PRO INF 12 665. Letter, Husband to Mayne, 25 March 1955.
[135] JBA CS7/36/5. Minutes of meeting, enclosed with letter, MVP to Rainford, 28 June 1956.
[136] JBA CS7/35/5. Letter, Lovell to Rainford, 6 April 1956. In particular 'approaches for the purchase of duplicate computors have already been made by the Americans'.
[137] JBA CS7/36/5. Letter, Lovell to Husband, 16 October 1956.
[138] JBA CS7/36/5. Letter, Lovell to Rainford, 16 October 1956.
[139] JBA CS7/36/5. Letter, Husband to Lovell, 20 October 1956.
[140] JBA CS7/36/5. Letter, Lovell to Rainford, 23 October 1956.

As the completion of the telescope drew near the conflict over responsibility for the instrument grew more intense. It was necessary to appoint and train four 'controllers' who would operate the control system within the nerve centre of the telescope: the 'Control Room'. However it was by no means clear how these new staff would fit in to the organisational structure of Jodrell Bank. Husband had a very definite view: there should be 'a single person' who would be *in charge of the telescope'*, involving all issues of 'maintenance and operation' of the instrument.[141] Husband drew an analogy:

> The telescope will be just about as difficult to look after as an airliner, and it should have at all times an acting captain, and certainly no divided responsibility between the control room and the main moving parts of the instrument.

Lovell replied with 'an appropriate family tree'[142]: headed by the nine senior members of the scientific staff who were named as 'supervisors'[143]; under them were the four controllers[144], and the seven on-site maintenance engineers.[145] The radio astronomer had brushed aside the suggestion of a senior engineer 'in charge of the telescope'.

Husband was not deterred, writing back with a description of a suitable applicant:

> My own feeling is that the type of man to be responsible for sailing and navigating the Telescope on any voyages which any of your scientists may order, might be an ex Navy or Merchant Marine Officer answerable only to yourself...A man of strong character accustomed to discipline and, above all things, working to rule should be in physical charge of the Telescope.[146]

Without such a man there 'would always be a grave danger with enthusiastic scientists who in order to complete an experiment might take some risk, and such a temptation must be removed'. It was clear to the Engineer that the scale and complexity of the new Telescope meant that it had to be in charge of a man of 'discipline', a quality not possessed by the 'enthusiastic scientists'.

Husband made his opinions known to Sir Charles Renold, chair of the Site Committee and its Construction Sub-Committee. Husband stated that his

---

[141] JBA CS7/36/5. Letter, Husband to Lovell, 10 August 1957.

[142] JBA CS7/36/5. Letter, Lovell to Husband, 13 August 1957.

[143] The 'Supervisors' were A.C.B. Lovell, R. Hanbury Brown, J.G. Davies, R.C. Jennison, S. Evans, R.D. Davies, C. Hazard, M.I. Large, and H.P. Palmer.

[144] Foulkes, Martin, Gibbs and Prior.

[145] Headed by A.W. Smith, the engineers were Dale, Dale, Isherwood, Harvey, Lacey, and Evered.

[146] JBA CS7/36/5. Letter, Husband to Lovell, 15 August 1957.

company's experience with the High Altitude Testing Plant at Burnley and British Iron and Steel Research Association's Sheffield Laboratories, places where 'in both cases expensive and *potentially dangerous* machinery of a type where no previous operating experience existed', demanded that 'the Radio Telescope requires a senior engineering officer' in charge control, maintenance and safety.[147]   This senior engineer would relieve 'Professor Lovell...of the necessity of taking purely engineering or financial decisions concerning the running and maintenance of the Telescope'. Husband informed Renold that this 'arrangement' was 'essential where large and complex engineering projects are used in the service of experimental scientists'.

However much Husband appealed to the laboratories at Burnley or Sheffield, it was by no means obvious that the arrangement was 'essential' because the organisation of large-scale science within British universities had not yet been settled, and was up for negotiation and argument. Lovell was furious, writing to the Vice-Chancellor that Husband's letter was 'an outrageous and intolerable document'.[148] He attempted to assert the university character of Jodrell Bank:

> I cannot allow my position or organisation to be discussed in this way by *outsiders*. This further *interference* by Husband in the *private* affairs of University organisation I must regard as personally insulting...I can say, straightaway, that the imposition of any organisation along the lines suggested by Husband would lead to my immediate resignation.[149]

This passage contains strong moral and spatial rhetoric: Lovell attempted to claim that Husband was an 'outsider' who must therefore not be allowed to 'interfere' with the organisation of Jodrell Bank. Such interference would be 'meddling with the basic tenets of University freedom'. The Vice-Chancellor contacted Renold, forwarding Lovell's complaint, and expressing his own 'very deep concern'.[150] The University viewed Husband's move as motivated by vested interest: 'none of us would ever have embarked on the building of the Telescope had we thought that in the end its existence was to be perpetuated *regardless* of the requirements of the Scientific programme'.

This exchange occured in the first weeks after Sputnik, and backs up my claim that disputes over possession and control lay behind the public proclamations of harmony between astronomer and engineer.

These disputes continued into 1958, centring on the date of transfer of the telescope from Husband & Co to the University, and the training of controllers. At times Lovell had to 'issue orders that all University staff must

---

[147] JBA CS7/36/5. Letter, Husband to Renold, 8 October 1957.
[148] JBA CS7/36/5. Letter, Lovell to Mansfield Cooper (VC), 16 October 1957.
[149] My emphasis.
[150] JBA CS7/36/5. Letter, Mansfield Cooper to Lovell, 17 October 1957.

be out of the control room'.[151] Husband, by mid January, would declare J.G. Davies only 'competent to make simple movements' controlling the Telescope[152]; even by April he considered that the scientist had 'not a very delicate touch on the hand controls - quite possibly because his brain is working ahead of his fingers'.[153] Husband refused to facilitate scientific work with the telescope (which always needed, until controllers were trained, a member of Husband's staff present): 'we want to help Lovell to use the telescope as much as possible, but until a full-time manager is appointed I sincerely hope he will limit his calls on us to a minimum'.[154]

In an attempt to break the deadlock Lovell wrote to the Professor of Engineering at Manchester University, J.A.L. Matheson (a member of the Site Committee). Matheson's opinion was that 'Husband's present tactics are...presumably connected with his jockeying for position in the political and financial mess that now bedevils us'.[155] He thought that Husband was aiming at an organisation structured into:

(i) an engineering team responsible for, and gradually building up a body of experience about, the structural mechanical and electrical mechanics of the instrument, and (ii) a team of radio-astronomers *using* the instrument for research.

Husband's 'secretiveness' stemmed, in Matheson's view, 'partly from the fact that (i) [had]...not been properly constituted' yet; and Husband was 'undoubtedly genuinely concerned for the future safe operation of the instrument and is...using the present impasse about hand-over to try and force the University to lay on the organisation that he believes to be necessary'.[156]

The stalemate could only be broken by an outside authority. With the approval of both the Vice-Chancellor and the DSIR, C. Scruton of the National Physical Laboratory was appointed to look into arrangements for the operation and maintenance of the radio telescope. Scruton, like Husband, had to appeal to analogous circumstances at non-University sites, and he looked into procedures at RAE Bedford and at Harwell, where there were 'similar problems of supervision of scientific equipment of considerable

---

[151] JBA CS7/36/5. Letter, Lovell to Rainford, 18 November 1957. This happened whenever the engineers said that 'tuning-up operations' were necessary.

[152] JBA CS7/39/1. Letter, Husband to Lovell, 15 January 1958.

[153] JBA CS7/39/1. Letter, Husband to Lovell, 16 April 1958.

[154] JBA CS7/39/1. Letter, Husband to Rainford, January 1958.

[155] JBA CS7/39/1. Letter, Matheson to Lovell, 22 January 1957 [in fact 1958]

[156] The engineer Matheson thought that Husband's 'hint ...that I should play a part in the permanent organisation...[to be] in line with the above diagnosis'.

engineering complexity'.[157] His conclusions on 'a suitable "hierarchy" of staff' was that *'The Director* of the Jodrell Bank Experimental Station shall be responsible to the University for the safety and maintenance of the telescope', but also that *'a Resident Engineer* shall be appointed...to whom the Director can delegate responsibility for the organisation of the operational and maintenance services'.

Scruton had essentially backed Husband's demands for a senior engineering post at Jodrell Bank. Lovell was unhappy but admitted defeat, as he complained to the Bursar: 'I think it is a pity that the University is being forced into this appointment which...I consider to be quite unnecessary'.[158] In revealing words Lovell thought that this was 'a serious *disturbance* in the workings of the technical staff at Jodrell Bank' and that 'it would be impossible to *infiltrate* a "resident engineer" who would be responsible for exercising *authority* over my technical staff including the telescope and other equipment on the station'.[159] Although Lovell admitted he might be forced into appointing a senior engineer, the inferior status of the engineer must be underlined: 'I am not...prepared to agree with the "free" kind of relationship suggested'.

An experienced ex-serviceman, Commander R.F. Tolson, was indeed appointed as Resident Engineer, managing engineering and control staff at Jodrell Bank. At least two of the Controllers also had both military and engineering experience.[160]

I have shown that there existed tension in the role of the engineer at Jodrell Bank. In the University's opinion Husband was motivated to assert his authority within Jodrell Bank by self-interest. This, strictly speaking, is unsustainable since Husband was only ever the consulting engineer for the telescope project, and therefore had, himself, no permanent position. However, the point can be productively broadened along two lines.

First, Matheson's diagnosis that Husband aimed to build up an engineering team at Jodrell Bank provides an insight: the experience accumulated would be applicable in Husband & Co's future projects. The engineering company moved on, in the early 1960s, to design lucrative large dishes both at Jodrell Bank, and for the British government at Goonhilly.

---

[157] JBA CS7/39/1. Scruton, *'The Manchester University Radio Telescope.* An enquiry into the arrangements for its operation and maintenance', 5 February 1958.

[158] JBA CS7/39/1. Letter, Lovell to Rainford, 19 February 1958.

[159] My emphasis.

[160] JBA CS7/39/1. Memorandum, 'The University of Manchester. Radio Telescope. Report on the appointment of Controllers', 1958. Mr Foulkes was ex-Royal Signals Corps and Post Office Engineering Department. Mr Gibbs served in the navy for nine and a half years on board HMS Ganges and the Admiralty Whitehall Wireless Station, as well as the BBC.

Second, as I argued in Chapter One, the post-war years were highlighted by scientific projects of greatly increased scale and complexity. As early as 1949 a meeting of the Board of the Faculty of Science of Manchester University had noted that:

> Certain pieces of special apparatus are now coming into use in the scientific laboratories of this country, for the use of which the services of highly skilled technical research assistants are essential ...Many of these are very expensive...[161]

The Board had in mind, in this case, UV, IR and mass spectrometers, ultra-centrifuges, electron microscopes and 'the electronic computing machine'. The point is that even these instruments demanded a permanent role for technicians and engineers at research assistant level. With the complex, large scale Radio Telescope these pressures were reinforced. Husband, as head of the design and engineering team, had made a substantial commitment (in terms of all resources) to the project: his and his employees' time and his company's money and experience, both at the expense of other possible projects. Now, at CERN and later 'big science' establishments engineers and instrument builders had a *permanent position* within the organisation, and were also *visibly accredited*. At Jodrell Bank, as I showed in the discussion above, there was no predecessor on which to model large scale university-based research: it had to be negotiated.

This analysis explains the two features of the actions of the engineer at Jodrell Bank that I have discussed throughout this chapter. First, since Husband was not visibly accredited at the press conferences, and not accredited enough, in his opinion, in *The Inquisitive Giant*, the analysis accounts for his persistance in claiming 'due credit' in the public realm. Second, the analysis accounts for Husband's challenge to Lovell's internal authority within Jodrell Bank. As Husband argued (although often couched in terms of 'dangerous equipment' and the need for 'discipline'), the scale and complexity of the telescope required a permanent authoritative position for a senior engineer.

What makes these events especially interesting is the attempted mobilisation of barriers and boundaries by the University in response to this threat to their authority. These mobilisations were linked to the construction of the authority of Lovell both within Jodrell Bank's organisation and outside, as the public figure identified with the instrument. For all his persistence in claiming his portion of the prestige from the Great Public Spectacle, Husband was effectively effaced by the insistence of the DSIR and the University that, because of PAC criticisms, his voice should not be primary at press conferences. The outcome was that the radio astronomer, Lovell, became *synonymous* with the prestige of the Radio Telescope.

---

[161] JBA UNI/10/1. Minutes of the Board of Faculty of Science, 8 November 1949. See also Chapter Two.

A CLEAR MESSAGE...: AUTHORITY AND
THE REITH LECTURES

The BBC's annual Reith lectures were invitations to a person of authority 'to undertake some study or original research on a given subject and to give listeners the results in a series of broadcasts'.[162] They had begun in 1948 with Bertrand Russell speaking on 'Authority and the Individual'. The following lectures were on similarly ponderable and serious subject matter, often on international relations: Robert Birley on Britain in Europe (1949), Cyril Radcliffe on the problems of power (1951), Arnold Toynbee on 'The World and the West' (1952), Sir Oliver Franks on Britain in world affairs (1954), and George Frost Kennan on 'Russia, the Atom and the West' (1957). However, in the topography of post-war intellectual culture that the Reith lectures represented, science also figured strongly: J.Z. Young on doubt and certainty in science (1951), J. Robert Oppenheimer on 'Science and the Common Understanding' (1953), and Edward Appleton on 'Science and the Nation' (1956). Indeed, only Nicklaus Pevsner talking on 'Englishness in Art' in 1955 touched neither on politics nor on science. It was therefore slightly surprising that Lovell should complain to Appleton, after congratulating him for being offered the lectures, that he could 'think of no better choice to rectify the rather dim deal which science has been given...so far'.[163] There were two themes that ran through the Reith lectures during the 1950s. Firstly, 'authority': this was both invested in the Reith lecturer through the eminence of the BBC platform, and also formed the subject of several of the talks (Russell, Young). The second theme was 'the position of post-war Britain': again two-sided as the talks were often presented as an analysis of Britain, but also used the discourses of nationalism.

These rhetorical resources were available to Lovell when in early 1958 the BBC offered him the position of Reith lecturer for the following Autumn. In *Authority and the Individual*, Bertrand Russell had summarised that 'our present predicament is due more than anything else to the fact that we have learnt to understand and control to a terrifying extent the forces of nature outside us, but not those that are embodied in ourselves'.[164] In *The Individual and the Universe*, Bernard Lovell, through claiming the authority of cosmic rhetoric, sought to support the construction of large dish telescopes, and control other embodied forces which lay outside Jodrell Bank. Cosmic authority was gained through a rhetoric of limits: questions (often existential) were framed that were presented as having answers located at the limits of

---

[162] Preface to Russell, B., 1949. *Authority and the Individual*, BBC Reith Lectures 1948, London: George Allen and Unwin.

[163] JBA CS7/39/4. Letter, Lovell to Appleton, 26 January 1956.

[164] Russell (1949), p. 125.

the universe, thereby bestowing authority on those who possessed the telescopic means to look. Thus, for example, Lovell spoke of a 'vast universe' and 'instruments [which] probe so far out into space and so far back in time':

> Today our telescopes are so powerful that they probably penetrate to the limits of the observable universe. We may therefore be near the limit of our scientific knowledge of the universe as regards its extent in time and space and the cosmological implications now in progress have assumed unparalleled significance.[165]

And again: at 'Jodrell Bank...we may now be in the process of probing the ultimate depths of space and time'.[166] The ability to be able to talk of events at great distance gave the centralised speaker an authoritative voice. Lovell deployed an analogous, but temporal effect in a historical reconstruction that took up the first three lectures (entitled 'Astronomy Breaks Free', 'The Origin of the Solar System' and 'The New Astronomy'). The account of theories of the development of the (nearby) solar system led linearly to satellites: Pioneer, the American satellite publicly tracked at Jodrell Bank in 1958, was 'a clear demonstration that man has already achieved sufficient technical ability to send his instruments into the vicinity of the moon'. By symmetry, 'The New Astronomy' told the linear story of the development of telescopes, passing through Herschel to the 'culmination of this line' of optical telescopes with Mount Palomar, after which came radio astronomy:

> The urge to build big radio telescopes is the same as the driving force behind the construction of large optical telescopes, namely the desire to penetrate far into space.[167]

The intersection between the study of 'far into space' and the historical lineage of telescopes lay at Jodrell Bank. Lovell, who (as the DSIR publicity officer had said) was the telescope as the telescope was him, was placed in a unique, and hence privileged, position.[168] In the following lecture 'Astronomy and the State', this authority was exercised. The format was

---

[165] Lovell, A.C.B., 1959. *The Individual and the Universe*, BBC Reith Lectures 1958, London: Oxford University Press, pp. 2-3.

[166] Lovell (1959), p. 55.

[167] Lovell (1959), p. 41.

[168] This constructed sense of 'uniqueness' was heightened by such comments as 'when I think of the enormous scientific and technological problems which had to be solved I still stand in awe when I reflect that *at this moment* at least four objects launched by man are relentlessly circling the earth' (my emphasis). Lovell (1959), p. 40.

again historical (whilst also being biographical): with Galileo and Newton 'the practical life of the astronomer became more and more involved in the striving to obtain better instruments for observing the heavens'.[169] This story of early, and partially British, success was one of 'individual initiative and private enterprise'. However, 'private benefactions' paid for a 'succession of telescopes of ever-increasing size by which American astronomers have captured the initiative in astronomical research'. To Lovell it was 'a mortifying thought that the largest telescope in Great Britain today is considerably smaller than the telescope which Herschel built'. But this national shame of 'the steady decay of British influence in astronomy' had 'been arrested by remarkable developments in the technical field...radio astronomy', on which 'Britain has spent over a million pounds during the last few years'. Lovell was 'filled with dismay' since this temporary advantage might be lost as both Americans and Russians now 'pursued [radio astronomy] with such vigour that they seem likely to establish precedence over our own efforts within a few years'. So 'why are the Great Powers willing to spend?'. Lovell answered:

> the technical devices which form the basis of the present economic and cultural strength of the Great Powers can be traced back within a few generations to fundamental scientific investigation which were carried out in the abstract, supported without thought of direct practical benefit.[170]

Lovell used satellite rhetoric to enforce this point, portraying Sputnik as a 'dramatic answer' to why Great Powers spent money on fundamental research. The link between satellites and radio astronomy had been publicly forged, and was reinforced throughout the lectures.[171] Lovell could consequently claim that although it was 'not part of my daily job to seek any possible practical outcome of my work' and that 'the large sums of money which have been given for radio astronomy in this country were invested in faith for the free investigation of the universe', it would within a 'few generations' lead not only to 'practical benefit', but even (in the days imperialist decay) to the recapturing of 'Great Power' status. Otherwise, and here the status of Britain was conflated with that of the West:

> Unless the West overcomes its present parsimonious attitude to science and

---

[169] Lovell (1959), p. 56.

[170] Lovell (1959), pp. 66-67.

[171] For example the lecture annotation states: 'At this point in his broadcast Professor Lovell introduced a recording' of the American Pioneer probe, and a few minutes later of 'a recording to prove to you that our voices transmitted by radio to the moon and back remained perfectly intelligible'. This latter was a 'free gift of the radio astronomer, to all the commercial and military organisations who will no doubt use it in the future'.

technology, then the relative quality of our civilisation will decline, and our influence will pass to other peoples.[172]

However, if satellites were to be used in an argument for the funding of radio astronomy, they had to be carefully managed. For example there was a division of scientists: of the pure, private and free 'brought up in the tradition of the peaceful isolation of the observatory dome under the starlit sky' who did not 'receive with enthusiasm these new developments...launched from the rocket range under the glare of publicity', and the 'others...happy to join in the initiation of this new era of observation which would be impossible but for the political and military divisions of the world'. The division was managed by strategies of expulsion throughout the lectures, delineating good astronomical practice by reference to all that it should not be. For example Russian cosmogony had strayed since 'philosophy has once more become part of scientific method'. Furthermore, science must be separated from military and commerce (the material benefits of pure science were, significantly, a 'free gift').

The rhetorical strategies of limits and of expulsion that grounded Lovell's authority also legitimated his discussion of cosmology. Cosmology in post-war Britain was characterised by a highly public debate between the iconoclastic Cambridge theoreticians supporting the steady state theory, and observational astronomers, specifically Ryle and the Mullard radio astronomers, supporting the big bang. This has been interpreted in terms of competition between groups in different institutional and social positions.[173] The post-war discussion of cosmology was carried out partially and necessarily in the popular forum, and that in order to be heard the discussant must be authoritative. For Lovell it was possession of the publicly-demonstrated telescope: 'the air is alive with new hope and expectancy, because our new instruments may be reaching out so far into space that we may soon be able to speak with more confidence'.[174] The telescope would be the unproblematic judge of the steady state theory: 'in the foreseeable future man will produce experimental tests which will either substantiate or destroy this picture'; and again: 'the great radio telescopes will give us the answer we require'.

The Reith Lectures were a manifesto for the funding of radio telescopes. The resources needed to construct and maintain the Jodrell Bank research establishment had initially been secured through the private machinery of

---

[172] Lovell (1959), p. 73.
[173] Martin, B., 1976. 'The origins, development and capitulation of steady-state cosmology: a sociological study of authority and conflict in science', MSc thesis, University of Manchester.
[174] Lovell (1959), p. 75.

government departments and scientific societies. When these mechanisms did not support radio astronomy to the desired degree, Lovell had turned to the public forum: the film, the press conference and the Reith Lectures. In part a public discourse of astronomy pre-existed, but it also had to be constituted by a series of strategies tailored to fit the specific requirements of Lovell. This discourse was therefore broad: the targeted message of telescope funding was contained within a wider broadcast. As such this message of the Reith Lectures could be resisted by the civil servants and scientific peer groups that Lovell had hoped to influence. Furthermore, to communicate through public lectures the discourse had to be partially shared with its audience. Lovell tried to communicate through the public, whilst holding them at arm's length:

> The main concern of the astronomer is with highly abstract and remote topics. Some of this work can still be pursued by the astronomers working in isolation from the daily turmoil of existence. But we are moving into a new epoch in which even the study of remote parts of the universe demand a close partnership between astronomer and the State.[175]

This was certainly an attempt to gain funds through association with national security, but it also contains a plea for seclusion from local disturbance: 'in isolation from the daily turmoil'. However, since the astronomers were forced to talk through the popular discourse of astronomy, their interpretations and actions could be contested by the very groups of 'visitors' and 'trespassers' that they sought to simultaneously address and distance.

...AND INTERFERENCE: PUBLIC ACTIONS AND THE ODD LETTERS

Interest in the activities at Jodrell Bank came from diverse sources, and the DSIR's set of six categories from elite visiting astronomer to the 'general public' both acknowledged and exploited this. The negotiations between promoters of radio astronomy and groups such as film makers have already been analyzed above, but the final conglomerate category of the public remains silent. However, by symmetrically examining correspondence it is possible to reconstruct and reanimate this popular interest.

Many incoming letters were benign, for example radio listeners thanking scientists for interesting talks they had heard. Professional astronomy intersected here with amateur astronomy. Amateurs were locally organised: almost all cities and major towns could boast regular meetings, and

---

[175] Lovell (1959), p. 72.

membership (from a high base) seems to have grown in the post-war years.[176] Often societies possessed telescopes for members' use: for example, Manchester Astronomical Society shared the Godlee Observatory with a local college from 1903.[177] With guided on-site visits and lecturers from Jodrell Bank, the MAS provided an occasional interface between amateur and professional.[178] Letters from amateur astronomers are found amongst Jodrell Bank correspondence. Some, respecting the authority of the professional astronomer, wrote asking for the explanation of observations they had made, or about the operation of radio telescopes. The latter interest was shared by radio hams, another network of science-orientated hobbyists.

While amateurs' letters were answered (at least before 1957), other letters also asking for the explanation of observations (or offering conclusions on the receipt of a reply[179]) were not.[180] Lovell, metonymically identified with Jodrell Bank, received a huge volume of correspondence, particularly with the publicised tracking of Russian and American satellites and after the Reith Lectures in 1958. The unanswered communications were labelled and filed as 'Odd letters'. Several characteristics of these letters can be noted: they were extremely diverse in subject matter and form and they came from highly distributed sources. All, with one notable exception, were from non-scientists.[181] Many of them challenged the authority of the Reith lectures, for example:

> I listened, with great interest to your lecture last night. However it was disappointing to hear you seeming to encourage these futile experiments for so-called "Space Travel"...[182]

---

[176] For example the British Astronomical Association, which had national and semi-professional aspirations, claimed a doubling of membership from its interwar target of 1,000 by 1948. See Kelly, H.L., 1948. *The History of the British Astronomical Association: the First Fifty Years*, A Historical Section Memoir.

[177] UMIST, 1992. *The History of Manchester Astronomical Society. The First Hundred Years*, Manchester: UMIST AVPU.

[178] Only very rarely and only in the early years, for example with J.P.M. Prentice of the BAA, were amateur astronomers a significant component of Jodrell Bank research.

[179] Occasionally also a personal visit by a member of the Jodrell Bank staff, or money.

[180] A standard reply was composed, acknowledging the letter and thanking the sender for the 'information which it contained', but regretting that the 'number of letters...received' prevented an answer. CS7/72/4.

[181] In the sense of not being attached to an academic, industrial or government institution as a scientist. The notable exception was Professor Joseph Rotblat inviting Lovell to answer a Pugwash Committee questionnaire. CS7/49/1. Letter, Rotblat to Lovell, 11 June 1959.

[182] JBA CS7/49/1. Letter, Stoddard to Lovell, 10 November 1958.

Others wrote about unexplained acoustic recordings, ultra-violet stars, 'new atomic construction theory', and rocket designs. A few correspondents were not discouraged by the lack of response. H.W. Poole wrote after the Reith lectures setting forth some discoveries 'at least as important as those of Kepler', and continued a few months later exclaiming that

> Our astronomers do not understand sunspots. They are not uprushes of expanding - and so cooled gas. On the contrary sunspots are the open ends of spiral movements of the solar material.[183]

The theories offered were not restricted to astronomy. One correspondent wrote about 'a method whereby all the sciences, material, social, economic and religious may be combined or unified into one "whole"'[184]

Not all letters reported new theories: the Reith lecturer also received astrological rebuttals and religious warnings.[185] A Fellow of the Federation of British Astrologers, amongst others, wrote defending the 'father of astronomy' against its murderous child.[186] Others prophesised the 'great and Dreadful Day of the Lord' brought on by scientific inventions[187], warned that the moon was the gateway to hell (the dangers of meddling with other worlds was a common theme[188]), or quoted scripture. The crash of the Luna 2 probe into the moon in September 1959, as tracked by the Radio Telescope, brought several denunciations, often conflating religious and anti-Soviet Cold War sentiments. Lovell's Reith argument (aimed at possible founders), that large radio telescopes could guarantee Britain a position of influence between the USA and USSR, was read by other listeners as evidence of unacceptable sympathy and concessions to the red menace: 'aiding and abetting the

---

[183] JBA CS7/49/1. Letter, Poole to Lovell, 28 January 1959.

[184] CS7/49/1. Letter, Rumball to Lovell, 30 November 1958. '...I have communicated this fact to the USA and the USSR and to many other people but as yet I have only had one reply (from the Liberal Party)'.

[185] Although theory and religious themes were often expounded together. As a brief example, one title of a 'reply to Professor A.C. Lovell' was 'The Biochemistry of the Mind. The Primordial Substance of Divine Thought in the Psycho-centric Conception of Man'.

[186] CS7/49/1. Mitchell to Lovell, 11 November 1958.

[187] 'Forgive this long letter; but I write to you; one of the brainier Scientists – in the hope you can use your vast knowledge to curb the activities of these lunatics "Scientists-so-called" who seem Hell-bent for total destruction of this planet!'. CS7/49/1.

[188] 'Before "playing fast and loose" with the Planet venus, there are two books I think you should read :- "WORLDS IN COLLISION" and "AGES IN CHAOS"'CS7/49/1. Letter, Bevis to Lovell, 11 November 1959. The books in question, by Immanuel Velikovsky, sold well in the late 1950s and 1960s.

"Commies"'.[189]
Spiritualist communication with the dead, or communion with 'higher intelligences', gave one regular correspondent direct observations of other planets (a private alternative to the possession of large telescopes as a means of legitimating cosmological knowledge):

> Your Television Programme on Wed. was attended by me together with Ashtar Sheran, chief of the IFO Fleet and Taonitas Commander of the Jupiter Fleet. The latter's judgement was: "I liked the man, but can you not inform him with exemplary brevity that nobody can prove how God has created the world, least of all those who have not even a correct picture of the nearest planets?"[190]

Revelatory or visionary communications were not uncommon in the 'odd letter' responses to Jodrell Bank. Occasionally, for example with a report on inhabitants of the moon who lived in 'three houses...extremely large and set together shaped in a way similar to the "dome" shaped building that covered...the Exhibition', the correspondents drew on other post-war spectacles of science.[191]

The textual challenges to interpretation and authority were sometimes translated into action.[192] For example in February 1958, a few months after the telescope's first movements and its association with the Russian satellite Sputnik, Husband wrote to Rainford requesting that 'an investigation' be made with regard to a 'practical joke':

> A student or students from Keele College planted a very large dummy Russian bomb or satellite on the telescope turn-table. It contained a woolly dog addressed to Professor Lovell and was not discovered until the telescope had rotated far enough to give a clear view from the Control Room.[193]

Like the abduction of the Stone of Scone from Westminster Abbey eight years before, with which this installation of a woolly version of Sputnik II's Laika has resonances, albeit in a different arena, the carnivalesque was a popular response to authority. The association of the telescope with satellites,

[189] CS7/49/1. Letter, unsigned to Lovell, 18 September 1959.
[190] CS7/49/1. Letter, Hohenner-Parker to Lovell, 26 February 1959.
[191] CS7/50/1. Letter, Kean to Lovell, 26 May 1962.
[192] These occasions support Cooter and Pumfrey's plea that 'a shift of focus is necessary if we are to recapture science in popular culture...away from texts and towards a greater plurality of signifiers of scientific activity'. Cooter and Pumfrey (1994), p. 255. This can be seen as part of a new attention to 'symbolic actions' in cultural history. See Hunt, L. 1989. 'History, culture, and text', in Hunt, L. 1989 (ed.), *The New Cultural History*, Berkeley: University of California Press.
[193] JBA CS7/31/4. Letter, Husband to Rainford, 22 February 1958.

a resource used by the astronomers to pursue funds, had been creatively taken up within certain groups outside, and could not be completely controlled.

Unanswered, categorised as 'odd', and filed separately from other correspondence this collection initially strikes the historian as diverse and dispersed offerings. However the categorisation which labelled them (and excluded them) as miscellaneous, or other, was crucial in ordering both visitors and correspondence. The 'oddness' was an essential *product* of the *organisation* of Jodrell Bank as a spectacle. They were also the necessary reverse of the centralised and authoritative broadcast of the Reith Lectures. The 'odd' letters illustrate again the theme of the problematic constitution and management of authority that runs through this chapter. The authors of the 'odd' letters were responding as much to the mystic ambiguities of cosmological discourse (for example, 'the origin of the universe' and 'all of time and space was originally concentrated in a super-dense primeval atom') as to the authority embodied in the Reith lecturer.

DISCUSSION: POSITION

In his Reith Lectures of 1958 Lovell spoke from a position that was the outcome of a decade of organisational growth, and accumulation of prestige and credit. His position of authority had been challenged in their different ways by engineers and the public. I have discussed these processes and conflicts at length in this chapter, and in this concluding section I wish to analyse their intersection with spatial management.

The Festival of Britain in 1951 had sought to dispel the gloom of austerity with the progressive and rational: science displayed in the Dome of Discovery the possibilities of a new planned nation. The DSIR, a small government department worried about its position with respect to the growing scientific responsibilities of rival departments, were looking during this period for a prestigious civil project. The proposal from Manchester University scientists, of good reputation in Whitehall as contributors to the war effort, to build a 'giant radio telescope' filled this niche. I have shown in this chapter how the DSIR, through print and film, promoted this project as their 'great public spectacle': an object of considerable public prestige.

I have also shown that this construction had two consequences: first that the prestige discharged back into matters of public accreditation; second that the public interest in the telescope, and their interpretation of it, had to be managed. These consequences found expression spatially.

In his organisation of the Great Public Spectacle, Hingston of the DSIR expanded a structure that he found in operation at the Californian observatories at Mount Palomar and Mount Wilson. This structure spatially separated the 'public' from the 'scientific' spaces: simultaneously allowing guidance of interpretation and marking off the scientific as a privileged and private site. With this organisational structure in place two important strategies were possible. First, suitably packaged interpretations of the telescope could be passed out into the public realm: the written releases to the press as they gathered on press days on this line, the photographs which were captioned and 'canalized', and the showings of *The Inquisitive Giant* to visitors all illustrate this point. Second, the visitors could be held back, away from the private internal spaces of Jodrell Bank where they could observe but not disturb the observatory's organisation. Where the pressure on the boundary became too 'threatening' the visitors were repeatedly described in terms of 'intrusion', 'interference', 'danger' and 'disturbance'. These descriptions made up a powerful and spatialised discourse that held the elements of the public presenting a threat to organisational authority back from the spectacle of science: for example trespassers or errant journalists. In the following chapter I show that the discourse also provided means of authorising and interpreting the products of the telescope. However, this management of the public through Hingston's organisational structure was only possible because there existed a recognisable repertoire of spaces: distinctions between public and private spaces that could be mobilised to distinguish the scientific from the non-scientific, the inside from the outside. These distinctions were not only physical, such as fences and walls, but embodied: skills and 'positions' within the research station.

I have shown that the activities of the engineer Husband presented another threat to the organisation of work at Jodrell Bank. I related the tension in the role of the engineer to the change in scale and complexity of research that the telescope represented, and further linked this to Husband and Lovell's disputes over public accreditation and organisational authority. There is indirect evidence to show that the public effacement of the engineer (and the simultaneous prominence given to the scientist) stood in contrast to American Big Science projects. Comparing 1950s CERN to Brookhaven, Galison has written that: 'American physicists had an entirely different relation to engineers than their European counterparts...in particular, the Americans considered the joint physics-engineering projects of accelerator building to be a worthy collaboration'.[194]

At the height of these disputes, Lovell had written to the Vice-Chancellor that he could not allow his 'position' and 'organisation' to be challenged by an 'outsider' such as Husband: the engineer's actions amounted to 'interference'. The appointment of a senior engineer was an 'infiltration' of Lovell's organisation. This is precisely that same discursive move that had

---

[194] Galison (1992). This view is echoed by Hevly more generally: 'scientists brush away the trail they leave on their way to scientific facts, and it seems they often remove evidence of the engineering contribution', Hevly (1992).

been mobilised against the intrusive public: a threat to organisational authority countered by a spatialised discourse of interference. However in this case it did not succeed. The engineers were defined as 'insiders' by the skills they embodied: such as the ability to control the telescope: hence the conflict over the 'Control Room' and training and organisation of controllers, and hence Lovell's concern to demarcate proper 'scientific' policy over Sputnik. While they could display insider status, the engineers possessed measured authority within Jodrell Bank, and could pass across the barriers that kept the public at bay.

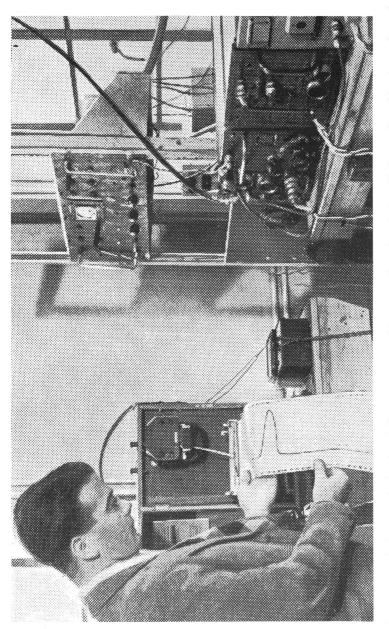

Figure 4.1. A posed photograph showing radio astronomer with a very clean inscription. Understanding this picture is at the heart of this book.

Source : Lovell, A.C.B., 1954a. 'The new radio telescope at Jodrell Bank' *Discovery* 15, p185.

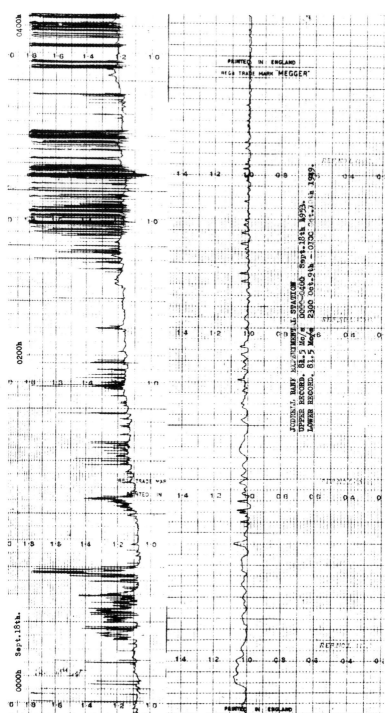

Figure 4.2. A 'before and after' illustration of the deleterious effects of radio interference, drawn up by the radio astronomers in their negotiations with govern-ment frequency bodies.
Source : PRO CAB 124 1773

CHAPTER 4

Clearing the Air (Waves): Interference and Frequency Allocation for Radio Astronomy

Radio astronomers at Jodrell Bank were faced with an interpretative problem (see Figure 4.1). A typical experiment on the reception of radio waves involved the following arrangement of apparatus: the signal received through the aerial (such as one placed at the focus of the 250 foot Radio Telescope, or in combination with other antennae) was amplified and compared to a known constant (a radio frequency noise generator). A pen-recorder then produced an inscription of the resultant signal: the output was therefore a pen-trace on a roll of paper. These inscriptions did not speak for themselves and required interpretation, but here is where the radio astronomer was presented with a fundamental dilemma: a 'spike' on the pen trace could either be interpreted as an indication of an astronomical object in the telescope's beam, or as a result of local interference. The acuteness of this dilemma depended on the particular experimental set-up. Aerials were frequently combined together as interferometers which mimicked the resolution of larger single dish telescopes. When aerials were placed at extremely large distances from each other, not only could resolution of astronomical objects comparable to optical telescopes be achieved, but also the instrument's in-built selection of similarly phased signals meant that local interference was somewhat negated as a source of interpretative trouble. However, this benefit could be wiped out by sufficiently powerful interference (see Figure 4.2). Thus, at Cambridge, which adopted interferometer arrays as their core experimental set-up, interference remained a severe problem: both as a disruptive problem, as I shall show in this chapter, and as an interpretative one, of which the pulsar 'discovery' in the 1960s is a startling example.[1]

The theory of the directional response of an aerial, or combination of aerials, was available to the radio astronomers of the 1950s through earlier

---

[1] Woolgar (1979). Edge and Mulkay (1976), pp. 228-230.

work by electrical engineers. The astronomers measured, and developed the theory of, these directional patterns.[2] A single dish gave a single 'beam' of sensitivity in the direction towards which it was pointed, whereas multiple aerial interferometers gave a more complex 'multi-beam' response, in which 'side-lobes' off the main direction could give an appreciable response. In neither case did the response entirely fall to zero in any direction.[3] It was this technical factor that could allow an interfering signal to merge with that from the astronomical object.

The astronomers' response to their output was, at one important level, a matter of skill: the accumulation of knowledge, often only expressible through manipulation of the electrical equipment with which they had experience, that allowed them to identify and 'read' the pen-recording traces. In several cases the expected and differing properties of interfering signal and astronomical radio source allowed 'filtering' circuits to automate these skills. For example, one method was to convolve a matrix of data with a 'suitably chosen function' to remove high-frequency fluctuations:

> There are many occasions in radio astronomy when it is necessary to carry out convolutions. One important use is in distinguishing signal from noise in the records. This is the mathematical equivalent of the observer drawing a pencil line through the noise ripple on his chart.[4]

However, as Woolgar (and the ethnomethodologists in their discussion of the discovery of a pulsar) have reminded us, the scientist's documents exist *before* the 'signal': only after the object is made to be a separate entity does it seem the other way around.[5] As emerges from the ongoing anxieties of the radio astronomers, the interpretative dilemma of interference was always present, even when minimised by automating strategies.

The discourse that interpreted pen-recordings separated the valued from the worthless: the astronomical radio source from the local signal. The valued trace underlay the data from which journal articles and symposium papers could be written, and, once embedded in explanatory text and approved by

---

[2] Jennison, R.C., 1966. *Introduction to Radio Astronomy*, London: Newnes.

[3] Hazard, C. and Walsh, D., 1959. 'An experimental investigation of the effects of confusion in a survey of localised radio sources', *Monthly Notices of the Royal Astronomical Society* 119, pp. 648-656.

[4] Haslam, Davies and Large (1962), p. 172.

[5] Woolgar, S., 1988. *Science: the Very Idea*, London: Tavistock, p68. Garfinkel, H., Lynch, M. and Livingston, E., 1981. 'The work of discovering science construed from materials from the optically discovered pulsar', *Philosophy of the Social Sciences* 11, pp. 131-158.

peers, be published. The worthless trace was privately discarded.[6]
Interference very rarely appeared in the published articles of the radio
astronomers. In the studies involving most sensitive measurement mention
was made of limitation by unrecognisable signals, for example the
'unidentified signals' of Hanbury Brown and Hazard.[7] However interference
was a problem for all radio astronomy measurements, even radar work.[8] If
strong enough the interference would obliterate a pen-recording of an
intensity measurement, if of the same order of intensity as the astronomical
signal then confusion and ambiguity was possible. Interference's rare
appearances in public print were usually methodological: to account for loss
of records[9], or constraints on observed frequencies.[10]

The interpreting discourse, drawn from electrical engineering, expressed
the trace in moral and spatial terms: 'interference' was an 'intrusion' and a
'disturbance', and should be 'excluded'.[11] In Chapter Three similar language
was used to counter contests of organisational authority at Jodrell Bank. In
Chapter Five I will discuss the public as identified by the radio astronomers
as an *embodied* source of interference. In many ways 'interference' can be
seen as relations that astronomers had with the outside world, in particular
the public, *translated* into, and from, radio astronomical language. In this,
and the following, chapter I examine the discourse of interference, in order
to uncover the relationships between authority, valuation and the spatial

---

[6] This valuation is taken over by commentators. Edge and Mulkay in *Astronomy Transformed* refer to interference only very occasionally: in the specialty's prehistory (Jansky was investigating "static and interfering noises", p. 10, also Reber's galactic work in 1937, p. 84), as part of lucky discovery accounts (for example with Hey's wartime discoveries, p12, with the identification of radio emissions from Jupiter, p. 226, and the Cavendish discovery of pulsars, pp. 228-230) or as a problem with a technical solution (p. 117). This is not a criticism of Edge and Mulkay, as the discourse stems the radio astronomers' own public valuation of their data that is iterated in their sociological interviews.

[7] Hanbury Brown, R. and Hazard, C., 1951a. 'Radio emission from the Andromeda Nebula', *Monthly Notices of the Royal Astronomical Society* 111, pp. 357-367. Also Chivers, H.J. and Wells, H.W., 1959. 'A new ionospheric phenomenon', *Nature* 183, p. 1178.

[8] Lovell, A.C.B. and Davies, J.G., July 1951. 'Radar tracks shooting stars', *Radio Electronics.* [9] Hanbury Brown, R., Palmer, H.P. and Thompson, A.R., 1954. 'Galactic radio sources of large angular diameters', *Nature* 173, pp. 945-946.

[10] Lamden, R.J. and Lovell, A.C.B., 'The low frequency specrum of the Cygnus (19N4A) and Cassiopeia (23N5A) radio sources', 1956. *Philosophical Magazine,* Series 8, 1, pp. 725-737.

[11] Although the metaphor and words came from electrical engineering (particularly ionospheric research), 'interference' held minor but importantly different meanings for the radio astronomers, especially in the context of relations with the public.

organisation of a spectacle of science, the major themes which I bring together in my conclusion.

Interference could be countered in two ways. First, the manipulative practices that I have outlined above were refined to identify and reduce its disturbing effect. For these skills to be effective considerable internal discipline, as I discuss in the next chapter, was necessary. The second strategy was for the astronomers to leave the observatory and change others' behaviour, to make a productive quiet space within Jodrell Bank.

In this chapter I examine a crucial part of this second strategy: the campaign to secure and 'protect' radio frequencies for use by radio astronomers. In parallel to their optical colleagues who required a dark sky, the radio astronomers wanted a 'quiet' site. Furthermore, astronomical objects appeared different at different frequencies (and hence energies): so they needed a set of interference-free frequencies on which to observe. The politics of frequency allocation can profitably be compared to the politics of funding that I discussed in Chapter Two. In both cases the radio astronomers had to strike alliances and compete to secure important resources in a framework that was defined by the machinery of government. However, whereas the radio astronomers had to make the case for their telescopes largely in competition with other scientific projects, in the case of radio frequencies they were in competition with far more powerful bodies, in particular the armed services and television.

I trace in this chapter the campaign for quiet and protected frequencies for radio astronomy through three levels: when radio astronomy was an outsider to the bureaucracy of allocation, its lobbying for admittance, and finally the mobilisation of international allies to ensure an undisturbed observatory. As radio astronomy became more institutionalised and permanent, the astronomers were able to organise and lobby for spectrum space. Radio astronomy was successfully recognised as a service with allocations in the Radio Regulations drawn up at Geneva in 1959. I will also show how the organisational politics of frequency allocation was inscribed back into the technology of radio telescopes.

THE NATIONAL AND INTERNATIONAL REGULATION OF RADIO

Commercial and institutional sites were rapidly found for the new 'wireless' technology that emerged at the end of the nineteenth century.[12] To begin with

---

[12] Aitken, H.G.J., 1976. *Syntony and Spark: the Origins of Radio*, New York: John Wiley and Sons, discusses the technological innovations of Hertz, Lodge and Marconi in detail. Headrick, D. R., 1991. *The Invisible Weapon: Telecommunications and International Politics 1851-1945*, London: Oxford University Press.

it was enthusiastically enlisted for maritime service, where it enabled all-weather ship-to-ship and ship-to-shore communication. The use of radio allowed merchant shipping to be move faster more safely and economically, their distress calls received, and contact kept with coastal stations. For navies, radio allowed the fast fleet battleships to be co-ordinated. Finally, radio telegraphy promised inter-continental communication both for governmental and private use, complementing and then displacing submarine telegraphy. Monopoly and congestion soon created a need for regulation. As one commentator has noted: it was 'only a few years after radio was first practically applied [that] an international conference was called in Berlin (1903)'.[13] The effective and unhindered use of radio was threatened by two factors. The prime motivation was that the Marconi Company's near monopoly be broken. The Company, which held key patents, had issued a directive that operators of Marconi equipment should refuse to respond to signals from non-Marconi sets, even distress calls.[14] The second factor, which became increasingly important, was inherent in the technology: in order that two sets could communicate they must have common technical standards, in particular the receiving circuit must be tuned to match the transmitter. The frequencies on which the communication was to take place had to be prearranged. A split emerged between the Marconi-supporting Great Britain and Italy and other countries who opposed Marconi's monopoly. A protocol was all that was agreed. However, the need for international agreement was strong, and the 1903 Protocol formed the basis of a Convention for an International Radiotelegraph Union and accompanying Radio Regulations, at the Berlin Radio Conference of 1906.

The International Radiotelegraph Union's Convention was closely modelled on that of the International Telegraph Union, a body set up in 1865 to regulate telegraphic communication. The Regulations directed the use of certain frequencies for certain services. 1000 kc/s and 500 kc/s were for public correspondence in the maritime service, below 168 kc/s for long distance communications by coast stations, and between 168 kc/s and 500 kc/s were for (non-public) military and naval stations.[15] Also, each administration (in most cases a governmental body) had to report to the Bureau of the ITU details on all stations[16] and enforce technical standards.

---

[13] Codding, G.A., 1952. *The International Telecommunications Union: an Experiment in International Cooperation,* Leiden: E.J. Brill, p. 81.

[14] A similar desire to break Marconi patents in America, due to worries that military interests were being compromised by allowing a European company such influence, led to the powerful Radio Corporation of America (RCA) to be set up. See: Lewis, P. and Booth, J., 1989. *The Invisible Medium: Public, Commercial and Community Radio,* London: Macmillan, p. 30.

[15] Codding (1952), p. 95.

[16] Including nationality, geographical location for coast stations, call letters, range, radio system used, wavelengths used, nature of service, and hours of operation.

The IRU held Radio Conferences at London (1912), Washington (1927) and, jointly with the International Telegraph Union, at Madrid (1932), where they merged to form the International Telecommunications Union (ITU). The radio spectrum was soon seen in terms of 'bands'. The size of bands was negotiated between physical, technological and political actors. The Conferences allocated and distributed of the spectrum bands to the various services. The extent of the spectrum allocated increased over the years: up to 1 Mc/s in 1912, 23 Mc/s in 1927, 200 Mc/s at the ITU Conference at Cairo in 1938, and 10,500 Mc/s at Atlantic City in 1947.[17] Their contested nature meant that frequency allocations were inscribed with their political contexts. The war dominated contexts of many of the Conferences,[18] the relative power of the military within the national administrations, and the typical development of radio technologies within military-government networks, meant a generous allocation of spectrum to the armed services.[19] The practical and bureaucratic difficulties in moving users from a frequency once they had invested equipment in its use gave an in-built 'conservative' resistance to later pressures to change.[20]

Once the ITU Conferences had divided the spectrum into bands and determined which services could use each band, each administration had the responsibility to assign individual frequencies within the band to stations. In the UK, the General Post Office (GPO), a government department, carried out the day-to-day civil work. A cabinet committee, called successively the Wireless Telegraphy Board and later the Radio Board dealt with 'communications problems' and directed the GPO's policy. Before the war the Radio Board was coexistent with the Imperial Communications Committee, and during and after the war with the Cabinet Frequency Committee (CFC). The CFC was the final arbiter of disputes and originated spectrum strategy. Its operational powers were devolved to the Admiralty-based British Joint Communications and Electronics Board (BJCEB) and thence to the BJCEB's Joint Frequency Planning Panel (JFPP). The GPO worked in close consultation with the JFPP and the Radio Board.

However, the actual process of frequency allocation was not as 'top-down'

---

[17] Levin, H.J., 1971. *The Invisible Resource: Use and Regulation of the Radio Spectrum*, Baltimore: Johns Hopkins Press, p. 19.

[18] London, Washington and Atlantic City in particular.

[19] The generous allocations to the armed services built on the early take up of radio by the navy. Within the UK military dominance was reflected in the adminstrative body in the interwar years being the Imperial Communications Committee of the influential Committee for Imperial Defence. Radar and navigation beacons provide striking examples of development of radio technology at government-military sites before the Second World War, communication satellites a good instance after.

[20] With a corollary that later services tended to use higher frequencies which only later technologies could exploit.

as the above description might suggest. The case of radio astronomy illustrates this. The radio spectrum had to accommodate more and more services, including amateurs, broadcasters, police, fire and local government services, private commercial radio, beacons for maritime and aeronautical navigation, and time signals. There was therefore competition for the use of radio frequencies. The GPO had to 'manage' the spectrum; it specified where transmissions could be made (this is easy for fixed stations but less so for mobile ones); if a frequency was shared, it limited the power of the transmissions, which, in effect, partitioned the country. Disputes that the GPO could not solve, for example if it did not have the security clearance to be able to judge the relative merits of each side, it passed upwards to the JFPP.

THE METAPHOR OF SPACE – THE SPECTRUM REIFIED

The radio frequency spectrum was and is spoken of as if it possessed an area. That is to say, actors used spatial metaphors. For instance, radio frequencies came in 'bands', different services had to be 'accommodated' or 'given room' in them, and if there was no room there might have to be a 'clearance'. The bands came in 'blocks', on which could be 'reservations' or even 'squatters'. In a particularly revealing example the armed services were said to 'occupy all the space' in a frequency band.[21] Why was this the case? The period during which such metaphors were used was coextensive with the regulation of the spectrum. Two separate factors can be noted. Firstly, radio transmitters did not transmit on a single frequency. There was always a degree of 'spread', which affected a range of frequencies. This might result in interference beween stations, which led to the second factor: the decision to 'manage' the spectrum. If the spectrum needed to be 'divided' and allocated then this process had to be institutionalised within a bureaucracy. The first factor necessitated the second, but the management may also be independent of technological constraint, for instance in allocating as yet unexploited frequencies. The use of spatial metaphors was therefore connected to the administrative process of frequency allocation: the work of the General Post Office, the Joint Frequency Planning Panel and the International Telecommunications Union. The radio spectrum was a space bureaucratically made and maintained at sites such as the GPO's Headquarters in Whitehall and the ITU's offices in Geneva.

There are two possible models to account for the genesis of this. First, that the radio spectrum was a politically important resource, and the government bodies were confronted with organising the continuous range of frequencies for a discrete set of favoured users. The language available to

---

[21] The above examples can be found in RCA 2622 Pt 1. Lovell, (1968), pp. 175-177, and Levin, passim.

describe electromagnetic radiation (the physicists' "spectrum" of "lines") was unsuitable, so the civil servants drew on a set of metaphors with clearly delineated and understood methods of discussing property: metaphors of land ownership and hence of boundaries and space. The second model turns this argument around: the processes of regulation, division and allocation of property and management of ownership itself produced spatial language. These processes produced spatial metaphor for land as for the radio spectrum.

The use of these spatial metaphors was not inevitable. Other alternatives were the 'highway' model, where frequencies were talked of as lines or routes of communication; the 'economic' model, where the spectrum was a 'resource' with 'stock and flow attributes'; and the 'engineers' model where there were 'stations' and 'circuits'. There was inevitably much mixing of metaphors. The dominant metaphor in a situation tied in with the context within which social groups worked with radio frequencies, and the context was dominated by the demands of bureaucratic management and administration. It is because the radio astronomers in this story had to pursue their aims through administrative channels that their negotiation of frequency allocation was also spatial. As will be seen, an outcome was that astronomers, in negotiating intangible frequency space, transformed[22] physical space.

RADIO FREQUENCIES AND THE NEW RADIO ASTRONOMY

During the second world war, radio frequency regulation continued as a component of the paper war effort: part of the bureaucratic organisation that held together personnel and military technology. However, the goals of regulation had changed. There were several factors at work here. First, armed service requirements were prioritised, and civil bands were appropriated. Innovative work, such as that carried out at the Telecommunications Research Establishment (TRE) at Great Malvern, was allocated portions of the spectrum for experimental use of frequency. Regulation was used to combat interference, the term here used to describe signals that disrupted military organisation.[23] Second, technical developments meant that research into radio

---

[22] In that there were recipocal effects between position and frequency the transform could be called a Fourier Transform.

[23] PRO AVIA 7 652. Letter, Ratcliffe to Under Secretary of State, Air Ministry (DCD), 20 May 1940. Ratcliffe, part of the establishment that was later to be moved to be TRE, wrote that 'inteference at Dunwich CHL Station which was considered as possibly due to enemy action was reported to us'. This instance, found to be 'caused by the first harmonic of the VHF transmitter of 17 Squadron', was resolved by a change of frequency allocation for the transmitter. Interference would be reported to the Director of Communications Development (DCD) at the Air Ministry or MAP. Frequency policy passed through the Wireless Telegraphy (WT) Board.

and radar technology was carried out at higher frequencies. The scale of this can be assessed from the extra frequency space that the first post-war conference, at Atlantic City in 1947, was required to allocate: 10-10,500,000 kc/s compared to 10-200,000 kc/s at Cairo in 1938.[24]

I argued in Chapter One that radio astronomy in Britain grew from the networks formed at war-time establishments such as TRE. The radar scientists who began the meteor astronomy programme operated on the frequencies available to their ex-military equipment. In the memorandum, 'Radio Astronomy at Jodrell Bank', Lovell described programmes on galactic noise, solar noise, meteors, the moon, aurorae and cosmic ray ionisation. In a further programme, 'A Proposal for a 250 foot Aperture Steerable Paraboloid for Use in Radio Astronomy',[25] Lovell added possible studies on 'echoes from the planets' and the 'gegenschein' to the list. The galactic noise and solar noise programmes would require licences and quiet frequencies for reception of radio waves. The meteor, lunar, aurora, planetary and gegenschein programmes would all require licences and quiet frequencies for both reception and transmission.

During these early years (1946-1950) of research at Jodrell Bank it seems apparent that the astronomers operated either on temporary three month licences from the Radio Branch of the Post Office Engineering Department[26] or pragmatically and illicitly operated where a quiet band could be found and was compatible with or desirable from their technology. In 1947 the problem was only dimly perceived: Jodrell Bank was an experiment of uncertain future. It could therefore use temporary licences or gaps in the congestion.

In 1948, however, interference from Manchester taxis created destruction and confusion in the inscriptions of meteors and galactic noise:

> in the galactic noise experiments, the interference appears as a deflection on the automatic pen record of much greater amplitude than the small sporadic variations being looked for. In the meteor studies, the interference...gives rise to a false 'echo'. In addition...there are numerous minor sources...which cause variations in the galactic noise records comparable with any true sporadic variations which may occur.[27]

There is evidence for interference between GCI, CHL and AI systems, see: PRO AVIA 7 652. Letter, W.B. Lewis to Chief Superintendent, RAE, 9 January 1941.

[24] Levin (1971), p. 241.

[25] PRO DSIR 2 497. Memorandum, 'A Proposal for a 250 foot Aperture Steerable Paraboloid for Use in Radio Astronomy', January 1950.

[26] JBA CS1/4/6. '10. Licences 1950-3'.

[27] PRO HO 255 174. Memorandum, 'Discussions with Dr Lovell and others at Jodrell Bank Experimental Station', 27 October 1948.

This disturbance proved so 'severe' that, with 'an extremely massive aerial' committed to the frequency in use, the astronomers sought official intervention.[28] To achieve this they went to the Post Office. The inquiry came as a surprise to the GPO: 'so far as this department is aware, no previous communication has been received from this experimental station, which appears to be run by Manchester University'.[29] Although concerned 'to know on whose advice an expensive array was constructed for use on a frequency used for land mobile services', the Post Office engineers considered the 'short-term problem' solvable by moving the taxis. However, a long-term solution to radio astronomy in the 20-200 Mc/s band would, in their estimation, require negotiation through the BJCEB and therefore with the armed services. Indeed 'a really long-term problem might demand consideration of whether the laboratory could not be better sited or the research be confined to the small hours of the morning'. Constructive sympathy from the Post Office was gained through the radio astronomers arguing that their work, despite being 'of a fundamental character', generated practical benefits: 'by-products...of direct interest to communications engineers'.[30] Post Office engineers visited Jodrell Bank and departed to write within Whitehall that 'we might be able to recommend portions of the frequency spectrum where the experiments can be carried out with the least risk of interference'[31], although 'the only really 100% satisfactory solution' would be 'to prevail upon the military of Ministry of Civil Aviation (MCA) to find these people 500 kc/s of spectrum space for the next few peaceful years'.[32]

Before helping the radio astronomers by moving the short-term problem of taxis and thereby 'accepting a serious limitation on the scope of 'business radio' frequency allocations'[33], the GPO engineers determined internally to ascertain the institutional importance of Jodrell Bank: 'to check the backing for this work at higher scientific level'.[34] This level was the Radio Noise Committee of the Royal Society, chaired by Ratcliffe, head of the Cavendish

---

[28] PRO HO 255 174, Letter, Lovell to Engineer-in-Chief (GPO Radio Branch), 5 October 1948.

[29] PRO HO 255 174. Notes between ED (W2) to OTD (Tp&RB), 7 October 1948.

[30] Ibid. Specifically: 'in certain bands galactic noise is several times greater than the nose inherent in a radio receiver and is in fact the predominant source of noise'; and investigating the possible connection between meteors and E-layer formation (used for high frequency long-distance communication).

[31] PRO HO 255 174. Memorandum of visit by Lillicrap (OTD, Tp&RB) to Jodrell Bank, 9 December 1948.

[32] PRO HO 255 174. Handwritten note.

[33] PRO HO 255 174. Memorandum by Horrox.

[34] PRO HO 255 174. Note, Creighton to Horrox, 24 March 1949.

radio group of which Cambridge radio astronomers were part. This Committee, whose role was to coordinate radio noise research, had no responsibility itself for frequency allocation. The Post Office informed it that the late-comers to the spectrum should have 'little hope of bands being reserved for noise measurement, even over restricted areas'.[35] A promise to find where interference was 'less' was 'quite well received but it was claimed nevertheless that an important new branch of science' was being 'severely handicapped by such frivolities as taxi-services'. It was decided that the case for 'the claims of pure research' had to be made through the DSIR.

STAGE ONE: OUTSIDERS SEEKING THE ALLOCATION OF FREQUENCIES

The civil (GPO) and military (BJCEB) authorities remained indifferent to the spectrum claims of the small-scale radio astronomy of the late 1940s and early 1950s, as the former wrote to the latter: 'we do not consider the frequency used for these measurements as having any kind of priority and any action to avoid interference would be without prejudice to the authorised services in the band'.[36] Lying outside of the bureaucracy of the spectrum, radio astronomy had no 'protection' from interference. The radio astronomers lacked a voice within Whitehall to argue their case.

A new beacon at Manchester Ringway airport, transmitting on 75 Mc/s, provided the immediate cause for action. It forced the closing down of a Jodrell Bank transmitter and aroused the suspicions of the Ministry of Civil Aviation, prompting Lovell to seek 'formal authority' for the use of radio frequencies. 'I am sure you will appreciate that the question of frequency allocation...is of fundamental importance to the future of the subject' wrote Lovell to the DSIR[37], the government department with the deepest investment in the success of Jodrell Bank. The frequencies required for transmission and reception were 36.6, 69, 71, 72 and 120 Mc/s. Lovell also presented a long list of frequencies for reception: '[a band in] 20-30, 30-40, 90-110, 150-160, 200-220 Mc/s and frequencies around 300, 400, etc, up to above 2000 Mc/s'. Lovell noted that, although these 'requirements might seem severe,...general clearance is only needed for a comparatively small radius around Jodrell Bank'. For frequencies above 27.5 Mc/s this 'comparatively small radius' was 50 miles. Such a clearance zone would also, of course, have to be

---

[35] Note by Lillicrap, 'Radio Noise Committee (DSIR)', to Creighton, Mumford, read also by Horrox and Abbot, 5 April 1949.

[36] RCA 2622 Pt 1. Letter, Lillicrap (for Engineer-in-Chief, GPO) to S/L Marks (for Secretary, BJCEB), 16 November 1949.

[37] JBA CS7/29/1. Letter, Lovell to Vernon, 11 March 1952.

applicable around Cambridge. Lovell concluded hoping that the DSIR would 'be able to enlist the sympathy of the Post Office authorities'. This the DSIR set about doing, with the result that the Post Office organised an exploratory meeting.

Both Cambridge and Manchester drew up lists of frequencies which they were either using or intending to use. These were discussed at a meeting on May 16 1952. Captain Booth and four other officials represented the GPO, with Martin Ryle of Cambridge and R. Hanbury Brown of Jodrell Bank attending. The frequencies recorded as being in use were:[38]

Table 4.1:   Frequencies in use at Cambridge and Jodrell Bank, 1952

Cambridge	Manchester	Use by Manchester
38±0.75 Mc/s	36.6±0.5 Mc/s	Meteor transmission and noise reception
81.5±1 Mc/s	69±0.5 Mc/s	Meteor transmission
164±2 Mc/s	71±0.5 Mc/s	Meteor transmission
250(about)±2 Mc/s	72±0.5 Mc/s	Meteor transmission
500(about)±2 Mc/s	73.5±0.5 Mc/s	Meteor transmission
1420-1405 Mc/s	74.5±0.5 Mc/s	Meteor transmission
	120 Mc/s	Meteor transmission and moon reception
	125 Mc/s	Noise reception
	158.5±1 Mc/s	Noise reception
	1420 Mc/s	Noise reception

The 1420 Mc/s hydrogen band was the only known emission line in the radio spectrum. Its frequency was the only one noted for radio astronomical priority at Atlantic City, and even then it was not exclusively allocated. Ryle stated that the wide band 1420-1405 was needed for 'detecting the doppler shifts in external galaxies', which would have cosmological (and hence prestigious) import. Ryle also noted that he was 'receiving aircraft transmissions...on 164 Mc/s' and was 'temporarily using 175 Mc/s'. Hanbury Brown registered interference 'on 36.6 Mc/s from some form of beacon, on 75 Mc/s from Ringway [Manchester airport], on 158.5 from Liverpool marine services [and] on 125 Mc/s from aircraft'. The meeting drew up a joint list of requested frequencies for reception:

---

[38] JBA CS7/29/1. Minutes of ad hoc meeting at Room 316, Armour House, 16 May 1952.

Table 4.2: Frequencies requested by Cambridge and Jodrell Bank

Frequency	Remarks
38±0.75 Mc/s	Manchester would prefer 36.6 Mc/s
81.5±1 Mc/s	
164±2 Mc/s	Manchester would support any frequency from 140-190 Mc/s provided it is clear of marine use at Liverpool
246.8±2 Mc/s	
400(about)±2 Mc/s	required by Manchester
500(about)±2 Mc/s	
A frequency between	required by Manchester
500-1420 Mc/s	
1420-1405 Mc/s	
3000(about) Mc/s	
9850 Mc/s	Proposed by Manchester tentatively

Futhermore, Manchester requested the following frequencies for transmission:

Table 4.3: Frequencies requested by Jodrell Bank for transmission

Frequency	Remarks
36.6 Mc/s	Could be 38 Mc/s in previous list
5 channels near 70 Mc/s,	GPO will investigate possibility
2 for use on big paraboloid	
120 Mc/s	GPO regard as impossible to get this allocation
240-300 Mc/s	Could be 246.8 Mc/s in previous list

Both the GPO and the radio astronomers recognised that the difficulty in obtaining a transmission licence was greater than to have a frequency cleared for reception, which could, if necessary, be shared with another intermittent user. Captain Booth 'undertook to discuss the proposed list of frequencies for radio astronomy with various agencies and to call another meeting'.

The DSIR attested to the prestigious national importance of radio astronomy, a view the GPO passed on to the Joint Frequency Planning Panel (JFPP) of the BJCEB:

> the Universities are about to embark on an extensive new programmes of work for which they are receiving assistance grants of between £1/4-1/2 million from Government and private funds. The work already accomplished by British workers in this field has won international appreciation and it is considered important that every assistance to the retention of this lead shall be given[39]

---

[39] RCA 2622 Pt 1. Memorandum by Merriman (GPO), 'Frequencies for radio astronomy', enclosed in letter, Mead (OTD, GPO) to S/L Shaw (BJCEB), 23 June 1952.

Weight was given to the frequencies suggested by tying them to the telescope technologies: 'the nature of the work planned is such that in some cases the design parameters of the equipment will be locked to the precise frequency that may be made available'.

The GPO informed the 57th meeting of the JFPP of the demands of the radio astronomers, along with their opinion that, despite the astronomers' support from 'the DSIR and other interested departments', they 'considered that the demand was excessive' and thought it could 'negotiate a reduction' in frequencies requested.[40] The GPO promised to investigate and return.

The GPO tabulated the requested frequencies, together with an 'explanatory memorandum'.[41] The 58th JFPP meeting considered it 'in detail'.[42] As the GPO reported back, the radio astronomers now found that the 'formal' use of radio frequencies was beset with problems. The Ministry of Civil Aviation (MCA) used 38 Mc/s for 'for certain navigational aids', but it could be used under sufferance. Likewise, 69 and 72 Mc/s could be used only 'on the understanding that [Jodrell Bank] would shut down in the event of interference' to either aeronautical services (69 Mc/s) or 'civilian land mobile communication services' (mostly taxis or radio dealers). The MCA found use of 74.5 Mc/s 'not acceptable', although 71 and 73.5 Mc/s were. The Home Office could not guarantee interference-free use of 81.5 Mc/s because of local police services. 164 Mc/s would be free except during 'military exercises' (JFPP suggested an alternative of 176 Mc/s). 246.8 Mc/s 'was not considered acceptable because it is already in use by the services'.[43] The Air Ministry allowed use of 210 Mc/s, but pointed out that it would be brought into use at 'certain locations in the near future', and anyway the whole band 174-216 Mc/s was 'allocated internationally for the broadcasting service', including 'high power television'. The JFPP considered frequencies of 400, 1420 and 9850, at the time too high for other services, to be unlikely to be subject to interference for the radio astronomers. 'Special note' was taken of the hydrogen line at 1420.4 Mc/s, and it was only this frequency which achieved 'exclusive allocation' to radio astronomy.[44] The Panel regretted that not much could be protected, 'but this seems inevitable since...these frequencies fall into parts of the spectrum which are particularly

---

[40] RCA 2622 Pt 1. Minutes, 57th JFPP, 24 June 1952.

[41] JBA CS7/29/1. Letter, Vernon to Fryer (Overseas Telecommunications Department, GPO), 22 October 1952.

[42] RCA 2622 Pt 1. Minutes, 58th JFPP, 29 July 1952.

[43] It was within the 'UHF tactical control band' and any other use of it was 'unacceptable'. RCA 2622 Pt 1. Ibid.

[44] Even this allocation was questioned by the following January, since the higher level 'Committee B' noted that 'world wide Air Navigation' was pencilled in the band 1418.9-1421.9 Mc/s. RCA 2622 Pt 1. 61st JFPP, 6 January 1953.

valuable for radio services of many kinds', and it repeated the query 'if it was practicable to carry out your observations in more remote locations'. The solution to exile from spectrum space could be exile in physical space!

Hanbury Brown replied for Jodrell Bank, noting the Panel's restrictions.[45] He also reported continued interference from the 'marine radio telephony at Liverpool' (probably tugs). He restated the request for 246.8 Mc/s, as it was planned to be used 'in conjunction with the new large paraboloid', the implication being that the DSIR ought to protect the prestigious project that it backed financially. It was also queried why the JFPP had not mentioned 'a frequency of about 500 Mc/s, a frequency between 500 and 1420 Mc/s and a frequency of about 3000 Mc/s'. Generally, Hanbury Brown said, 'we regard the problem of frequency allocation with considerable anxiety'. Suitably chastised, the DSIR sought out the Post Office again, to see 'if we can do anything else to help our friends the radio astronomers'.[46]

A New Ally: the Royal Society

The radio astronomers required more leverage. To achieve this they had to take two approaches. They had to make their position more consistent and organised: this would result in Cambridge and Jodrell Bank jointly preparing and coordinating frequency stakes (except on the rare occasions that they themselves clashed). These would be argued at the appropriate level by a single representative (see below). Secondly, more powerful allies were enlisted. Blackett and Lovell had found this invaluable three years before when, as discussed in Chapter Two, using Blackett's and Appleton's influence, a one-off sub-committee of the Royal Astronomical Society had been formed which recommended the massive financial backing for the Radio Telescope. This recommendation, in the form of a resolution of the Royal Astronomical Society, had proved instrumental in securing funds for the project from the DSIR. So, finding their own power insufficient to obtain frequency space, the radio astronomers mobilised a more powerful voice, the Royal Society. Lovell's letter to the Royal Society Secretary, D.C. Martin, portrays a science in crisis:

> [the GPO's] limited action is however quite insufficient to safeguard any successful future for radio astronomy in Great Britain. In support of this contention I might add that we have recently been forced off three frequencies which were considered 'safe' in the GPO's letter...[47]

Lovell called for 'a progressive policy' that would 'give priority to the

[45] JBA CS7/29/1. Letter, Hanbury Brown to Greenall (DSIR), 8 January 1953.

[46] JBA CS7/29/1. Letter, Greenall to Fryer, 15 January 1953.

[47] JBA CS7/29/1. Letter, Lovell to Martin, 23 April 1953.

reasonable claims of radio astronomy', darkly warning that a threat to the subject which 'now formed an important part of the country's scientific effort...might well influence the future of radio communications'. Lovell's rhetoric, tailored to hold together the alliance necessary to secure frequency resources for the Jodrell Bank, is strikingly similar to that he used arguing for funding.

Martin, who described himself as knowing 'too little about the respective authorities who allocate these frequencies' sought the advice of R.L. Smith-Rose, director of the Radio Research Station at Slough. Martin noted that it appeared that 'some positive action on a high level [was] called for, if the advance of radio astronomy [was] not to be endangered'.[48] He suggested 'that Sir Edward Appleton, as chairman of the British National Committee for Scientific Radio [a Royal Society sub-committee], should make the recommendation to the council of the Royal Society, and the Council will approach the Post Master General'.

Soon after Lovell had contacted Martin, he received a copy of the letter from the Post Office to the DSIR.[49] Here were the decisions of the Joint Frequency Planning Panel again, but presented in a more 'discouraging' way:

> The position in brief is that it would be quite impracticable to reserve a frequency which the astronomers could use for transmission at Cambridge or Jodrell Bank, or even to offer them a 'reception only' frequency that was reasonably free from interference...

The astronomers, the GPO went on, ought to be made aware of 'the situation right away in case they propose to spend more on equipment for a frequency which...will be subject to a lot of interference later on'. The expansion of their instrumentation was, of course, precisely what the astronomers intended to do.

Lovell lost no time in forwarding the offending letter to the Royal Society: 'I think this epitomises the point which I was trying to make...The [GPO] are perfectly willing to fit in frequencies for Radio Astronomy after other interests have first attention'.[50] To the DSIR, Lovell expanded the point: 'Unless we are given top priority for the allocation of frequency, Great Britain will have to give up the subject entirely within the next ten years'.[51]

The resolution to go before Appleton's BNCSR was written and rewritten three times by Lovell before being passed to Ratcliffe at Cambridge. Out from the early drafts went details of the cost of the Jodrell Bank programme (already growing rapidly) and a favourable quote from a Royal Astronomical

---

[48] JBA CS7/29/1. Letter, Martin to Smith-Rose, 25 April 1953.
[49] JBA CS7/29.1. Letter, Greenall (DSIR) to Lovell, 14 May 1953.
[50] JBA CS7/29/1. Letter, Lovell to Martin, 15 May 1953.
[51] JBA CS7/29/1. Letter, Lovell to Greenall, 15 May 1953.

Society resolution ('In drafting this memo, I have had to bear in mind...that it was to be a short document which might be read by the Post Master General'[52]). The memorandum reiterated the theme of national prestige, noting that whilst the 'early leadership which British science attained in observational astronomy was unfortunately lost to America'[53], radio astronomy could wrest this prize back to cloudy Britain, if only the 'serious hindrance by radio interference from commercial and military systems' could be removed. The memorandum called for the Royal Society to persuade the Post Office to refrain from issuing licences on certain frequencies to any service within a 'clear area [covering] a radius of 50 miles from each observatory'. Ratcliffe redrafted the memorandum to emphasise that the astronomers were aware that the frequencies were already allocated, that they only asked for 'the refusal of licences in certain limited areas'[54], that they were willing to negotiate and that they were aware of possible security aspects.

Although the astronomers presented unified demands, this did not mean that they had identical interests. Here, this is revealed by the different attitudes towards transmission licences between Cambridge and Jodrell Bank. As Ratcliffe stated: 'we have no need for transmitting and do not feel that the case for granting a transmission licence is anything like so good as the case for refusing transmitting licences to others'. This was due to the different research programmes, a 'division of labour' noted by Edge and Mulkay. Cambridge (primarily) developed interferometry techniques for passive observation, which required no transmission, whereas Jodrell Bank had won early credit for its meteor echo work, which did. Lovell accepted Ratcliffe's modified version as a final draft. The table of frequencies was also negotiated between Cambridge and Manchester. Lovell's early draft included the extra frequencies: 'about 500 +/-3 Mc/s, about 1000 +/-3 Mc/s...[and] about 3000 +/-3 Mc/s'. These were pulled by Ratcliffe since they were more than what had previously been requested. Lovell again withdrew: 'I do not think it worth confusing the issue at this stage, since we are fighting a matter of principle'.[55]

The BJCEB were able to get advance warning of the Royal Society actions. An internal note written on Martin's circular to members of the BNCSR expressed concern: 'whatever the rights and wrongs of it, this could cause

---

[52] JBA CS7/29/1. Letter, Lovell to Ratcliffe, 19 May 1953.

[53] JBA CS7/29/1. Lovell, third draft of memorandum for the British National Committee for Scientific Radio of the Royal Society.

[54] JBA CS7/29/1. Letter, Ratcliffe to Lovell, 28 May 1953. 'To make room for this I suggest that we omit the pieces about the size and cost of your equipment, which I think is well known'.

[55] JBA CS7/29/1. Letter, Lovell to Ratcliffe, 11 June 1953.

trouble if it eventually gets to the Lord President (Cabinet)'.[56]

The resolution passed through the BNCSR, helped by strong backing from Appleton, its chairman: 'I can say without hesitation that I am sure the BNCSR will support the representations made...and I do so hope that Council will feel able to do the same'.[57] This was indeed the case and the Royal Society Secretary, Sir David Brunt, sent the document to the Lord President, the Marquess of Salisbury, with a covering letter.

Territorial Expansion, Occupation of the Spectrum and a Suggested Salient

Independently of this starting up of Royal Society machinery, there was some 'promising'[58] movement from the JFPP about the extra high frequencies requested by Lovell in his letter to the DSIR in January and left off the Royal Society resolution. The DSIR forwarded copies of the letter from the GPO requesting information on these frequencies, to both Lovell and Ryle. The radio astronomers took this limited opening as an opportunity for much wider territorial expansion. 'I am sure that you will agree that we should correlate our answers to this letter', wrote Ryle, 'I think we should get as many frequencies as possible...although these frequencies are not included in the documents which are going to the Royal Society'.[59]

The astronomers were determined to make a concerted effort: '...now the Royal Society document is in circulation, the time is ripe for a *really comprehensive* list of frequencies to be applied for'.[60] Ryle had three objectives: reopen 'the question of the lower frequencies which Mead seems to think is settled'. This should be closed again before other interests appeared: 'I think we should move fast before commercial television gets going!'. Second, they should aim at 'two frequencies per octave' which would meet 'any requirement' without loss of 'efficiency'. Also, if they adopted this approach they could have a good claim on a frequency within the '100-250 Mc/s region, where... it is going to be most difficult'. Third, the frequencies of emission lines should automatically be protected.[61] Ryle

---

[56] RCA 2622 Pt 1. Note, Stewart to Finch, 10 July 1953.

[57] JBA CS7/29/1. Letter, Appleton to the Royal Society Council, 8 July 1953. The clearance of the following frequencies in 50 mile radii around Jodrell Bank and Cambridge was requested: 38, 81.5, 164, 246.8, ~400, 1420.4, 9850 (receiving only, all in Mc/s); 36.3, 69, 71, 72, 73.5, 210 or 246.8 (receiving and transmitting, all in Mc/s).

[58] JBA CS7/29/1. Covering letter, Greenall to Lovell, 8 July 1953, for letter Mead to Greenall, 4 July 1953.

[59] JBA CS7/29/1. Letter, Lovell to Ryle, 16 July 1953.

[60] JBA CS7/29/1. Letter, Ryle to Lovell, 19 July 1953.

[61] This led to the deuterium line being allocated to radio astronomy whilst not being used or even detected.

encapsulated these frequencies in a suggested list.[62] Lovell's reply to the DSIR reflected this list closely.[63]

These approaches led to a meeting 'of a fact-finding nature only' held at Post Office Headquarters on 20 October 1953.[64] Present were E. Sharpe (GPO, chairman), Lovell, Hanbury Brown, Ryle, and representatives from the Lord President's Office, the DSIR, the Home Office, the Ministry of Transport and Civil Aviation (MTCA), the BJCEB, the War Office, the Air Ministry, the Post Office Engineering Department and the GPO Overseas Telecommunications Department. At this stage, no reaction had been revealed by the Lord President's Office to the radio astronomers about the Royal Society's resolution. At the meeting the government departments who occupied frequency space gave little ground to the astronomers. The suggestion that 'a more remote location for their observations' be found was raised again. Lovell replied that this would be a 'great inconvenience', and, interestingly, that 'the Cheshire plain ...was particularly suitable for radio astronomy, not only as regards topography, but also from the point of view of weather conditions', in contrast to the standard argument that Britain ought to fund radio astronomy since it was independent of climate. The departments reiterated the objections which they had given before through the BJCEB.

The frequencies 36.3, 69, 71, 72 and 73.5 Mc/s were considered 'satisfactory' for transmissions so long as other services were not interfered with. There were more serious problems with finding a high frequency 'anywhere between 200-270 Mc/s, with 4 Mc/s total bandwidth. Both Cambridge and Jodrell Bank had planned 'expensive equipment'[65] around this allocation. However the '[armed] Services have very extensive commitments which *occupy* all the space between 235-350 Mc/s' (my emphasis), whereas 'various [civil] aeronautical services' and soon 'high power television stations' were allocated 200-235 Mc/s.

For reception, 38, 81.5, 164, 400 and 9850 Mc/s were available, but the Post Office could not guarantee that they would be free from interference.

---

[62] The 'arrangement...planned to include existing equipment and the atomic lines' was 38.0 ± 0.75, 81.5 ± 1, 110-140 ± 1, 164 ± 2, 177.5 ± 1, 230-270 ± 2, 354 ± 2, 500-600 ± 2.5, 800-1100 ± 2.5, 1420.4 ± 2, 2200-3300 ± 5, 5000-6000 ± 5 and 9850 ± 5 (all in Mc/s). 38 and 81.5 Mc/s were 'essential' because 'large amounts of apparatus [was] already built'. 'Some' apparatus was built for 164 Mc/s, and 177.5, 354, 1420.4 and 9850 Mc/s were atomic lines, of which only hydrogen 1420.4 Mc/s had been detected.

[63] JBA CS7/29/1. Letter, Lovell to Greenall, 24 July 1953.

[64] JBA CS7/29/1. Minutes of meeting, 'Frequencies for Radio Astronomy', held on 20 October 1953 at GPO HQ.

[65] The 'new large paraboloid at Jodrell Bank and for the new interference system at Cambridge'.

Lovell made his feelings known to the DSIR: 'the whole affair is...
fundamentally unsatisfactory and it is absurd that we should have to plead
in this manner. It seems to me that the requirements of the radio telesope
must be regarded as having equal priority with any of the equipments used
by the services, MCA or the Home Office'.[66] He wrote to Ryle saying that
he was 'still appalled at the attitude that we might be fixed in when everyone
else has had their pick', continuing that it 'is our intention to maintain the
utmost pressure on the authorities and I hope you will feel like doing the
same'.[67] A letter written to the Royal Society the same day made similar
points, but caged in less strident tones: the meeting was 'useful in that it
assembled in one room all...[the] authorities' and 'further action must
obviously await the official reply to the Royal Society's communication'.[68]

As we have seen, the radio astronomers could not obtain a frequency
between 200-400 Mc/s, even though large systems (the Radio Telescope and
a Cambridge interferometric array) had been planned around its use. This
band then became a focus for argument:

> the best line to take is to press for something in the [RAF's] 250-400 Mc/s band,
> as this is symbolic of the whole problem, i.e. we only want a small fraction of
> the band; we know it to be used by others; we don't necessarily believe these
> other users to be any more vital than ourselves. This same problem occurs
> elsewhere, but this is an obvious focus as it is a very serious gap from our point
> of view.[69]

The argument suggested by Ryle was that it was 'quite inconceivable that
[the RAF's band] would not be able to stand pruning by 2-5%. if this is
impossible the whole system would appear to be operationally too marginal
to be of use'. Ryle also suggested writing 'personally to [the ex-TRE]
Cockburn, you know he is Scientific Advisor to the AM...and see whether he
can make any private arrangements'. Lovell soon put this strategy in to
operation. In a letter to Greenall he reports a (putative) opinion of a
representative of the Lord President's Office:

> Wilson did say to me...that he regarded the question of a frequency between 200
> and 400 Mc/s as critical. This seemed to me to show great insight...that frequency
> band obviously holds a vital principle which is at stake...The argument that...2
> % cannot be spared...is absurd...something is desperately wrong with the defence
> planning in that such a little margin of error has been allowed...[70]

---

[66] JBA CS7/29/1. Letter, Lovell to Greenall, 21 October 1953.
[67] JBA CS7/29/1. Letter, Lovell to Ryle, 21 October 1953.
[68] JBA CS7/29/1. Letter, Lovell to Martin, 21 October 1953.
[69] JBA CS7/29/1. Letter, Ryle to Lovell, 29 October 1953.
[70] JBA CS7/29/1. Letter, Lovell to Greenall, 3 November 1953.

Lovell concluded by saying that 'Ryle and I feel very strongly that we should fight this to the bitter end, not only because we badly want a frequency in that wave band but also because...it contains the germ of the whole dispute'. These territorial arguments were reciprocally connected to a wider campaign, which I shall discuss in the next chapter. As Lovell wrote to Ryle: 'I gave an address to the Manchester Luncheon Club last week and took the opportunity of dealing quite severely with Manchester's overspill, electricity grid lines and frequency reservations, as they affect the future of the radio telescope'. Frequency negotiations, although fought on the bureaucratically created space of the radio spectrum, were attempts to change the activities of organisations around Jodrell Bank and Cambridge. Thus the motivation of enquiries such as Lovell's to Ryle: 'do you have any worries about encroachment of population or grid lines?' can be seen to be part of the important spatial politics that underpinned the observatories.

Meanwhile Ryle had approached Cockburn who was 'fairly optimistic that something could be arranged' and had suggested Group Captain Powell 'who is responsible for the allocation of VHF frequencies'. After bringing up the question of two 4 Mc/s bands in 225-400 Mc/s with Powell, Ryle found the situation 'fairly hopeful', 'providing that we can tie [the Air Ministry] down somewhat - with the GPO's help - to some agreement of permanency'.[71] The outcome was a meeting arranged with Powell, missed by Lovell because of an 'engine derailment...north of Lichfield'. Powell undertook to analyse the 'very real difficulties' that an allocation presented[72] and forward any recommendations to the JFPP, though Ryle felt that if 'action could be taken now, when equipment for only a relatively small fraction of the total channels [have] actually been installed', obtaining the bands would be possible.[73]

Also in December the GPO communicated to the radio astronomers the decisions made by the JFPP on the frequencies presented at the meeting in October.[74] Police and maritime services operated in 81.5 and 164 Mc/s so Sharpe suggested alternatives of 79 and 161.7 Mc/s. Importantly he could not suggest anything within the key band 200-400 Mc/s. 408 and 132 Mc/s were available but possibly subject to interference. However, where the frequencies requested were high or for short periods the radio astronomers were assured quiet bands. For instance the frequency space 5250-5270 Mc/s was allocated to radio astronomy and 'noted in the National Frequency Plan'. The clustering of the older services in the lower frequencies allowed this.

Cambridge and Manchester again collaborated in their response to the JFPP's decisions. Both noted the suggested alternatives and restrictions, the

[71] JBA CS7/29/1. Letter, Ryle to Lovell, 18 November 1953.
[72] JBA CS7/29/1. Letter, Powell to Lovell, 14 December 1953.
[73] JBA CS7/29/1. Letter, Ryle to Sharpe, 17 December 1953.
[74] JBA CS7/29/1. Letter, Sharpe to Lovell, 8 December 1953.

only difference lying in Cambridge's attitude to 81.5 and 164 Mc/s to which they were 'already committed very seriously and would therefore have no wish to change'. Both laid emphasis on the frequencies below 400 Mc/s: 'none of [these]...represent permanent allocations and it is therefore difficult to plan the construction of equipment for use with the telescope'.[75] In particular, 'the failure to obtain allocations in the band 200 to 400 Mc/s [is] extremely serious and we shall continue to press as strongly as possible for frequencies in this range'.

Although the Air Ministry were reported as being 'naturally windy' about the radio astronomers claims on the 200-400 Mc/s band[76], a meeting arranged at the Ministry by Powell admitted the possibility of accommodation in two sub-bands, within 320-360 Mc/s and 250-260 Mc/s.[77] There is evidence that the subject was discussed at high level: 'between the Minister of Defence and the First Lord of the Admiralty and the Secretaries of State for War and Air'.[78] The Air Ministry gave up two bands, 258-262 and 338-342 Mc/s, but qualified the offer: 'although all three Service Departments will do their best to avoid their use near Jodrell Bank and Cambridge they are...unable to...guarantee that you will not experience some interference...from over-flying aircraft or continental users'.[79] This widening of the space that the radio astronomers had to seek to control and quieten caused alarm 'if...aircraft carrying equipment operating in these bands are going to fly over this country, the interference could be impossible'.[80] Ryle suggested a new argument involving the postulated and undetected deuterium line, at 354 Mc/s within the key band, tacitly drawing upon the the analogy of the full protection for radio astronomy afforded to the 1420 Mc/s hydrogen line:

---

[75] JBA CS7/29/1. Letter, Lovell to Sharpe, 22 December 1953.

[76] RCA 2622 Pt 1. Note by Stewart appended to note by Finch, 12 January 1954.

[77] RCA 2622 Pt 1. Note, G/C Powell (Air Ministry) to Chair BJCEB, 26 January 1954. In 320-360 Mc/s the AM had planned air/ground communication, these 'could be rearranged to reduce interference risk from ground transmitters', but not from 'over-flying aircraft'. 250-260 Mc/s was 'more difficult' because 'limited range communication equipment...for use by all Fighter and Ground Attack aircraft' was planned, as well as 'nine Army channels, 5 Naval channels, and two shared Army/Naval channels'.

[78] JBA CS7/29/1. Smith Rose, 'Memorandum on the Allocation of Frequencies for Radio Astronomy', 28 May 1954.

[79] A JFPP report noted: 'though every effort would be made to protect Radio Astronomy use of them (sic) the wide bandwidth requested covered 40 channels of the NATO plan...Not only is [this plan] channelled at 100 kc/s but Navy, Army and Air Force channels are allotted adjacent to each other, making such a requirement a tri-service problem'.

[80] JBA CS7/29/1. Letter, Ryle to Lovell, 18 March 1954.

I have not really followed the literature closely enough to know how likely its detection is, or whether it is likely to prove anything that cannot be derived more easily from the Hydrogen line. It does seem however that the ratio of Deuterium/Hydrogen is related to various cosmological theories.

Results with cosmological implications impressed funding bodies and other authorities. So Ryle's comment that 'the big paraboloid may be the only instrument capable of doing worthwhile observations at 354 Mc/s...' was therefore a strong hint to Lovell of a possibly useful argument.

By equating the deuterium line with the secure hydrogen line an argument could be made for its increased protection. Lovell took this up in a letter to the GPO: 'As a general principle we regard it as extremely important to keep the few spectral frequency lines clear'.[81] When this drew an unpromising response, Lovell called in support: '...the successful observation of the deuterium line at this frequency might become very important in radio astronomy...the Radar Research Establishment at Malvern is interested...[and] is building an equipment [sic] to search for this emission line. This presumably might support our case for a reservation'.[82] However, by the time this argument could be put an important change in the representation of radio astronomy on spectrum committees had been made.

The Outsiders Come In

During mid to late 1953 the GPO and BJCEB composed a robust response to the Lord President's Office, arguing that the frequency allocation bodies had never been 'asked to clear away frequencies in the full sense', but had done their practical best to 'accommodate' the new user, even though:

> from the point of view of civilian communications alone it will be appreciated that some of the most important areas of the country are within 50 miles of the two observatories.[83]

In February 1954, Jodrell Bank heard of the results of the Royal Society's approach to the Lord President. The Lord President's argument that 'ideally radio astronomers should be put on terms of equality with the other users who had shared out the frequency spectrum' put to the Post Master General, Service Ministers and Minister of Defence[84] had led to no new reservations

---

[81] JBA CS7/29/1. Letter, Lovell to Sharpe, 22 March 1954.

[82] JBA CS7/29/1. Letter, Lovell to Sharpe, 13 May 1954.

[83] RCA 2622 Pt 1. Draft memorandum, 'Frequencies for radio astronomy. For the Lord President's Office', August 1953. Included with letter, Mead to BJCEB, 7 August 1953.

[84] RCA 2622 Pt 1. Minutes of CFC, FQ(54) 1st meeting, 29 July 1954.

secured for radio astronomy. The one tangible result was that the Lord President had 'found that hitherto there had been no direct representation on these [the interdepartmental frequency] Committees of which I might call the "radio astronomy interest", and agreed to the addition to these committees of representatives from the DSIR.[85] Although Lovell thanked Martin, the Secretary of the Royal Society, for the Society's assistance, his letter reveals disappointment that 'considerable bands were being held in reserve for commercial television, and yet radio astronomy had no priority with which to claim even a fractional part of [the 30-1000 Mc/s] band'.[86] However, the appointment of a representative of the 'radio astronomy interest' at high level was a crucial organisational change. The astronomers 'naturally [hoped] that the representatives will be from the personnel at DSIR Headquarters who are in very close touch with the problems in radio astronomy'.[87] The appointee was R.L. Smith-Rose who had recently taken over from Appleton as director of the Radio Research Station at Slough.

Unknown to the radio astronomers, however, the lobbying of the Lord President had gained another concession: recognition by the highest body dealing with spectrum policy, the Cabinet Frequency Committee (CFC).[88] A BJCEB civil servant noted that with respect to 'a draft of a paper which GPO would submit to CFC in the event that the discussion between the Lord President and Post Master General made it necessary': 'the important points are...CFC to agree that radio astronomy be accepted as a new user and that exclusive "wavebands be allocated"...within 50 miles of each University'.

This concludes one broad stage in the effort of radio astronomers to secure a quiet space around Jodrell Bank and Cambridge for their observations. These efforts were not at first altogether successful. The only assurances they had achieved for interference-free radio bands were at extremely high frequencies which other services did not use, or licences to use temporary gaps. Without a permanent allocation they could not be sure of preventing encroachment from tugs, beacons, the police, over-flying aircraft or other potential sources of interference. The power relations changed with the appointment, using Royal Society pressure, of a representative on the powerful interdepartmental and cabinet committees of the 'radio astronomy interest'.

---

[85] JBA CS7/29/1. Letter, Marquess of Salisbury (Lord President of the Council) to Sir David Brunt, 29 January 1954.

[86] JBA CS7/29/1. Letter, Lovell to Martin, 5 February 1954.

[87] Ibid. The GPO agreed to sponsor the DSIR as a member of both CFC and the JFPP. They did this after discussion which concluded 'it was OK – if it is not we would have to veto'. RCA 2422 Pt 1. Note by Finch, 12 January 1954.

[88] RCA 2622 Pt 1. Note by Finch, 1 January 1954.

STAGE TWO: INSIDERS

The spokesperson for radio astronomy, R.L. Smith-Rose was not a radio astronomer. The Radio Research Station at Slough, of which he was director, was a government establishment. Its work involved research on the ionosphere and radio propagation through the atmosphere. To carry out his new responsibilities Smith-Rose wrote to Lovell and Ryle to discover the astronomers' requirements. With these he planned to prepare 'a statement for the Lord President to send to the Postmaster-General...[and] an appropriate paper for the next meeting of the Cabinet committee on frequencies'.[89] The original table sent by Smith-Rose for up-dating dated from before the October 1953 meeting. He also mis-spells Ryle's surname ('Ryall') suggesting that Smith-Rose had beforehand little connection with radio astronomy.

Smith-Rose received the opinions of Manchester and Cambridge and built them into 'A memorandum on the allocation of frequencies for radio astronomy' to go to the Postmaster-General. It was 'intended to present a survey of the position which has been reached during the past year or two'[90], and cited a report of Appleton's British National Committee for Scientific Radio (BNCSR) saying 'that while some improvement had been obtained regarding the allocation of frequencies... there was still a great deal more to be done'. The memorandum divided the frequencies into three tables. Table I listed 'frequencies...determined by natural resonant phenomena'. This included the protected hydrogen 1420 Mc/s line, and the proposed but undetected 177.5 (H), 354 (D) and 9850 (H) Mc/s lines, 'about which there can be no question of discussing alternative allocations'. The second table held 'those frequencies...the use of which a considerable measure of agreement has already been reached'.[91] However, 'recent experience shows... the limitations of the present form of agreement'. The third table listed frequencies 'for which there were rival claimants', including those contested between radio astronomy and the Services.[92] The memorandum made three recommendations:

(a) to obtain agreement for the exclusive use by radio astronomers of the frequencies given in Table I...
(b) to obtain assurance that all the frequencies in Table II can be assigned for an indefinite period so that astronomers...may safely embark on...long-term

---

[89] JBA CS7/29/1. Letter, Smith-Rose to Lovell, 15 May 1954.

[90] JBA CS7/29/1. Smith-Rose, 'Memorandum on the Allocation of Frequencies for Radio Astronomy', 28 May 1954.

[91] This included 36.3, 69, 71, 72, 73.5, 81.5 and 164 Mc/s, and the bands in the ranges 17.9465-17.985, 85-110 annd 110-142 Mc/s.

[92] Table III lists: bands in 210-246.8, 408, 500-600, 800-1100, 2200-3300 and 5000-6000 Mc/s.

...observations (c) to have a full and frank discussion with representatives of the interested parties of the frequencies given in Table III.

Lovell described this as an 'excellent summary'.[93]

Smith-Rose took the radio astronomer's case to the Joint Frequency Planning Panel on 29 June 1954. The JFPP composed a separate report for consideration by the Cabinet Frequency Committee. It noted that the 'difficulty in accommodating the Radio Astronomy requirements is increased by the relatively wide bandwidths for which protection is sought...and by the high protection ratios required due to the very low signal strengths'[94], and summed up:

> From both the civil and military point of view the areas within fifty miles radius of Jodrell Bank and Cambridge embrace many important parts of the country in which there are already high demands on the frequency spectrum; furthermore, in order to provide protection from aircraft transmissions and particularly aircraft flying at high altitude, the protection area has to be considerably extended. The problem of accommodating Radio Astronomy would have been much simpler had more remote locations been selected.

The conclusions reached were unsympathetic: 'it is not, in general, possible to guarantee freedom from interference', indeed the 'departmental measures so far taken in each specific case represent the best arrangement that can be made...at JFPP level at present'. Three possible directions were noted: that 'work in Radio Astronomy were carried out at more remote locations', 'the bandwidth and...degree of protection sought ...be reduced', and that the 'requirements of Radio astronomy should be considered for the next ITU Administrative Radio Conference'.

The Cabinet Frequency Committee considered the JFPP's report, a report by the DSIR (Smith-Rose's memorandum) and a report from the Air Ministry. Smith-Rose replied to a number of questions on the number of frequencies required, the relative importance of frequencies, the effect of some degree of interference, reduction of bandwidths and the location of research in 'less congested' areas.[95] Smith-Rose spoke of the resources that the DSIR had committed to the observatories, of the 'construction work [that] had been done' meaning that 'it was not feasible to move them at this juncture', and also that:

> the equipment at the centres was the most sensitive search equipment in the

---

[93] JBA CS7/29/1. Letter, Lovell to Smith-Rose, undated.

[94] JBA CS7/29/1. 'Report by the Joint Frequency Planning Panel: Allocation of Frequencies for Radio Astronomy', 20 July 1954.

[95] JBA CS7/29/1. 'Extract of Minutes of Meeting of Cabinet Frequency Committee - 29 July 1954'.

country, indeed in the whole world, and might be of very great value in a future war.[96]

The Committee invited Smith-Rose to 'prepare a paper with particular reference to time-sharing, band width and acceptable level of interference' for the JFPP, which was then to report again to the CFC. It also recommended that the JFPP 'arrange for the representation of radio astronomers on the Panel, whenever matters of interest to them were being discussed'.

There was again little concrete in the outcome of this approach. The relocation of observatories, even though the Radio Telescope and Cambridge interferometers were half-completed and Smith-Rose considered the matter a 'waste of time', was still being raised. Smith-Rose did feel however that 'the meeting...served a useful starting point in educating many of the other users of radio, civilian and Service alike, that radio astronomers are now seeking a place on equal terms...in the radio spectrum'.[97] He suggested the upcoming Union Radio Scientifique Internationale (URSI) meeting in The Hague as a place where 'a short memorandum' could be drawn up by Ryle, Lovell and himself, to go to the next JFPP meeting in September. The URSI meeting represented part of the international organisation of radio astronomers to include bands for radio astronomy in the next ITU regulations, which I discuss later.

Although the September meeting considered a brief memorandum[98], the main aim of securing quiet frequencies waited until the following meeting. A working party was set up to consider 'radio astronomy requirements'. The only representative of radio astronomy out of eight was Smith-Rose.[99] This made a second report for the JFPP to take to the Cabinet Committee.[100] The classification system again follows the familiar three-way split, but this time another division into four categories is made: secure, temporarily secure, insecure and not yet dealt with. Five frequencies (1420, 9850, 17.946 and 17.985, 408 and 2295 Mc/s) were made secure, and five were temporarily secure (177.5, 1400-1422, 36.3, 38 and 95.1 Mc/s). This left eleven insecure (354, 69, 71, 72, 73.5, 79, 81.5, 132 or 125, 164 and 207.5 Mc/s) and one (in 800-1100 Mc/s) not yet dealt with. The report recommended that the

---

[96] RCA 2622 Pt 1. Minutes, CFC FQ(54) 1st Meeting, 29 July 1954.

[97] JBA CS7/29/1. Letter, Smith-Rose to Lovell, 6 August 1954.

[98] JBA CS7/29/1. Smith-Rose, DSIR memorandum, 'The Allocation of Frequencies for Radio Astronomy', 9 September 1954.

[99] The others were: DSD Admiralty, D Signals War Office, ACAS Air Ministry, Sharpe (GPO), Tels 4 Ministry of Transport and Civil Aviation, the Home Office and the BBC.

[100] JBA CS7/29/1. 'Second Report by the JFPP on the Allocation of Frequencies for Radio Astronomy' (draft), 8 January 1955.

Cabinet Frequency Committee consider the secure frequencies 'satisfactorily protected', examine the temporarily secure bands 'with a view to resolving those cases where it considers that the protection for Radio Astronomy is inadequate', and deal with the insecure bands when international planning allowed it. This was tied to local arrangements between Jodrell Bank and Cambridge and the Services to share time and avoid interference within 50 miles. The Cabinet Committee agreed to these recommendations.

Smith-Rose communicated the conclusions to Ryle and Lovell remarking that he was 'very satisfied with the progress that has been made'.[101] Lovell replied that he was 'certainly impressed', and that it represented 'a fundamental safeguard for the future of radio astronomy in Great Britain'.[102] However, Smith-Rose's reported satisfaction and Lovell's anticipations of security contrasted with the Cabinet committee's chairman's judgement that:

> On the question of the siting of the radio astronomy stations...it should be stressed that the question should be looked at with a view to providing not for the next few years only, but for the next fifty or 100 years; and, with this in mind, if it was not absolutely essential for the astronomy station to be tied to universities,...the possibility of finding suitable sites, far removed from main centres of population, should be thoroughly examined.[103]

Thus by gaining representation at the highest levels determining national frequency allocation, the radio astronomers had obtained a degree of security for the parts of the spectrum they wished to observe. This was only possible because they had the status to persuade the Royal Society to pursue the matter, and they were organised enough to correlate their responses. However, few of the reservations were permanent. Smith-Rose, Lovell, Hanbury Brown and Ryle had to be constantly prepared actively to protect their areas of spectrum. Also, they had fallen short of their 'one frequency per octave' target. Although frequency allocation was (and is) an on-going process, there was one more important stage that the astronomers pursued in order to secure spectrum space. This was the building of international borders around their frequency allocations: the inclusion of radio astronomy in the next ITU Administrative Conference's Radio Regulations. This Conference was called in 1959 in Geneva. Such international space-making required international collaboration and effort and is described in the section after next. Before this, there is an interlude in which a conflict occurs within the radio astronomers' ranks.

---

[101] JBA CS7/29/1. Letter, Smith-Rose to Lovell, 15 January 1955.

[102] JBA CS7/29/1. Letter, Lovell to Smith-Rose, 25 January 1955.

[103] RCA 2622 Pt 2. Minutes, CFC FQ(55) 1st meeting, 30 June 1955.

INTERLUDE: CAMBRIDGE, JODRELL BANK AND THE GEE CHAIN

The following episode concerned four frequencies, 81.5, 79, 69.5 and 73.8 Mc/s, the use of which was contested by Jodrell Bank, Cambridge and the Air Ministry. The Gee system was one of several radio navigational aids developed during the war. By comparing the time delays of radio pulses from different radio beacons arranged in chains, the locations of which were known, an aircraft could calculate its own position. This allowed landing, taking off and bombing at night or in poor visibility.[104] In 1945 there existed five chains: the Northern chain situated in the far north of Scotland and the Shetlands, the North-Western chain, in Northern Ireland and the Western Isles, the Eastern chain, in central England, and the Southern and South-Western chains along the south coast. Each chain had its own frequency to avoid interference. Gee was combined with a second system, Gee-H: 'the standard Blind Bombing System for Bomber Command and 2nd TAF'.[105] From the early 1950s, Gee formed 'the basis of a European Network controlled and operated by SHAPE [NATO]'.

Both Cambridge and Manchester used 81.5 Mc/s for investigating 'cosmic noise'. In 1952, before the permanent protection of frequencies described above, the Post Office considered: '81.5 Mc/s has been used without trouble...for two years...[the radio astronomers] should continue to use it'.[106] By 1953, Lovell reported that 81.5 Mc/s 'now suffers severe interference'[107] from police radio in Manchester. Ryle, in a list of requested frequencies, stated that it was 'Essential - large amount of apparatus already built'[108], it being 'the operating frequency of the new large Cambridge telescope'.[109] He, too, soon found interference from 'harmonics and local oscillator radiations' originating from Gee transmitters. The inter-body discussion meeting of 20 October 1953 agreed 'that efforts should be made to find an alternative between 75-85 Mc/s'.[110] Such an alternative was found, the JFPP suggesting 79 Mc/s as an 'improvement' despite it being:

---

[104] Hall, J. S. (ed), 1947. *Massachusetts Institute of Technology Radiation Laboratory Series, Volume 2: Radar Aids to Navigation*, New York: McGraw-Hill, pp. 60-64.

[105] RCA 2622 Pt 1. Memorandum by Air Ministry, 'Frequencies for Radio Astronomy', 3 March 1954.

[106] JBA CS7/29/1. Letter, Fryer to Vernon, 22 October 1952.

[107] JBA CS7/29/1. Letter, Lovell to Martin, 23 April 1953.

[108] JBA CS7/29/1. Letter, Ryle to Lovell, 19 July 1953.

[109] RCA 2622 Pt 1. Letter, Ryle to Sharpe, 17 March 1954.

[110] JBA CS7/29/1. Minutes of meeting held at Post Office Headquarters, 20 October 1953.

in use for certain aeronautical and land mobile services...The frequency...is also to be used to meet a further Services requirement, but the Department concerned will endeavour to avoid its use near Jodrell Bank.[111]

So Jodrell Bank accepted 79 Mc/s instead of 81.5 Mc/s. Cambridge could not make such an easy decision because a 'long-term series of observations on the sun' were funded for, and their choice of frequency had already begun to be built into their apparatus: 'We are already committed very seriously to these bands and would therefore have no wish to change to the bands you suggest'.[112] With the Barkway Gee beacon transmitting on 79 Mc/s only 15 miles from Cambridge, the interference on 81.5 Mc/s at Cambridge was demoralisingly severe:

> The power is so great that...we get about 2 millivolts in a simple aerial a few feet off the ground. One gives up hope of these meetings doing any good when this sort of thing can happen without the GPO knowing of it.[113]

This caused a series of exchanges between Ryle and the Air Ministry. The problem lay in the expansion of the Gee chains and the introduction of new transmitters. Both the Air Ministry and the Cambridge radio astronomers had invested in expensive equipment and were unwilling to change it. Eventually they reached a compromise in which the frequency (79 Mc/s) of the Eastern Gee chain (which included Barkway) was exchanged with that of the Scottish chain (73.8 Mc/s). Here the matter momentarily rested with 73.8 Mc/s built into the Eastern Chain, 81.5 Mc/s into the Cambridge interferometer, and 79 Mc/s built 'with considerable expense and trouble'[114] into equipment at Jodrell Bank and (unknown to Manchester) the Scottish Gee chain.

Jodrell Bank soon found problems with 79 Mc/s. First there was a relatively minor event: interference from local land mobile services. The Post Office could point out that:

> There are...only three private business radio services using frequencies between 78 and 80 Mc/s which are licensed to operate within 50 miles of Jodrell Bank...We have not...licensed any new...services...nor authorised an extension of any of the existing services.[115]

This could be accommodated by a 'slight down shift in our frequency'.[116]

---

[111] JBA CS7/29/1. Letter, Sharpe to Lovell, 16 November 1953.

[112] JBA CS7/29/1. Letter, Ryle to Sharpe, 17 December 1953.

[113] JBA CS7/29/1. Letter, Ryle to Lovell, 18 March 1954.

[114] JBA CS7/29/1. Letter, Lovell to Sharpe, 7 September 1954.

[115] JBA CS7/29/1. Letter, Sharpe to Lovell, 13 September 1954.

[116] JBA CS7/29/1. Letter, Lovell to Sharpe, 13 October 1954.

The frequencies used were incorporated into the concerted lobbying of the Committees reported above. The JFPP noted:

> GEE will have slave stations as close as 75 nautical miles from Jodrell Bank. This is not expected to cause interference, due to the nature of the terrain.[117]

This turned out not to be the case. The 'terrain' did indeed allow interference from the Eastern chain at Stenigot. Furthermore, as part of the Gee expansion, the Air Ministry wished to resite its Gee-H chain. This involved the introduction at Camphill (near Newcastle-under-Lyme, 10 miles from Jodrell Bank) of a beacon transmitting on 69.5 and 79 Mc/s. Smith-Rose, who 'was not present at the meeting of the Panel which discussed [the] matter'[118], pointed this out to Lovell.

To summarise: due to interference at Cambridge on 81.5 Mc/s from 79 Mc/s transmissions from Barkway, the Eastern chain (including Barkway) and Scottish chain frequencies were exchanged. Stenigot, also on the Eastern chain was therefore also changed, which interfered with reception at Jodrell Bank on 73.5 Mc/s. The Camphill Gee-H Station interfered with Jodrell Bank on 69 and 79 Mc/s.

Lovell replied to Smith-Rose: 'we are distressed to hear about these new developments since they seem likely to obliterate nearly 50% of the work done at Jodrell Bank'.[119] This, Lovell reminded Smith-Rose obliquely, included work for the the Ministry of Supply and the International Geophysical Year, 'I therefore think you should draw the attention of the authorities to the great importance of avoiding any interference with our programme'. With regards to 79 Mc/s:

> ...we are only just about to bring the 79 Mc/s equipment into use. We have been involved in a delay of nearly two years and an expense of several thousand pounds in making this change. It seems to me incredible that we are now to be faced with a powerful transmitting station only 15 miles from Jodrell Bank after having acted on the advice of the Post Office authorities...even if we could afford the expense and the time we cannot move back...[as] there are television transmitters by commercial dealers in Stockport and the band above...is completely occupied by Police communications...

Smith-Rose protested to the JFPP, deploring the resiting of the Gee stations and the changes in frequency, and using the arguments that Lovell provided.[120]

---

[117] RCA 2622 Pt 2. Memorandum, 'Second report by the JFPP on the allocation of frequencies for radio astronomy', 8 January 1955.

[118] JBA CS7/29/1. Letter, Smith-Rose to Lovell, 30 March 1955.

[119] JBA CS7/29/1. Letter, Lovell to Smith-Rose, 1 April 1955.

[120] JBA CS7/29/1. Letter, Smith-Rose to the Secretary of the JFPP, 5 April 1955.

The Air Ministry would not stop transmission, although it considered the possibilty of changing to 40 or 84 Mc/s. The point was also 'stressed' within Whitehall that there was:

> no easy solution without jeopardising defence requirements, not only for the UK but also of Western Europe; any change in the UK's plan for the use of the equipment in question, be it geographical or frequency-wise will have a chain effect throughout the whole of Western Europe.[121]

The Gee problem represented an extremely sensitive example of the reciprocal spatial relations between geographical and spectrum space. Again: 'Unless Gee-H can adjust frequency or re-site to avoid radio astronomy, or unless radio astronomy can somehow be accommodated elsewhere it seems impossible to avoid this interference'.[122]

The JFPP reported that 'no change of Gee-H from 69.5 and 79 Mc/s can be anticipated even in the most favourable circumstances for many months'[123], and asked for more information on the old 81.5 Mc/s near Manchester. The Cabinet Frequency Commitee considered the conflict between Gee and astronomers. The 'inability of Air Ministry to clear one type of interference at Cambridge without causing consequential interference at Jodrell Bank' was 'strongly deplored' by Smith-Rose.[124] The Air Ministry said that it was 'unable to meet the expenses arising from the proposed exchange of frequency' and asked for the DSIR to pay (an unsuccessful tactic). The result was 'somewhat of an impasse'.

Faced with the congested 81.5 Mc/s, Lovell opted for 73.5 Mc/s, pending tests on the interference from the Stenigot station. Such an agreement would of course mean that Cambridge escaped interference from any changes to Barkway. Ryle therefore sought to persuade Lovell pointing out that the Manchester noise experiments would suffer if Stenigot was 79 Mc/s, and that the meteor programme, being directional, could avoid the beacon,

> If you are in agreement with the above conclusions it would seem reasonably safe to accept a frequency at Stenigot of 73.8 Mc/s...it might also be possible to...move down 0.5 Mc/s or so. If you would agree to this it would solve what is a very serious problem indeed for us.[125]

---

[121] RCA 2622 Pt 2. Memorandum, 'BNCSR meeting', 30 March 1955.

[122] RCA 2622 Pt 2. Note by Finch 'Summary of factors related to Gee-H plan', 14 April 1955.

[123] JBA CS7/29/1. Letter, Smith-Rose to Lovell, 6 June 1955.

[124] JBA CS7/29/1. Letter, Smith-Rose to Lovell and Ryle, 2 July 1955. This includes an 'Extract from Paper on "Allocation of Frequencies for Radio Astronomy"', presented to the Cabinet Frequency Committee.

[125] JBA CS7/29/1. Letter, Ryle to Lovell, 6 July 1955.

Ryle was capable of making such a detailed argument because Cambridge had undertaken 'extensive trials...to determine the probable interference from a number of individual Gee stations...[including] the field strength from Stenigot'. It is interesting to note that because the two 50 mile radius 'territories' of Cambridge and Jodrell Bank nearly overlapped (Stenigot was 'almost exactly the same distance from Jodrell and Cambridge'), Ryle and Lovell were able to negotiate over frequency space.

Ryle also argued extensively with Smith-Rose to protect Cambridge's 'only satisfactory frequency (81.5 Mc/s)'[126]:

> The sheer labour of converting those equipments to an alternative frequency, even if such could be found, would be sufficient to ensure that the lead which Jodrell and Cambridge have given the country would be lost.

Ryle used technical aspects, such as the 'phenomenal field strength' and the 'poor stability' of the Gee transmitter to prevent its proposed proximity. If the JFPP approved 73.8 Mc/s for Stenigot and Barkway then expansion of the Cambridge radio telescope system would be possible: 'we should then get definite clearance for the proposed site at Lord's Bridge, 5 miles SW of Cambridge, from all users'.[127]

This left the disputed 69 and 79 Mc/s. In the same letter proposing the compromise over 73.5 Mc/s, Lovell stated that 'concern over the proposal to operate Gee-H on 69.5 and 79 Mc/s at Camp Hill remains undiminished'. Change from these frequencies was 'impossible' without 'major reconstruction' and more 'manpower'. Worse, 'in the case of two of the programmes (73.5 and 79 Mc/s) the equipments are being duplicated in the Antarctic [for IGY]'.

The JFPP considered the affair in the light of the astronomers' remarks. The Air Ministry confirmed the change of the Stenigot and Barkway frequency to 73.8 Mc/s. Tests would be carried out on Camp Hill transmissions on 69 Mc/s and Stenigot on 73.8 Mc/s with respect to interference to Jodrell Bank. Finally, the Air Ministry 'would explore the possibility of using a frequency different from 79 Mc/s at Camp Hill'.[128] Smith-Rose hoped this provided 'some progress on a very thorny problem'.

Jodrell Bank and the Air Ministry carried out the 69 Mc/s tests in April

---

[126] JBA CS7/29/1. Letter, Ryle to Smith-Rose, 6 July 1955.

[127] Note the spatial metaphor for frequencies has caused ambiguity here: 'site' refers to a location (where?), whereas 'clearance' refers to the 'users' (of frequency). Ryle was engaged with a tortuous search in 1954-1955, involving the GPO and JFPP, for an interference-free site near Cambridge after being forced to move when a lease renewal was refused. The search was particularly complicated by the presence of nearby USAAF bases, such as Mildenhall and Lakenheath. RCA 4622 A.

[128] JBA CS7/29/1. Letter, Smith-Rose to Lovell, 13 July 1955.

1956. The result was 'severe interference' so bad that it 'caused [the Jodrell Bank] recording mechanism to trip continuously'.[129] This continued throughout the summer, after which the JFPP reconsidered the matter and suggested 68-68.5 Mc/s (in 'the upper limit of Broadcasting Band 1'[130]), which proved acceptable to Manchester: 'although the interference from Camphill is still present the pulses are reduced to about one and a half times our noise level...we are prepared to adjust our triggering level'.[131]

The Air Ministry took some time to bring the Gee stations on air, during which time Jodrell Bank carried on their observations on 79 Mc/s unhindered. However by June 1956, Lovell reported interference. This, the GPO reported was due to a Gee station at Great Dunfell in the Scottish chain starting fulltime operation.[132] Experiments continued intermittently after this but the interference proved too much and the frequency was not requested in the next round of allocations.

This concluded the rather convoluted negotiations of frequency, the 'thorny problem', between the Air Ministry and the Cambridge and Jodrell Bank radio astromomers. In this case the demands of the two observatories were different and conflicting so the usual 'mutual front' could not be presented to the allocating bodies. Compromise was reached not just through the official channel of radio astronomical interests, Smith-Rose, but also in direct negotiation with the Air Ministry, through the series of 'tests'. Many familiar arguments were mobilised: that radio astronomy was an asset to the country, that change was impossible because frequency decisions had been 'hard-wired' into the technology, that there were not the resources (money and manpower) to affect the change. The solution was indeed a compromise as neither the astronomers nor the Air Ministry survived with their initial plans unchanged. The actions of the radio astronomers caused substantial change in the Gee networks near them. As a remark by Lovell in 1958 reinforces, the frequency assignments were a negotiation over the surrounding local space:

> The present differences between our own demands and those of Ryle are not very significant. Where they exist it is nearly always because we have been asked to try different frequencies to suit local conditions, eg., the allocations at 79 and 81.5 Mc/s.[133]

However, the Air Ministry could call on stronger institutional allies. It was carrying out a 'national defence plan' and it was well represented on the

[129] JBA CS7/29/1. Letter, Lovell to G/C Passmore, 21 April 1956.

[130] JBA CS7/29/1. Letter, Golothan (Radio Services Department, GPO) to Lovell, 5 December 1956.

[131] JBA CS7/29/1. Letter, Lovell to Golothan, 12 December 1956.

[132] JBA CS7/29/1. Letter, Golothan to Lovell, 1 July 1957.

[133] JBA CS3/14/2. Letter, Lovell to Ratcliffe, 6 October 1958.

important committees. Against such an opponent, the radio astronomers were always likely to have to vacate frequency space, as 79 Mc/s bears out.

STAGE THREE: THE INTERNATIONAL ALLOCATION OF FREQUENCIES

No matter how persuasively Lovell, Ryle and Smith-Rose represented certain frequencies (such as the 354 Mc/s deuterium line) as naturally important for radio astronomy, the lists that were agreed were shaped by many contingent factors. Radio astronomers in other countries, such as Australia, the Netherlands and the USA, pursued national frequency space in a different context, and hence negotiated different lists. This created extra difficulties for the process of international allocation of frequencies for radio astronomy.

The position of the radio astronomers with respect to frequency allocation before 1959 was summed up by Lovell in a letter to Ratcliffe of the Cambridge observatory:

> I think we all take the attitude that it is no good proceeding with further individual requests for frequencies, but that we must accept the allocations which are made by the national or international bodies. The important thing is to strive to get these allocated one per octave, and then Ryle and ourselves and any other organisation will have to fall into line with these allocations.[134]

Security for radio astronomy's bands lay in their inclusion in the Radio Regulations, drawn up by the full ITU Conferences. The ITU scheduled the next Ordinary Administrative Radio Conference (OARC) to be in Geneva in 1959, the first since Atlantic City in 1947. Before Geneva, other international bodies had recommended the protection of frequencies for radio astronomy. Commission five of the International Scientific Radio Union (URSI), passed the following resolution seeking:

> ...by international agreement (via IAU and CCIR) to reserve for [radio astronomy]...one or more frequency bands on which radio traffic is prohibited.[135]

The ITU's radio International Radio Consultative Committee (the CCIR) passed a far stronger resolution the following year, recommending:

> That the attention of the various Administrations should be drawn to the desirability of reserving, where feasible, for the international study of solar

---

[134] JBA CS3/14/2. Letter, Lovell to Ratcliffe, 6 October 1958.
[135] JBA Proceedings, IXth URSI General Assembly, Zurich, 1950, Commission V, resolution 5.

radiation and of galactic radio noise, one particular exclusive frequency in each of several parts of the radio spectrum...[a list followed].[136]

Futhermore these actions should be made 'in preparation for the next Ordinary Administrative Radio Conference'. URSI then urged:

> that the CCIR ask the Frequency Allocation authorities to give all possible protection to those engaged in radio astronomical measurements in the radio spectrum from 10 Mc/s to 30,000 Mc/s.[137]

The CCIR responded stating that:

> ...Administrations should afford all practicable protection from interference to radio astronomical measurements, particularly on frequencies around 1420 Mc/s.[138]

The URSI met the following year in the Hague, present at which amongst others were Smith-Rose, Lovell and Ryle. It again commented on the CCIR's decisions:

> The URSI wishes to emphasise the importance of making adequate frequency allocations for radio astronomy. It is recommended that both the CCIR and the National Committees of URSI should take every possible step to obtain the necessary reservations. It is envisaged that at least one frequency per octave will be required with a bandwidth of between one and two percent...The URSI wishes to emphasise again the importance of reserving internationally a frequency band around the spectral line of neutral hydrogen.[139]

The DSIR warned the Cabinet Frequency Committee of these claims in 1955.[140] The CCIR adopted a very similar line at their 1956 General Assmbly in Warsaw. The URSI's lobbying of CCIR then came to a rest.

The external actions of such bodies as the URSI were not the most persuasive factors to the JFPP and the Cabinet Committee in Britain (despite the CCIR's appeals to the national 'Administrations'). The British frequency committees were more concerned with managing the national users of the radio spectrum, and the protection of British interests abroad, in particular the

---

[136] JBA Proceedings CCIR, Geneva 1951, Recommendation 56.

[137] JBA Proceedings Xth URSI General Assembly, Australia, 1952, Commission V, Resolution 1.

[138] JBA proceedings, CCIR, London, 1953, Recommendation 118.

[139] JBA Proceedings of the XIth General Assembly, The Hague, 1954, Commission V, Resolutions 4 and 5.

[140] RCA 2622 Pt 2. Memorandum, 'Summary of the action taken by the JFPP and the CFC to provide frequencies for radio astronomy', 18 October 1957.

defence interests tied up with NATO. However, the adoption of radio bands for the astronomers in the Radio Regulations, provided an important rhetorical resource for the radio astronomers to use in appeal to these committees.

Radio astronomers in the United States, Britain and the Netherlands shared news and strategies of their national attempts to secure quiet radio frequencies. Jan Oort, in Holland, wrote to Lovell requesting 'data on what has been reached in Great Britain and what is still being asked for'[141]; John Hagen, of the Naval Research Laboratory and later the National Radio Astronomy Observatory, wrote:

> I have become engaged in attempting to obtain clear channels for radio astronomy use in this country. I recall at the URSI Assembly that you said you were doing the same thing in England...could you let me know your progress and [your] list of bands you chose to ask for. In so far as possible I think we should attempt to coordinate our requests looking forward to a future international agreement...[142]

Such coordination was to difficult to achieve, as is revealed by comparing the frequencies used by American observatories with the British lists: there is very little overlap.[143]

The BJCEB and JFPP, reluctant in assigning frequencies internally to the radio astronomers, remained to be convinced of the advantages in seeking secure international frequencies for astronomy at the ITU. The planning within Whitehall for the Geneva conference had begun in 1957 with the setting up of an Interdepartmental Steering Committee (ISC), along with its Frequency Allocation Sub-Committee (FSC). Late in that year the FSC requested from Smith-Rose 'details of the frequencies now in use at Jodrell Bank and Cambridge and details of those frequencies requiring national protection'.[144] Lovell and Ryle passed revised lists of frequencies through Smith-Rose to Colonel Severin of JFPP and BJCEB. The request for comments from departments on these lists was interpreted by some as a 'reopening' of the question of frequencies for radio astronomy.[145] The lists provoked queries over bandwidths, and closer correlation between Cambridge and Manchester lists, both of which would have reduced the total request. Lovell resisted. The bandwidths were 'realistic...they should not be reduced', and conceded frequency sharing except where 'it is not practicable for us...we

[141] JBA CS7/29/1. Letter, Oort to Lovell, 6 September 1954.

[142] JBA CS7/29/1. Letter, Hagen to Lovell, 17 December 1954.

[143] JBA CS7/29/1. Table, 'Requested Frequency Allocations for Radio Astronomy', 1 September 1956.

[144] RCA 2622 Pt 2. Minutes, 90th JFPP, 10 December 1957.

[145] RCA 2622 Pt 2. Letter, Best (Home Office) to Chair BJCEB, 28 March 1958. The Home Office thought that the 50 mile frequency zones around Jodrell Bank needlessly restricted police and fire services in Yorkshire and Lancashire.

have a wide range of transmission activities on [38 or 36.3] and Ryle receives only'[146]. Some departments, including the GPO and Home Office, continued to view the information from the radio astronomers as insufficient. With these divisions to manage, the JFPP set up a Working Party to examine the claims. The radio astronomers were excluded from membership of the Working Party, and were allowed only representation via the DSIR. Severin justified this decision to Smith-Rose as enabling 'certain requirements of the Armed Forces and other users to be discussed more freely than would be the case' otherwise.[147] The Working Party meetings stalled over demands for 'precise guidance concerning the protection [radio astronomers] require...in terms of field strengths', a demand that Smith-Rose deflected, relaying the counter-demand for 'complete protection'.[148]

The radio astronomers did not just request frequencies that tied in with the programmes and equipment already in progress. They also linked them in with future concerns. Ratcliffe wrote expansively to Lovell on 'two matters which are most important for both of us', the first was 'Frequencies for Radio Astronomy', the second the 'Future of Radio Astronomy':

> Has not the time come when we should all be thinking about the future of Radio Astronomy in this country, in 8 or 10 years' time, and getting others to plan? Are we to have National Observatory, or what?.[149]

The National Observatory was seen as the next step in the progressively more expensive line of radio telescopes: 'I believe that we should be thinking of capital expenditures of the order of 20 to 50 million pounds in order to plan telescopes which can combine all the advantages of the Ryle and Jodrell techniques'[150]. Ratcliffe's plan drew inspiration from two new joint university institutions: the British nuclear physics facilities, NIRNS, and the American National Radio Astronomical Observatory (NRAO) in West Virginia. The campaign utilised the nationalist argument again: 'If we fail to do this we may be subject to severe criticism in the future for allowing British Radio Astronomy to decline'. Avenues used were both internal to the funding machinery ('I had intended to raise this question at an early meeting of Blackett's sub-committee [for] astronomy applications to the Scientific Grants Committee of the DSIR'), and external, such as Lovell's 1958 Reith Lectures discussed in Chapter Four.

This ambitious plan chimed with the expansionist strategies in the radio spectrum. The astronomers pursued this along familiar routes. Cambridge

---

[146] JBA CS3/14/2. Letter, Lovell to Smith-Rose, 24 September 1958.
[147] RCA 2622 Pt 2. Letter, Severin to Smith-Rose, 7 May 1958.
[148] RCA 2622 Pt 2. Letter, Smith-Rose to Severin, 15 May 1958.
[149] JBA CS3/14/2. Letter, Ratcliffe to Lovell, 2 October 1958.
[150] JBA CS3/14/2. Letter, Lovell to Ratcliffe, 6 October 1958.

and Jodrell Bank composed a joint letter to Smith-Rose (also signed by Hey of the Army Operational Research Group at the Royal Radar Establishment at Malvern). In this they aimed to 're-state our requirements for frequencies in this field of work and relate them to the recommendations of interested international bodies'.[151] It drew attention to the International Astronomical Union (IAU) statements that emission bands and 'bands of width 2-3% centred roughly on the harmonic series of frequencies 40, 80, 160, 320, 640, 1280 Mc/s and so on (the 'one per octave' demand) should be protected. Although they conceded that 'it may prove necessary, for local reasons, to choose a frequency differing somewhat from the exact harmonic relationship', the astronomers reiterated their desire 'to preserve the harmonic series as far as possible since there will then be less trouble with harmonics of transmitters on lower frequencies', a technical argument that allowed a greater claim on spectrum space to be made.[152] The statement included a list of requested frequencies, many of which are the familiar ones, now re-interpreted and matched to the IAU harmonic pattern. It is clear what was happening: the international list was enlisted as yet another argument to protect astronomy's existing frequencies and annex further ones. International allies were recruited to solve local disputes. This is again shown in the two 'matters which urgently require consideration', first:

> The frequency 178 Mc/s, on which the large aerial at the Mullard Observatory works, appears to be in serious danger from the extension of Television. There will then be no frequncy near the 'international' 160 Mc/s.

The second summed up the astronomers demands that the 'authorities should go to Geneva...with a precise statement how they propose to assist radio astronomy in this country, in line with international requirements so that ...they can get frequencies assigned on a world-wide basis'.

With Smith-Rose thus notified, Ratcliffe widened the strategy: 'I think the next move should be that we put as nearly as possible simultaneously, through the DSIR and Royal Society, an official demand for precisely the same frequencies, making a case in general terms that frequencies should be allocated for purely scientific purposes, in addition to commercial purposes'.[153] One reason for such a widening of strategy seems to be a lack of faith in the commitment of Smith-Rose, voiced by Ratcliffe: 'I have had a rather disappointing talk with him about [the joint letter]. He is certainly

---

[151] JBA CS7/29/2. Copy of joint letter signed by Lovell to Smith-Rose, 15 December 1958.

[152] Also an argument that does not hold on close examination if divergences due to 'local conditions' are allowed.

[153] JBA CS3/14/2. Letter, Ratcliffe to Lovell, 23 December 1959.

not a very strong advocate for us'.[154] Ratcliffe's letter reflected the inter-mingling of international spectrum requests, internal Royal Society machinery, specific local frequency disputes, public protestations, and the National Observatory. The local dispute was the use of 178 Mc/s by the Cambridge interferometer which was threatened by television expansion: 'we intend to preserve the frequency...by direct action with BBC and ITA to get them to delay allocation of that channel'. However 'to prepare the background for this manoeuvre', Ratcliffe urged that:

> there should be a leading article in, for example, *The Observer*, drawing attention to the importance of Radio Astronomy for this Country and the danger in which it is because no frequencies are allocated for Science. It has to step into the (unused) TV bands...it has nowhere else to go. The only solution is to stop work, or move, at great cost, to a remote site...Postponement of interference from TV is essential, if the present equipment which has been constructed at a cost of about £50,000 is not to be put out of use.

This article, which Ratcliffe suggested Lovell write since 'after the Reith lectures it will come best from you', would also 'pave the way for the provision of finances for the ultimate National Observatory'. The article was not written: after discussing it with Hanbury Brown, Lovell 'concluded that it might be a very risky and dangerous manoeuvre. First it would probably annoy the frequency allocation people, and second it might provide another excuse for not financing radio astronomy'.[155] With the prestigious Radio Telescope now successfully publicly demonstrated, a project that required careful distancing from the Cambridge programme, Lovell was also not likely to be enthusiastic about the loss of control that a future National Observatory might represent.

Smith-Rose drew up a document for circulation outlining the present and future frequency requirements for radio astronomy. He was 'unoptimistic' about the IAU proposal for a harmonic series:, saying 'it would seem to be impracticable at the present time to make the various changes in other services which would be necessary'.[156] Furthermore on certain frequencies, for instance 178 Mc/s, radio astronomers would have to 'face the fact' that the frequencies were lost and 'prepare their plans for future research accordingly'. To the radio astronomers this did not 'state our case strongly enough'[157], and

---

[154] JBA CS3/14/2. Letter, Ratcliffe to Lovell, 12 January 1959.

[155] JBA CS3/14/2. Letter, Lovell to Ratcliffe, 22 January 1959.

[156] JBA CS7/19/2. Letter, Smith-Rose to Lovell, 28 January 1959. This is the covering letter to the document Smith-Rose, 'Allocation of Frequencies for Radio Astronomy', 27 January 1959.

[157] JBA CS3/14/2. Letter, Ratcliffe to Lovell, 3 February 1959.

Ratcliffe drew up a new memorandum, backed up by Lovell.[158] This memorandum reiterated the IAU call for a harmonic list, and presented a table of frequencies in use. For these it *'strongly urged that they be now clearly assigned for Radio Astronomy'.*[159] A special case was made for 178 Mc/s to be withheld from television: the 'disappearance of this frequency would completely jeopardise the very important work on the cosmological aspect of Radio Astronomy', which was combined with an inducement offered that Cambridge would sacrifice 81.5 Mc/s as long as 'present services in the band are not reorganised in frequency or geographically in a way which would increase the interference to Radio Astronomy'.

The first step in the Royal Society approach was the passing of a resolution through its BNCSR, the chair of which had passed from Appleton to Ratcliffe. The resolution recommended the protection of the emission lines and 'a band in each octave above 30 Mc/s'[160] at the 'forthcoming meeting of the ITU at Geneva'. The Committee decision was communicated to the President of the Royal Society with an accompanying explanatory paper from Ratcliffe. He urged that the President 'forward [the resolution] to the authorities at the highest level, if possible direct to the Post Master General and the Lord President'.[161] Ratcliffe included five arguments for the resolution: radio astronomy produced results of cosmological importance; the maximal size of the existing telesopes argued for minimising interference; the 'important part of astronomy' that measured the 'spectral distribution of the radiations' implied that 'one frequency per octave is a bare minimum'; progress would open up the need for higher and higher frequencies; and finally,

If this country is to keep the lead already established in radio astronomy it must plan for the future, possibly for a central radio astronomy observatory. Unless action is taken now there will be no frequencies available, and the initiative will pass to other countries.

The Council of the Royal Society passed on these resolutions demanding 'one frequency per octave' to the Post Master General and the Lord President of the Council. The bodies working on frequency policy for Geneva rebuffed the move:

---

[158] 'I have agreed with him a brief for your use which you will be receiving immediately'.

[159] JBA CS7/19/2. Document, 'Allocation of Frequencies for Radio Astronomy', with rider 'For S-R to put to the Cabinet Committee'.

[160] JBA CS7/19/2. Document, 'Radio Frequencies for Scientific Purposes', with rider 'For royal Society to send to the PMG'.

[161] JBA CS7/19/2. Document, 'Allocation of Radio Frequencies for Scientific Purposes', from the BNCSR Chair to the President of the Royal Society, 7 February 1959.

> This recommendation [of one frequency per octave] has been considered briefly by the Panel [JFPP], the FSC and the Interdepartmental Steering Committee. In each case the view was expressed that there would be little likelihood of obtaining international protection for these bands.[162]

This brevity stemmed in part from irritation that the details of the radio astronomers' demands were known in early 1959, disturbing 'over a year of intensive study and negotiation' in which 'the UK proposals for international allocations [had been] completed'.[163] Arguments in the subject's favour that met approval within the JFPP and FSC were the 'intrinsic value of radio astronomy and the important defence aspects of certain research'.[164] The consensus was that 'the Service Ministries and other Government Departments [had] already gone out of their way to help'[165], and that 'in view of the difficulties facing the legitimately established users of the radio spectrum in trying to make way for the radio astronomers, the [arrangements so far]...can be regarded as a very satisfactory accomplishment'. The policy response of the frequency committees in rebuffing the Royal Society was to reject the harmonic series (as 'quite impractical') and to work with the DSIR-supplied list of working frequencies and deal with these as best they could:

> of 11 frequency recommendations, 11 suitable alternatives were agreed upon; 2 frequencies were of a very doubtful nature...one fell in the NATO military UHF communications band...no alternatives could be suggested; the last frequency falls into a band in which a new defence requirement is now being discussed at Foreign Office - State Department level ...[and] was therefore deferred.

Protection for the very lowest frequencies in the list was to be sought at international level, whereas interference on the other frequencies was only to be minimised by national rearrangement.[166] Not even a letter from the Lord

---

[162] RCA 2622 Pt 2. Memorandum by Severin (BJCEB), 'Frequencies for radio astronomy', 9 March 1959.

[163] RCA 2622 Pt 2. Memorandum by Severin, 'Comments by the BJCEB on the letter dated 23 March 1959 from the Lord President of Council to the Postmaster General', 7 April 1959

[164] RCA 2622 Pt 2. Draft memorandum to chair of ISC, 'Provision of frequencies for radio astronomy', 6 April 1959.

[165] The sentence carried on 'but the radio astronomers appear to have remained very much a law unto themselves', but this was later crossed out. Elsewhere, the radio astronomers were said to 'clearly not understand that, in the general interest, users of radio frequencies accept a discipline without which there would be chaos in the...spectrum'. RCA 2622 Pt 2. Memorandum, 'Frequencies for radio astronomy', prepared for CDS staff, 2 April 1959.

[166] The frequencies taken to Geneva were around: 38, 81.5, 178, 322, 408, 600, 900, 1400-1427, 1645-1675, 2295, 5260, and 9850 Mc/s for reception only, of which

President of the Council, Lord Hailsham, urging that 'when the allocations of these frequency bands are being made, it is important to try to meet the request put forward by the radio astronomers to the fullest extent possible', could undo this policy decision.[167]

The policy was taken to Geneva in 1959, with Smith-Rose accompanying the British delegation as a representative of scientific radio. Lovell and Ratcliffe communicated its outcome to radio astronomers in the US and Holland. Findlay of the NRAO, as chairman of Commission V, coordinated the URSI approach to Geneva, for which it achieved the IAU's blessing at their Moscow 1959 meeting. This involved putting the IAU 'harmonic' proposal to the ITU radio Consultative Committee (CCIR), and preparing a lengthy document of arguments for radio astronomy. URSI produced arguments based on practical spin-offs of fundamental research to support the harmonic claim. The Dutch radio physicist and mathematician, Prof Dr Balth van der Pol, represented the URSI and IAU position at Geneva.

What were the results of this carefully planned attempt to secure international protection for radio astronomy's frequency bands? A number of frequencies were indeed allocated for radio astronomy. These were different in the different Regions[168], which relieved some of the international tensions between radio astronomy groups' requests. The ITU allocated the following in Region 1 (which included Britain): 2.5, 5, 10, 15, 20, 25, 38.0, 40.68, 79.75-80.25, 150.05-153, 322-329 (the deuterium line), 404-410, 606-614, 1400-1427 (the hydrogen line), 2690- 2700, 4990-5000 Mc/s and 10.68-10.7, 15.35-15.4, 19.3-19.4, 31.3-31.5 Gc/s. There are several points to notice. First, the ITU allocated almost one frequency per octave. Second, the frequencies actually secured have diverged from the harmonic series that the IAU recommended. This is not surprising considering the bargaining nature of the Conference. Third, there was little overlap with the lists touted by the British radio astronomers. This had several consequences. Where the frequency was in use, such as 38 Mc/s at Cambridge, 'the band [was to be]

---

only 322 (Deuterium line search) and 1645-1675 (OH line search) were taken direct from NCSR suggestions. Transmission and reception frequencies were also taken based around: 36.3, one of 68, 72 and 73.5, 100 and 410.25 Mc/s.

RCA 4622 Pt 3. Minutes of JFPP Working Party on 'Frequencies for radio astronomy', held on 18 and 24 March 1959.

[167] RCA 2622 Pt 2. Letter, Lord Hailsham (Lord President of the Council) to Rt Hon Ernest Marples (Post Master General), 23 March 1959.

[168] The International Administrative Radio Conference at Atlantic City in 1947 divided the world into three 'Regions' for the purposes of frequency allocation. Region 1 consisted of Africa, Europe and Russia; Region 2, the Americas; and Region 3 non-Russian Asia and Oceania.
Post Office Electrical Engineering Journal (1950) 43, p. 202.

protected as far as practicable'.[169] Where there were plans for use, for instance 150-153 Mc/s, then the authorities allocated the band 'in such a way as to afford maximum protection when services at present using the band [in this case fixed and mobile services] are withdrawn'.

The allocation of the Deuterium band of 322-329 Mc/s, the original 'germ' of radio astronomers' expansionist strategies, was bitterly contested. The radio astronomers pleaded that 'they had expensive equipment (about £100,000 worth at Cambridge and nearly £1 million worth at Jodrell Bank)' based on this frequency.[170] A calculation by the BJCEB put the capital investment of defence equipment in 225-400 Mc/s at £35 million.[171] Ratcliffe, demanding 'suitable national allocation' along with 'some agreement with France, Holland and Belgium to protect the band', was reported as being 'prepared to press his case to the highest levels'. The Ministry of Defence expressed worry, and sought an ally in the United States: it requested the British Joint Scientific Mission (BJSM) in Washington to communicate its 'national policy...that the UK will not repeat not support any international or national allocation for radio astronomy if it falls within 225-400 Mc/s band' which was reserved for NATO communications.[172] The MOD said that the 'UK military was suffering intolerable pressure to allow broadcasters' into the band.[173] The US agreed to protect NATO at Geneva.[174] The radio astronomers could be unknowing allies of the cold war enemies, as the MOD put it:

> either...NATO nations and their friends sit back and allow Soviet Bloc and others to negotiate the international allocation of the Deuterium Line, or [allow]...UK military [to] vigorously oppose this.[175]

However, with support from other Western European nations the Geneva conference resolved that national 'Administrations should bear in mind the

---

[169] JBA CS3/14/2. Document, 'Administrative Radio Conference 1959: Frequency Allocations for Radio Astronomy'.

[170] RCA 4622 Pt 3. Memorandum, 'Note to the file 2622', 23 April 1959.

[171] RCA 2622 Pt 2. Memorandum, 'Frequencies for radio astronomy', 2 April 1959.

[172] RCA 4622 Pt 3. Telegram Sepia 18, Ministry of Defence to BJSM, Washington, 16 July 1959.

[173] RCA 4622 Pt 3. Telegram Purple 45, MOD to BJSM, 7 August 1959. It continued: 'once a breach is made in the 225-400 band, the flood gates will be opened. This will be serious in area of NATO Europe...'.

[174] RCA 4622 Pt 3. Telegram Mauve 646, BJSM to Ministry of Defence, 6 August 1959.

[175] This unwitting alliance reoccurred in one-off problems during the early 1960s, such as the American plan to launch an orbiting belt of metal 'needles' as part of the West Ford communication system, or the high level 'Rainbow Bomb' nuclear explosion.

needs of radio astronomy in future planning of this band'.[176] This was in effect a commitment to organise a shared band, a partial success for the radio astronomers which fell far short of the UK and US hopes. The defeat prompted the UK military to allow less discussion of its frequencies even in internal negotiations.[177]

So here, as with a few others, the ITU allocations enabled the radio astronomers to gain spectrum space. In bands like 178 Mc/s, around which Cambridge had constructed their large interferometer and the ITU had not allocated, there carried on the precarious local agreements 'until the band is required for television'. In bands which had been allocated but where British radio astronomers had no existing plan (such as 40.68 Mc/s) 'no protection could be given'. Here the astronomers lost ground. The authorities considered the use of very high frequencies as unproblematic. The result was therefore some strengthening of protection of frequencies, but also the continuing negotiation and pragmatic assignment of others.

CONCLUSION

Before World War II, the high incidence of fog, smoke and dust in the atmosphere led to the construction of the 200" optical telescope on Mount Palomar well away from interference sources such as industrial and domestic complexes. The United Kingdom possesses an exceedingly sophisticated and dense electronic environment in which noise and signal levels are very high. The wisdom of constructing expensive radio astronomy observatories in the heart of this environment is open to question...[178]

---

[176] RCA 4622 Pt 3. Letter, G/C Gaine to Chair European Military Communications Co-ordinating Committee (EMCCC), 6 January 1960.

[177] RCA 4622 Pt 4. Minute sheet, 27 September 1961. This records: 'I mentioned the antagonism at international conferences to the provision of frequency bands for military requirements...the Soviet Bloc is opposed to NATO and there are countries who are opposed even to civil requirements of a nation such as ours. For example, at the 1959 OARC, the only Commonwealth countries who supported the UK when the latter was in difficulties, were Australia, New Zealand, South Africa and Canada...It seems to me that it is unwise to allow information on NATO military use of the band 225-400 Mc/s to be disseminated under unclassified cover. Scientists are not people who are much concerned with or worried about such mundane matters as security – the recipients of the CCMs are bound to talk to other scientists – and all this helps spread the word that the scientists are prevented from securing exclusive use of the Deuterium Line...by the NATO military (a matter which was concealed at the OARC, Geneva, 1959) – and this will lead to others (who are not friends of NATO) making their demands for the use of the band for services other than radio astronomy'.

[178] RCA 2622 Pt 2. Memorandum, 'Frequencies for radio astronomy', prepared for CDS staff, 2 April 1959.

Nationally we are now going into this thing [radio astronomy] in a big way...We shall look ridiculous politically if, this expensive apparatus having been financed by the Government, we prevent its effective use by letting the ether in its neighbourhood get hopelessly overcrowded. There is already...a certain amount of public comment on this question.[179]

Geographical location is a determining factor, of course, and unfortunately the astronomers could hardly have chosen a worse site that Jodrell Bank from the point of view of avoiding interference...[180]

In this conclusion I will first summarise the stages by which radio astronomers found a secure position within the hostile 'electronic environment' of Britain. Second, I discuss the strategies that they used in this campaign, drawing comparisons to the efforts to secure funding. Last, I investigate how this campaign was played out on two intersecting geographies: the physical and the radio spectrum.

The radio astronomers began as outsiders to the bureaucracy of radio frequency allocation: their research programmes had barely begun when the spectrum was divided and reallocated at Atlantic City in 1947. Frequencies were already allocated, largely by government departments: the political geography of Whitehall was imprinted on the geography of the radio spectrum. As radio astronomy observatories, new organisations within an already structured environment, expanded there was soon a conflict: disturbances expressed in terms of 'interference'. I showed how Cambridge and Jodrell Bank radio astronomers began to counter this 'threat': by coordinating lists of requested frequencies and mobilising what powerful allies they could, in particular the Royal Society. The lobbying by the Royal Society of the Post Master General and Lord President of the Council, led to no totally 'secure' frequencies, but did gain both recognition of radio astronomy as a legitimate new 'user' and representation on the important frequency committees.

In the second stage of the campaign, I showed how the possession of a voice inside the frequency allocation process allowed the demands of the radio astronomers to be heard. Negotiations on committees such as the Joint Frequency Planning Panel and the Cabinet Frequency Committee led to 'arrangements' whereby the activities of government departments within 50 miles of Jodrell Bank and Cambridge were deflected to minimise interference.

The third stage continued the project of securing and extending a productive quiet within the observatories, this time by recruiting a new international resource: inclusion in the Radio Regulations hammered out at

---

[179] PRO CAB 124 1773. Letter, 'Bobbety' (Marquess of Salisbury, Lord President to 'Buck' (The Earl De La Warr, Post Master General), 22 December 1953.

[180] PRO CAB 124 1773. Letter, 'Buck' to 'Bobbety', 19 January 1954.

the 1959 Ordinary Administrative Radio Conference of the ITU. The third stage utilised four avenues: Smith-Rose's representation on the committees, lobbying through the DSIR and Royal Society, using the recommendations of international scientific bodies such as the IAU, and coordinating efforts with radio astronomers abroad. The ITU fulfilled the radio astronomers wishes of allocations of at least 'one frequency per octave' for their use. However, international allocation was only an argumentative resource, and did not translate directly into secure and quiet frequencies: assignment and clearance of frequencies still had to be achieved through the national administration.[181]

The campaign for spectrum space linked with the campaign to secure funding, in particular for the expensive projects such as the large interferometer arrays at Cambridge and the Radio Telescope at Jodrell Bank. The frequencies that were allocated as a result of the contested process I have described were built into the radio technology of the telescopes, such as the aerial and amplifier design. The pressure on the newcomer to settle for higher frequencies reinforced other motivations such as the scientific rewards of hydrogen line research and the utility of the defence interpretation of the Radio Telescope as a possible radar installation. The claim that the frequency had been built into the radio telescope was also made rhetorically: in order to persuade others in committee that the telescope would be more difficult and expensive to change. The deuterium emission line provides an excellent example of this: chosen by the radio astronomers in an attempt to breach the broad military band 200-400 Mc/s.[182] Both campaigns for funding and frequencies advanced by the construction of broad alliances: the mobilisation and lobbying of key allies that went beyond the strict official routes of securing resources. A precondition of building these broad alliances was the position of the radio astronomers in the networks of contacts and influence that linked scientific, governmental and military bodies. Like the effort to support the Radio Telescope financially, the arguments that carried the broad alliance to gain frequencies included predicted practical applications, national prestige symbolised by leadership in the field, and hinted defence implications.

I argued that the radio spectrum represented a bureaucratically-created

---

[181] This was always an ongoing process: 'there can never be finality in this field; the technological position is changing frequently and the various committees have to do their best to meet equitably, at any given time, the needs of various claimants'. RCA 2622 Pt 1. Letter, Lord Salisbury to Sir David Brunt, 29 January 1954.

[182] The strategy could break down if the scientific importance of the specific band could be unpacked. This happened with the deuterium band at one stage when the British military realised that no emission on that line had even been detected: 'Earlier this year an *honest* radio astronomer *admitted* that the Deuterium line had not been located by observers in UK and even if achieved the emission line would be so weak that little advantage would be gained from observation'. RCA 4622 Pt 3. Telegram, Ministry of Defence to British Joint Scientific Mission, 16 July 1959 (my emphasis).

space, and offered two models to account for this. Since spatial metaphor was used to discuss the radio spectrum the campaign to secure frequencies for radio astronomy was an expansionist one. There was a reciprocal interaction between the geographies of the radio spectrum and of physical space. This interaction was because a change as a result of a negotiation over the committee-defined spectrum reciprocated a rearrangement in physical space. The cure for interference required either movement in physical space or in the spectrum. At many instances in this chapter the radio astronomers, foregoing an entirely clear and quiet frequency, agreed a compromise with a government department. This compromise would involve the deflection of activities, such as the flights of aircraft or the construction of radio beacon networks, away from the sensitive observatories. This settlement found spatial expression in the fifty mile zones that radiated from Jodrell Bank and Cambridge: a boundary built to separate disruptive and intrusive sources from the productive and quiet astronomical sites.[183] The boundary, and the borders within the spectrum that separated designated bands, was a managed and negotiated expression of power struggles. The radio astronomers were aware of the consequences if this struggle was lost, and their opponents on the frequency committees won: made known in the repeated high-level suggestions that they consider moving altogether from Cambridge and Jodrell Bank.

Constant activity was thus necessary to hold the observatories in position within the intersecting geographies of physical space and the radio spectrum. A stable quiet observatory was a precondition of the production of signals rather than noise. The interpretative dilemma discussed at the beginning of this chapter meant that this production was an acute ontological and epistemological problem for radio astronomers. The work needed to establish the precondition (building alliances and persuading government bodies to protect frequencies) meant the epistemological and ontological was enmeshed with the social. The activities of the radio astronomers spread productive and disciplined quiet outwards from Jodrell Bank: a social project I examine from a different angle in the next chapter.

---

[183] The 50 mile boundary was not a given: it could be, and was, contested. For example the Home Office, aware that several police and fire services operated within 50 miles of Jodrell Bank, argued: 'This [limit] has always appeared to be unrealistic and so vague that it might lead to unnecessary inconvenience to other users. A 100 W transmitter from a hill 60 miles away might well produce a stronger field at the radio astronomy receiving point than a 1 W transmitter ten miles away, while a 5 W transmitter from an aircraft at appreciable height could easily cause more interference than a 25 W transmitter at ground level'. RCA 2622 Pt 2. Letter, Best to Chair JFPP, 28 March 1958.

CHAPTER 5

Clearing the Ground: Bodily Control, the Radio Telescope and its Environment

Jodrell Bank is not our Big Brother[1]

This chapter follows up Chapter Four's focus on locality and interference. The scientific practices of radio astronomy could not exist in isolation from the practices and ways of life of its other neighbours in the North West. There occured several confrontations over the planning and nature of local land use and development throughout the period in which the telescope was built and put to use. In particular this chapter will discuss the expansion of nearby villages, towns and cities, the electrification of the railways, and the laying down of power lines, all with resultant changes in the social patterns of the inhabitants of Cheshire. In Chapter Four, I showed that constant activity outside the observatory was needed from the radio astronomers to ensure that a quiet productive space existed within it. This activity resulted in quiet extending from the observatory out to a negotiated zone around Jodrell Bank and Cambridge of fifty mile radius. An analogous outcome of the conflicts over local development was the codification of the negotiations in the form of planning regulations. These codifications, which, like the frequency politics, deflected and transformed surrounding ways of life, also spread outwards from Jodrell Bank. I discuss the restrictions at the centre of this zone in terms of the 'internal discipline' of the observatory.

In Chapter Three I showed how the promotion of the Radio Telescope as the DSIR's Great Public Spectacle, and the subsequent 'hordes' that visited to witness the instrument from the local centres of population, conflicted with the astronomers' assertions that only a secure, uninterrupted site would be scientifically productive. This assertion found expression in what I called the discourse of interference: a way of talking in terms of 'disturbance', 'intrusion', and dangerous 'interference' that both held the visiting public

---

[1] JBA CS7/28/1. *Crewe Chronicle (Sandbach Edition)*, 12 June 1969.

back at the boundaries of Jodrell Bank, and evaluated and interpreted the output of the telescope. In this chapter the discourse of interference is shown to define a distance between the observatory and the *urban* public: a group, seen as *embodying* destructive interference, made visible by encroaching 'overspill towns' and transport systems.

After examining the internal restrictions of action within Jodrell Bank, I discuss the tensions of the telescope within its physical environment in three stages. I first consider the developments in the 1940s and 1950s: the planned expansion of nearby towns as Manchester 'overspills' which caused a clash between the desires of astronomers and local business. The outcomes of this collision, as achieved through the processes of local government were the codification of activities, such the planning of new housing, the construction of buildings and the operation of certain machinery, and the division of the land: different areas of Cheshire were now different (and marked as such) because of the existence of the observatory. I also look at other spatial disputes that concerned the astronomers: for example the electrification of the railways and the expansion in the use of the automobile. Second, I continue the account of codification and division by considering the public appeals brought against the planning restrictions in the 1960s.[2] Here, the representational and textual strategies deployed to 'protect' the telescope are examined. Thirdly, I follow how these attempts to break the zonal planning agreements that bounded developers near Jodrell Bank prompted the University to seek ever more solid legal protection of their observatory.

INTERNAL DISCIPLINE

The initial choice in 1945 of Jodrell Bank, a few fields near Chelford 18 miles south of Manchester, as the location of some temporary radar experiments on cosmic ray showers was taken on pragmatic grounds. The apparatus was heavy, bulky but transportable: it was housed in trucks such as the 'Port Royal'. However, the cosmic ray experiments could not be sited within Manchester, urban activities such as the running of electrical trams causing interference.[3] The Manchester University Botany Department only partially used the Jodrell Bank site, the location of the first cosmic ray experiments there being determined by the contingent availability of a third unused field.[4] As the research programme developed in the first few years at

---

[2] It is unfortunate that the loss of files, before deposition at the Jodrell Bank Archives relating to local development in the 1950s, means that a suitably detailed account is impossible.

[3] Lovell (1968), p. 2.

[4] Lovell (1968), p. 30.

Jodrell Bank, the astronomers' time, money and careers began to be more and more heavily invested in the site. The location was materially transformed: new aerials were built, huts and roads constructed. Such changes were coextensive with the growth and reformation of organisational structures. Under Blackett's regime the organisational emphasis was placed on fast expansion in a clutch of professor-led teams: the (now) radio astronomy group grew distinct from the Manchester University Physics Department sited within the University's centre along the Oxford Road. The contacts and credibility built up before and after 1945 ensured that the radio astronomy group would not have an inferior relation to the Physics Department as perhaps its peripheral physical location might imply.

As more credit was sunk into organisational growth at Jodrell Bank, so more attention was paid to protecting the site as a productive scientific space. Instructions had to be issued telling the growing numbers of staff how to behave if the observatory was to be productive. From May 1950 it was 'strictly forbidden for any member of Jodrell Bank to drive a car or motor-cycle on the premises unless it is satisfactorily suppressed'.[5] This measure, along with 'arrangements...made to prevent any vehicles entering the premises', was made 'to reduce all disturbing traffic to a minimum'. Soon, other activities within the observatory had to be disciplined:

> The inteference during the daytime from machines and other apparatus in use on the station has become so serious that very urgent action must now be taken to remove it.[6]

A 'systematic investigation of all sources of interference, such as electrical drills, calculating machines, etc' was carried out, 'to suppress them where possible'. Anything unsuppressible was 'banned from use'. The elimination of disturbing interference in order to secure a quiet laboratory meant being carefully attentive to what staff *did*.

This internal discipline was automated wherever possible. In response to a query over telescope design from the Leiden radio astronomer Jan Oort, Lovell had replied:

> In designing our new Radio Telescope, we set ourselves the task of reducing the intensity of the interference by 400 times...[7]

This was achieved by the 'use of a focal plane design which effects an improvement of 20 times' because the spill from the primary feed over the

---

[5] JBA JBM/1/5. Notice, 18 April 1950.

[6] JBA JBM/1/5.Notice, 20 November 1953.

[7] JBA CS7/15/2. Letter, Lovell to Oort, 12 March 1953.

edge of the dish was reduced[8], and 'by siting the new instrument' at a greater distance from 'the nearest road point'.

THE FIRST CONFLICTS OVER LOCAL DEVELOPMENT

The application and granting of planning permission to build the 'new paraboloid' were relatively painless considering the size and location of the instrument, although Lovell records that it was not 'given almost instantly'. Three conditions were made: '(1) we must preserve the trees and replant, (2) we must discuss the colour of the telescope with the Council for the Preservation of Rural England [CPRE], (3) we must inform the Air Ministry...'.[9]

A letter from the Cheshire County Planning Department wrote that the CPRE's view on the telescope's colour was 'that the lower portion of the structure should be painted in a rural green colour, and the upper portion...should be painted grey or silver'.[10] The Air Ministry needed to be notified because of a disused aerodrome nearby.[11]

The construction of new housing was an emotive political issue in post-war Britain with both Labour and Conservatives promising hundreds of thousands of new homes. 'Overspill' housing near the big cities, in particular the New Towns, were an exciting expression of the possibilities of planning. The radio astronomers first became aware that the land near the telescope could be developed as part of the rehousing of Manchester's overspill population in the Autumn of 1952 (at the time the telescope's first foundations were being laid):

> Seven miles to the South West were the salt towns of Sandbach and Middlewich and the danger of subsidence was so great that no one entertained the idea of extensive building there. At the same distance South east was Congleton...Envious eyes were cast on this region by the planners: the Congleton Borough Council wanted development, but to us it was vital that Congleton should not grow a great conurbation towards the telescope.[12]

---

[8] Other design aspects sought to minimise interference generated by the instrument itself, for example in a description of the Radio Telescope, Lovell stated 'there are no slip rings so that the danger of interference is avoided'. Lovell, A.C.B., 1959. 'The Jodrell Bank Radio Telescope', *Nature* 180, p. 60.

[9] Lovell (1968), p. 160

[10] JBA CS7/15/2. Letter, Assistant Area Planning Officer, County Planning Department of Cheshire County Council to Lovell, 2 July 1952.

[11] Lovell (1968), p. 161.

[12] Lovell (1968), p. 161.

Lovell made his concerns known to the Ministry of Housing and Local Government. He records the political bargaining of this period as follows: Manchester 'wished to extend its territory by absorbing Mobberley and Lymm', to which encroachment Cheshire County Council was opposed. The Cheshire County Council 'in cooperation with the Congleton Borough Council' therefore offered Congleton as an alternative site. The University's response was ambivalent: 'the urgent need for extending the University premises...could not be done until the people were rehoused'.[13] On the astronomers' side was the Rural District Council who opposed the expansion of Congleton. The Minister of Housing and Local Government called a Public Inquiry in October 1953. A local MP, Colonel F.J. Erroll attempted to raise the question of the siting of the telescope and satellite town development in parliament.[14] With the only material evidence of the construction of the telescope at this time being the reinforced concrete foundations, the astronomers were vulnerable to suggestions that they should move. A year before, in October 1952, the Joint Frequency Planning Panel had asked whether, because of radio interference, 'if it was practicable to carry out your observations in more remote locations'.[15] Lovell was aware of the dangers to the radio telescope project as is revealed in his angry remonstrations to the DSIR:

> it has occurred to me that in each of the three major discussions, ie frequencies, grid lines and new towns, there has been a suggestion that the telescope might be shifted. This is, of course, fatuous.[16]

Lovell gave the DSIR five reasons why such a move could not be contemplated, only the first being money (a large part of which, of course, came from the DSIR): it was 'not a question of merely wasting the £100,000 which has already been spent...but it would involve the shifting of the entire establishment at a cost which I would not like to contemplate'. Secondly, it would be an 'impossibility' to run 'the telescope in a remote district'. Thirdly, it would only (Lovell complained to a civil servant!) be done to ease the Minister of Housing and Local Government's life: 'I can well understand that the politicians might readily contemplate the wastage of a few thousand pounds to help them out of these various difficulties'. The fourth reason was an appeal to an authority which had impressed the DSIR before (in the

---

[13] Lovell (1968), p. 162. Also JBA CS7/15/1. Letter, Lovell to Cawley (DSIR), 22 October 1954.

[14] Lovell (1968), p. 162

[15] see Chapter Four: Quotation contained in JBA CS7/29/1. Letter, Vernon to Fryer, 22 October 1952

[16] JBA CS7/15/1. Letter, Lovell to Greenall (DSIR), 7 December 1953.

funding of Jodrell Bank[17]), the Royal Astronomical Society: 'the siting of this instrument was discussed exhaustively by the Committee which originally considered the proposal'. Lastly, the telescope was 'likely to yield its most significant results in the first few years of its use' so therefore 'nothing should be put in the way of its rapid completion', an argument of scientific prestige that would resonate with the strategies of national prestige deployed with success over the telescope's funding.

The Manchester Guardian composed a piece that was checked, amended and approved word-for-word by Lovell. In the draft, Erroll was reported as having not been in touch with Manchester University, and that the University was more concerned about 'developments to the south (of the Telescope...) for it was in that direction that "the most important region of the universe" lay. Prompted by the *Manchester Guardian's* reporter saying: 'you don't feel that you would like to use any stronger expression than that he has not been in touch with you so you don't know what is causing him concern?', Lovell suggested the content of a suitable article:

> MG:...Professor Lovell expressed surprise at the phrasing of the question. He considered that the project was of such national importance.
> Lovell: You would say that in view of the accepted national importance of the project - otherwise we would not be given the money.
> MG: Quite - In view of the accepted national importance of the project he considered that
> Lovell: a more appropriate question would be to ask the Minister to make sure that no satellite town development would interfere with the Radio Telescope[18]

The response of the Parliamentary Secretary to the Ministry of Works, relaying the views of the Minister of Housing and Local Government to Colonel Erroll's question was confidence that any local development could be arranged so as not to interfere with the radio telescope.[19] The Minister saw 'no reasons to believe that any town development which may be proposed in the Congleton area could not be sited as to avoid electrical interference with the Radio Telescope'.[20]

---

[17] See Chapter Tow.

[18] JBA CS7/41/1. Transcript, 'Telephone conversation between Professor A.C.B. Lovell and a Representative of *The Manchester Guardian*', undated (November 1953). The transcript also contained the exchange:
Lovell: Now look, is there any means of making sure Col. Errol sees that?
MG: One can only assume that he does look at the *Guardian*.

[19] Lovell (1968), p. 163.

[20] Parlimentary Debates (Hansard), 5th Series. Vol 520. House of Commons Official Report, Session 1953-54, comprising period 3 November to 20 November 1953. Erroll's question had been to ask 'the Parlimentary Secretary to the Ministry of Works, as representing the Lord President of the Council, whether he will instruct

In October 1954, the Minister of Housing gave a boost to the hopes of Congleton's expansionists by rejecting Manchester's 'bill for re-housing its overspill population in Mobberley and Lymm'.[21] In February 1955, Manchester appeared to be interested in Congleton. Lovell contacted the DSIR again. In their reply the DSIR sought to reassure the astronomers that the 'Parliamentary reply of November 1953 was not overlooked when discussions at the Ministry [of Housing and Local Government] touched on these matters.[22] Indeed with Manchester's attentions returning to 'make another attempt at Mobberley and Lymm', the telescope seemed safer since as Lovell wrote: the development of 'neither...[Mobberley or Lymm] would worry us'.[23]

However, the temperature of the debate over the Congleton expansion soon rose sharply. There were two main reasons for this. First, local industrialists (in particular a Mr L.S. Hargreaves who had spent '£100,000 on the purchase of an existing factory and land in [the]...area'[24]) applied pressure on Congleton Borough Council through mobilising a business-friendly local paper, *The Congleton Chronicle,* and local organisations such as the Congleton Rotary Club, to support their cause.[25] Second, another local MP, Air Commodore A.V. Harvey raised the question in the House of Commons.[26] Lovell told the first meeting of the Telescope's Board of Visitors that 'the expansion of building in the neighbourhood of the telescope', along with the 'lack of frequency allocations', made up 'two serious threats to the use of the new telescope'.[27] The Ministry of Housing and Local Government sought to settle the matter through meetings between

---

the Department of Scientific and Industrial Research to withhold any further grants from its funds for the construction of the radio telescope which is being built south of Manchester until he is satisfied that the public money so expended will not be wasted by satellite town development reducing the value of the telescope'.

[21] JBA CS7/15/1. Letter, Lovell to Cawley (DSIR), 22 October 1954.

[22] JBA CS7/15/1. Letter, Greenall to Lovell, 10 October 1955.

[23] JBA CS7/15/1. Letter, Lovell to Greenall, 14 February 1955.

[24] Lovell (1968), p. 166.

[25] Lovell (1968), p. 166. When invited to give a talk to the Congleton Rotary Club, Lovell stated that: '...instead of a dozen or so people as I had expected, the meeting had been transferred to the large hall of Danesford School which was packed to the doors'.

[26] Parlimentary Debates (Hansard). 5th Series. Volume 542. House of Commons Official Report, Session 1955-56, comprising 7-24 June 1955, written answers, pp. 53-54. Duncan Sandys as Minister of Housing and Local Government replied. Also: ditto, Vol 543, comprising 27 June to 15 July 1955, written answers, pp. 163-164.

[27] JBA CS1/2/2. Minutes, Board of Visitors of the Radio Telescope, 23 June 1955.

the Ministry, representatives of Congleton Borough and Cheshire County Councils, the DSIR, Manchester University and the astronomers.[28]

These conflicts solidified in the form of codifications on the use of land: different planning regulations for different areas in relation to the telescope. We can now study this process of solidification (and the reification of the conflict's arguments in the form of planning code) as it unfolded in the antagonistic context discussed above.

The first emergence of the concept of 'zones' was probably as a rule of thumb for the astronomers. Interference obviously got worse the nearer the source was to the telescope, but the astronomers could not hope to attempt to combat every source that could cause problems. Furthermore there were factors other than distance: strength and direction of the signal, the topography between the signal and the telescope, the effects of changing atmospherics, the proximity of other buildings, the sensitivity of the receiver, the nature of the research, even the skill of the astronomer.[29] However, it was very important in conflicts over radio frequencies and radio interference to be clear and unequivocal: a 'sphere of influence' needed to be defined requiring quick closure over the numerical radius of this area. Such closure could not and was not technically determined (although it was technically informed). Although the adoption (before 1955) of a fifty mile radius for radio interference, and an (about) six mile radius for interference from urban activities (sparks, car ignition) were strategic rules of thumb, the closure of these zones were through social, political and technical processes.

The area near Congleton that Hargreaves and the other business interests proposed to develop, called West Heath, lay just within six miles from Jodrell Bank. The meetings between the Councils and the astronomers presided over by the Parliamentary Secretary to the Ministry of Housing and Local Government resulted in the recognition (and the first step in reification) of the six mile zone in a modified form. The modification was a concession to the business interests:

> As a result of the meeting a compromise was reached. A line was drawn on a map showing the West Heath area of the borough, and it was agreed that the borough council would not seek to develop to the north and west of the line...known as the F line.[30]

---

[28] Lovell (1968), p168. Also: JBA CS7/28/1, transcript of the Judgement of Mr Justice Cooke on 'Geoffrey Harold Spencer v. The Minister of Housing and Local Government, The Cheshire County Council, the Congleton Rural District Council', at Royal Courts of Justice, 3 July 1970. Also: JBA CS7/34/1. Letter, Greenall to Lovell, 15 July 1955.

[29] For example, astronomers learnt that certain 'shapes' of line in a pen-drawing were due to certain forms of interference: car ignition, carrier waves, and so on.

[30] JBA CS7/28/1. Transcript of the Judgement of Mr Justice Cooke, see fn (28).

An area in the shape of a nearly circular D was made, within which processes of 'consultation' with the Ministry would have to be made. Outside, the area the existence of Jodrell Bank would have no effect on building regulations. This did not (and could not) bring closure to the planning, since all parties could interpret the situation differently. That such action happened in this period can be seen from the historical account in a Judge's ruling in a later case: Lovell presented the line as 'prohibiting development within our six-mile zone...In fact, the Minister was not exercising any statutory power of making decisions and he did not prohibit anything'. Furthermore, there was 'a letter...in which an officer of the Science Research Council [the successor to the DSIR] displays a misconception similar to that contained in Sir Bernard's book'.[31] Congleton Borough Council was also able to interpret the ruling, soon after the first inscribing of the F line it was slightly modified:

> it was agreed between the Jodrell Bank directorate and the Congleton borough council that the Jodrell Bank directorate would raise no objection to development in a *defined* area to the north and west of the original F line.[32]

Therefore, by a mixture of territorial negotiation and pragmatic compromise the Jodrell Bank observatory first became settled (and hence more indefeasible) within the local authorities' regulations over land use.

THE ELECTRIFICATION OF THE RAILWAYS AND GRID LINES

Territorial negotiation was also the strategy used by the astronomers to deflect two other electrical disturbances within the environment of Jodrell Bank: the construction of overhead high-voltage electricity grid lines and the electrification of the Manchester-Crewe railway (which was adjacent to the Jodrell Bank site).

The initial proposal in 1952 for extending the 275 kilovolt 'Supergrid' to Cheshire involved an overhead line from Drakelow to Carrington which

---

[31] Mr Justice Cooke, see fn (28), quoted Lovell's passage from Lovell, op cit, p. 168. This shows again that *The Story of Jodrell Bank* has to be carefully analysed to uncover the purpose and direction of its rhetoric. The Judge was being slightly disingenuous in presenting Lovell's sentence and the SRC assertion as merely two unconnected examples.

[32] JBA CS7/28/1. Transcript of the Judgement of Mr Justice Cooke. My italics. The Minister of Housing and Local Government encouraged these local negotiations over areas 'in which development is likely to intrefere with the use of the telescope, the intention being that such areas should be defined from time to time by agreement between the [Jodrell Bank] directorate and the local authority'.

would pass 'within 7000 yards of the telescope'.[33] As Lovell wrote to the East Cheshire Area County Planning Office:

> We are rather worried about the proximity of this line to Jodrell bank. The corona discharges from such a high voltage line would be a most desperate form of interference and are most likely to occur in conditions of high humidity which otherwise usually give us our best results.[34]

After discussion with the Electricity Authority it was agreed to simulate the effect of the proposed line by turning on and off a slightly more distant lower voltage line. The measurements took place within the controlled environment of Jodrell Bank; furthermore, what was to count as interference also had to be regulated, the astronomers sought (in this case) to deny that other forms of interference were comparable.[35]

Such disputations ended (in Lovell's words) in 'deadlock' until a meeting called by the Ministry of Fuel and Power 'instructed [the Electricity Authority] to re-route this supergrid line away from the telescope'. The reasons for this decision are hard to uncover, except to note that the astronomers had won the backing of the DSIR (with whom the Ministry would have consulted) for the scheme.[36] The cases of the grid lines (a similar episode occured in 1954 over a 33 kilovolt line to serve a nearby salt works) demonstrates again that the astronomers, in order to control and 'quieten' the area within the observatory, had to concern themselves with the wider milieu.

The threat perceived by the astronomers to come from the electrification of the railway line was confronted in a similar manner. In 1955 it was mooted that the very first railway line to be electrified would be the line from Manchester Piccadilly Station to the large rail depot at Crewe, passing very close to the telescope. Although the time scale envisaged was 'fifteen years' before the electrification would happen, the astronomers immediately notified the DSIR. However in March 1956, '...it was announced that the Crewe-Manchester line [was] to be electrified with an overhead system and that it [was] to come into operation by January 1959'.[37] Lovell protested to the DSIR again, saying the telescope would be 'seriously handicapped' and unless 'we...fail to obtain the full cooperation of the authorities the telescope may well prove unworkable'. He gave four 'essential requirements':

---

[33] Lovell (1968), p. 170.

[34] JBA CS7/15/2. Letter, Lovell to Kettle (County Planning Department, East Cheshire Area, Area Planning Office), June 1952.

[35] 'I objected to the inclusion of uninformed comments about the level of interference to be experienced from other sources in the neighbourhood with which the writer [of the minutes of the meeting] tried to justify [the proposed line]'. Lovell (1968), p. 171.

[36] Lovell (1968), p. 172.

i) A simple wire-netting screen to be erected close to the overhead wires for the few miles of the track which is in the immediate view of the telescope.

ii) Special attention to...insulators on the overhead line.

iii) The automatic transmission of a signal from two pre-determined points on the railway track so that the necessary suppression is automatically applied to the telescope.

iv) The planting of additional screening, such as trees adjacent to the line in the immediate vicinity of the telescope.

These were attempts to change and control the telescope's environment and were pursued through the channels of the civil service bureaucracy: 'I imagine that an official approach from your department to the Ministry of Transport...might ensure that we are put in touch with the personnel who have the necessary authority to attend to our worries'. Of particular interest is requirement iii) where the action taken outside the observatory can be seen 'feeding back' into the operation of the instrument. However, in this instance the DSIR, its 'previous successful interventions on [the astronomers] behalf notwithstanding', suggested that 'the University (not DSIR) should put the case to British Railways (not the Ministry) at first'.[38] This the astronomers asked the University to do[39], with the result that a meeting was arranged between the astronomers and British Railways in June. At the meeting special insulators, electrical screening of track '1000 yards either side of the telescope', the suppression of 'local signalling arrangements', the power feed to the line, and 'an automatic indicator in the Jodrell Bank control room to show the position of trains' were all considered.[40] A series of such meetings enabled the astronomers and the University to delay electrification until the 1960s and ensure that British Railways made measures to suppress the accompanying interference.[41]

LOCAL DEVELOPMENT AGAIN

Although the electrification of the railways was regarded with unease by the astronomers and prompted them into action, they were 'much less concerned

---

[37] JBA CS7/31/2. Letter, Lovell to Cawley, 7 March 1956.

[38] JBA CS7/31/2. Letter, Greenall to Lovell, 13 March 1956.

[39] JBA CS7/31/2. Letter, Lovell to Rainford, 17 March 1956.

[40] JBA CS7/31/2. Minutes of meeting 'to discuss the problems arising in connection with the electrification of the railway line in the neighbourhood of the radio telescope', 4 June 1956. Representation for British Railways came from the British Transport Commission and London Midland Region. The astronomers present were Lovell, R. Hanbury Brown, J.G. Davies and H.P. Palmer.

[41] JBA CS9/1/4. Minutes, Board of Visitors to the Radio Telescope, 2 June 1959.

about this than the possibility of any uncontrolled spread of population in the neighbourhood'.[42] I discussed above how the astronomers' concern over development within the 'rule of thumb' six miles of Jodrell Bank resulted in a conflict at this distance with Congleton Borough Council's scheme for expansion. The result (after Ministerial intervention) was an agreement that no land would be developed on the Jodrell Bank side of the 'F line' (tangential to a circle of radius six miles). With the radio telescope finally becoming operational in 1957, moves were begun to codify land development in the its entire neighbourhood. In January 1959, a meeting 'attended by representatives of Manchester University, including Professor Lovell, of Cheshire County Council, of Congleton Borough Council', and a number of district councils:

> ...had before it a map showing an area coloured pink...[that] extended to a distance of six miles from the telescope on its southern, eastern and western sides, but in other directions was more restricted. Within the pink area was a shaded area extending in part to a distance of two miles and in part to a distance of four miles from the telescope.[43]

At this meeting it was negotiated that:

> ...the University should be consulted about all proposed development within the shaded area, and about all proposed development elsewhere in the pink area except where the proposal was for an individual building for non-industrial use. It...should be left to the discretion of area planning officers as to whether they should consult the University about proposed development outside the pink area.[44]

Tracing the borders of these zones reveals some of the considerations that went into drawing them. The astronomers sought to reduce local development as far out, and as completely, as possible. However, other interests (commercial, the Borough Council planners, land-owners), mediated through the Council representatives, sought to restrict this move. The zones and borders therefore reflect the compromises in the negotiations between the two groups. For example the astronomers obtained a measure of regulation out to six miles. But why six miles? The examination of a map reveals an answer: a disc of six miles covered an area that almost, but not quite, reaches the outskirts of the nearest small towns: Middlewich, Sandbach, Congleton and Macclesfield (only the smaller Holmes Chapel lies inside). The influence of the astronomers was therefore enough to secure restrictions out to this distance (being mostly agricultural land) but not in the politically more

---

[42] JBA CS7/15/1. Letter, Lovell to Greenall, 2 February 1955.
[43] JBA CS7/28/1. Transcript of Mr Justice Cooke, see fn (28).
[44] Ibid.

difficult locations of the existing small towns. The Councils could not concede regulation of industrial (and other) activities within their urbanised areas. Within the six miles zone, the astronomers secured strict regulation in the smaller 'shaded area'. However, both zones extended further to the south: astronomical objects attain their greatest elevation from the horizon in the southerly direction, and so the concession by the University astronomers to the developers of a relatively unregulated northern area was part of the bargaining to secure a protected south.

The shape and extent of the zones around the Jodrell Bank observatory were therefore forged in the particular context of its location. The 'six mile' interference-free zone was a concept with a meaning specific to Jodrell Bank. At Cambridge, there was a different set of contextual pressures from which a different patterning of development occured. This different patterning is analogous to the different 'local arrangements' made between observatories and radio spectrum users that I considered in Chapter Four.

The consultation process, demanded by the agreements outlined above for development within the two zones, can be seen in action in the discussion between Manchester University and the planners over the growth of the nearby villages of Holmes Chapel and Goostrey. A meeting was held between H.W. Kettle, the Area Planning Officer at Macclesfield, Lovell and his assistant R.G. Lascelles, and R.S. Lloyd of the University's Bursars Office, in November 1965.[45] Development in three areas was discussed: Congleton Borough, Goostrey Village and Holmes Chapel Village. On Congleton, the Area Planning Officer first 'wished to know whether development on the south-west side of Padgbury Lane could be released; and secondly...whether there could be agreement to a change in the 'F' line... [as] the present population of Congleton was 18,000 and was expected to rise to 35,000 by 1985'. The astronomers used the 'Ministerial decision' on the consultative process relating to the environment of Jodrell Bank to insist that 'no change be made to the restriction on development beyond the 'F' line'.[46] On the village of Goostrey, the university conceded to the building of a small amount of new housing, 'provided the development was phased and infilling of the original village zone was encouraged'. The concern over Holmes Chapel centred on traffic patterns.[47] Lovell's suggestion showed how the presence of a radio observatory could affect social action (in this case the driving of vehicles):

---

[45] JBA CS7/28/1. 'Report of Meeting held at Jodrell Bank on Tuesday 16 November 1965'.

[46] This excepted 'the 21 acres of industrial development already agreed'.

[47] 'First, attention would be given to the A50/A54 cross roads. secondly, a by-pass of motorway standard was proposed from the M6 to the North of the village, then linking with the A50 to pass along the south side of the Dane valley, finally swinging south t rejoin the A50'.

...to safeguard the telescope, signs should direct traffic to use the A34. From Monks Heath northbound traffic could be routed to the Knutsford interchange via Chelford, and southbound traffic could be routed via the Congleton by-pass and A534 to the Arclid interchange...

The University agreed to the 'general plan for Holmes Chapel village', provided 'implementation of the proposals was phased up to 1990 and development of the area [away from the telescope] was encouraged'. Futhermore, it used its agreement sanctioned by the Minister to restrict completely some activities: 'the University would object strongly to any apparatus of a nature which might involve radio frequency heating or similar processes'. The question of radio frequency (microwave) heating became particularly acute in the the 1960s and 1970s when the white goods industries pushed mass-produced microwave ovens for the domestic market.

A further example of how the University sought to prevent the building of houses near the telescope was a second attempt to expand Goostrey two years later in 1967. The Rural District Council put forward a proposal to build '25 houses per annum' which they considered desirable for a variety of reasons ('a good class of development', 'a reasonable freedom of choice of design', 'a large children's playspace', 'road improvement', and 'a contribution to the Rural District Council sewerage scheme').[48] However, this was greater than the agreement in 1965, and so the astronomers objected. After discussions, Lovell was 'prepared to withdraw his objection to the proposed development', but only if a list of 'points were agreed by written resolution of the authorities concerned'. Such points included: phasing of the building until later dates and the discouragment and opposition by the Council of development of other areas in the 'hatched zone'. These points were agreed, and an 'Undertakings' was signed by the Congleton Rural District Council, the Cheshire County Council and the University.[49]

The University exploited the restrictions on local development that were codified by the intervention of the Minister of Housing and Local Government in 1959 to 'protect the instrument from the intrusion of sources of electrical interference'.[50] However, with the growth in population in the telescope's environment and the pressure to locate industry in areas well placed for

---

[48] JBA CS7/28/1. Minutes, 'Meeting at Jodrell Bank', 8 March 1967. Present were: Hollinshead, Rigby, Richardson, Rogers, Birtwhistle, Molyneux (all of the Congleton Rural District Council), Kettle (Area Planning Officer), Lovell and Lascelles.

[49] JBA CS7/28/1. 'Undertakings given to Manchester University in relation to future development of that part of the consultation (hatched) zone within the Congleton Rural District for the protection of the radio telescope at Jodrell Bank', 20 March 1967.

[50] JBA CS7/28/1. 'Confidential memo from Sir Bernard Lovell to Mr J.F. Hosie (SRC) on recent planning problems concerning Jodrell Bank', 6 August 1969.

transport and communication, it was always likely that the University's powers within the zones would be challenged.

THE CODIFICATION IS CHALLENGED: APPEALS AGAINST THE ZONES

In December 1967, the Congleton Rural District Council objected to the University's involvement in three innocuous proposed developments, including housing at Brereton Heath.[51] As its Clerk reported to the Bursar of Manchester University: 'my Council is extremely disappointed to note that the University is now planning to express views on detailed matters relative to planning'.[52] In their feeling of 'strong exception' the Council passed a resolution 'that any agreements made with the Jodrell Bank Authorities in the past should be regarded as revoked'. In particular, the Council wanted to challenge and diminish the University's power in local development, and sought to:

> ...clarify the respective responsibilities of the Authorities concerned and to emphasise that the Cheshire County Council is the Local Planning Authority and the Rural District Council the delegated Authority.

The University replied that it was 'deeply concerned' about the RDC's actions, and the Bursar reminded the RDC's Clerk that the agreement revoked had been signed 'only nine months ago'.[53]

What had caused Congleton Rural District Council to rescind suddenly on agreements? The astronomers claimed that it was the personal involvement of one of the Councillors 'who is also a member of various County committees, [and] is personally involved in negotiations for clients who have interests in the areas considered'.[54] These allegations were sharpened: 'Indeed...there would appear to be a close parallelism between the development of this person's private business and the agitations for the changes in the planning arrangements'. By couching the opposition in terms

---

[51] JBA CS7/28/1. Letter, Molyneux (Clerk of the Council) to Rainford, 13 December 1967. The developments were: a caravan site at Somerford Hall Farm, and houses at two farms near Holmes Chapel.

[52] JBA CS7/28/1. Ibid. It is not known what specifically the Council was objecting to in the University's letter (not found).

[53] JBA CS7/28/1. Letter, Rainford to the Clerk of Congleton RDC, 21 December 1967.

[54] JBA CS7/28/1. 'Suggested draft letter from the Busar to Mr J.K. Boynton, Clerk to the Cheshire County Council', March [?] 1968.

of corruption, the astronomers sought to incite the County Council (to whom this letter was directed) to halt the Rural District Council's actions. As Lovell wrote to the Bursar: the 'evidence on which the substance of this letter is based is incontrovertible, and according to [the Area Planning Officer], Boynton [the Clerk of the County Council] has already warned the individual concerned'.[55]

The proposal to build at Brereton Heath went to a Public Inquiry. From the reports in the local newspapers the voice of the Rural District Council (to whom, as representatives of local business interest, the newspapers were sympathetic) can be recovered. The *Sandbach Chronicle* reported the story under the frontpage headline: 'Jodrell Bank in News Again: Its "victims" should be compensated, inquiry told'.[56] The *Chronicle* informed its readership that planning permission had been refused for three reasons: 'close proximity to Jodrell Bank, no 'mains drainage' and 'no adequate nearby outlet for surface water'. However, the case for the appeal was given by 'Mr. H.C. Rigby' (coincidentally, although passing unmentioned by the *Sandbach Chronicle*, a member of Congleton Rural District Council), who stated:

> ...indications had been given by county officials at an earlier date that permission to develop the land would be given, and the problem of drainage could be "quite easily" overcome. The problem of Jodrell Bank was "not a valid objection, either morally or in law".

The Chronicle then detailed some of the appellant's previous developments and repeated twice that he felt 'badly let down'. The article discussed and dismissed an argument that the planning was refused because spending cuts had delayed drainage of the area: the 'problem' was the radio telescope. The newspaper reported Lovell's presentation 'showing diagrams to illustrate his point', and it followed this, in bold type, with:

> Mr Rigby suggested that Sir Bernard "could not care less" what happened to the area unless the telescope was affected, but Sir Bernard refuted this as being "totally untrue".

Further arguments not against development at Brereton Heath were put forward by the County Surveyor's Department and the Rural District Council's Engineer and Surveyor. Finally, in large type, the newspaper printed:

> Mr Rigby asked that if Jodrell Bank was "above the Law", parliament should

---

[55] JBA CS7/28/1. Letter, Lovell to Rainford, 11 March 1968. The individual was Rigby.

[56] JBA CS7/28/1. *Sandbach Chronicle*, 13 September 1968.

make it law and properly provide for those Districts and individuals who were "being robbed".

Rigby drew parallels with the Coal Board and the British Rail Board who did offer compensation for 'stopping development'. 'This is a test case to the powers of Jodrell Bank' he proclaimed, 'neither he nor anybody could prove that it was straight over Brereton Heath where these marvellous things in the sky are happening'.

Thus the picture becomes a little more symmetrical. As constructed from the astronomers' papers the situation was one of corrupt local officialdom attempting to override fair and equitable agreements without a thought for fundamental science. The newspaper article showed that there were arguments (not mentioned by the astronomers) in favour of development, that the conflict was not necessarily motivated by avarice.[57] However, it can be said that the presence and influence of the nearby telescope was the intended target of Rigby and the RDC: 'the time has now come to determine Jodrell Bank's *authority*'.[58]

The *Congleton Chronicle* communicated the Inquiry's decision that the 'proximity of the telescope' could be given as the 'SOLE reason for dismissing a planning application'.[59] The decision had the consent and backing of the Minister for Housing and Local Government. As the reporter asked rhetorically: 'Why is Jodrell Bank the only party able to sterilise land without having any liability for compensation?' The article repeated the arguments of the *Sandbach Chronicle*, and quoted Rigby again saying that it was a 'test case' for the influence of Jodrell Bank. The developer at Brereton Heath, a Mr Stringer, decided to appeal to the courts against the Minister's decision.

Although the description 'test case' is best reserved for the Brereton Heath appeal, the next dispute reveals the network and coalition building between the developers and their opponents. In the Autumn of 1968, Mr and Mrs Winkle made a planning application to add a dining room to their pub, the 'Swettenham Arms', which lay two miles directly south of Jodrell Bank (and coincidentally adjacent to Lovell's house 'The Quinta'). Buoyed up by 'the remarkable strengthening of our position as a result of the Brereton decision' Lovell decided to 'take a stiff line' against the proposal.[60] Internally, the

---

[57] The article stressed the values of the appealant: 'he ran a small business firm with his wife. He started on his own about 20 years ago and employed a dozen men. Most of the appeal site near to his home at Brereton Heath had been part of his father's estate'.

[58] My italics.

[59] JBA CS7/28/1. Congleton Chronicle, '"Test Case" on Jodrell Bank: Sets a precedent fo future development', 17 January 1969.

[60] JBA CS7/28/1. Internal note, Lovell to Lascelles, 30 January 1969.

reason discussed was 'the influence which such developments would have on the magnitude of the traffic and the direction of its flow'. The pub extension would 'greatly enhance traffic movements around the lanes in the immediate vicinity of the telescope', and furthermore there would be a dangerous change in the social habits of the telescope's neighbours:

> ...the licensing rules are such that the bulk of movement of traffic is over by 2300 hrs. The introduction of...dinners and dinner dances would...remove this important constraint. The hours between...2300 and 0600 are vital to the...high sensitivity observations with the radio telescope, and it is of the utmost importance that we continue to make every safeguard against the increase in...traffic

Lovell repeated these arguments in a letter to the Area Planning Officer of Cheshire County Council, adding complaints that the decision appeared a 'fait accompli' by the RDC and about the 'grave danger' of 'processes which are used in modern restaurant practice' (microwave ovens).[61] The astronomical practices surrounding the telescope were therefore in conflict with the social practices of its neighbours, and the contested (symbolic) site of the clash was a dining room of a Swettenham pub. The University made a formal objection in February 1969, on the grounds that it contravened the 'Undertakings' signed in March 1967.[62]

The worry about increased traffic was echoed locally by the Campaign for the Protection of Rural England (CPRE), in particular its Chairman of the Cheshire Branch (who coincidentally lived in Swettenham[63]), Mr G.D. Lockett. Lockett, whose last campaign had been against the sign for the Swettenham 'Tartan Bar', brought local arguments to bear against the 'the sort of traffic that visits such places and at such hours of darkness is not catered for by the road...[which] is narrow and on areas of it are blind spots

---

[61] JBA CS7/28/1. Letter, Lovell to Kettle, 6 February 1969. Also JBA CS7/28/1. Letter, Lovell to Hosie, 19 May 1969: 'you will be well aware of the acute anxieties which face radio astronomers today in view of the new devices which are being installed in such premises'.

[62] JBA CS7/28/1. Letter, Rainford to Kettle (Area Planning Officer, CCC), 18 February 1969. Letter, Rainford to Male (County Planning Officer, CCC), 18 February 1969. These were strengthened when the astronomers could later claim that not only was the proposal for a restaurant but also for a 'dwelling house...for Mrs Wincle's (sic) son': 'two weeks ago [Boynton] assured me that if a house had been in question and not an extension to an inn there would have been no question that the University's opposition would have been respected'. JBA CS7/28/1. Letter, Lovell to Rainford, 30 May 1969.

[63] 'The fact that my son resides in the cottage nearest to the Church on the north side and Sir Bernard Lovell on the other is not the determining factor'. From JBA CS7/28/1. Letter, Lockett to Collins, 26 February 1969.

and sharp bends'.[64] He wrote to County Hall at Chester pointing out that although he knew 'privately that Jodrell Bank [would] represent this matter strongly to the Clerk [of the RDC]' it was in his 'capacity as Church Warden' and Chair of the CRPE to make it known that 'other residents [would] be prepared to go the whole way as objectors'.[65] To Lockett the telescope was a means to prevent an 'expensive roadhouse' in his 'small and remote village', the 'interference angle' gave him common ground with the astronomers, and he hoped 'thereby [to force] a Ministry inquiry'.[66] The telescope rested on such networks of local political influence:

> While I have twice met the Chief Constable during my brother's year as High Sheriff, I am sure that...if this letter was passed to him he would agree that this matter does concern the police and road safety in the County.

However, attempts to appeal to such higher authorities were only part of the active process of ally-recruiting by both sides in the dispute. The Parish Council was split: 'Taylor and Tomlinson have made an issue that this is an act of malice..[they] regard what is happening to the Arms as 'progress'', Lockett reported to Lovell, 'What is now essential is that local residents directly affected join in signing an agreed letter'.[67] Taylor, the Swettenham member on the RDC, was portrayed by Lockett as 'behaving most strangely' and being 'unrepresentative' in Lockett's attempt to win the backing of another local grandee, Sir Clyde Hewlett.[68] Hewlett, managing director of Anchor Chemicals, erstwhile president of Conservative Party bodies, member of the Committee of Governors of Manchester University (and Baron of Swettenham from 1972) was a powerful ally.[69] A four page letter of his[70] circulated through the anti-extension network stated that he had moved to Swettenham 'with the special purpose in mind of living in the country' and not to live next to 'a casino'. His reasons were traffic ('I have already had cause to write twice to the Chief Constable complaining about the standard of driving'), 'change of character of the village' particularly the church (even though he was 'not home frequently enough to be able to attend the church with any great regularity'), and 'litter'.

---

[64] JBA CS7/28/1. Letter, Lockett to Molyneux (Clerk of Congleton RDC), 1April 1969.
[65] JBA CS7/28/1. Letter, Lockett to Collins, 26 February 1969.
[66] JBA CS7/28/1. Letter, Lockett to Cornwall-Legh, 26 February 1969.
[67] JBA CS7/28/1. Letter, Lockett to Lovell, March [?] 1969.
[68] JBA CS7/28/1. Letter, Lockett to Hewlett, 3 March 1969.
[69] *Who was Who*, 1971-1980.
[70] Although unsigned it can be identified by 'I am so heavily committed in business and national politics...'.
JBA CS7/28/1. Letter to Andow, 3 March 1969.

The Rural District Council found it possible to resist the interpretation that the extra dining area meant heavier traffic, since as its Clerk reported the view of the County Surveyor: 'the intention [was] merely to provide more comfortable surroundings for the people who [wished] to have a meal with their drinks'.[71] Also, the RDC could dismiss the accusation that they were unrepresentative ('a matter of opinion'[72]). The supporters of the development launched a petition, which 1500 approving persons signed. The Swettenham Arms case was one in which the developers held as strong a hand as they were likely to possess in their attempts to overturn the influence of the Telescope. In a letter to the Manchester University Bursar, Lovell aired his view that it was 'a reasonable assumption that the individuals agitating against the Jodrell restrictions have chosen to fight this particular issue in the knowledge that it would be a very embarrassing one for me' (recall that Lovell's house, The Quinta, adjoined the Swettenham Arms).[73]

Lovell asked the University that the decision on the Swettenham Arms be referred to the Minister for Housing and Local Government.[74] Also, the astronomers replayed a strategy that had brought success in previous disputes and excursions: securing the support and utilising the resources of a sympathetic government department, here the Science Research Council (SRC). The SRC was formed in 1965 when the government apparatus dealing with science was reformed (the responsibilities of the old DSIR were dissolved and redistributed). Furthermore, for five years from the beginning of the Council, Lovell was chair of the Astronomy Space and Radio Board of the SRC. He was therefore closely tied to the networks distributing resources for science in this period. The SRC were aware of the Brereton Heath appeal and had provided Lovell with details of the Cambridge radio astronomy group's similar problems over re-siting and interference.[75] Lovell

---

[71] JBA CS7/28/1. Letter, Molyneux to Lockett, 28 February 1969.

[72] JBA CS7/28/1. Letter, Molyneux to Hewlett, 19 March 1969.

[73] JBA CS7/28/1. Letter, Lovell to Rainford, 8 December 1969.

[74] JBA CS7/28/1. Letter, Lovell to Rainford, 13 May 1969. Lovell uses a financial argument to supplement his case to the Bursar: 'Clearly it does not make sense to be spending over half a milllion pounds on the Mk I telescope [so] that its life can be extended...if we ourselves cannot guarantee to be able to use it efficiently during that period'.

[75] JBA CS7/28/1. Letter, Hosie to Lovell, 14 May 1969. The specific worry was over liability for claims for compensation arising out of the planning restrictions imposed. The University, after due consideration, came to the conclusion that claims directly against the University were 'not very likely', but the danger that the Local Planning Authority might seek to pass claims against the LPA onto the University, had to be assessed. As the University put it to the SRC: 'If this were the case, I feel sure...the University would look to the Government for assistance' (in effect the SRC). JBA CS7/28/1. Draft letter, Rainford to Hosie, May 1969.

now contacted the SRC again over the Swettenham Arms case. After describing the 'major development and the consequential effect on the protection of the zone around the telescope', Lovell requested that the SRC 'take urgent on this matter and establish contact with the appropriate officer in the Ministry [of Housing and Local Government]'.[76] The SRC, having approached the MHLG, wrote to Lovell that 'you have the assurance of the LPA [Local Planning Authority] that planning permission will not be granted until [the MHLG] has considered the case'.[77]

In June 1969, Congleton Rural District Council, as reported by the approving local press, publicly '[threw] down the gauntlet to Jodrell Bank on terrestrial development': '...they said firmly, 'Jodrell Bank is not our Big Brother'.[78] A RDC Councillor, 'Cheshire County Alderman John Hollinshead' portrayed the nearby presence of the astronomers as a threat to Holmes Chapel's prosperous expansion of trade and population, the telescope versus housing: 'We want development at Holmes Chapel to go along with the influx of population and not be governed by Jodrell...'.

The astronomers reacted to this heightening of tension, as Lovell wrote to the University Bursar: 'I do feel that we should not allow these attacks to pass without some kind of response since there is the grave danger of an erosion of the goodwill which we have laboriously built up over the past 20 years'.[79] The University made an official complaint, drawing attention to the 1967 signed agreement on development.[80]

With the Swettenham Arms development now certain to go to a public inquiry and the Holmes Chapel/Brereton Heath case to be decided at court, the astronomers marshalled all their information together. An internal Jodrell Bank note asked Lascelles, the Jodrell bank publicity officer, 'to make a list of the public pronouncements which Hollinshead and Rigby have made against us', gather 'photocopies of the newspaper reports', and even 'a list of similar inns and restaurants like...the Swettenham Arms which lie in the vicinity'.[81] These were incorporated into a four page memo outlining a history of the 'urgent need to protect the instrument from the intrusion of sources of

---

[76] JBA CS7/28/1. Letter, Lovell to Hosie, 19 May 1969.

[77] JBA CS7/28/1. Letter, Essex (SRC) to Lovell, 20 May 1969.

[78] JBA CS7/28/1. *Crewe Chronicle (Sandbach Edition)*, 12 June 1969. *The Sunday Express* also picked up on the story: 'Jodrell Bank fights pub's plan for new dining room: cookers "would interefere with giant radio telescope"', 22 June 1969.

[79] JBA CS7/28/1. Letter, Lovell to Rainford, 16 June 1969.

[80] JBA CS7/28/1. Letter, Rainford to Lovell, 17 June 1969. Letter, Lovell to Rainford, 19 June 1969. Draft letter, Rainford to Male (County Planning Officer), 17 June 1969.

[81] JBA CS7/28/1. Internal note, Lovell to Lascelles, 29 July 1969. Also internal note, Lovell to Lascelles, 16 September 1969.

electrical interference' (with twenty pages of carefully chosen documents) and sent to the SRC.[82] In a rhetorically characteristic conclusion Lovell stated that 'the rate of development in the consultation zones would be such as to put an effective end to the work of the telescope at Jodrell Bank'. In an accompanying letter, there are clues as to how the astronomers intended the SRC to interpret the material:

> This memorandum has been marked as a personal one from me to you but it is intended that you should use your own judgement as to the extent to which you wish to convey its contents to the Minister...[83]

However, having saluted the impartiality of the SRC, Lovell then guided the reading against the Councillors:

> When you read this memorandum...you will, I think, conclude that there is an implication that part of the trouble may be that a certain individual has not declared his interest...[84]

Lovell supplemented the carefully chosen and interpreted documentation with an argument that had proved successful in earlier attempts to secure funding and frequency allocations: the hinting at shadowy defence connections:

> ...the important interest of another department in the use of the telescope and its consequential international associations. ...One thing is certain to me; of all our uses of the telescope that use would probably be most damaged by the interference which we are seeking to contain.

The date for the Swettenham Arms Inquiry was set first for December 1969. The astronomers took the unusual step of being represented by the University's Solicitor, an indication of the seriousness with which they viewed the affair.[85] The astronomers had also collated information (including seeking

---

[82] JBA CS7/28/1. Memo, 'Memo from Sir Bernard Lovell to Mr J.F. Hosie, SRC, on recent planning problems concerning Jodrell Bank', 6 August 1969.

[83] JBA CS7/28/1. Letter, Lovell to Hosie, 6 August 1969.

[84] The bulk of the letter refered to a 'matter of some delicacy': the adjacency of Lovell's house to the Swettenham Arms. Lovell also issued a two page internal memo to persons working at Jodrell Bank: 'I do not want my personal involvement to be discussed unless absolutely necessary but if a situation arises...then the relevant facts are...': there followed a list of 'facts'. The ninth point was: '...anyone with a grain of imagination who studies *The Story of Jodrell Bank* must realise that my whole life for the last 20 years has been controlled by the telescope and the desire to protect and use it as one of the world's great and unique scientific instruments'. JBA JBM/1/4. Internal memo from Lovell, 2 February 1970.

[85] JBA CS7/28/1. Internal letter, Lascelles to Lovell, 5 December 1969.

'reinforcement of the evidence' from the Cambridge group[86]), and attempted to guide the possible readings. Smith-Rose, who was a figure familiar and sympathetic to the astronomers, was chosen as an independent Assessor for the Inquiry.[87] Lovell was to be called as an 'expert witness'.[88] The other objectors were the Council for the Protection of Rural England. On the developers' side were the applicants, Mr and Mrs Winkle, represented by Councillor Rigby (who was a Solicitor by profession), and Congleton Rural District Council. They were supported by the local press: for example the *Crewe Chronicle* ran a story entitled 'Can the Boffins Still Oppose Housing', in which the reporter juxtaposed the planned expanded Jodrell Bank visitors' centre ('Jodrell Commercial Enterprises Inc...I can see it now - a huge neon sign embellished with these words, casting a brash Coney Island brilliance on the Cheshire Plain') with the land around made 'sterile' for business.[89] The Inquiry was twice delayed: from December 1969 to February 1970, and from February to April, whilst Lovell undertook a lecture tour of the United States.

The Swettenham Arms Inquiry took place on the 19th to the 23rd April 1970. The forty-seven pages of written testimony that Lovell submitted, along with diagrams, books and documentation, can be analysed for the textual and representational strategies used to 'protect the telescope'.[90] The evidence can be divided into two parts. The first half placed the Jodrell Bank observatory in a wider context in which it could be seen as useful and even economically desirable.[91] The second half demonstrated how 'sources of interference...could so easily and rapidly destroy the working of this telescope'. The evidence began with a listing of Lovell's own honours and 'professional qualifications', followed by brief hints at his war-career developing radar. The move to Jodrell Bank was simply attributed to 'electrical interference' being 'so great' in Manchester (other factors such as availability of space were passed over). The story of the emergence of radio astronomy in Britain was told in national terms that strongly echo the 1950s publicity such as *The Inquisitive Giant*: of a cloudy country recapturing 'pre-eminence' in astronomy from the United States. The Evidence illustrated scientific worthiness by lists of papers generated at Jodrell Bank, and stories of discoveries some 'of supreme importance to our understanding of the Universe'. Institutional support was

---

[86] JBA CS7/28/1. Letter, Lovell to Ryle, 6 January 1969?.

[87] JBA CS7/28/1. Letter, Lovell to Smith-Rose, 15 December 1969.

[88] JBA CS7/28/1. Letter, Rainford to Messrs. Tatham, Worthington & Co., Solicitors, 15 December 1969.

[89] JBA CS7/28/1. Newspaper artcle, *Crewe Chronicle*, January 1970.

[90] JBA JBM/1/4. 'Proof of Evidence Submitted by Sir Bernard Lovell, FRS', April 1970.

[91] Similar strategies were used to obtain funding, see Chapter Two.

indicated by including approving documents from the SRC, in particular the Fleck Report which recommended that money for radio astronomy be concentrated just at Cambridge and Manchester.[92] The contextual arguments used, against which Jodrell Bank could be seen as beneficial, were of the 'spin-off' variety. For example:

> ...we recruit young men [sic] of ability and promise to join us in our researches at Jodrell Bank, but we also maintain a flow of young people through the establishment who move out and play important parts in British industry.

Statistics on training were aligned to disprove the belief that 'Jodrell Bank exists to enable a few of us to carry out abstract researches on the nature of the Universe'. The study of the recently identified quasars provided an example of how 'the forefront of astrophysics' could have 'fundamental significance to our understanding of physics in the terrestrial world': since the astronomers 'may be exploring new sources of energy'. Benefits were not confined to science: 'the United Kingdom has derived considerable benefit because of the experience of the engineers', particularly Messrs. Husband & Co. of Sheffield'.[93] Research on the other novel astronomical object of the late 1960s, the pulsar, demonstrated the 'versatility and adaptability of the telescope'.[94] However, linking the two halves of the Evidence, the:

> recordings of these phenomena are...very easily confused with the regular impulsive signals which are generated by the ignition of cars and other devices in the neighbourhood of the telescope.

As I argued in Chapter Four, the 'danger of confusion' between interfering signal and astronomical object derived from an fundamental ambiguity in the astronomers' representational practices. However, in Lovell's Proof of Evidence these same representational practices formed part of a display aimed at bringing the interference to the Inquiry room and demonstrating its adverse effects. After going through some simple calculations of power levels, Lovell stated:

> I have laboured these points because...in this room I have heard speakers deny that our researches with the radio telescope can be interfered with by local sources

---

[92] Science Research Council, 1965. *Radio Astronomy*, London: HMSO.

[93] The telescope at Goonhilly 'which enables many of you to enjoy clear phone calls and television sent across the ocean from America', a copy of the Jodrell Bank Mark II telescope was given as an example. Lovell went on: ' sometimes think that this kind of benefit to British engineering and industry...[for which] there is now a considerable market...is under-rated'.

[94] Cf the discussion of interpretative malleability of the telescope in Chapter Two.

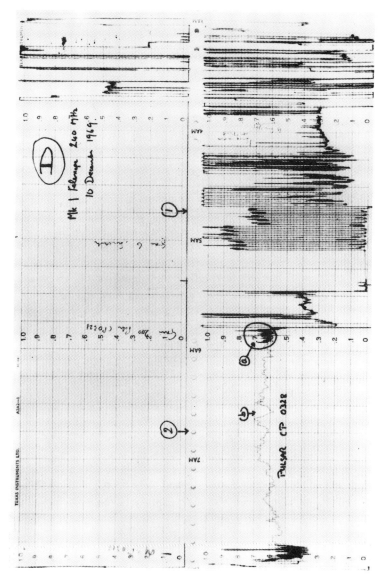

Figure 5.1 Lovell had the skills to interpret the products of the Radio Telescope which his local opponents did not possess. At the Swettenham Arms inquiry he could say: 'the recordings of these phenomena are therefore themselves very easily generated by the ignition of cars or other devices in the neighbourhood of the telescope. That is clear from a comparison of teh signals whch I have shown on the charts A, B and C with that from the pulsar on Chart D. [pictured here]'.
Source: JBA JBM/1/4. Lovell, 'Proof of evidence'.

of interference. In case anyone still doubts the validity of these calculations...I will...produce some practical examples of the disasters which can occur in our research programmes.

The astronomers (presumably surreptitiously) measured 'noise' levels at the Swettenham Arms car park, as well as from at their 'own property at Jodrell Bank' using 'a motor vehicle equipped with suitable interference measuring apparatus with which we commonly explore our sites'. This apparatus generated charts that became the centre of Lovell's argument.[95] He could point out with precision 'the enormous concentration of noise during the opening hours of the Inn, beginning in the evening and ending at closing time'. Further pen-recordings were shown, demonstrating how rare astronomical events could be 'inextricably confused' or even 'completely obliterated'.[96] All these illustrations would, of course, have been entirely unintelligible to the Inquiry, and required Lovell's interpretive commentary (see Figure 5.1). The link between the social activities of the telescope's neighbours and the interference ('which could so easily and rapidly destroy [its] working') was therefore made visible through the familiar discourse of interference: simultaneously interpreting the output of the telescope while holding the public at a distance. Lovell wound up with a plea that in 'one of the greatest and most exciting ages of astronomy...we...be allowed at Jodrell Bank to continue to develop to the full our researches into the Nature of the Universe'.

The responses of the developers to the stategies used by Lovell can be uncovered in the report of the *Congleton Chronicle*. Faced with the displays of interference, the one retreat was to personalise the Evidence. Rigby pointed out: 'Sir Bernard is an individual, and the only evidence called by the University was Sir Bernard's who has a dual interest in this'.[97] The impartiality of the 'independent' Assessor, Smith-Rose, was questioned, and the Councillor sought the moral highground of the underdog: the astronomers and the CPRE were hiding 'behind powerful influences ...[they] had employed Queen's Counsel to put their cases... which was "using a sledgehammer to crack a nut"'. The solicitor for Cheshire County Council attempted to limit the damage done, the council planning sub-committee, he said, 'could accept the Inspector giving judgement for the University, but the County could not accept quotation of this case by the University in future as a precedent in planning appeals'.[98]

---

[95] JBA JBM/1/4. Proof of Evidence, Exhibits A, B and C.

[96] JBA JBM/1/4. Proof of Evidence, Exhibits D, F, G and H.

[97] JBA CS7/28/1. Newspaper article, 'Going to Develop Despite Inquiry, Final Day of the Swettenham Arms Extension Appeal', 24 April 1970.

[98] JBA CS7/28/1. Transcript of Thomson (Solicitor's Department, Cheshire County Council), 23 April 1970, enclosed in letter, Lovell to Hosie, 1 May 1970.

The Inquiry came to a close after five days, but it was several months before its conclusions were known. With the networks of influence thus supporting the telescope and with the evidence displayed and deployed with skill it was no surprise when the Inquiry found against the developers. In the meantime, the case of the proposed extra housing at Brereton Heath (known as the Stringer Appeal after its appealant) reached the High Court.

The Stringer Appeal was heard on the 3rd July 1970. Documents relating to the history of planning around Jodrell Bank were available to the Judge, Mr Justice Cooke. He ruled that the 1967 agreement between astronomers and local councillors was ultra vires the local authority's powers, and therefore without 'legal effect'.[99] However, in response to the applicant's claim that the Minister of Housing and Local Government was not entitled by the terms of the Town and Country Planning Act 1959 to intercede in the case, the Judge stated 'that the likelihood of interference with the work of the telescope [was] a planning consideration'. The Judge upheld the Minister's decision to prevent the building of houses at Brereton Heath, and therefore protected the telescope's zones.[100]

THE LEGAL 'SAFEGUARDING OF JODRELL BANK RADIO TELESCOPES'

The astronomers, however, viewed the protection as still weak: 'whereas a judgement against the Minister's decision would have been a disaster for us this favourable outcome merely leaves the situation as it is...we will have to fight every single issue'.[101] There was also dismay 'at the Judge's conclusion that the documents which exist between the University and the Cheshire County Council [were] void'. Such a precarious position prompted the University to use its influence: 'A direction from the Minister...would seem to be the next step that should be taken, and I feel we should be pressing the County to obtain such a direction, as well as exerting any pressure we can through SRC on the Minister'.[102] The Minister of Housing and Local Government could make such a 'Direction' under Article 11 of General

---

[99] JBA CS7/28/1. Transcript of Judgement of Mr Justice Cooke, see fn (28).

[100] The outcome was widely reported in the national press the following day (4 July 1970): *Daily Mirror*, 'Builder Loses - Science Wins'; *The Daily Express*, 'The Planets Have It'; *The Daily Telegraph*, 'Ban Stays on Houses near Jodrell Bank'; *Manchester Guardian*, 'Jodrell Housing Ban is Upheld'; *The Daily Mail*, 'Jodrell Bank Stands Alone'; *The Times*, 'Jodrell Bank Building Ban', reported: 'It was said that sparks from a housewife's electric cleaner might be confused with an intergalactic explosion'.

[101] JBA CS7/28/1. Letter, Lovell to Lockett, 13 July 1970.

[102] JBA CS7/28/1. Letter, Rainford to Lovell, 13 July 1970.

Development Order, 1963. This would 'require the Planning authority to consult with Jodrell Bank and have regard to their views in reaching a decision', but it also 'would not make it mandatory for the County Council to agree', final responsibility in the case of disagreement would be the 'Minister's...fairly and squarely'.[103]

A meeting held at the newly-named Department of Environment between DoE, Cheshire County Council, Manchester University and the SRC, had the purpose in its chairman's words to replace the "gentleman's agreement' of the County Council to consult with the University' with 'something more 'statutory".[104] The meeting resolved to 'formulate a Jodrell Bank policy and have it publicised' (in essence 'a reinforcement of the '1967 agreement" that had been dismissed as ultra vires by the High Court), and subsequently adopted into the Cheshire 'Structure Plan'. These actions would be accompanied and enforced by the Ministry issuing a Direction under Article 11. The astronomer's erstwhile opponents were spent: a meeting at County Hall Chester between County Council and the University noted that 'the draft Policy Statement on Jodrell Bank had been discussed with the Rural District Councils concerned and had had a friendly reception'.[105] The Town and Country Planning (Jodrell Bank Radio Telescope) Direction 1973 was finally issued in April of that year. This Direction regulated planning on the basis of the zones contingently drawn up as an expression of the relative balance of power at the very local level: between the astronomers and the Rural District Councils. It stated that the local planning authority had to 'consult the University before granting planning permission' within the zones, except for specified minor developments.[106] Furthermore, the telescope was written into the 'Policy of the Local Planning Authority' of Cheshire County Council, and the local Local Plans of the Congleton and Macclesfield Borough Councils.[107]

CONCLUSION

This chapter followed the last, 'Clearing the Air (Waves)', in its analysis of

---

[103] JBA CS7/28/1. Transcript of Thomson, see fn (97).

[104] JBA CS7/28/1. Minutes of meeting held at the Department of Environment, 18 March 1971.

[105] JBA CS7/28/1. Minutes of meeting at County Hall Chester, 30 November 1971.

[106] Cheshire County Council, Town and County Planning Act 1971, the Town and Country Planning General Development Order, the Town and Country Planning (Jodrell Bank Radio Telescope) Direction 1973, 6 April 1973.

[107] Cheshire County Council, 'Jodrell Bank Telescopes: Policy of the Local Planning Authority with Regard to the University of Manchester and the Nuffield Radio

interference. Like the visitors who came from nearby towns and cities to witness the Radio Telescope, the bodies and businesses of local inhabitants were thought to be the source of destructive interference. The two chapters also shared a spatial theme, although in this case the geography was perhaps more physical rather than that of the bureaucratically-sustained radio spectrum. It sought to follow the claim that scientific practice could not live in isolation from the practices and ways of life of nearby inhabitants by looking at where the neighbours conflicted.

Efforts to rehouse the 'overspill' population from Manchester created pressures for the radio astronomy observatory. Locations proposed for building houses were sometimes in areas (such as Congleton) to which the astronomers objected. The possible nearby presence of these urban extensions was seen as a 'threat' to the productive working of the observatory. I looked at the resources that the astronomers had to hand in order to 'defend' and 'protect' their site. I then argued that the concern of the astronomers for nearby practices of other inhabitants was translated into a discourse of 'zones'. The shape and size of these zones expressed the balance of local power and were therefore contingent and geographical: it was the *distribution* of power that was important. The closure of the debate around protected zones at four and particularly six miles was explained in terms of such a distribution.

I then discussed two further developments that the astronomers attempted to counter: the electrification of the railways and the laying down of electrical grid lines. The astronomers did not try to deflect the M6 motoway partly because they thought that the motorway would 'take away traffic from the consultation zone', but also because major shifts of road policy were beyond their influence.[108] Again institutional, technical, and other resources were used to protect the radio astronomers' interests. One suggestion emerging from the meetings on railway electrification, that a mechanism could be fitted to the telescope to suppress interference when trains passed, showed how activities in the telescope's environment could directly 'feed-back' into the scientific processes of data production and interpretation.

I analysed next how the zones were gradually and calculatedly contested by those who felt their restrictions: local business and developers, the Rural District Councils who saw their areas of jurisdication eroded, amongst others. The cases of a proposal to build 23 extra houses at Brereton Heath near Holmes Chapel, and the attempt to enlarge a dining hall at the Swettenham Arms public house, were discussed in detail, for they had implications (for both institutions and persons) beyond their seeming parochiality. As

---

Astronomy Laboratories'; Congleton Borough Local Plan; Macclesfield Draft Local Plan; Vale Royal Borough Council Local Plan.

[108] JBA CS7/28/1. Minutes of meeting at Department of Environment, 18 March 1971.

symmetrical account as possible was given, outlining how each side had prepared and presented its arguments, and how they had operationalised their strategies (by for example enlisting local networks, the local press, and government departments). In particular, the rhetorical, textual and representational strategies of Lovell in presenting evidence at the Appeals were dissected. He was found to be utilising the same discourse of interference that I have delineated in the previous chapter.

In the final part, I showed how the University pressed on after its 'victories' in the planning Appeals and court hearings to secure tighter and legally-binding protection for the astronomers. The telescope was included and written in to numerous local plan. It had security in its finding an unchallenged textual location.

However, how did this affect scientific practice, without which the above discussion was merely so much local gossip? First of all there was the purely negative effect that the telescope had been grounded: scientific practice was only possible at all because the astronomers and their allies (in this case government departments, the University and the CPRE) had successfully thrown off challenges to them remaining at Jodrell Bank. Such actions should not be dismissed lightly since the astronomers had to make full use of their 'symbolic capital' (contacts, reputations, status) that they had accumulated over the previous decades. Second, the astronomers had to undergo a certain discipline within Jodrell Bank. I showed how the quiet induced by suitable internal discipline was spread out into the surrounding country by the astronomers' campaigns. This internal discipline was part of the refining of bodily skills to identify and counter confusing interference and was connected to the skills which the astronomers developed to value and interpret their pen-recording output of their telescopes that I discussed in Chapter Four. Lovell gave one example of the interpretative dilemma in his evidence in the Swettenham Arms inquiry:

> about a year and a half ago...there was a high degree of confusion with the emissions from an electric fence which were occuring with a precisely defined interval of about half a second. These became so inextricably confused with the signals which we were expecting to receive from the Pulsars that for some time the electric fence was mistaken as a Pulsar.[109]

The response of the astronomers to the 'threat' of interference, a 'threat' because it was on valued interference-free inscriptions that the allocation of credit and criticism within the astronomical community depended, was to attempt to account for it either mechanically (as in the railway interference suppressor), or in practice (through learning and distinguishing types of interference). Lovell, in his Evidence to the Swettenham Arms Appeal, not

---

[109] JBA JBM/1/4. Proof of Evidence for Swettenham Arms.

only utilised the representational possibilities open to him but also spent some time calculating minimum levels of interference. These levels were an outcome of the local conflicts and negotiations over land-use, and reflected the local distribution of power. The quoted figure of 10^{-17} Wm^{-2} was contingent on all these geographical factors.[110] Interference of this order of power could not necessarily be distinguished from an astronomical object: it was therefore at the level of the interpretation of the raw data generated at the heart of the laboratory that the outcomes of geographical disputes can be seen to enter scientific practice. This chapter has shown further how this geographical dispute was resolved through the use of the spatialised discourse of interference that distanced the urban public.

---

[110] JBA JBM/1/4. Proof of Evidence for Swettenham Arms.

CHAPTER 6

Conclusion: a Spectacle of Science

The scene changes...to heavy North Midland ploughland. There is probably a grey sky overhead and puddles lie in the earth. A farmer is driving his tractor, spreading fertiliser...Some of the hedges are white with May blossom. It is the England which everyone expects; the world of the *Times* calendar. Suddenly the camera swings round to show the gaunt shape of the Jodrell Bank radio telescope; the huge, fantastic wire bowl swinging slowly round on its railway bogies. This is another Britain of the explorers and inventors....We watch the farmer at his work and take a look at the intricate mechanism of the radio telescope and the people who are operating it. A pen traces on a roll of paper a chart of the invisible radio stars.[1]

The above quotation comes from a letter written in 1958 to the Director of Jodrell Bank from the Production Manager of Rayant Pictures ltd, whose firm were making a film to be shown at the Brussels Exhibition for the Central Office of Information. It captures well several of the themes of this book: the construction of a spectacle of science, its mobilisation as a progressive national symbol at particular moments of post-war change, and also as a site where research work is organised and astronomical knowledge produced.

The development of Jodrell Bank cannot be fully understood without locating it in the dynamic context of post-war Britain. Expenditure on both civil and military research had grown immensely in comparison to pre-war funding. This increased finance passed through a loose, non-centralised funding structure that had remained largely unchanged since the reforms of Haldane. The stasis was not the result of stagnation but of tense compromise: between the expansionary radicals and the financial moderates who made up the Barlow Committee of 1946. The increased funding reflected the post-war regard for 'boffins' and for rational planning, both popularly and within

---

[1] CS7/36/4. Excerpt from proposed film treatment. Letter, Hardie Brown to Lovell, 23 April 1958.

government. It sustained the closer connections between government, military and academic science that had been forged at war-time sites such as TRE and Bletchley Park, and could be continued and justified by Cold War tensions. The war-time research projects shaped the growth subject areas of post-war civil science. Radio astronomy and nuclear physics represent the clearest examples of this trend. These large-scale projects were prestigious and capital-intensive, requiring large instruments, increased manpower, and programmes of research that were relatively long-term. Alongside the transformation of the organisation of the largest-scale research was an expansion of education, in particular the production of qualified scientists and engineers at the universities.

Manchester University viewed itself as leading this movement. The physics department was directed by Professor Patrick Blackett, ex-member of the Maud and RDF Committees and scientific advisor to the Admiralty, and now member of the Barlow Committee. Blackett and Manchester physics were therefore particularly well-placed within the post-war networks of science, military and government to be a site for expansion. One research direction in which Blackett enthusiastically supported expansion was radio astronomy. In Chapter Two I examined how the research programme at Jodrell Bank in the 1950s came to be dominated by the promotion of a project to build a huge new instrument: a steerable radio telescope with a dish 250 feet in diameter.

I discussed how support for the instrument, amongst bodies such as the Royal Astronomical Society, was constructed, and how this support was used to persuade the Department of Scientific and Industrial Research to fund the Radio Telescope. The Telescope was initially approved for three reasons: its scientific 'timeliness and promise', the alliance of support that depended on the post-war networks of contacts between academia and government, and (recurringly) 'prestige'. One of the reasons that makes justifications by prestige difficult to analyse is also precisely what gave the term its usefulness: no actor feels the need to unpack its meaning. For the RAS national prestige implicitly referred to the relative standing of British science, whereas for the DSIR the term denoted any symbolic project which demonstrated British prominence and was recognised as such by other government departments (and also projects that were difficult to stop). For the astronomers prestige was a resource that could be recycled when applying for further grants. The looseness of the term was its strength.[2]

Like many prestigious technical projects the Radio Telescope rapidly came to have problems with its budget. Extra money and a financial appeal to industry were needed. The interest of other groups had to be secured in order to hold the project together. The Nuffield Foundation, the armed services,

---

[2] Lowy, I, 1992. 'The strength of loose concepts - boundary concepts, federative experimental stratagies and disciplinary growth: the case of immunology', *History of Science* 30, pp. 371-396, discusses a similar case with the term 'self'.

industrial companies, and civil government departments such as the DSIR and the University Grants Committee, did not have coinciding interests. This account of the technical commitment at Jodrell Bank differs from that given by Edge and Mulkay. In *Astronomy Transformed* they argue that the technical choice of large steerable radio telescopes can be explained by appealing to the dynamics of the social group of radio astronomers. I have shown that a much larger set of social bodies was involved.

Central to Chapter Two was the analysis of how the problems of the Radio Telescope related to the questioning during the 1950s of the universities as suitable sites for scientific research. Doubts over the institutional form for the radio astronomy observatory were expressed early in the decade by the DSIR's permanent secretary, Lockspeiser. Here, as with CERN, Brookhaven was looked to as a successful organisational innovation. The trenchant criticisms that the Public Accounts Committee made of the funding of the telescope again caused the UGC and DSIR to contemplate whether expensive, long-term scientific machines should perhaps be run exclusively by government. The PAC had picked upon the Radio Telescope because it was well publicised, and was therefore a good vehicle for continuing its wider campaign which was to ensure that the increased channelling of public money to the universities was matched by more careful and secure financial practice. The PAC's goal was access to the Bursar's office: the opening of the finances of the universities to inspection by the Treasury.

I therefore placed the funding of the Radio Telescope in a much wider context: the disputes over control of government money. These disputes were expressed at sites on the border between academia and government. I supported this claim by showing how battles, analogous to the conflict over Jodrell Bank, were fought at certain Units of the Agricultural and Medical Research Councils. The site for science within the institutional geography of post-war Britain was in flux. Other bodies were also affected, for example the role of the Royal Society as a distributor of grants was threatened by the Treasury's opinion that it was not capable of handling and accounting the increased funds of post-war science. The DSIR stood to gain in influence as its budget expanded, and other government departments warned the universities of this increased 'finger in the pie'. The universities mobilised the rhetoric of academic 'freedom' on which the Haldanian system of autonomous research councils was based; freedom, of course, also meant a continuation of university control and privilege, as well as preserving the university as a site for scientific research.

In this heterogeneous context, the interpretation and presentation of the instrument was malleable. Interpretative malleability of the telescope was facilitated by the loose, uncentralised funding context of post-war Britain. This malleability, combined with prestige (which as I have noted was another quality operable by many groups) must be central to any explanation of the construction of the Radio Telescope. Prestige, an accumulated cultural capital of public credit, was useful both outside and inside government. In Chapter Two I demonstrated how the promotion of the prestigious telescope was of particular importance internally to the DSIR. However, the collapse of the approach by the telescope's allies to Macmillan for funding showed how prestige could be destructively dissected by skilled hands.

The high public profile that the Radio Telescope possessed was given as an explicit reason within Whitehall why the project could not be cancelled. This passive protection was therefore one important process that associations of national prestige allowed. In Chapter Three, however, I showed how the construction of the telescope as an instrument of public prestige played a more active and important part in its history.

The DSIR promoted the Radio Telescope as its Great Public Spectacle. The instrument was presented, for example in the quality film *The Inquisitive Giant*, as a demonstration of national prestige and continuing scientific and technical leadership, at a time when Britain's status as a world leader was questioned. The identification of the Radio Telescope with official national identity[3] was manufactured.[4] As the opening quotation illustrates, transformations associated with science might be profound, but they were also benign and continuous with national history (interestingly, other important objects of national myth also present authority as a benign presence[5]). The promoters of the Radio Telescope displayed the meaning of the telescope at the boundary, or screen, between the observatory and the outside world: at press conferences, planned opening ceremonies, and in spaces reserved for visitors, where *The Inquisitive Giant* was projected outwards for visitors to see.

The boundary was, however, both a creative resource and constraint. A problem lay in how to ensure that the spectacle was read correctly by its audience. The DSIR imported a spatial fix from the Californian optical observatories of Mount Wilson and Mount Palomar. Visitors were categorised and managed differently. A scientific space was distinguished, into which only *valued* visitors were allowed access, and which was only passively

---

[3] Official national identity as expressed, in one more example, in the illustrations of the Central Office of Information's *Britain: an Official Handbook* of 1965, self-proclaimed 'mainstay of the reference facilities provided by the British Information Services in many countries'. The Radio Telescope is accompanied on the front cover by other new and old emblems of Britain: such as new towns, St Pauls and the English Bobby. The inside covers, a page before Queen Elizabeth, display images of forty four British Nobel Prize winners.

[4] A corollary of this argument is that the often posed question about reasons for 'late' American development of radio astronomy is probably miscast - it is the British case which is unusual, although clearly the histories of the specialty in other countries, with respect to national context, have to be investigated.

[5] Porter, R. (ed.), 1992. *Myths of the English*, Cambridge: Polity, p. 5.

viewable by visitors categorised as belonging to the 'general public'. This protective screen was crucial to the operation of the private observatory at a time when its finances were secured by public appeal, since it enabled the interests of a mass audience to be enrolled without its admission into the observatory.

As political movements representing scientists in Britain, such as the Association of Scientific Workers, declined in influence in the post-war years, so semipopular publications, such as *New Scientist*, representing science grew. A popular post-war audience for science through reading journals or the imprints of the Scientific Book Club, or by visiting the sites of spectacular scientific display, such as the Festival of Britain, would not have been surprised by the association of science and technology with national progress. This linkage therefore existed as a resource, both for ambitious scientists, keen to build up a research centre, and for politicians and civil servants: at the moment when Harold Wilson waxed resonantly about forging a new Britain in the 'white heat' of science and technology[6], the position of radio astronomy by committee chaired by ICI Chairman Lord Fleck: 'the UK therefore finds itself in a leading position in a new fields of science...[As a matter of policy] the UK should press forward with research in radio astronomy at the existing centres, giving it generous treatment'.[7]

But the popular audience was not necessarily content with the role cast for it as mere viewer and consumer of telescopic messages. In the trespassing of the Jodrell Bank site, the written response to public lectures such as Lovell's BBC Reith Lectures, and in particular as personified (by the astronomers) in the form of journalists, the public actively reinterpreted the significance of the telescope. In correspondence between the radio astronomers, the DSIR and the University, the uncontrolled public were described in 'threatening' terms of 'interference', 'intrusion', 'disturbance' and 'infiltration'. This discourse of interference enabled the public (who were not articulate in its use) to be held back from Jodrell Bank and placed in the role of spectators. With the discourse of interference central in the operation of Jodrell Bank as a spectacle of science, the post-war relations of science and public is a significant intensification of earlier relations. Shapin has summarised the work of F.M. Turner, amongst others: 'orientations to nature not accredited

---

[6] For Wilson's rhetoric examined in context, see: Edgerton, D. 1996. 'The "White heat" revisited: the British government and technology in the 1960s', *Twentieth Century British History* 7, pp. 53-82, also: Horner, D. 'The road to Scarborough: Wilson, Labour and the scientific revolution', in Coopey, R., Fielding, S. and Tiratsoo, N., 1993. *The Wilson Governments, 1964-1970*, London: Pinter, and Coopey, R. 1991. 'The white heat of scientific revolution', *Contemporary Record* 5, pp. 115-127.

[7] SRC, 1965. *Radio Astronomy: Report of the Committee appointed by the Lord President of the Council under the chairmanship of Lord Fleck 1961-1964*, London: HMSO, p. 6.

by the sanctioned scientific community did not have to be eliminated; it was sufficient...that they have no public forum and no political purchase'.[8] Unwanted visitors to Jodrell Bank were not merely devalued and excluded, but they also had to be reconfigured as an audience if the spectacle of national prestige was to operate.[9]

In my Introduction I compared the ways in which historians discussed display by scientists and natural philosophers. They had shown how the authority of a natural philosopher was tied to the deployment of spectacle from which moral and theological lessons were drawn. Specific spatial relations were used to make distinctions: between the performer and audience, and thence to the trustworthiness of the performer's pronouncements. Although much of this work is on the eighteenth century, it has analogies to the processes of screening at Jodrell Bank. There, too, spatial management was used to create a spectacle and produce distinctions: between the radio astronomer and the public audience in particular. The sharp difference between display in the eighteenth and mid-twentieth centuries lies in the dissimilarity of the organisational context. The distinctions created at Jodrell Bank must be related to the politics of large-scale instrumentation, such as the securing of resources or the disputes between the rival claims of engineer and radio astronomer. Many of these distinctions, in particular denotations of prestige, had significance for distant bodies such as civil and military government departments. Moreover, the display of the Radio Telescope was via many media, some of which, such as film, were largely new. The processes of separation and valuation provide examples of the dynamics of mediated display within a large-scale scientific organisation.

With the telescope constructed as an instrument of public prestige, the question was raised how and on *whom* the credit would be bestowed. The key tension here was between the rival claims of Lovell, the radio astronomer director of Jodrell Bank, and Husband, the consulting engineer. Husband claimed that his contribution to the design and construction of the Radio Telescope should have been duly and visibly recognised. The engineer complained when he was excluded from press conferences on grounds that he would call attention to the problems highlighted by the PAC. He pressed for quick action to be taken over Sputnik, in order to demonstrate the technical wonder of the telescope, and fought for an equal billing with Lovell in the film. The tensions over the position of the engineer came to a head with the conflict over 'control' of the telescope. Lovell responded to this threat to his organisational 'authority' by stating that he would not tolerate

---

[8] Shapin (1990), p. 997.

[9] This was a re-categorisation: the one category of 'odd' letter writers contained a bewildering array of types of correspondent. It is a reminder of Latour's observation that reordering and recategorisation is a root of the power of a laboratory. Latour (1983).

'interference'. The interference of the public had been a 'threat' to organisational authority and a spatial solution had been found. With the engineers, the conflict was also spatial, although this time in an internal area inaccessible to the public: the possession and training of bodily skills of telescope control within the control room (equivalent in their metaphors to the bridge of a ship).

The dispute over who received credit by public association with the instrument was resolved, in the actions to limit PAC criticism, in the radio astronomer's favour: 'Lovell is the telescope, and the telescope is Lovell' as was declared at a press conference. Lovell recycled this authorised credit back into further arguments for the support of radio astronomy, for example those made in his Reith Lectures. However, the arguments over the position of the engineer were also located in the same wider context in which I accounted for the dissonances over funding and siting of large-scale British research. The arguments over Husband can be seen as part of the processes whereby the visible accreditation and permanence of the on-site instrument builders was negotiated for large-scale establishments such as CERN.

I found that in two cases conflicts over external public prestige and internal organisational authority were intertwined with spatial management and rhetoric of interference. I therefore examined spatiality and interference at Jodrell Bank in more detail.

The product of the Radio Telescope (understood as a system involving aerials, drives, servo-mechanisms, pre-amplifiers, amplifiers, mixers, technicians, radio astronomers and so on) was an inscription: a trace generated by a pen-recorder. At this point the radio astronomers were faced by a dilemma: any spike in the trace could be attributed either to an astronomical object or to the result of a signal of more local origin. The traces that were taken to be of astronomical origin were *valued*: they were analysed, and formed the basis of the articles and papers on which credit was allocated within the public community of radio astronomers. The traces that were attributed to local signals were *valueless* and were privately discarded. This separation, or screening[10], was achieved by a discourse in which the valued pen-recordings became astronomical objects, whereas the valueless ones were described in terms of 'interference', which again was said to be 'intrusive' and 'destructive'. The screening achieved in this discourse about inscriptions can be summarised in the following table:

---

[10] For analysis of the spatiality of this screening, see: Agar, J., 'Screening science: spatiality and authority at Jodrell Bank', in Agar, J. and Smith, C.W. (ed.), *Making Space for Science*, London: Macmillan, forthcoming.

Table 6.1   Discourse of interference

valued	valueless
distant	local
astronomical object	interference
natural	human
quiet	noisy
productive	destructive

Interference was tackled in two ways. First, visual and manipulative skills of identification were refined as astronomers built up experience of radio electronics and signal shapes. However, interference could never be eradicated: as the sensitivity of receivers increased there was always a limit at which astronomical object and noise became 'inextricably confused'. Furthermore, powerful interference could obliterate the record of an astronomical object. Therefore the radio astronomers responded in a second way to 'protect' the Radio Telescope from interference: by internal discipline and attempts to discipline others outside Jodrell Bank. Within Jodrell Bank actions that might give rise to interference were suppressed. This was not enough and the radio astronomers had to leave their observatory and change others' local behaviour in order to produce a quiet productive space within.

An important part of this second strategy which I discussed in Chapter Four was the securing of 'quiet' radio frequencies for radio astronomy. Radio technology had co-evolved through the twentieth century alongside bureaucracies of regulation and control. I argued that the regulation of radio frequencies by processes of division and allocation had created a new space: the radio spectrum. The radio spectrum was a space dominated by the armed services because the military was often the site for radio technology innovation, and because issues of national security dominated the international conferences that determined the broad division and allocation of spectrum space.

Radio astronomy was a small-scale enterprise at the time of the first post-war Ordinary Administrative Radio Conference (OARC) at Atlantic City in 1947. However, as commitments of people, equipment, money and time to radio astronomy grew at places such as Jodrell Bank and Cambridge, radio astronomers could no longer work temporarily or illicitly in gaps in the radio spectrum. The campaign to gain allocation of a plot for radio astronomy within the spectrum was pursued in three stages. In the first stage the radio astronomers failed to persuade the civil (General Post Office) or military-dominated (British Joint Communications and Electronics Board) bodies to make space for a 'new user'. In the second stage, the radio astronomers at Cambridge and Jodrell Bank collaborated to present a united front to the allocatory authorities. They also enlisted a new and powerful ally to argue for their cause. A motion, passed through the British National Committee for Scientific Radio, asked the Royal Society President to take the matter up

with the Lord President of the Council and Post Master General. With this
alliance the radio astronomers advanced a 'one-frequency-per-octave' strategy
of territorial expansion, a strategy that mirrored the expansion in
instrumentation and research programmes. Whilst some assignments were
made to radio astronomy, the most significant gains for the astronomers from
this move were recognition by the Cabinet Frequency Committee of radio
astronomy as a legitimate new user and representation on the key committees.
In the final stage, Manchester and Cambridge radio astronomers worked with
their foreign counterparts to seek inclusion within allocations of the next
OARC at Geneva in 1959. I argued that the outcome of these international
negotiations were significant, not for the specific frequency decisions that
were made, but as a resource to use on the national committees to solve local
conflicts.

In several ways the campaign for a place in the spectrum was analogous
to the lobbying to secure funding. The claim that radio astronomy represented
British leadership was made to the Joint Frequency Planning Panel and other
committees in the British preparations for Geneva, just as it had been made
to funding bodies. Likewise possible military uses and economic spin-offs
were suggested. Alliance-building and malleability in the interpretation of
the telescope marked both campaigns.

The outcome of these bureaucratic negotiations, frequency assignments
for radio astronomy in the spectrum, was intimately connected to changes in
the observatories' localities. First, the frequency authorities at several points
during the meetings with the radio astronomers suggested that an alternative
to admission to the spectrum space was the moving of the observatories to
quieter locations. Second, when assignments were made, they meant that the
trajectories of other local users, in particular government departments and
the armed services, were deflected. These deflections were reified as 50-mile
zones around both Cambridge and Jodrell Bank. Screened off at the centre
of each zone was a productive quiet space.

This pattern of constant activity and intervention in the observatories'
neighbourhoods was also found in the disputes over local development, the
electrification of the railways, and the laying of power lines, that I discussed
in Chapter Five. The tensions over local development began in the 1950s
when through negotiation and pragmatic compromise a series of restrictions
on land use were introduced. This, in effect, reified the struggle between
local developers and Jodrell Bank in the form of legal zones, the spatial
divisions reflecting the settlement of disputed authority. The Minister of
Housing and Local Government confirmed these zones after agitation against
them from two Members of Parliament.

The zones that 'protected' the Radio Telescope were legally challenged in
the 1960s by an alliance of local business, local councillors and the local
press. They were opposed by another local alliance of radio astronomers and
rural conservationists. The connections between locality, authority and

interference were visible in the evidence for the appeal hearings. The aim of restrictions of the use of local space, according to Lovell who prepared a detailed and lengthy submission of evidence, was to 'protect the instrument from the intrusion of sources of electrical interference'. The 'destructive' power of interference was brought to the court-room in the form of numerous pen-recording inscriptions. These inscriptions needed expert interpretation, authority which only Lovell himself (and Smith-Rose, radio astronomy's voice on the frequency committees) could provide. The discourse of interference provided the unchallengeable means of interpretation. So, again, the discourse of interference was used simultaneously to interpret and make value-judgements about the output of the Telescope, and be used to hold the unwanted urban public back.[11]

In Chapter Two I showed that repetitive computational work was involved the production of cosmological knowledge such as surveys of radio sources. People and equipment within Jodrell Bank had to be carefully organised so that valued traces could be interpreted as useful data, reduced, analysed and possibly published. Local interference (human and non-human) disrupted this production of order, and immense hidden effort was expended to maintain this production: the allocation of stable, quiet frequencies, the disciplining of local urban activities (within and without the observatory), and the exclusion of unwanted visitors. Only by intense ongoing negotiations could universal knowledge claims be made.

Two major presentations given by Lovell in 1958 provide valuable illustrations of these points. His Reith Lecture series was broadcast by the BBC, and subsequently published as *The Individual and the Universe*. They were a popular exposition how a new specialty, radio astronomy, had contributed to new cosmologies, the speaker authorised because of his identification with the prestigious Radio Telescope. However the Reith Lectures also operated on other registers: in a telling passage Lovell reflected that, while once the astronomer could work 'in isolation from the daily turmoil', now 'even the study of remote parts of the universe demands a close partnership between astronomer and State'. The surge of odd letters after the Reith lectures was a reminder that the interfering disturbance of the 'daily turmoil' was never far away. Lovell second presentation was a review

---

[11] While it is something of a paradox: on one hand the observatory was protected with anti-urban rhetoric, on the other Jodrell Bank was a spectacle of British science, and the institutions of science (universities, societies, and so on) were largely urban. However, as Nicholas Green and Raymond Williams both remind us: rural values were co-constructed with the urban, and the countryside-as-spectacle was embedded in urban networks. Williams, R., 1973. *The Country and the City*, London: The Hogarth Press. Green, N., 1990. *The Spectacle of Nature*, Manchester: Manchester University Press.

paper for the Eleventh Solvay Conference in June 1958.[12] He summarised observations and surveys of radio sources made at Cambridge, Sydney and Jodrell Bank, and the discussion which followed involved many of the world figures of astronomy and cosmology, including Walter Baade, Jan Oort, Thomas Gold, Hermann Bondi and Hendrik van de Hulst. The astronomical content of the presentation is interesting as a minor intervention from the Manchester group into the Cambridge-Sydney sources controversy which has been expertly analysed by Edge and Mulkay. However, what was not said is as interesting as what was: the repetitive computation, and the interpretative difficulties, and the local organisation of the observatory were effaced. The only mention of 'spurious sources' was a discussion of the problem of separating two distant sources when using an interferometer. The ground work at Jodrell Bank, and other radio astronomical sites, to establish them as productive sites for science and to authorise particular inhabitants to speak, was in hand or had already been done.

The Jodrell Bank Radio Telescope, as a spectacle of science, held a unique place in British culture in the 1950s and 1960s. Even now, interpretation of the instrument is mutating: as a scientific instrument it is embedded in interferometry networks, such as the cross-Britain Multi-Element Radio Linked Interferometer (MERLIN), whereas as a political instrument it has received one of the very large lottery grants justified by 'public understanding of science' rhetoric. It is important to remember that the meaning of the instrument varies for different audiences and was (and is) unstable: interpretation changed before and after Sputnik, for example. I have examined the operation of the instrument during a particular period of time, and sought to show how it worked: as a national spectacle of science, permanent (unlike the Festival of Britain), and dependent on difficult relations with a heterogeneous crowd cast as spectators. The mundane research practices of the scientists and technicians, on the 'micro-level', of constructing a low-noise amplifier or handling pen-recordings, say, had to be aligned to the reproduction of the observatory's organisation at higher levels. The processes of valuation can therefore be seen it organising who was a credible insider, or what trace was to be valued, kept, ordered, and perhaps published. Finally, valuation as an organising process also shaped the filing system, later the archive, of the observatory. The historian must take care, by explicitly describing the processes of valuation, not to have the narrative actively shaped by them.

---

[12] Lovell, A.C.B., 1958b. 'Radio-astronomical observations which may give information on the structure of the universe', 11th Solvay Conference, Universite de Bruxelles.

BIBLIOGRAPHY

Unpublished Sources

Public Records Office (PRO)

PRO AVIA 7 652	Allocation of operating wavelengths for RDF systems	1938-1941
PRO DEFE 11 15	Defence research and development	1947-1953
PRO DSIR 2 270	Advisory Council 21 March 1951	1951
PRO DSIR 2 295	Advisory Council 20 May 1951	1951
PRO DSIR 2 497	Scientific Grants Committee 22 June 1950	1950
PRO DSIR 2 501	Scientific Grants Committee 2 May 1951	1951
PRO DSIR 2 512	Scientific Grants Committee 6 May 1953	1953
PRO DSIR 17 182	Minutes to Lord President	1945-1959
PRO DSIR 17 265	Manchester University. (a) Professor Hartree's application for grant reference Differential Analyser in the Physical Laboratories. (b) Loan of Differential Analyser to NPL	1939
PRO DSIR 17 615	Ad hoc committee to consider long-term support for research in universities minutes	1958
PRO HO 255 174	Radio astronomy frequencies: Jodrell Bank Experimental Station; interference from taxi stations	1948-1950
PRO INF 12 664	Film Division. Production of Shorts and Features. The Inquisitive Giant	1954
PRO INF 12 665	Film Division. Production of Shorts and Features. The Inquisitive Giant	1954-1955
PRO INF 12 666	Film Division. Production of Shorts and Features. The Inquisitive Giant	1955-1958
PRO PREM 11 2484	Note to Prime Minister by Lovell	1958
PRO T 218 132	Grants for maintenance and operation of the Jodrell Bank Radio Telescope	1958

PRO T 218 191	DSIR grants for special research at universities and colleges	1956-1960
PRO UGC 2 36	Minutes and agenda for meetings of the University Grants Committee	1955-1956
PRO UGC 7 152	Jodrell Bank. Manchester University	1951-1957
PRO UGC 7 548	Inspection of accounts by the Comptroller and Auditor General	1952-1959
PRO UGC 7 549	Parliamentary control of finance	1954-1956
PRO UGC 7 550	Gater Committee	1956-1958
PRO UGC 7 771	Transfer of research projects from Research Councils to universities; division of responsibility between UGC and DSIR	1952-1959
PRO WO 195 14270	Radar and Signals Advisory Board. The radar detection of the Russian earth satellite and carrier rockets and its bearing on the missile detection problem	1958

Radiocommunications Agency (RCA)

RCA 2622 Pt 1	Frequency Allocations and Assignments for Radio Astronomy, 11.11.49 - 1.2.55	1949-1955
RCA 2622 Pt 2	Frequency Allocations and Assignments for Radio Astronomy, 8 January 1955 - 15 May 1959	1955-1959
RCA 4622 Pt 3	Frequency Allocations and Assignments for Radio Astronomy, 6 April 1959 - 7 December 1960	1959-1960
RCA 4622 Pt 4	Frequency Allocations and Assignments for Radio Astronomy, 19 January 1961 - 17 November 1964	1961-1964
RCA 2622 A	Frequency Allocations and Assignments: Sites for Cambridge Radio Astronomy	1954-1955

Jodrell Bank Archive (JBA)

JBA CS1/2/2	Board of Visitors, 1959 & 1960	1958-1962
JBA CS1/4/6	10. Licences: 1950-1953	1950-1953
JBA CS3/14/2	Frequency Allocations, 1957-1962	1957-1962
JBA CS7/3/3	(Untitled - Radio Telescope Fund)	1955-1950
JBA CS7/14/2	69. DSIR Paraboloid. 1950-1952	1950-1952
JBA CS7/15/1	Paraboloid 1953-1956 DSIR	1953-1956
JBA CS7/15/2	67. Paraboloid Misc. 1949/53	1949-1953

JBA CS7/15/3	Press Releases Mark I	1957
JBA CS7/19/1	RAS Committee	1949-1954
JBA CS7/19/2	Scintillation 1949-1950	1949-1950
JBA CS7/23/7	(Untitled: The Inquisitive Giant)	1954
JBA CS7/28/1	Local Development 1969-1971	1969-1971
JBA CS7/29/1	Frequencies 1952-1963	1952-1963
JBA CS7/29/2	Frequencies to 1964	1959-1964
JBA CS7/31/2	Radio Telescope Miscellaneous 1956	1956
JBA CS7/31/3	Radio Telescope Miscellaneous 1957	1957
JBA CS7/31/4	Radio Telescope Miscellaneous 1958	1958
JBA CS7/33/1	Paraboloid 1965/55 Husband & Co	1953-1956
JBA CS7/34/1	Paraboloid Miscellaneous 1954-55	1954-1956
JBA CS7/35/2	Paraboloid Husband & Co	1953
JBA CS7/35/5	Ministry of Supply and USAAF Meteor and Lunar Echo Programme	1957-1958
JBA CS7/36/2	Satellites: MoS/Royal Society Contracts	1957-1962
JBA CS7/36/5	Radio Telescope: Control 1956-1957	1955-1957
JBA CS7/39/1	Radio Telescope: Control/Maintenance	1958
JBA CS7/39/4	Radio telescope: Films	1954-1956
JBA CS7/39/5	Lovell/Vice-Chancellor 1954-1960	1954-1960
JBA CS7/41/1	27. Press 1951-1953	1951-1953
JBA CS7/41/3	Radio Telescope: Publicity 1957	1957
JBA CS7/41/4	Radio Telescope: Publicity	1958-1959
JBA CS7/49/1	Odd Letters - 1961	1958-1961
JBA CS9/1/4	Telescope. Board of Visitors	1958-1960
JBA JBM/1/4	Proof of Evidence etc Swettenham Arms	1951-1959
JBA JBM/1/5	Notices 1950-1956 Sept	1950-1956
JBA JBM/2/4	Press Releases (Firms) 250 ft Radio Telescope	1957
JBA UNI/10/1	32. Board of Faculty/Science 1954/55	1954-1955

Cheshire County Council

Cheshire County Council, Town and County Planning Act 1971, the Town and Country Planning General Development Order, the Town and Country Planning (Jodrell Bank Radio Telescope) Direction 1973, 6 April 1973.

Cheshire County Council, 'Jodrell Bank Telescopes: Policy of the Local Planning Authority with Regard to the University of Manchester and the Nuffield Radio Astronomy Laboratories'; Congleton Borough Local Plan; Macclesfield Draft Local Plan; Vale Royal Borough Council Local Plan.

Books, Articles and Theses

Agar, J., 'Screening science: spatiality and authority at Jodrell Bank', in Agar, J. and Smith, C.W. (eds.), *Making Space for Science*, London: Macmillan, forthcoming.

Agar, J., 'Lunar echo experiments at Jodrell Bank', in Butrica, A., *Beyond the Ionosphere*, NASA History, forthcoming.

Aitken, H.G.J., 1976. *Syntony and Spark: the Origins of Radio*, New York: John Wiley and Sons.

Almond, M., 1950. 'On interstellar meteors', *The Observatory* 70, p. 112-116.

Almond, M., 1951. 'The summer daytime meteor streams of 1949 and 1950. III. Computation of the orbits', *Monthly Notices of the Royal Astronomical Society* 111, pp. 37-44.

Alter, P., 1987. *The Reluctant Patron: Science and the State in Britain, 1850-1920*, London: Berg

Anon, 1940. *Science in War*, Harmondsworth: Penguin Books.

Anon, 1952. *The Story of the Festival of Britain 1951*, London: HMSO.

Arnold, L., 1992. *Windscale 1957: Anatomy of a Nuclear Accident*, Dublin: Gill and Macmillan.

Aspinall, A., Clegg, J.A. and Hawkins, G.S., 1951. 'The radio echo apparatus for the delineation of meteor radiants', *Philosophical Magazine* 42, pp. 504-514.

Aspinall, A., Clegg, J.A., Lovell, A.C.B., and Ellyett, C.D., 1949. 'The daytime meteor streams of 1948. I Measurement of the activity and radiant positions', *Monthly Notices of the Royal Astronomical Society* 109, pp. 352-358. Ibid, ditto 'II Measurements of the velocities', *Monthly Notices of the Royal Astronomical Society* 109, pp. 359-364.

Aspinall, A., Davies, J.G. and Lovell, A.C.B., 1951. 'The velocity distribution of sporadic meteors II', , *Monthly Notices of the Royal Astronomical Society* 111, pp. 585-608.

Aspinall, A. and Hawkins, G.S., 1951. 'The summer daytime meteor streams of 1949 and 1950. I. Measurement of the radiant positions and activity', *Monthly Notices of the Royal Astronomical Society* 111, pp. 18-25.

Baigrie, B.S., 1995. 'Scientific practice: the view from the tabletop', in Buchwald, J.Z. (ed.), 1995. *Scientific Practice: Theories and Stories of Doing Physics,* Chicago: Chicago University Press, pp. 87-122.

Banham M. and Hillier B. (eds), 1976. *A Tonic to the Nation: the Festival of Britain 1951*, London: Thames & Hudson.

Barlow, Sir A. (ch), Scientific Manpower: Report of a Committee Appointed by the Lord President of the Council, Cmd 6824, 1946.

Barnes, T.J. and Duncan, J.S., 1992. *Writing Worlds: Discourse, Text and Metaphor in the Representation of Landscape,* London: Routledge.

Barnett, C., 1986. *The Audit of War: the Illusion and Reality of Britain as a Great Nation,* London: Papermac.

Biagioli, M., 1990. 'The anthropology of incommensurability', *Studies in History and Philosophy of Science* 21, pp. 183-209.

Bijker, W., Hughes T.P. and Pinch T. (eds), 1987. *The Social Construction of Technological Systems: New Directions in the Sociology and History of Technology,* London: MIT Press.

Blackett, P.M.S. and Lovell, A.C.B., 1941. 'Radio echoes and cosmic ray showers', *Proceedings of the Royal Society of London A* 177, p. 183.

Bourdieu, P. and Passeron, J.-C., 1977. *Reproduction in Education, Society and Culture,* London: Sage.

Bowen, E.G., 1987. *Radar Days,* Bristol: Adam Hilger.

Briggs, A., 1969. 'Development in higher education in the United Kingdom', In Niblett (1969), pp. 95-116.

Bud, R. and Cozzens, S. (eds), 1992. *Invisible Connections: Instruments, Institutions, and Science,* Bellingham: Spie.

Cahan, D., 1989. 'The geopolitics and architectural design of a metrological laboratory: the Physikalisch-Technische Reichanstalt in Imperial Germany'. In James (1989), pp. 137-154.

Cairncross, A., 1992. *The British Economy since 1945: Economic Policy and Performance,* Oxford: Basil Blackwell.

Calder, A., 1969. *The People's War: Britain 1939-45,* London: Cape.

Callon, M., 1987. 'Society in the making: the study of technology as a tool for sociological analysis'. In Bijker, Hughes and Pinch (1987), pp. 83-103.

Campbell, D., 1986. *The Unsinkable Aircraft Carrier,* London: Paladin.

Capshew, J.H. and Rader, K.A., 1992. 'Big science: Price to present', *Osiris* 7, pp. 3-25.

Cathcart, B., 1994. *Test of Greatness: Britain's Struggle for the Atomic Bomb,* London: John Murray.

Chartier, R., 1984. 'Culture as apprpriation: popular cultural uses in early modern France', in Kaplan, S.L. (ed.), 1984. *Understanding Popular Culture: Europe from the Middle Ages to the Nineteenth Century,* Berlin: Mouton, pp. 229-254.

Chivers, H.J., 1960. 'The simultaneous observation of radio star oscillations on different radio frequencies', *Journal of Atmospheric and Terrestrial Physics* 17, pp. 181-187.

Chivers, H.J. and Greenhow, J.S., 1959. 'Auroral ionization and absorption and scintillation of radio stars', *Journal of Atmospheric and Terrestrial Physics* 17, pp. 1-12.

Chivers, H.J. and Wells, H.W., 1959. 'A new ionospheric phenomenon', *Nature* 183, p. 1178.

Christie, J.R.R., 1993. 'Aurora, Nemesis, Clio', *British Journal for the History of Science* 26, pp. 391-405.

Clark, R.W., 1962. *The Rise of the Boffins,* London: Phoenix House.

Clark, R.W., 1965. *Tizard,* London: Methuen.

Clark, R.W., 1972. *A Biography of the Nuffield Foundation,* London: Longman.

Cleaver, A.V., 1974. 'European space activities since the war: a personal view', *Spaceflight* 16, p. 220.

Clegg, J.A. and Davidson, I.A., 1950. 'A radio echo method for the measurement of the heights of the reflecting points of meteor trails', *Philosophical Magazine* 41, pp. 77-85.

Clegg, J.A., Hughes, V.A., and Lovell, A.C.B., 1947. 'The daytime meteor streams of 1947 May-August', *Monthly Notices of the Royal Astronomical Society* 107, pp. 369-378.

Closs, R.L., Clegg, J.A. and Kaiser, T.R., 1953. 'An experimental study of radio reflections from meteor trails', *Philosophical Magazine* 44, pp. 313-324.

Clifford, J. and Marcus, G.E., 1986. *Writing Culture: the Poetics and Politics of Ethnography*, London: University of California Press.

Codding, G.A., 1952. *The International Telecommunications Union: an Experiment in International Cooperation*, Leiden: E.J. Brill.

Collins, H.M. and Pinch, T.J., 1979. 'The construction of the paranormal: nothing unscientific is happening', *Sociological Review Monograph* 27, pp. 237-270.

Collins, H.M., 1988. 'Public experiments and displays of virtuosity: the core-set revisited', *Social Studies of Science* 18, pp. 725-748.

Coopey, R. 1991. 'The white heat of scientific revolution', *Contemporary Record 5,* pp. 115-127.

Cooter, R., 1992. 'The politics of spatial innovation: fracture clinics in inter-war Britain'. In Pickstone (1989), pp. 146-164.

Cooter, R. and Pumfrey, S., 1994. 'Separate spheres and public places: reflections on the history of science popularization and science in popular culture', *History of Science 32,* pp. 237-267.

Cosgrove, D. and Daniels, S., 1988. *The Iconography of the Landscape: Essays on the Symbolic Representation, Design and Use of Past Environments*, Cambridge: Cambridge University Press.

Council for Scientific Policy, Report on Science Policy, appendix II, Cmnd 3007, (1966); and Advisory Council on Scientific Policy, Ninth Report, Cmnd 11, (1956).

Cox, I., *1951. The South Bank Exhibition. A Guide to the Story in Tells,* London: HMSO.

Dagg, M., 1957a. 'The correlation of radio star scintillation phenomena with geomagnetic disturbances and the mechanism of motion of the ionospheric irregularities in the F region', *Journal of Atmospheric and Terrestrial Physics 10,* pp. 194-203.

Dagg, M., 1957b. 'Radio star ridges', *Journal of Atmospheric and Terrestrial Physics* 11, pp. 118-127.

Darwin, J., 1991. *The End of British Empire: the Historical Debate:* Oxford: Basil Blackwell.

Davies, J.G., 1963. 'The use of computers in radio astronomy', in Palmer, H.P., Davies, J.G. and Large, M.I., 1963. *Radio Astronomy Today,* Manchester: Manchester University Press.

Davies, J. G. and Ellyett, C. D., 1949. 'The diffraction of radio waves from meteor trails and the measurement of meteor velocities', *Philosophical Magazine* 40, pp. 614-626.

Davies, J. G and Greenhow, J. S., 1951. 'The summer daytime meteor streams of 1949 and 1950. 11 The measurement of the velocities', *Monthly Notices of the Royal Astronomical Society* 111, pp. 26-36.

Davies, J.G. and Lovell, A.C.B., 1955a. 'The Giacobinid meteor stream', *Monthly Notices of the Royal Astronomical Society* 115, pp. 23.

Davies, J.G. and Lovell, A.C.B., 1955b. 'Radio echo studies of meteors', *Vistas in Astronomy* 1, pp. 585-598.

Davies, R.D., 1956. 'The relation between interstellar gas, dust and the emission from neutral hydrogen at 21cm', *Monthly Notices of the Royal Astronomical Society* 116, pp. 443-452.

Davies, R. D., 1957. 'On the nature of Cyg-X radio source as derived from observations in the continuum and at the hydrogen-line frequency', *Monthly Notices of the Royal Astronomical Society* 117, pp. 663-679.

Davis, N.Z., 1975. *Society and Culture in Early Modern France,* Stanford: Stanford University Press, p. 225.

Dingle, H. (ed.), 1951. *A Century of Science, 1851-1951,* London: Hutchinson's Scientific and Technical Publications.

Dolby, R.G.A., 1982. 'On the autonomy of pure science: the construction and maintenance of barriers between scientific establishments and popular culture'. In Elias, Martins and Whitley (1982), pp. 267-292.

Douglas, M., 1966. *Purity and Danger: an Analysis of Conceptions of Pollution and Taboo,* London: Routledge and Kegan Paul.

Edge, D.O. and Mulkay, M.J., 1976. *Astronomy Transformed: the Emergence of Radio Astronomy in Britain,* London: John Wiley and Sons.

Edgerton, D., 1991. *England and the Aeroplane: an essay on a militant and technological nation,* London: Macmillan.

Edgerton, D. 1996. 'The "White heat" revisited: the British government and technology in the 1960s', *Twentieth Century British History* 7, pp. 53-82.

Edgerton, D., 1996. *Science, Technology and the British Industrial "Decline ", 1870-1970,* Cambridge: Cambridge University Press.

Edgerton, D.E.H. and Horrocks, S.M., 1994. 'British industrial research and development before 1945', *Economic History Review* 47, pp. 213-238.

Elias, N., Martins, H. and Whitley, R. (eds), 1982. *Sociology of the Sciences Yearbook 1982: Scientific Establishments and Hierarchies,* Dordrecht and London: Reidel.

Ellyett, C.D., 1950. 'The influence of high altitude winds on meteor trail ionization', *Philosophical Magazine* 41, pp. 694-700.

Ellyett, C.D. and Davies, J.G., 1948. 'Velocity of meteors by diffraction of radio waves from trails during fortnation', *Nature* 161, pp. 596-597.

Evans, J.V., 1957. 'The electron content of the atmosphere', *Journal of Atmospheric and Terrestrial Physics 11,* pp. 259-271.

Forgan, S., 1986. 'Context, image and function: a preliminary enquiry into the architecture of scientific societies', *British Journal for the History of Science* 19, pp. 89-113.

Forgan, S., 1989. 'The architecture of science and the idea of a university', *Studies in History and Philosophy of Science* 20, pp. 404-434.

Forgan, S., 'Festivals of science and the two cultures: science, architecture and display in the Festival of Britain 1951', forthcoming.

Forgan, S. and Gooday G., undated. '"A fungoid assemblage of buildings": diversity and adversity in the development of college architecture and scientific education in nineteenth-century South Kensington', unpublished paper.

Fraser, R., 1957. *Once Around the Sun: International Geophysical Year 1957-1958*, London: The Scientific Book Club.

Galison, P., 1992. 'The many faces of big science'. In Galison and Hevly (1992), pp. 1-17.

Galison, P. and Hevly, B., (eds), 1992. *Big Science: the Growth of Large Scale Research*, Stanford: Stanford University Press.

Galt, J.A., Slater, C.H. and Shuter, W.L.H., 'An attempt to detect the galactic magnetic field using Zeeman splitting of the hydrogen line', *Monthly Notices of the Royal Astronomical Society* 120, pp. 187-241.

Garfinkel, H., Lynch, M. and Livingston, E., 1981. 'The work of discovering science construed from materials from the optically discovered pulsar', *Philosophy of the Social Sciences* 11, pp. 131-158.

Gieryn, T.F., 1983. 'Boundary-work and the demarcation of science from non-science: strains and interests in professional ideologies of scientists', *American Sociological Review* 48, pp. 781-795.

Gilbert, G.N., 1976. 'The development of science and scientific knowledge: the case of radar meteor research'. In Lemaine, MacLeod, Mulkay and Weingart (1976), pp. 187-204.

Golinski, J., 1989. 'A noble spectacle: phosphorus and the public culture of science in the early Royal Society', *Isis* 80, pp. 11-39.

Golinski, J., 1990. 'The theory of practice and the practice of theory: sociological approaches in the history of science', *Isis* 81, pp. 492-505.

Gooday, G., 1991a. '"Nature" in the laboratory: domestication and discipline with the microscope in Vicorian life science', *British Journal for the History of Science* 24, pp. 307-341.

Gooday, G., 1991b. 'Edifice, artifice and artifact: the social architectonics of physics laboratories in late nineteenth century Britain', paper for conference, St Johns College, Cambridge, April 1991.

Gorst, A., Johnman, L. and Scott Lucas, W. (eds.), 1989. *Post-war Britain, 1945-64: Themes and Perspectives*, London: Pinter.

Gourvish, T. and O'Day, A. (eds.), 1991. *Britain Since 1945*, London: Macmillan.

Gowing, M., 1964. *Britain and Atomic Energy, 1939-1945*, London: Macmillan.

Gowing, M., 1974. *Independence and Deterrance, Britain and Atomic Energy, 1945-52*, 2 Vols, London: Macmillan.

Green, N., 1990. *The Spectacle of Nature: Landscape and Bourgeois Culture in Nineteenth-Century France*. Manchester: Manchester University Press.

Greenhow, J.S., 1954. 'Systematic wind measurements at altitudes of 80-100 km using radio echoes from meteor trails', *Philosophical Magazine* 45, pp. 471-490.

Greenhow, J.S. and Hawkins, G.S., 1952. 'Ionizing and luminous efficiencies of meteors', *Nature* 170, pp. 355-357.

Greenhow, J. S. and Neufeld, E. L., 1955. 'The diffusion of ionized meteor trails in the upper atmosphere', *Journal of Atmospheric and Terrestrial Physics* 6, pp. 133-140.

Gummett, P., 1980. *Scientists in Whitehall*, Manchester: Manchester University Press.

Hall, J. S. (ed), 1947. *Massachusetts Institute of Technology Radiation Laboratory Series, Volume 2: Radar Aids to Navigation*, New York: McGraw-Hill.

Hall, P., Breheny, M., McQuaid, R. and Hart, D., 1987. *Western Sunrise: the Genesis and Growth of Britain's Major High Tech Corridor*, London: Allen and Unwin.

Hanbury Brown, R., 1953. 'A symposium on radio astronomy at Jodrell Bank', *The Observatory* 73, pp. 185-198.

Hanbury Brown, R., 1954. 'The remnants of supernovae as radio sources in the Galaxy', *The Observatory* 74, pp. 185-194.

Hanbury Brown, R., 1959. 'Discrete sources of cosmic radio waves', *Handbuch der Physik* 53, p. 210.

Hanbury Brown, R., 1984. 'Paraboloids, galaxies, and stars: memories of Jodrell Bank', in Sullivan (1984), pp. 213-236.

Hanbury Brown, R. and Hazard, C., 1950. 'Radio-frequency radiation from the Great Nebula in Andromeda (M31)', *Nature* 166, pp. 901-902.

Hanbury Brown, R. and Hazard, C., 1951a. 'Radio emission from the Andromeda Nebula', *Monthly Notices of the Royal Astronomical Society* 111, pp. 357-367

Hanbury Brown, R. and Hazard, C., 1951b. 'A radio survey of the Cygnus region. I. The localized source Cygnus (1)', *Monthly Notices of the Royal Astronomical Society* 111, pp. 576-584.

Hanbury Brown, R. and Hazard, C., 1951c. 'A model of the radio-frequency radiation from the galaxy', *Philosophical Magazine* 42, pp. 939-963.

Hanbury Brown, R. and Hazard, C., 1951d. 'A radio survey of the Cygnus region. 1. The localized source Cygnus *(1)*', *Monthly Notices of the Royal Astronomical Society* 111, pp. 576-584.

Hanbury Brown, R. and Hazard, C., 1952a. 'Radio-frequency radiation from Tycho Brahe's supernova (AD 1572)', *Nature* 170, pp. 364-365.

Hanbury Brown, R. and Hazard, C., 1952b. 'Extra-galactic radio-frequency radiation' *Philosophical Magazine* 43, pp. 137-152.

Hanbury Brown, R. and Hazard, C., 1953a. 'A survey of 23 localized radio sources in the northern hemisphere', *Monthly Notices of the Royal Astronomical Society* 113, pp. 123-133.

Hanbury Brown, R. and Hazard, C., 1953b. 'A radio survey of the milky way in Cygnus, Cassiopeia and Perseus', *Monthly Notices of the Royal Astronomical Society* 113, pp. 109-122.

Hanbury Brown, R. and Hazard, C., 1953c. 'Radio-frequency radiation from the spiral nebula Messier 81', *Nature* 172, p. 853.

Hanbury Brown, R. and Hazard, C., 1953d. 'An extended radio frequency source of extragalactic origin', *Nature* 172, p. 997-998.

Hanbury Brown, R. and Hazard, C., 1959. 'The radio emission from normal galaxies. 1. Observations of M31 and M33 at 158 Mc/s and 237 Mc/s', *Monthly Notices of the Royal Astronomical Society* 119, pp. 297-308.

Hanbury Brown, R., Jennison, R.C. and Das Gupta, M.K., 'Apparent angular sizes of discrete radio sources', *Nature* 170, pp. 1061-1063.

Hanbury Brown, R. and Lovell, A.C.B., 1955. 'Large radio telescopes and their use in radio astronomy', *Vistas in Astronomy* 1, pp. 542-560.

Hanbury Brown, R. and Lovell, A.C.B., 1957. *The Exploration of Space by Radio*, London: Chapman and Hall.

Hanbury Brown, R., Palmer, H.P. and Thompson, A.R., 1954. 'Galactic radio sources of large angular diameters', *Nature* 173, pp. 945-946.

Hanbury Brown, R., Palmer, H. P. and Thompson, A. R., 1955a. 'Polarization measurements on three intense radio sources', *Monthly Notices of the Royal Astronomical Society*, pp. 487-492.

Hanbury Brown, R., Palmer, H.P. and Thompson, A.R., 1955b. 'A rotating-lobe interferometer and its application to radio astronomy', *Philosophical Magazine* 46, pp. 857-866.

Hanbury Brown R. and Twiss, R.Q., 1954. 'A new type of interferometer for use in radio astronomy', *Philosophical Magazine* 45, pp. 663-682

Hanbury Brown R. and Twiss, R.Q., 1956. 'Correlation between photons in two coherent beams of light', *Nature* 177, pp. 27-29.

Hard, M., 1993. 'Technological drift in science: Swedish radio astronomy in the making, 1942-1976'. In Lindqvist (1993), pp. 378-397.

Hartcup, G. and Allibone, T. E., 1984. *Cockcroft and the Atom*, Bristol: Adam Hilger.

Haslam, C. G. T., Davies, J. G. and Large, M. I., 1962. 'A system of digital analysis for radio astronomy using a fully steerable telescope', *Monthly Notices of the Royal Astronomical Society* 124, pp. 169-178.

Hawkins, G. S. 1956. 'A radar echo survey of sporadic meteor radiants', *Monthly Notices of the Royal Astronomical Society* 116, pp. 92-104.

Hawkins, G.S. and Almond, M., 1952. 'Radio echo observations of the major night-time meteor streams', *Monthly Notices of the Royal Astronomical Society* 112, pp. 219-233.

Hazard, C. and Walsh, D., 1959. 'An experimental investigation of the effects of confusion in a survey of localised radio sources', *Monthly Notices of the Royal Astronomical Society* 119, pp. 648-656.

Headrick, D. R., 1991. *The Invisible Weapon: Telecommunications and International Politics 1851-1945*, London: Oxford University Press.

Hendry, J., 1989. *Innovating for Failure: Government Policy and the Early British Computer Industry*, Cambridge MA and London: MIT Press.

Hendry, J. and Lawson, J. D, 1993. *Fusion Research in the UK, 1945-1960,* London: HMSO.

Hennessy, P., 1989. *Whitehall,* London: Fontana.

Hermann, A., Krige, J., Mersits, U and Pestre, D., 1987. *History of CERN,* 2 Vols, Amsterdam and Oxford: North-Holland Physics Publishing.

Hevly, B., 1992. 'Reflections on big science and big history'. In Galison and Hevly (1992), pp. 355-363.

Hey, J.S., 1973. *The Evolution of Radio Astronomy,* London: Elek.

Horner, D. 'The road to Scarborough: Wilson, Labour and the scientific revolution', in Coopey, R., Fielding, S. and Tiratsoo, N., 1993. *The Wilson Governments, 1964-1970,* London: Pinter, pp. 48-71.

Hughes, J., 1996. Plasticine and Valves: industry, instrumentation and the emergence of nuclear physics', in Gaudillere, J.P., Lowy, 1. and Pestre, D., 1996. *The Invisible Industrialist: Manufactures and the Construction of Scientific Knowledge,* London: Macmillan,

Hughes, T.P., 1982. *Networks of Power: Electrification in Western Society, 1880-1930,* Baltimore: Johns Hopkins University Press.

Hughes, T.P., 1987. 'The evolution of large technological systems'. In Bijker, Hughes and Pinch (1987), pp. 51-82.

Inkster and Morrell (eds), 1983. *Metropolis and Province: Science in British Culture, 1780-1850,* London: Hutchinson.

Jay, K., 1956. *Calder Hall: the Story of Britain's First Atomic Power Station,* London: Methuen.

Jennison, R.C., 1958. 'A phase interferometer technique for the measurement of the Fourier transformns of spatial brightness distributions of small angular extent', *Monthly Notices of the Royal Astronomical Society* 118, pp. 276-284.

Jennison, R.C., 1959. 'The detection of coherent harmonics in certain solar outbursts', *The Observatory* 79, pp. 111-113.

Jennison, R.C., 1966. *Introduction to Radio Astronomy,* London: Newnes.

Jennison, R.C. and Das Gupta, M.K., 1953. 'Fine structure of the extra-terrestrial radio source Cygnus I', *Nature* 172, pp. 996-997.

Jennison, R.C. and Das Gupta, M.K., 1955a. 'The measurement of the angular diameter of two intense radio sources. I. A radio interferometer using post-detector correlation'. *Philosophical Magazine* Series 8 1, pp. 55-64.

Jennison, R.C. and Das Gupta, M.K., 1955b. 'The measurement of the angular diameter of two intense radio sources. II. Diameter and structural measurements of the radio stars Cygnus A and Cassiopeia A'. *Philosophical Magazine* Series 81, pp. 65-75.

Jennison, R.C. and Latham, V., 1959. 'The brightness distribution within the radio sources Cygnus A (19N4A) and Cassiopeia A (23N5A)', *Monthly Notices of the Royal Astronomical Society* 119, pp. 174-183.

Jukes, J.D., 1959. *Man-Made Sun. The Story of Zeta,* London: Abelard-Schuman.

Kaiser, T.R., 'A symposium on meteor physics at Jodrell Bank', *The Observatory* 74, pp. 195-208.

Kaiser, T.R. and Cross, R.L., 1952. 'Theory of radio reflections from meteor trails I', *Philosophical Magazine* 43, pp. 137-152.

Kelly, H. L., 1948. *The History of the British Astronomical Association: the First Fifty Years,* Historical Section memoir.

Kelly, M. and Sanchez, R., 1991. 'The space of ethical practice of emergency medicine', *Science in Context* 4, pp. 79-100.

Knorr-Cetina and Mulkay (eds), 1983. *Science Observed: Perspectives on the Social Study of Science,* London: Sage.

Kopal, Z., 1986. *Of Stars and Men: Reminiscences of an Astronomer,* Bristol: Adam Hilger.

Krige, J., 1989. 'The installation of high-energy accelerators in Britain after the war: big equipment but not "Big Science"', in De Maria, M., Grilli, M. and Sebastiani (eds.), *The Restructuring of Physical Sciences in Europe and the United States, 1945-1960,* Singapore: World Scientific, pp. 488-501.

Krige, J. and Pestre, D., 1992. 'Some thoughts on the early history of CERN', in Galison and Hevly (1992), pp. 78-99.

Lamden, R.J. and Lovell, A.C.B., 'The low frequency specrum of the Cygnus (19N4A) and Cassiopeia (23N5A) radio sources', 1956. *Philosophical Magazine,* Series 8, 1, pp. 725-737.

Large, M.I., Mathewson, D.S. and Haslam, C.G.T., 1959a. 'A high-resolution survey of the Andromeda nebula at 408 Mc/s', *Nature* 183, pp. 1250-1251.

Large, M.I., Mathewson, D.S. and Haslam, C.G.T., 1959b. 'A high-resolution survey of the Coma cluster of galaxies at 408 Mc/s', *Nature* 183, pp. 1663-1664.

Latour, B., 1983. 'Give me a laboratory and I will raise the world'. In Knorr-Cetina and Mulkay (1983), pp. 141-170.

Lemaine, G., MacLeod, R., Mulkay, M., and Weingart, P. (eds.), 1976. *Perspectives on the Emergence of Scientific Disciplines,* The Hague: Mouton & Co

Leslie, S., 1993. *The Cold War and American Science: the Military-Industrial-Academic Complex at MIT and Stanford,* New York: Columbia University Press.

Levin, H. J., 1971. *The Invisible Resource: Use and Regulation of the Radio Spectrum,* Baltimore: Johns Hopkins Press.

Lewis, P. and Booth, J., 1989. *The Invisible Medium: Public, Commercial and Community Radio,* London: Macmillan.

Lindqvist, S., 1993. *Center on the Periphery: Historical Aspects of 20th-Century Swedish Physics,* Canton: Science History Publications.

Little, C.G., 1951. 'A diffraction theory of the scintillation of stars on optical and radio wavelengths', *Monthly Notices of the Royal Astronomical Society* 111, pp. 289-302.

Little, C.G. and Lovell, A.C.B., 1950. 'Origin of the fluctuations in the intensity of radio waves from galactic sources', *Nature* 165, pp. 423-424.

Little, C.G. and Maxwell, A., 1951. 'Fluctuations in the intensity of radio waves from galactic sources', *Philosophical Magazine* 42, pp. 267-278.

Little, C. G. and Maxwell, A., 1952. 'Scintillation of radio stars during aurorae and magnetic storms', *Journal of Atmospheric and Terrestrial Physics* 2, pp. 356-360.

Lovell, A.C.B., 1946. 'Cosmic rays and their origin', *Endeavour* 5, p. 74-79.

Lovell, A.C.B., 1947a. 'New metwor shower', *BAA Circular 282*.

Lovell, A.C.B., 1947b. 'Radio echoes from the aurora, daytime meteor showers', BAA *Circular 285*.

Lovell, A.C.B., 1947c. 'Meteors, comets and meteoric ionization', *Nature* 160, pp. 76-78.

Lovell, A.C.B., 1947d. 'Electron density in meteor trails', *Nature* 160, pp. 670-671.

Lovell, A.C.B., 1948a. 'BeQvars meteor stream', *BAA Circular 292*.

Lovell, A.C.B., 1948b. 'The daytime meteor streams, 1948, June-July', *BAA Circular 300*.

Lovell, A.C.B., 1948c. 'Combined radar, photographic and visual observation of the Perseid meteors of 1947', *Nature* 161, pp. 278-280.

Lovell, A.C.B., 1948d. 'Meteors and their effect on radio', *Journal of the Institution of Electrical Engineers* 95, p. 324.

Lovell, A.C.B., 1950a. 'Radio waves from the milky way', *The Listener,* 6 July 1950.

Lovell, A.C.B., 1950b. 'Meteor ionization in the upper atmosphere', *Science Progress 38,* p. 22.

Lovell, A.C.B., 1951a. 'Radio astronomy', *Discovery* 12, p. 7.

Lovell, A.C.B., 1951b. 'The new science of radio astronomy', *Nature* 167, pp. 94-97.

Lovell, A.C.B., 1951 c. 'Report on Jodrell Bank to the RAS Council 1950', *Monthly Notices of the Royal Astronomical Society* 111, pp. 196-200.

Lovell, A.C.B., 1952a. 'Britain's giant radio telescope', *London Calling,* 21 August 1952.

Lovell, A.C.B., 1952b. 'Report on Jodrell Bank to the RAS Council 1951', *Monthly Notices of the Royal Astronomical Society* 112, pp. 302-305.

Lovell, A.C.B., 1952c. 'The radio telescope. A new tool of astronomical research', *Times Science Review,* Winter Supplement.

Lovell, A.C.B., 1952d. 'The radio astronomer's universe', Norman Lockyer Lecture, *The Advancement of Science* 8, p. 351.

Lovell, A.C.B., 1953a. 'Report on Jodrell Bank to the RAS Council 1952', *Monthly Notices of the Royal Astronomical Society* 113, pp. 327-330.

Lovell, A.C.B., 1953b. 'Radio astronomy at Jodrell Bank. Part 1', *Sky and Telescope* 12, pp. 94-96.

Lovell, A.C.B., 1953c. 'Radio astronomy at Jodrell Bank. Part II', *Sky and Telescope* 12, pp. 122-124.

Lovell, A.C.B., 1954a. 'The new radio telescope at Jodrell Bank', *Discovery* 15, p. 185.

Lovell, A.C.B., 1954b. 'Report on Jodrell Bank to the RAS Council 1953', *Monthly Notices of the Royal Astronomical Society* 114, pp. 318-322.

Lovell, A.C.B., 1954c. 'Britain's giant radio telescope', *Proceedings of the Royal Institution* 35.

Lovell, A.C.B., 1954d. *Meteor Astronomy,* Oxford: Clarendon Press.

Lovell, A.C.B., 1955a. 'Radio astronomy', *Journal Royal Society of Arts* 103, pp. 666-682.

Lovell, A.C.B., 1955b. 'Report on Jodrell Bank to the RAS Council 1954', *Monthly Notices of the Royal Astronomical Society* 115, pp. 151-156.

Lovell, A.C.B., 1956a. 'Radio astronomy and the fringe of the atmosphere', *Quarterly Journal of the Royal Meteorological Society* 82, pp. 1-14.

Lovell, A.C.B., 1956b. 'Radio astronomy and the Jodrell Bank Telescope', *Proceedings of the Institution of Electrical Engineers* 103, pp. 711-721.

Lovell, A.C.B., 1957. 'The Jodrell Bank Radio Telescope', *Nature* 180, p. 60.

Lovell, A.C.B., 1958a. 'Report on Jodrell Bank to the RAS Council 1957', *Monthly Notices* of the Royal Astronomical Society 118, pp. 331-336.

Lovell, A.C.B., 1958b. 'Radio-astronomical observations which may give information on the structure of the universe', 11th Solvay Conference, Université de Bruxelles.

Lovell, A.C.B., 1959a. *The Individual and the Universe,* BBC Reith *Lectures* 1958, London: Oxford University Press.

Lovell, A.C.B., 1959b. 'Radio astronomical measurements from earth satellites' *Proceedings of the Royal Society* A 153, p. 494.

Lovell, A.C.B., 1959c. 'The Jodrell Bank Radio Telescope', *Nature* 180, p. 60.

Lovell, A.C.B., 1962. *The Exploration of Outer Space,* London: Oxford University Press.

Lovell, A.C.B., 1967. *Our Present Knowledge of the Universe,* Manchester: Manchester University Press.

Lovell, A.C.B., 1968. *The Story of Jodrell Bank,* London: Oxford University Press.

Lovell, A.C.B., 1973. *Out of the Zenith,* London: Harper & Row.

Lovell, A.C.B., 1976. *P.M.S. Blackett: a Biographical Memoir,* Bristol: John Wright & Sons.

Lovell, A.C.B., 1985. *The Jodrell Bank Telescopes,* Oxford: Oxford University Press.

Lovell, A.C.B., 1991. *Echoes of War: the Story of H2S Radar,* Bristol: Adam Hilger.

Lovell, A.C.B., 1992. *Astronomer by Chance,* Oxford: Oxford University Press.

Lovell, A.C.B., 1993. 'The Blackett-Eckersley-Lovell correspondence of World War Two and the origins of Jodrell Bank', *Notes and Records of the Royal Society of London* 47, pp. 119-131.

Lovell A.C.B. and Banwell, C.J., 1946. 'Abnormal solar radiation on 72 Mc/s', *Nature* 158, p. 517-518.

Lovell, A.C.B., Banwell, C.J. and Clegg, J.A., 1947. 'Radio echo observations of the Giacobinid meteors 1946', *Monthly Notices of the Royal Astronomical Society* 107, pp. 164-175.

Lovell, A.C.B., Clegg, J.A. and Ellyett, C.D., 1947. 'Radio echoes from the aurora borealis', *Nature* 160, p. 372.

Lovell, A.C.B. and Davies, J.G., July 1951. 'Radar tracks shooting stars', *Radio Electronics.*

Lowy, I, 1992. 'The strength of loose concepts - boundary concepts, federative experimental stratagies and disciplinary growth: the case of immunology', *History of Science* 30, pp. 371-396.

Lynch M. and Woolgar W. (eds), 1990. *Representation in Scientific Practice*, Cambridge, MA: MIT Press.

McDougall, W. A., 1982. 'Technology and statecraft in the Space Age: toward the history of a saltation', *American History Review* 87, pp. 1010-1040.

McGucken, W., 1984. *Scientists, Society and State: the Social Relations of Science Movement in Great Britain 1931-1947*, Columbus: Ohio State University Press.

Maddox, J., 1958. *A Plain Man's Guide to Zeta,* Manchester Guardian Pamphlet.

Markus, T.A., 1993. *Buildings and Power: Freedom and Control in the Origin of Modern Building Types*, London: Routledge.

Martin, B., 1976. 'The origins, development and capitulation of steady-state cosmology: a sociological study of authority and conflict in science', MSc thesis, University of Manchester.

Martin, B. and Irvine, J., 1983. 'Assessing basic research: some partial indicators of scientific progress in radio astronomy', *Research Policy* 12, pp. 61-90.

Massey, D., 1984. *The Spatial Divisions of Labour: Social Structures and the Geography of Production*, London: Macmillan.

Massey, H. and Robins, M., 1986. *History of British Space Science*, Cambridge: Cambridge University Press.

Mathewson, D. S., Large, M. I and Haslam, C. G. T., 1960. 'A spectral analysis of the radio sources in Cynus X at 1390 Mc/s and 408 Mc/s', *Monthly Notices of the Royal Astronomical Socieiy* 120, pp. 242-247.

Maxwell, A., 1951. 'Radio emission from the sunspot of central meridian passage, 1950, June 14', *The Observatory* 71, pp. 72-74.

Maxwell, A. and Dagg, M., 1954. 'A radio astronomical investigations of drift movements in the upper atmosphere', *Philosophical Magazine* 45, pp. 551-569.

Maxwell, A. and Little, C.G., 1952. 'A radio-astronomical investigation of winds in the upper atmosphere', *Nature* 169, pp. 746-747.

Morrell, J.B., 1972. 'The chemist breeders: the research school of Liebig and Thomas Thomson', *Ambix* 19, pp. 1-46.

Morrell, J. and Thackray, A., 1981. *Gentlemen of Science: Early Years of the British Association for the Advancement of Science*, Oxford: Clarendon.

Morris, D., Palmer, H.P. and Thompson, A.R., 1957. 'Five radio sources of small angular diameter', *The Observatory* 77, pp. 103-106.

Morus, I.R., 1993. 'Currents from the underworld: electricity and the technology of display in early Victorian England', *Isis* 84, pp. 50-69.

Mukerji, C., 1989. *A Fragile Power: Scientists and the State*, Princeton: Princeton University Press.

Murray, W.A.S and Hargreaves, J.K, 1954. 'Lunar radio echoes and the Faraday effect in the ionosphere', *Nature* 173, pp. 944-945.

Needell, A.A., 1987. 'Lloyd Berkner, Merle Tuve, and the federal role in radio astronomy', *Osiris* 2nd series 3, pp. 261-288.

Niblett, W.R. (ed), 1969. *Higher Education: Demand and Response*, London: Tavistock.

North, J.D., 1994. *The Fontana History of Astronomy and Cosmology*, London: Fontana Press.

O'Connell, J., 1993. 'Metrology: the creation of universality by the circulation of particulars', *Social Studies of Science* 23, pp. 129-173.

Oort, J.H., Kerr, F.J. and Westerhout, G., 1958. 'The Galactic System as a spiral nebula', *Monthly Notices of the Royal Astronomical Society* 118, pp. 379-389.

Palmer, H.P., Davies, J.G. and Large, M.I., 1963. *Radio Astronomy Today*, Manchester: Manchester University Press.

Parliamentary Debates (Hansard), 5th Series. Vol 520. House of Commons Official Report, Session 1953-54, comprising period 3 November to 20 November 1953.

Parliamentary Debates (Hansard). 5th Series. Volume 542. House of Commons Official Report, Session 1955-56, comprising 7-24 June 1955, written answers, pp. 53-54. Also: ditto, Vol 543, comprising 27 June to 15 July 1955, written answers, pp. 163-164.

Pickstone, J.V. (ed), 1989. *Medical Innovations in Historical Perspective*, Basingstoke: Macmillan.

Pinch, T.J. and Bijker, W.E., 1987. 'The social construction of facts and artifacts: or how the sociology of science and the sociology of technology might benefit each other', in Bijker, W.E., Hughes, T.P. and Pinch, T.J. (eds.) (1987), pp. 17-50.

Platt, H., 'City lights: the electrification of the Chicago region, 1880-1930', in Tarr, J.A. and Dupuy, G., 1988. *Technology and the Rise of the Networked City in Europe and America*, Philadelphia: Temple University Press, pp. 246-281.

Porter, R. (ed.), 1992. *Myths of the English*, Cambridge: Polity.

Prentice, J.P.M., Lovell A.C.B. and Banwell, C.J. 1947. 'Radio echo observations of meteors', *Monthly Notices of the Royal Astronomical Society* 107, pp. 155-163.

Robertson, P., 1992. *Beyond Southern Skies*, Cambridge: Cambridge University Press.

Rose, H. and Rose, S., 1969. *Science and Society*, Harmondsworth: Penguin.

Rouse, J., 1987. *Knowledge and Power: Towards a Political Philosophy of Science*, Ithaca: Cornell University Press.

Rowe, A.P., 1948. *One Story of Radar*, Cambridge: Cambridge University Press.

Rowson, B., 1959. 'Angular diameter measurements of the radio sources Cygnus (19N4A) and Cassiopeia (23N5A) on a wavelength of 10.7cm', *Monthly Notices of the Royal Astronomical Society* 119, pp. 26-33.

Russell, B., 1949. *Authority and the Individual*, BBC Reith Lectures 1948, London: George Allen and Unwin.

Ryle, M., 1971. 'Radio Astronomy: the Cambridge Contribution'. In Wilson (1971), pp. 11-54.

Saward, D., 1984. *Bernard Lovell: a Biography*, London: Robert Hale.

Schaffer, S., 1983. 'Natural philosophy and public spectacle in the eighteenth century', *History of Science* 21, pp. 1-43.

Schaffer, S., 1988. 'Astronomers mark time: discipline and the personal equation', *Science in Context* 2, pp. 115-145.

Schaffer, S., 1991. 'The eighteenth brumaire of Bruno Latour', *Studies of History and Philosophy of Science* 22, pp. 174-192.

Schaffer, S., 1992. 'Late Victorian metrology and its instrumentation: a manufactory of Ohms'. In Bud and Cozzens (1992), pp. 23-56.

Schaffer, S., 1995. 'Accurate measurement is an English science', in Wise, M.N. (ed.) 1995. *The Values of Precision,* Princeton: Princeton University Press, pp. 135-172.

Seidel, R., 1992. 'The origin of the Lawrence Berkeley Laboratory'. In Galison and Hevly (1992), pp. 21-45.

Shapin, S., 1990. 'Science and the public', in Olby et al (eds.), *Companion to the History of Modem Science,* London: Routledge, pp. 990-1007.

Shapin S. and Schaffer, S.J., (1985). *The Leviathan and the Air-pump: Hobbes, Boyle and the Experimental Life*, Princeton: Princeton University Press.

Simon, E.D., 1944. *The Development of British Universities*, London: Longmans.

Smith, C.W. and Wise, M.N., 1989. *Energy and Empire: a Biographical Study of Lord Kelvin*, Cambridge: Cambridge University Press.

Smith, R.W., 1989. *The Space Telescope: a Study of NASA, Science, Technology and Politics,* Cambridge: Cambridge University Press.

Smith, R.W., 1992. 'The biggest kind of big science: astronomy and the Space Telescope', in Galison and Hevly (1992), pp. 184-211.

SRC, 1965. *Radio* Astronomy: *Repotl* of the Committee appointed by the Lord President of *the Council under the chairmanship of Lord Fleck 1961-1964,* London: HMSO.

Staff of Jodrell Bank, 'Radar observations of the first Russian earth satellite and carrier rocket', *Nature* 180, p. 941.

Star, S.L. and Griesemer, J.R., 1989. 'Institutional ecology, "translations" and boundary objects: amateurs and professionals in Berkeley's Museum of Vertebrate Zoology, 1907-39', *Social Studies of Science* 19, pp. 387-420.

Streat, R. (Dupree, M. ed.), 1987. *Lancashire and Whitehall. The Diary of Sir Raymond Streat. Volume Two: 1939-57,* Manchester: Manchester University Press.

Sullivan, W., 1961. *Assault on the Unknown: the International Geophysical Year,* London: Hodder and Stroughton.

Sullivan III, W.T. (ed), 1984. *The Early Years of Radio Astronomy: Reflections Fifty Years After Jansky's Discovery*, Cambridge: Cambridge University Press.

Tatarewicz, J.N., 1986. 'Federal funding and planetary astronomy, 1950-1975', *Social Studies of Science* 16, pp. 79-103.

Traweek, S., 1988. *Beamtimes and Lifetimes: the World of High Energy Physicists*, Cambridge, MA: Harvard University Press.

254 Science and Spectacle

UMIST, 1992. *The History of Manchester Astronomical Society. The First Hundred Years,* Manchester: UMIST AVPU.

Varcoe, I., 1974. *Organizing for Science in Britain: a Case Study,* Oxford: Oxford University Press.

Vig, N., 1968. *Science and Technology in British Politics,* Oxford: Pergamon Press.

Walkland, S.A., 1965. 'Science and Parliament: the role of Select Committees of the House of Commons', *Parliamentary Affairs* 18, pp. 266-278.

Walsh, D. and Hanbury Brown, R., 'A radio survey of the great loop in Cygnus', *Nature* 175, pp. 808-809.

Warwick, A., 1992 and 1993. 'Cambridge mathematics and Cavendish physics: Cunningham, Campbell and Einstein's Relativity, 1905-1911', 2 parts, *Studies in History and Philosophy of Science* 23, pp. 625-656 and *ditto* 24, pp. 1-25.

Wilkie, T., 1991. *British Science and Politics since 1945,* Oxford: Blackwell.

Williams, D.R.W. and Davies, R.D., 1954. 'A method for the measurement of the distance of radio stars', *Nature* 173, pp. 1182-1183.

Williams, D.R.W. and Davies, R.D., 1956. 'The measurement of the distance of radio sources by interstellar neutral hydrogen absorption', *Philosophical Magazine* Series 81, pp. 622-636.

Williams, F.E., 1976. 'The story of Dollis Hill', *Post Office Electrical Engineering Journal* 69, pp. 140-145.

Williams, M.E.W., 1989. 'Astronomical observatories as practical space: the case of Pulkowa'. In James (ed), pp. 118-136.

Williams, R., 1973. *The Country and the City.* London: The Hogarth Press.

Wilson, J.P (ed), 1971. *Search and Research,* London: Mullard.

Wilson, J.T., 1961. *IGY: the Year of the New Moons,* London: Michael Joseph, 1961.

Wise, M.N. (ed.) 1995. *The Values of Precision,* Princeton: Princeton University Press.

Woolgar, S., 1979. 'The emergence and growth of research areas in science with special reference to research on pulsars', unpublished PhD, Cambridge University.

Woolgar, S., 1988. *Science: the Very Idea,* London: Tavistock.

Zuckerman, S., 1988. *Monkeys, Men and Missiles: an Autobiography, 1946-88.* London: Collins.

Index

255

DATE DUE
